D0261651

Princess Margaret

PRINCESS MARGARET

A LIFE UNRAVELLED

Tim Heald

Weidenfeld & Nicolson
LONDON

First published in Great Britain in 2007
by Weidenfeld & Nicolson

1 3 5 7 9 10 8 6 4 2

© 2007 Tim Heald

A CIP catalogue record for this book
is available from the British Library.

hardback ISBN: 978 0 297 848202
export trade paperback ISBN: 978 0 297 85342 8

Typeset by Input Data Services Ltd, Frome

Printed and bound at Mackays of Chatham plc, Chatham, Kent

The Orion Publishing Group's policy is to use papers that
are natural, renewable and recyclable products and made
from wood grown in sustainable forests. The logging and
manufacturing processes are expected to conform to the
environmental regulations of the country of origin.

Weidenfeld & Nicolson

The Orion Publishing Group Ltd
Orion House
5 Upper Saint Martin's Lane
London, WC2H 9EA
An Hachette Livre UK Company

www.orionbooks.co.uk

For Emma, Alexander, Lucy and Tristram,
dispersed now to Miami, London, Auckland and
London but still a constant inspiration to
the Old Man of Fowey

CONTENTS

ILLUSTRATIONS

SECTION ONE:

Princess Margaret's christening, 1930 (Topham Picturepoint)

Princesses Elizabeth and Margaret on a rocking horse, 1932 (Spice/Fred & Hubert Thurston/The Royal Collection/Camera Press)

Princess Margaret, Princess Elizabeth and their mother Queen Elizabeth arriving at Olympia, 26 June 1934 (Spencer Arnold/Getty Images)

The royal family on the balcony of Buckingham Palace after the Coronation ceremony, 12 May 1937 (Central Press/Getty Images)

Princess Margaret watching the pantomime of *Red Riding Hood* at Covent Garden, 3 February 1939 (Press Association)

Photographs by Lisa Sheridan from *Our Princesses at Home* (John Murray, 1940)

Elizabeth and Margaret after they broadcast on *Children's Hour* from Buckingham Palace during the war (Press Association)

Elizabeth and Margaret rehearsing a Christmas pantomime of *Cinderella* in 1941 (Studio Lisa/Camera Press)

Gala Ball at Government House, Cape Town to celebrate Elizabeth's twenty-first birthday, 21 April 1947 (Topham Picturepoint)

Royal family picnicking at Balmoral, October 1945 (Bonham Carter family)

Princesses Margaret and Elizabeth on the Royal Estate at West Newton, Norfolk, 1948 (Camera Press)

The Royal family leaving St Paul's after attending a church service on a National Day of Prayer, 6 July 1947 (Press Association)

SECTION TWO

Princess Margaret in Italy, 1949 (The Royal Collection)

Twenty-first birthday portrait, 1951 (Cecil Beaton/Camera Press)

Waving to crowds from the balcony of Mansion House, 8 May 1955 (Keystone/Getty Images)

With John Betjeman at a party for the Duff Cooper Memorial Prize, 18 December 1958 (Topham Picturepoint)

Billy Wallace, Lord Porchester and Colin Tennant with Princess Margaret at a film premiere, 7 June 1955 (Topham Picturepoint)

Robin Douglas-Home (IMS/Camera Press)

Launch of RMS *Edinburgh Castle* at Belfast, 16 October 1947 (The Royal Collection)

Launch of HMS *Otago*, 11 December 1958 (The Royal Collection)

With Yves St Laurent at Blenheim Palace, 12 November 1958 (Reg Birkett/Getty Images)

With Valentino at the Savoy Hotel, 6 November 1968 (Topham Picturepoint)

Twenty-ninth birthday portrait, 1959 (Snowdon/Camera Press)

Princess Margaret beside her new portrait by Annigoni, February 1958 (Victoria & Albert Museum)

Princess Margaret and Lord Snowdon on their wedding day, Buckingham Palace, 1960 (Cecil Beaton/Camera Press)

The Snowdons with their children at Kensington Palace, 1965 (Cecil Beaton/Camera Press)

SECTION THREE

Princess Margaret being presented with flowers (Private collection)

Meeting Rudolf Nureyev at a film premiere, October 1977 (The Royal Collection)

Touring a tennis ball factory during her visit to the Philippines, 1980 (The Royal Collection)

Watching local dancing in Tuvalu (Private collection)

ACKNOWLEDGEMENTS

Any book is ultimately the responsibility of the author so none of my acknowledgements constitute any form of disclaimer. Any errors of fact or judgement are down to me and in no way the fault of those who helped me.

My first debt is, of course, to Her Royal Highness, Princess Margaret. I met her just twice and at no time discussed the possibility of my writing a book about her. I have no idea what she would have made of the idea but she has proved a wonderfully complex and intriguing subject and a constant challenge. Like any interesting human being there are aspects of her life which some may find unappealing. I never got the impression that she would have wanted these played down but it seems to me that the bad qualities in her life – if we are being judgemental which I'd rather not – are more than balanced by the good. I was once asked about a biographical subject whether I felt better for having known them. In the case of the Princess I can say, with some hesitation, that I do feel better for having known her, however fleetingly and vicariously. I hope that I have begun to do her justice.

Writing about her has been made incomparably more interesting by the permission of her sister, Her Majesty the Queen, to allow me to consult the papers relating to Princess Margaret which have been deposited in the Royal Archives at Windsor. This permission does not in any way make this an 'authorized' or 'official' book but the papers have been invaluable and have given me an unparalleled insight into Princess Margaret's official life and the other life which went on behind it and which made it possible. For this I am grateful to Her Majesty.

It is invidious, I know, to single out others, not least because there are those who only helped me on condition that they were not identified. They know who they are and my gratitude is none the less in the face of their anonymity. I know that this can pose problems for outsiders who will think this is a bluff and that no such secret informants actually exist. I understand this and sympathize but can only emphasize that there are sources who simply do not wish to be revealed.

Of those who helped me I hope it will not seem too unfair if I single out one or two whose contributions have been particularly special. I am especially grateful to Sir Brian McGrath whom I first encountered years ago when I wrote a biography of Prince Philip. Sir Brian was, at the time, the Duke of Edinburgh's private secretary, and among other things was responsible for acting as an interface between me and my subject. From time to time my editor, then as now the incomparable Ion Trewin, used to sit round a table at Buckingham Palace with Sir Brian and Brigadier Clive Robertson, the assistant private secretary. For hours we would argue about my text – rigorously and in detail – to such an extent that at the end of the exercise I would feel completely wrung out and want only to lie down and sleep. Brian, on the other hand, would rub his hands with glee and say, 'I must say, boys, I'm enjoying this. Let's go and have a drink.' He has become a much valued adviser and guide to what sometimes seem like the Byzantine intricacies of life at court and I thank him for his always discreet advice and for his patience.

Lord Napier and Ettrick, who was for a quarter of a century Princess Margaret's private secretary, has gone out of his way to help me present a fair and accurate portrait of his complicated former boss. He and Lady Napier have been unfailingly hospitable and courteous and I shall miss the visits to their elegant house in Wiltshire as well as the frequent phone calls and the exquisite courtesy with which Lord Napier always expressed his reservations. The Princess's old friend Lady Penn, widow of the splendid Sir Eric, whom I knew many years ago when I was reporting on the Investiture of the Prince of Wales at Caernarvon and he was a senior official in the Lord Chamberlain's Office, invited me to stay at her lovely home in Scotland and has let me use one or two of her revealing – and very professionally executed – photographs. I am also particularly grateful to two of the Princesses' former ladies-in-waiting: Anne, Lady Glenconner, who has not only been amusing and helpful but has, like Lady Penn, allowed me to use some of her private photographs; and Elizabeth Vyvyan, the wife of my old university friend, Major-General Charles Vyvyan. I remember telling the Princess, once, that I was a friend of Charles and Lizzie's and she said, characteristically, 'Isn't it grand to have a lady-in-waiting who's married to a general?'

Here I think it is time to stop singling people out and simply to list some of those who have helped me with the writing of this book. They are, in alphabetical order:

Lady Alexander; Judy Bennet; Lt. Col. Freddy Burnaby-Atkins; Major-General David Burden; Jeremy Catto; Ros Chatto; Pam Clark and everyone at the Royal Archives at Windsor; Charles Collingwood; Sir Hugh Cortazzi; Colin Dexter; the Dowager Duchess of Devonshire; Sir John Dankworth; the Hon. Mrs Dawnay (Iris Peake); Andrew Duncan; Lady Antonia Fraser; Jonathan Gathorne-Hardy; Lord Gladwyn (Miles Jebb); Lady Glenconner; Sir Edmund Grove; Selina Hastings; Sir William Heseltine; Angela Huth; the late Lt. Col. John Johnston; Maurice Keen; James Kidner; Terry Jones; Penny Junor; James Leith; Peter Martin (James Melville); Sir Brian McGrath; Peter Miller; Lord Montagu of Beaulieu; Kate Mortimer; John Moynihan; Lord Napier and Ettrick; Dr Alastair Niven; John Julius Norwich; Michael Palin; Lady Penn; Lee Prosser; Ned Ryan; the Hon. Margaret Rhodes; Kenneth Rose; John Snodgrass; Lord Snowdon; the Dowager Countess of Strathmore; the late John Timbers; Giles Townsend; Lord Ullswater; Hugo Vickers; Elizabeth Vyvyan; Christopher Warwick; David Wilkinson; Anne Wilmore; the late Anita Wilson; the Hon. Annabel Whitehead; Lord Wigram; the late Sir Michael Wilford; Henry Wrong; Margaret Yorke; Philip Ziegler.

ACKNOWLEDGEMENTS

I have been lucky with my publishers, Weidenfeld & Nicolson, who have an extraordinary record of publishing the biographies, diaries and letters of public and royal figures, and particularly with my editor, Ion Trewin. Ion and I go back a long way. In fact we date our relationship to more than thirty years ago when he was the Literary Editor at *The Times* and I was one of his reviewers. Since then we have worked together on several projects and he is not only a good friend, but one of the safest pairs of hands imaginable. I wish they made more editors like him. Others at Weidenfeld who have been valuably supportive include Bea Hemming, Keith Egerton and David Atkinson.

I should also add my agent, Michael Motley, not only for his negotiating skills but also for his knowledge of royal and aristocratic circles, and his constant cheerfulness.

Finally I must acknowledge my debt to my long-suffering wife. I know that it cannot have been easy to share a house with me as well as Princess Margaret, her friends, family, enemies and acquaintances. It cannot be much fun being married to a writer but Penny hardly ever complains and at least she has the consolation that I am keen on cricket and she is Australian.

INTRODUCTION

The Queen's husband, Prince Philip;[1] the romantic novelist Barbara Cartland;[2] the cricketer Denis Compton,[3] and the broadcaster Brian Johnston[4] at first glance this is a disparate quartet with little or nothing in common. They are, however, the four people about whom I have written full-length biographies.

It was certainly not my original intention to complete this curious little hand. When I embarked on Prince Philip, the first of these subjects, at the very end of 1989, I did not look any further into the future. When I did actually arrive at the other three commissions they all came about in quite different ways and were, incidentally, all published by different companies. Barbara Cartland was my own idea; Denis Compton was suggested by a publisher, and in the case of the recently deceased Brian Johnston I was approached by his widow, Pauline. Prince Philip, incidentally, was also a publisher's idea, based on the fact that I had written about royalty in general and the Duke of Edinburgh in particular for over twenty years.

----

1 Prince Philip (1921–). Husband of Queen Elizabeth II. Charismatic young naval officer turned into elder statesman/grumpy old man depending on point of view.
2 Barbara Cartland (1901–2000). Prolific romantic novelist famous for pink outfits and relentlessly quotable instant opinions.
3 Denis Compton (1918–1997). Debonair Brylcreem Boy, dazzling England batsman and a footballer good enough to win FA Cup with Arsenal.
4 Brian Johnston (1912–1994). Mellifluous Old Etonian broadcaster and cricket commentator, universally known as 'Jonners', with trademark passion for cake.

This serendipitous little group used to seem haphazard and disconnected but gradually I have come to realize that, in their white middle-class way, they are all representative of that increasingly elusive concept: Englishness. It's true that Compton started with few obvious advantages and was demonstrably working-class by birth and upbringing. By the time he died in 1997, however, he was as middle-class as the others, even down to the slightly plummy accent and his habit of signing off telephone calls with the phrase 'Goodbye, old boy, God bless.'

Compton was utterly English and while Prince Philip could be described as German, or at any rate European, his mother-in-law, Queen Elizabeth, once told me he was 'an English gentleman'. Barbara Cartland claimed, improbably and vaguely, some sort of Norman ancestry that came over with the Conqueror but had an aura that was totally English, even if of a preposterous nature, and despite his Lowland Scottish antecedents you could say the same about Brian Johnston. All four represented a sort of Englishness that was alive and well during the second two-thirds of the twentieth century even though in perpetual retreat.

Nor was it only my biographies. *Old Boy Networks – Who We Know and How We Use Them* was a look at a quintessentially English institution; so was *Village Cricket. Beating Retreat – Hong Kong under the Last Governor* was an account of what life was like in the last significant colony under imperial rule. Even my fiction is in part a celebration of Englishness: a story set in a boarding prep school during 1956, the year of the ill-fated Suez adventure; ten whodunnits featuring a clever but miscast investigator at the Board of Trade who tramples through the stately home industry, Oxford, Fleet Street diaries, provincial cities and other expressions of twentieth-century Englishness, not to mention my latest sleuth, Doctor Tudor Cornwall of Wessex University, who even finds himself starring in an updated version of Thomas Hardy's English classic *Tess of the D'Urbervilles*.

In that sense Princess Margaret was a perfect fit. Born in 1930, she lived out the century but did not long survive it, dying in 2002. Despite being part of a Hanoverian dynasty and having a Scottish mother, she, like her sister, the Queen, was the epitome of a certain sort of Englishness that was in the ascendant in 1930 but in terminal decline by 2002.

Like the other four biographical subjects she was also a household word in her day This had nothing to do with hard work and natural ability – as, I would argue, it did in the other four cases – and everything to do with the accident of birth. The other four were all, with the possible exception of Compton, prodigiously hard workers and they all had exceptional talents, deployed in often original forms. Princess Margaret was not a spectacularly hard worker and possessed no out-of-the-ordinary ability. She was famous because, at a time when it still seemed to matter, she was the daughter of a king and queen and the sister of a queen. This was enough to make her a celebrity at a time when no one knew what a celebrity was and it also ensured that her life would be a strange paradox. On the one hand she was immensely privileged; on the other she was a classic also-ran, second best.

She was largely forgotten when I first began to pursue the idea and people under the age of about forty had only a vague idea of who she was. Nor did they seem to care much. Over the few years since she died that seems to have changed as her life has become viewed as a whole and images of her as a young and glamorous princess, a Diana before Diana, have come to obscure or at least colour the prevailing picture of a sad and enfeebled elderly woman in a wheelchair.

Princess Margaret thus fulfils that necessary requirement of a biographical subject. She had been famous in her day and people were curious to know more. She was also complicated and contrary, almost a saint to some and definitely a sinner to others. Those who knew her and even those who just knew *of* her, were seldom ambivalent. She was either loved or loathed.

Once I had convinced a publisher of this truth I set about my researches. Much has been written about her and, apart from the numerous books in which she features as a member of the supporting cast, she has also already attracted four full-length biographies, one of them 'authorized' by her in her lifetime. Newspapers and magazines also wrote fully about her. Tantalizingly she kept a diary, which, if it still exists, must be in the possession of her two children but it is highly unlikely anyone else will ever see it.

A valuable source is the archive of papers, mainly from her private office between the late 1940s, when she first started to undertake official royal duties, and her death. One day I was advised by a friend at court (literally) to phone one of Her Majesty the Queen's staff at Buckingham Palace. I had never met the person concerned and knew nothing about them, so I was slightly surprised to be cordially greeted and told that the secretary had 'read all the correspondence'. I wasn't aware that there existed anything that could be dignified by the term 'correspondence', but as a result, apparently, Her Majesty the Queen had graciously allowed me to go to the Royal Archives in Windsor Castle and study Princess Margaret's papers.

This was, of course, good news and I spent happy days in the Archives leafing through the huge number of files regarding the engagements undertaken by Princess Margaret in Britain and abroad over a period of more than half a century. This enabled me to build up a detailed picture of her public life and the deliberations that lay behind the façade. The Archives have everything from scribbled alterations to suggested menus to carefully phrased caveats from the Foreign and Commonwealth Office on the advisability of visiting certain countries. In those files are letters from Archbishops and Ambassadors, from all parts of the globe and, of course, from the Princess herself. It's a treasure trove.

Written sources are invaluable but I wanted to balance them with the testimony of people who had known the Princess during her lifetime. The first great love of her life, Peter Townsend,[1] was dead, but I was able to read his book, listen to tape recordings of his interviews and talk to people who knew him. The Princess's husband, Lord Snowdon,[2] one of the great British photographers

---

1 Peter Townsend (1914–1995). Wartime fighter ace who became courtier and pivotal figure in eponymous 'affair' with the Princess, only to marry young Belgian and live happily ever after but elsewhere.
2 1st Earl of Snowdon (1930–). Brilliant, raffish Old Etonian photographer married to Princess Margaret from 1960 to 1978.

of his time and a fascinating if elusive character, was very much alive when I was writing this book and I met him for long lunches as well as talking to him on the telephone.

On the subject of Lord Snowdon I found it fascinating that so many people disliked him in a visceral way that sometimes applied to his wife as well. Cecil Beaton, the designer, photographer and diarist, was one acquaintance who seemed gratuitously vituperative.[1] His bile could, perhaps, be attributed to professional and personal jealousy; but he was not the only one. Another vicious bystander was another diarist, James Lees-Milne.[2] On 4 April 1978, visiting a friend, Michael Rose, in a Nuffield nursing home, Lees-Milne and he 'Talked of PM and Tony, the latter having been to see Michael the evening before. Michael said the tragedy was that both of them only liked second-rate people. Their friends were awful.' This is unfair since their circle included people such as John Betjeman and Gore Vidal, who may have seemed 'awful' to Lees-Milne but could hardly be described as 'second-rate'. Nevertheless it is a persistent, snobbish criticism that surfaces time and time again, applied particularly to Lord Snowdon but also, almost as often and almost as viciously, to his countess, Princess Margaret.

I talked, inevitably, to some who shared this view but I also spoke to ladies-in-waiting, to private secretaries, to people who encountered her just the once at a formal dinner and to those who knew her intimately for decades. Some of these liked Snowdon as much as Princess Margaret – sometimes more. After their separation and divorce there was the usual tendency to take sides. Interestingly, even those who liked Snowdon were inclined to blame him more than Princess Margaret for what went wrong. There was an almost universal sense that, charming though he might be, he was also not

---

1 Cecil Beaton (1904–1980). Assiduously camp photographer, diarist and designer who took many of the best photographs of Princess Margaret but who conducted a mutual love–hate relationship of equally compounded worship and disdain, even more obviously with his photographic rival, Snowdon.

2 James Lees-Milne (1908–1997). Feline diarist of gay taste with professional interest in historic houses and their inhabitants, enhanced – or tainted – by innate snobbery.

easy. I was very struck, though, by how intensely loyal many of Princess Margaret's friends remained to her memory. This was at least as true of her women friends as of men.

She was a household word in England from well before World War II until the rule of New Labour. She could be chillingly regal, putting people down with an icy hauteur; but she might also traipse down to Bermondsey market looking for bargains at crack of dawn or play the piano and sing huskily with a cigarette in a holder, a large Scotch at her elbow and a bevy of adoring friends gathered round. She was a friend of poets and playwrights and prima ballerinas but often went out of her way to be nice to quite ordinary people. You might even say that, in a perverse way that some refused to accept, she walked with kings yet kept the common touch.

Above all, if you really want to know what it was like to live in England through from the age of Ramsay MacDonald[1] to the time of Tony Blair,[2] from the world of J. M. Barrie[3] to that of J. K. Rowling,[4] from crackling crystal sets to flat-screen telly, to see deference replaced by new money and new attitudes – then she is an invaluable case history.

There will never be another princess like her, for she was *sui generis* and of her own time and place. She was not like the rest of us, for she was distant and unknowable, and yet she wanted to be close and caring. She was the ultimate enigma and yet also the key to understanding the changes in England that marked the three score years and ten of her life.

---

1 Ramsay MacDonald (1866–1937). Old Labour Prime Minister whose perceived move to the right alienated the party which he had done much to create.
2 Tony Blair (1953–). New Labour Prime Minister whose perceived move to the right alienated the party which he had done much to create.
3 J. M. Barrie (1860–1937). Scottish novelist and playwright best known for his play, *Peter Pan*, first performed in 1904.
4 J. K. Rowling (1965–). Fabulously successful children's bookwriter whose *Harry Potter* series earned her so much money that she was alleged by *Forbes* magazine to be the world's highest-paid female entertainer after chat-show host, Oprah Winfrey.

ONE

THE THIRTIES

'Birth of a daughter –
Mother and Child doing well'

S he was born at her mother's historic Scottish family house,
Glamis Castle, on the evening of 21 August 1930. Glamis,
incidentally, is pronounced with all the stress on the first vowel
and none on the second so that it sounds like the composer
Brahms and not like 'army' or the French for 'friend'. It belonged
then and belongs now to the Bowes-Lyon family, whose head for
the past four centuries has been the Earl of Strathmore.

The twenty-first of August was a 'dark and stormy night'. The
whole of Britain was lashed with storms and far away off the
south-west coast there was a tragedy that quite overshadowed any
euphoria that might have surrounded the royal birth.

'Severe Gale' reported *The Times* in its main news story, inside
the paper, which, of course, still had advertisements on the front.
'Yacht Sunk off Cornwall. Six Lives Lost. Commodore King
Drowned'. Commodore King was the Member of Parliament for
South Paddington, so his death precipitated a by-election.[1] It was
one of those tragedies made more poignant by the fact that would-
be rescuers were eyewitnesses to the event but were unable to
sling a rope from shore to ship. After the bald facts *The Times*
added: 'An account of the wreck was given yesterday by Sir Arthur
Quiller-Couch[2] whose house at Fowey is within five miles of the
rocks on which the boat went to pieces.'

---

1 Commodore King (1877–1930). Won a DSO and Croix de Guerre in Great
War, was MP for North Norfolk (where he had a large house, now a country-
house hotel), as well as Paddington. Served as Financial Secretary to War Office.
2 Sir Arthur Quiller-Couch (1863–1944). Novelist, playwright, compiler of
first *Oxford Book of English Verse* and creator of School of English at Cambridge

'Q', editor of the first *Oxford Book of English Verse* and Professor of English Literature at Cambridge, was a literary lion of the times, now barely remembered even in his native Cornwall. Getting the great man to write a piece for *The Times* would have been a considerable scoop.

From Scotland the simultaneous but comparatively unexciting royal birth was announced in the fashion in which royal births were traditionally reported in those distant days, namely with a column lead headed 'Duchess of York/Birth of a daughter/Mother and Child doing well', followed by the laconically deferential announcement: 'Her Royal Highness the Duchess of York was safely delivered of a Princess between 9 and 9.30 last night.' The story was placed between French strikes in Lille and an Afridi attack on Peshawar. The statement was signed by three doctors, one of whom, Sir Henry Stimson, later issued a statement denying widespread rumours that the royal birth had been assisted with a dose of morphine to dull the pain of childbirth.

Although undeniably and incontestably a royal birth, it was widely regarded as a relatively minor one. True, the six-pound-eleven-ounce infant was fourth in line to the succession after her elder sister Elizabeth, but few people seriously supposed that either of the little girls would actually wear the crown and rule the Empire.

Their grandfather, King George V,[1] was in his sixties and had been seriously ill with a lung infection the year before but exuded an air of stolid permanence. In war and subsequently turbulent political times he was seen as a symbol of stability and unity, not especially inspired or inspiring but a safe pair of hands and, generally speaking, a man of unimpeachable goodwill. As with other post-Victorian monarchs, George managed to conceal his political beliefs and enjoyed apparently cordial relationships with prime ministers such as Lloyd George and Ramsay MacDonald who held views that would have been quite unlike those held, privately, by the Royal Family.

University, and a great Cornishman.
1 King George V (1865–1936). King of England from 1910 until his death and grandfather of Her Royal Highness Princess Margaret.

At the time of Margaret's birth the King was not only regarded with affection but also as a fixture for at least the foreseeable future. However, in the event of his death he would be succeeded by his elder son David, Prince of Wales.[1] The Prince had been born in June 1894 so was only in his thirties at the time of his second niece's birth. He was still unmarried but popular, virile and likely not only to succeed his father smoothly and without incident but also long to reign over us. As he actually lived until 1972, actuarial estimates of his comparative longevity were well founded. There seemed absolutely no reason why he shouldn't marry and have children who would in due course succeed him as kings or queens of Great Britain.

In these circumstances the birth of a princess, even though one who would notionally be fourth in line of succession, was something of a sideshow – one reason why it was sandwiched between news of industrial unrest in France and revolting natives in India.

Historical parallels are seldom wholly precise but the modern equivalents of Margaret and her older sister Elizabeth are the Princesses Beatrice and Eugenie of York.[2] Although the daughters of the present Duke of York and his detached duchess are technically close in line of succession, are indubitably royal princesses and appear regularly in glossy magazines and on the balcony of Buckingham Palace, no one at the time of writing seriously supposes that either of them will ever become queen. Such an eventuality would involve at least two relatively premature deaths and the abdication of a much-loved if controversial uncle. Stranger things have happened but we don't expect them. This helps to explain why the birth of Princess Margaret Rose of York in 1930 was not much more widely and eagerly greeted than that of Princess Eugenie of York sixty years later.

Nevertheless Margaret's was still a royal birth and law dictated

---

1 David, Prince of Wales (King Edward VIII, later Duke of Windsor) (1894–1972). Abdicated the throne, uncrowned, and died in exile after marrying American divorcee Wallis Simpson. Uncle of HRH Princess Margaret.
2 Princesses Beatrice (1988–) and Eugenie (1990–) of York, great-nieces of HRH Princess Margaret.

that it must be solemnly validated by a minister of the Crown. The man appointed for this task was the Home Secretary, J. R. Clynes.[1] Clynes, described by one contemporary (David Kirkwood) as 'small, unassuming, of uneven features and voice without colour', was a wonderfully inappropriate choice for such a task. The son of a labourer who himself began work in an Oldham cotton mill at the age of ten, Clynes had set up the Lancashire Gasworkers' Union and had only been narrowly beaten by Ramsay MacDonald in the election for leadership of the Labour Party. He was the epitome of the socialist working man. In his memoirs he wrote: 'Collarless, moneyless, almost wordless, we earnestly believed that it was wrong for the ill-educated to be exploited for the benefit of the aristocrats.'

This was the man responsible for confirming the royal birth at Glamis Castle. Arrangements for his visit to Scotland were undertaken by Mabell, Countess of Airlie.[2] He was attended on his mission by Harry Boyd,[3] the Ceremonial Secretary, a pernickety career civil servant who was later made a Knight Commander of the Royal Victorian Order and was thoroughly suspicious of the birth taking place north of the Border. He thought it 'irregular' and something that might be construed as 'hole-in-the-corner'. There is no reason for thinking that Boyd was particularly anti-Scottish but it is true that this was the first royal birth in Scotland since those of King Charles I, at Dunfermline in 1600, and his brother Robert, Duke of Kintyre, two years later. Even if the Establishment did not harbour strongly anti-Scottish feelings there was a definite sense that the Royal Family was English and she should be seen to be so. When, for instance, the Duchess of York suggested that her infant daughter be christened in the private chapel at Glamis, this was quickly ruled out on the grounds that the monarch was Head of the Church of England and the Church

---

1 J. R. Clynes (1889–1949). Labour MP for 35 years, lifelong rival of Ramsay MacDonald, leader of the party in 1922.
2 Mabell, Countess of Airlie (1866–1956). Became Lady of Bedchamber to Queen Mary in 1901 and remained close confidante thereafter.
3 Sir Harry Boyd (1876–1940). Home Office official created Ceremonial Secretary in 1926 and Registrar to the Baronetage in 1932.

of Scotland was not at all the same thing – positively Presbyterian, in fact.

In the event the Princess arrived several days late, which meant that Clynes and Boyd had to spend several days with various Scottish aristocrats including a whole night, that of 11 August, sitting up drinking coffee with Lady Airlie in the confident expectation – predicted by Sir Henry Stimson – that the arrival of the Princess was imminent. Eventually Boyd, dressed in a blue kimono that he had picked up on a recent diplomatic posting in China, fielded the crucial phone call from Glamis at the very last minute and the two improbable official witnesses arrived at the castle with only half an hour to spare. They apparently brought their own sandwiches with them.

There was no doubting the newly arrived Princess's royalty. After all, her uncle was the King. From time to time in later life, however, enemies have suggested that the Bowes-Lyons were not as grand as they liked to make out. Kitty Kelley, the controversial American author of a best-seller called *The Royals*, referred to the Yorks as 'stolid and middle class' and made much of the way in which the Duke and Duchess referred to Queen Elizabeth as 'Cookie'. Kelley says that this was because of Queen Elizabeth's generally acknowledged liking for food, but it seems much more likely that the elegant Mrs Simpson professed to finding her great enemy 'common'.

If so – and she wasn't the only one – she could hardly have been wider of the mark.

'In the nineteen thirties the family only used it [Glamis Castle] for a couple of months each year,' said Lord Napier and Ettrick,[1] the Scots baron and one-time Scots Guards officer who served as Princess Margaret's private secretary for a quarter of a century. 'It was not much more than a shooting lodge as far as they were concerned.' The principal home of the Earls of Strathmore and their family was the fine red-brick Georgian mansion at St Paul's

---

1 Major the Lord Napier and Ettrick (1930–). Equerry to HRH the Duke of Gloucester from 1958 to 1960 and private secretary to HRH Princess Margaret from 1974 to 1998.

Walden Bury in Hertfordshire. There was also an imposing town house in St James's Square, used mainly during the London season. None of these was a remotely middle-class dwelling.

After being effectively snubbed over where to hold the christening the Duchess of York took her daughter south to Buckingham Palace in October. There the ceremony was performed by Cosmo Gordon Lang, the Archbishop of Canterbury, a close friend of the King. She was, properly, styled 'Her Royal Highness, The Princess Margaret Rose' and in later life she attached great importance to the three-letter pronoun. 'The' distinguished her from other, less regal 'Royal Highnesses' and she insisted on its use at all times.

The baby Princess was formally christened Margaret Rose. Her godparents were the Prince of Wales, who was not present but represented by his younger brother Prince George, Duke of Kent; her aunt Princess Victoria; Princess Ingrid of Sweden, later to be Queen of Denmark but absent from the ceremony and represented by her aunt, Lady Patricia Ramsay. The Bowes-Lyons were represented by her aunt Lady Rose Leveson-Gower and her uncle the Hon. David Bowes-Lyon. Hugo Vickers, unofficial biographer of Queen Elizabeth, says that there were persistent rumours that the 'relentless' society hostess Mrs Ronnie Greville was also a godmother, but this was not the case. The rumours presumably came about because when she died in 1942 Mrs Greville, who left a staggering sum of over a million and a half pounds in all, bequeathed £20,000 to the twelve-year-old Princess Margaret. Attempts at translating old money into modern equivalents tend to be misleading but most formulae suggest that to produce an early-twenty-first-century sum that approximates to a 1940s one you should multiply by about twenty. In any event this was more than she left to any of her actual godchildren. She also left fabulous jewels to Princess Elizabeth, who seems to have been somewhat embarrassed by the lavishness of the bequest.

The year of Princess Margaret's birth seems in some ways so very distant and yet in others quite eerily familiar. G. K. Chesterton and John Dos Passos published new novels; Players Navy Cut were ten for sixpence or twenty for eleven-pence-halfpenny; a letter-writer complained: 'No effort is made in the Schools today to give training in the considered use of words'; Australia won the Ashes two tests to one and Donald Bradman made centuries at Trent Bridge, Lord's and Headingley, with a double ton at the Oval just to rub it in. For the first half-dozen years of the little girl's life her parents were, in the words of one royal biographer (Hector Bolitho), 'still able to guard their domestic life from the splendour and fuss associated with high station'.

The curious notion that the princesses' childhood was 'normal' or 'modest' was effectively fostered by the redoubtable Marion Crawford, universally known as 'Crawfie'.[1] Crawfie served the family as a much-loved and trusted governess until, in 1950, she published 'the intimate story' of her little charges when her job was done and she was pensioned off – meanly she thought – with a grace-and-favour residence and a CVO. Her memoirs caused consternation among her erstwhile employers, in particular Queen Elizabeth, later the Queen Mother, who attempted, rather ineffectually, to have them suppressed or at least doctored. Other writers have scorned what Crawfie wrote and alleged, convincingly, that even if what she wrote was not actually rewritten it was certainly given a very heavy edit. Her writing is admittedly mawkish or Pooterish at times, but I have never seen it suggested that what she wrote about her little charges' childhood was all inaccurate. They did not like it, but they did not dispute it. The reliability of Crawfie is a bit of a red herring, but I have returned to the subject in my notes at the end of the book.

'The house', wrote Crawfie of the family's Piccadilly mansion, was 'neither large nor splendid. It might have been the home of any moderately well-to-do young couple starting married life.'

This was a dubious opinion. Even in the 1930s moderately well-to-do young couples starting married life would be unlikely to live in a four-storey mansion two doors down from Number One, London, the house given to the Duke of Wellington as a

---

1 Marion Crawford ('Crawfie') (1909–1988). Governess to Princess Elizabeth and Princess Margaret who published a memoir of their time together in 1950 and was consequently shunned by her erstwhile employers, to her lasting chagrin.

thank-you for winning the Battle of Waterloo. The address was 145 Piccadilly and it was only the London house. At weekends they repaired to Royal Lodge, the mansion in the middle of Windsor Great Park given to them by King George V in 1931. Queen Victoria had vainly attempted to persuade the Prince and Princess of Wales to take on the Lodge in 1865, but the offer had been declined. From 1873 until 1931 it was a grand grace-and-favour residence for members of the Household culminating with a Major Fetherstonhaugh, manager of the Royal Stud, who occupied it from 1926 until his death in 1931.

When they moved into Royal Lodge the Yorks worked hard to turn it into the sort of retreat that they could enjoy. For example, they restored the drawing room to its original elegant self by removing the partitions that had transformed it into three distinct smaller rooms. In a cupboard at Windsor Castle the Duke found some old shields, which he put round the cornice. Eric Savill, whose eponymous gardens remain a feature of the park, now open to the public, redesigned the lodge gardens, packing them with abundant azaleas and rhododendrons, both of which flourished. Despite being close to the castle and effectively in the middle of the London stockbroker belt, the Great Park was and is a brilliant imitation of feudal English parkland in the depths of the countryside. Royal Lodge was a typical large English country house and was not only a valued retreat for the Yorks throughout Margaret's childhood but remained her mother's home during her widowhood. It became the nearest Princess Margaret ever had to a country place of her own.

For summer and other holidays they went up to Birkhall in Scotland, the house near Victoria and Albert's castle of Balmoral.

Crawfie describes the household into which she moved in 1932 as 'homelike and unpretentious', but again these judgements are relative. The children's out-of-school life was supervised by Nanny, Mrs Knight, always known as 'Alah', which was presumably a corruption of her real name, which was Clara. In this she was assisted by an under-nurse and a nursemaid. These were the MacDonald sisters, Margaret – or 'Bobo' – and Ruby, both of whom were to continue as faithful and influential retainers well into adult life. Once again Crawfie's assessment strikes a jarring note in an age when this sort of nursery has surely vanished completely, at any rate in all but the most unusual – and anachronistic – households. She may have thought it 'homelike and unpretentious', but regarded from a twenty-first-century viewpoint it seems extraordinarily privileged and odd.

From the very first, Margaret Rose was keen on music. Even at this early age she was able to hold a tune and pick one out on the piano keyboard. Not everyone was enthusiastic about this. Alastair (Ali) Forbes,[1] the feline American journalist, who was a shrewd observer and acquaintance, thought that her talents were roughly on a level with *Opportunity Knocks* and certainly no better. Her cousin Margaret Elphinstone, later Rhodes,[2] and an almost exact contemporary of Princess Elizabeth remembers, one night at Birkhall, lying in the next-door room to Margaret's. The walls were very thin and the little girl was singing 'Old Macdonald Had a Farm'. As every child knows, the song can go on and on with its repetitive and ever-growing refrain of animal noises. Margaret Elphinstone found herself listening to an incessant chant from the next-door room. She prayed that the Princess would please stop and let her sleep.

Years later Margaret Rhodes confirmed a widespread opinion that the Princess was very indulged, especially by her father. If she did do anything naughty she generally managed to defuse the situation by making everyone laugh. The original offence seemed invariably to be forgotten if not forgiven.

The little Princess celebrated her third birthday at Glamis and the guest of honour was the playwright J. M. Barrie, who lived nearby. Barrie later wrote a description of the occasion for his friend Cynthia Asquith, which was quoted in her book *The King's Daughters.*

---

1 Alastair (Ali) Forbes (1918–2005). Well-connected Bostonian anglophile who specialized in waspish gossip about British royalty and aristocracy.
2 Margaret Rhodes (née Elphinstone) (1925–). Daughter of 16th Lord Elphinstone and his wife Mary, sister of Queen Elizabeth the Queen Mother. Lived in grace-and-favour house in Windsor Great Park, was with her aunt Elizabeth at Royal Lodge when she died in 2002; close friend of her royal cousins.

'Some of her presents were on the table,' wrote Barrie, 'simple things that might have come from the sixpenny shops, but she was in a frenzy of glee over them especially about one to which she had given the place of honour by her plate. I said to her as one astounded, "Is that really your very own?" and she saw how I envied her and immediately placed it between us with the words: "It is yours and mine."'

A little later someone mentioned Barrie's name in the Princess's hearing and she turned and said, precociously, 'I know that man. He is my greatest friend, and I am his greatest friend.'

Barrie was much taken with these two phrases – so much so that he edited them into his next play, *The Boy David*. Confessing this to the little Princess he promised that he would pay her a penny each time the lines were spoken on stage. A royalty for royalty.

The play finally appeared in 1937 by which time the Duke of York was King and Barrie assumed that a payment of the pennies would be an act of lese-majesty. He was surprised and gratified, therefore, when a message came from Buckingham Palace saying, in jocular terms, that Princess Margaret was owed money by the playwright and if it was not forthcoming a solicitor's letter would follow shortly.

In collaboration with his solicitor, Sir Reginald Poole, Barrie drew up a solemn agreement. It was the last thing he ever wrote and began as follows: 'WHEREAS. This Indenture made the tenth day of June one thousand and nine hundred and thirty seven BETWEEN James Matthew Barrie so called Author and HER ROYAL HIGHNESS THE PRINCESS MARGARET WITNESSETH as follows: WHEREAS the above-mentioned henceforward to be called the said Barrie did write and otherwise indite a play of short and inglorious life called *The Boy David* and basely produce the aforesaid play as exclusively the work of his own hand ...'

This was 'engrossed on parchment' (Cynthia Asquith) and officially stamped. The idea was that when pennies had been procured from the bank Barrie would take them round to Buckingham Palace and present them to Princess Margaret in return for her signature discharging the debt. Sadly, however, Barrie died before this could be done, though the pennies were presented, posthumously, by Cynthia Asquith herself.[1]

The early years of Princess Margaret's life were tranquil and undemanding. Not until 1936 was her life thrown into turmoil, when her mother and father unexpectedly became Queen and King. She and her sister Elizabeth were brought up together and behaved as a close-knit and exclusive little team. As one of the many cosily deferential accounts of her early life (*The Pitkin Princess Margaret's Nineteenth Birthday Book*) remarked, with a bland smile which almost, but not quite, concealed the underlying reality: 'This close companionship was to continue for a handful of happy, homely years until, as 1936 drew to its dramatic close, the unexpected Accession of their parents to the Throne foreshadowed – at first gently, but none the less relentlessly – the different destinies of the Royal sisters.'

The Pitkin author, Catherine Birt, added: 'The first variation in the pleasant pattern of their lives came in the schoolroom when the studies of Princess Elizabeth, destined one day to be Queen, became more specialised than those of Princess Margaret.' This sometimes rankled with the younger sister.

As little girls the two princesses had a close and affectionate relationship with their Uncle David, whose London residence, York House, was a part of St James's Palace and therefore within easy walking distance of their own London house at 145 Piccadilly. Uncle David was charming and entertaining. He had recently installed elevators and the engineer responsible, who had also put in the lifts at Broadcasting House, enjoyed giving the excited girls rides in the new machine. His name was Maurice Denham[2] and he later became a celebrated actor. Years afterwards Princess Margaret attended a Sadler's Wells performance of *Hamlet* in aid

---

1 Lady Cynthia Asquith (1887–1960). Daughter of Earl of Wemyss and novelist and biographer who was J. M. Barrie's secretary for more than twenty years.

2 Maurice Denham (1909–2002). Elevator engineer who turned to acting as performer in radio hits such as *ITMA* and royal favourite *Much Binding in the Marsh*, and went on to be popular star of TV and films such as *Day of the Jackal*.

of an Aids charity. Denham played the gravedigger. 'Oh! It's the lift man!' cried the Princess, pleased.

The story of the Abdication is familiar in its outline and in its outcome but, perhaps inevitably, its effect on the life of the younger sister is sometimes overlooked. For Elizabeth the abrupt departure of the charming and entertaining Uncle David was obviously transforming. She went, in one traumatic moment, from being a privileged little girl whose apparent destiny was to be a very superior sort of British aristocrat to being the heiress presumptive. At the beginning of the year she seemed destined to end up as a grand but little-known old lady surrounded by dogs, horses, servants and a large family. Such people still exist, a formidable class-within-a-class lurking, as it were, in the west wing. By the end of 1936, however, the little Princess was to be Queen. She was the heiress presumptive and would have yielded that position only if her parents had produced a son. This, of course, they never did.

The historic events of 1936 were presaged by a grim-sounding family Christmas at Sandringham at the tail end of the preceding year. The King was in such poor health that he needed oxygen to enable him to sleep at night. His doctor, Lord Dawson,[1] had already told the Prime Minister, Baldwin,[2] that George was packing his bags prior to departure into the unknown and the King himself was fretting about the prospect of his eldest son inheriting the Crown. He thought, with some perspicacity, that the volatile, weak and selfish Prince of Wales would ruin himself within six months of succeeding. He confided as much to his old friend Cosmo Gordon Lang, the Archbishop of Canterbury, and prayed that the Crown would pass to his second son, Bertie, then to the attractive and sensible 'Lilibet'. Princess Margaret's elder sister

---

1 Lord Dawson of Penn (1864–1945). Doctor who was first appointed to the Royal Household during reign of King Edward VII and continued to treat the Royal Family until his death.
2 Stanley Baldwin (1867–1947). Stolid–seeming Midland businessman who was One Nation Conservative Prime Minister between wars and tarred, perhaps unfairly, with appeasement brush.

was always known as 'Lilibet' throughout childhood, the result of an early inability to pronounce 'Elizabeth' correctly.

Throughout the Sandringham festivities of Christmas 1935 the Prince of Wales seemed to sulk and slip away as often as possible to telephone his mistress, the American divorcee Wallis Simpson, who was the symptom if not the cause of his problems. Bertie's two other brothers were also at Sandringham for the holiday. George, the Duke of Kent,[1] was there with his duchess, the glamorous Marina of Greece.[2] The Kents had their newborn son Prince Edward with them. The jovial Henry, Duke of Gloucester,[3] was there too with his new bride, Lady Alice Montagu-Douglas-Scott,[4] whose quiet, rather shy Anglo-Scottish aristocratic mien was more to the Yorks' taste than Marina's foreign exoticism.

In this rather tense and depressed atmosphere the five-year-old Princess Margaret was a bouncing, unconcerned presence and when her grandfather did finally pass on, less than a month later, she apparently remained a blithe, unconcerned little body 'unconscious of everything' though 'intrigued' by the fact that Alah kept bursting into tears. Their governess later recalled that she did her best to obey the Duchess's injunction not to let the girls be depressed by playing noughts and crosses with them in the nursery. Years later she complained that she could never even contemplate noughts and crosses without being reminded of the Dead March from *Saul*.

The 'Year of the Three Kings' was, for the most part, a period of Wallis Simpson's ascendancy. She did not care for either of the

---

1 George, Duke of Kent (1902–1942). Most artistic and intellectual of Princess Margaret's uncles, killed in still-mysterious Sunderland flying boat accident in Caithness while serving with RAF.

2 Marina, Duchess of Kent (1906–1968). The last foreign princess to marry into the British Royal Family was a beautiful member of Greek Royal house and of Russian extraction.

3 Henry, Duke of Gloucester (1900–1974). Bluff, military royal uncle who served for two years after World War II as Governor General of Australia but was happier on Northamptonshire farm.

4 Alice, Duchess of Gloucester (née Montagu-Douglas-Scott) (1901–2004). Longest-lived member of Royal Family, Scottish aristocrat and part of the Buccleuch dukedom, pretty, modest and self-effacing.

Yorks but was particularly ill-disposed towards the Duchess, whom, as we've seen, she mocked as 'Cookie' because, supposedly, she thought her dowdy and fat whereas she herself was famously fashionable and skinny as a pencil. Actually the sobriquet reeks of insecurity on the part of a foreign interloper who was never really accepted by a British society that was famously xenophobic and staid. Margaret herself was to complain of this years later, referring (to me, actually) to the 'men with moustaches' who epitomized all that was most reactionary at the summit of social life in Britain. As uncrowned queen in all but name Wallis busied herself excluding her enemies, having old servants sacked and hogging Edward VIII's attentions for herself.

Elizabeth, the elder sister, attended both the lying-in-state of the girls' grandfather and his funeral. Between King's Cross station and the lying-in-state at Westminster Hall the Maltese Cross on the Imperial Crown broke loose and fell into the gutter causing the new King to exclaim loudly, 'Christ, what's going to happen next?' Company Sergeant Major Carver of the King's Company 1st Battalion Grenadier Guards picked it up and put it in his pocket.

At home, life in the princesses' nursery did not always run on an even keel. They often fought. Elizabeth had a mean left hook but Margaret liked to get in close and was known to bite. The elder girl seemed the more dignified and able to control her temper well whereas Margaret was naughtier but adept at kissing and making up as if nothing had happened. Elizabeth used to complain, 'Margaret always wants what I want,' and rows invariably started when they were ordered to wear hats, which they both hated. Their father was proud of his elder girl but Margaret, more tactile and demonstrative, 'brought delight into his life' and almost made him what he was not – demonstrative.

Not until early December 1936 did 'a grim headline' finally appear in the British press and reveal what the insiders of the Establishment already knew: 'The King and his Ministers. Great Constitutional Crisis'. This sounds like a line from Sellar and Yeatman's classic 1066 and All That. Because the basic source material involving the young princesses tends to be from Crawfie and Pitkin Pictorials there is a terrible temptation to view these momentous times in nursery-rhyme terms. We learn little of the obvious fears and premonitions of the young princesses in the 1930s but we know that they bit their fingernails – encouraged by the vision of Neville Chamberlain doing the same; that they learned to chew gum while waiting for the Aberdeen fish express at Glamis railway station and that when they went to the Bath Club for swimming lessons with Amy Daly, doyenne of swimming instructresses, Elizabeth was long and slender with good legs while Margaret looked like a plump navy-blue fish. When the Abdication took place the heading of Miss Crawford's chapter was pure Enid Blyton: 'We Move to Buckingham Palace'.

Yet the dramas were real and life-changing. The uncrowned King Edward VIII actually told his brother the Duke of York in mid-November that he intended to marry the newly divorced Wallis Simpson whether the government approved or not. Popular adulation for him remained apparently undimmed and at the same time he made a famous trip to South Wales, where he said fatuously but popularly, 'Something must be done.' It wasn't.

Euphoria surrounding Edward VIII was short-lived, for when the news broke, thanks to some innocuous questions from the Bishop of Bradford about the King's failure to go to church, the public reaction was shocked. A week after the first revelations the King signed the Instrument of Abdication in front of his brothers, the Dukes of York, Gloucester and Kent.

On Friday, 11 December Bertie, Margaret's beloved father, was formally proclaimed King George VI. When he came home to 145 Piccadilly for lunch that day he did so as king. It was that moment which seemed to make him realize for the first time precisely what had happened and what he had become. Margaret's main complaint seems to have been that she had only just learned to write the word 'York'. Now that she was the King's daughter that word was consigned to history.

One of Princess Margaret's most tantalizingly ambiguous relationships is that with her grandmother Queen Mary, for whom the Abdication was the worst experience of her life. Those who remember her recall the Queen as being tall, austere and alarmingly regal. In later life Margaret used to say that she disliked her grandmother, remarking variously to people such as Kenneth Rose[1] and Christopher Warwick[2] that she 'couldn't stand' her. She apparently used to say that her grandmother was jealous of the two little princesses because they, being daughters of a king, were more royal than she, who had merely married one. There is also evidence that Queen Mary[3] considered her younger granddaughter 'spoiled' and unduly short. Both these opinions got back to the Princess, who resented them. It is at least arguable, however, that she resented them more as an adult looking back on childhood than as a child at the time.

Whatever 'spin' she chose to put on the relationship in later life the evidence in the Royal Archives suggests that both granddaughter and grandmother were loving and dutiful. The documents that survive are, for the most part, bread-and-butter letters of the kind that any well-brought-up child would be required to write as a matter of course. They would almost certainly have been read by one or other or possibly both parents before being dispatched. And failing that – unlikely – they would definitely have been read by nanny or governess.

For her part Queen Mary seems to have been a conscientious and loving grandmother whose Christmas and birthday gifts were generous and punctilious. They were in turn always dutifully acknowledged by her granddaughter.

After her sixth birthday, for instance, Margaret wrote in pencil block capitals from Birkhall, 'DARLING GRANNY, THANK YOU VERY MUCH FOR THE LOVELY BRACELET. I LOVE IT, AND IT WAS VERY KIND OF YOU TO GIVE ME SUCH A BEAUTIFUL PRESENT. I HAD A VERY NICE BIRTHDAY. I HOPE YOU ARE QUITE WELL. LOTS OF LOVE FROM MARGARET.'

Gifts such as this were not confined to these special occasions and sometimes arrived quite unexpectedly and for no apparent

---

1 Kenneth Rose (1924–). Founder of the *Sunday Telegraph* 'Albany' column, biographer of King George V, taught Antony Armstrong-Jones while Eton beak, royal expert and apologist.

2 Christopher Warwick. Friend and biographer of HRH Princess Margaret.

3 HM Queen Mary (1867–1953). Wife of King George V, mother of King George VI and grandmother of HRH Princess Margaret.

reason except a grandmother's fancy. On 12 June 1937, for instance, Margaret wrote from Buckingham Palace: 'Darling Grannie, Thank you very much for my sweet little tea-pot. Everyone wonders what it is. I don't know if scent tea-pot is the right name. But I love it very much. With love from Margaret.' The little girl's signature is supported by eighteen small crosses and four big ones.

A few days later Lilibet wrote to thank their grandmother for a joint present of Canadian coins and stamps. For her birthday that year Margaret was able to acknowledge 'a luvely brooch'. At Christmas it was mugs, in celebration of 'Papa's Coronation'. 'When we lifted them out of the box,' wrote Elizabeth, 'they both began playing "God save the King" at different parts.'

The old Queen's love and interest were not just manifested in present form. All through the autumn of 1937 she treated the girls to 'wonderful Monday afternoons' and one afternoon in October she took them to the Tower of London. Her 'very loving granddaughters' thought that 'the ravens were so funny the way they galloped about' and 'would have hated to have lived in those dungeons. They must have been horrible.'

Grannie's 1938 birthday present was a 'sweet little jug', which Margaret promised to display in her cabinet as soon as she returned to London. A few days later it was 'the most beautiful tea-pot – I feel very grown up with a tea-pot all my own'.

A year later the presents began to take on a more practical form. On 9 February it was 'useful little notebooks'. She decided to keep one for money because 'Papa is going to give me sixpence a week'. In May she and Elizabeth were both sent 'a ruler, pencil and rubber' and Margaret wrote on behalf of her sister 'as she is very busy'. The educational visits continued. 'We went for a very interesting expedition in the Tube and we went on the escalator which we liked very much.' A few weeks later Grannie sent photographs of them together at Bekonscot, the model village at Beaconsfield in Buckinghamshire.

As Margaret grew older her presents became more beautiful and more valuable. In 1939 she had her party a day early because Papa would be away on the day itself. 'Mummy gave me the most lovely brooch. It is supposed to be a bunch of lily-of-the-valley, the bells are made of pearls, and the leaves enamel.' That Christmas Queen Mary sent her a watch from Badminton, where she lived throughout the war as the permanent house guest of the Duke and Duchess of Beaufort.[1] Margaret told her that she 'never expected anything so beautiful. I love the diamonds and sapphires in it.' She also wrote: 'We all missed you very much, especially when we go passed (*sic*) your door and you are not there.'

That same year Queen Mary gave her granddaughter a fan of Honiton lace in a box with a handwritten note saying: 'Honiton lace fan made to order of Victoria Mary, Princess of Wales, for the St Louis Exhibition, USA, given to Princess Margaret by her grandmother Queen Mary in 1939'. The letter together with the fan and the box was listed in the Christie's sale of Princess Margaret's effects in 2006 as Lot 326. The estimated value was between £300 and £500, but in the event it sold for £14,400.

If 145 Piccadilly could be described, even erroneously, as an ordinary middle-class sort of house, the same could not be said of Buckingham Palace. It was huge, public and doubled up, as it still does, as an office block and a private dwelling. It even had its own post office.

The children's nursery quarters had been repainted and were relatively bright and cheerful. Each sister had a bedroom looking out over the Mall. Elizabeth shared hers with Bobo McDonald[2] and Margaret roomed with Alah. There had been a schoolroom in the Palace, but it was one of the darkest and gloomiest rooms in the entire building with a balustrade outside that was reminiscent of prison bars. It had a fireplace at each end but felt cold and seemed 'regal but oddly dead'. The King took one look

---

1 Duke of Beaufort ('Master') (1900–1984). Master of the Horse from 1936 to 1978 but enjoyed the sobriquet Master because of his Mastership of the Beaufort Hunt. His Duchess was Princess Mary of Teck, daughter of the 1st Marquess of Cambridge.
2 Bobo MacDonald (1905–1993). Worked for Princess, later Queen Elizabeth, since the 1920s, ending as her much-loved dresser, feared by many if not all at court. Sister of Princess Margaret's maid, Ruby.

and agreed that it wouldn't do. Instead a smaller but sunnier room overlooking Constitution Hill was found and converted. It had once been used as a temporary nursery for Elizabeth when her parents were away.

Despite the pervading gloom and the oppressive size of the place – it took the girls five minutes just to get into the gardens — they ran free. Visiting dignitaries from the Prime Minister down became used to finding two little girls tearing down the interminable corridors with the plumpish younger sister always lagging behind and panting, 'Wait for me, Lilibet. Wait for me!' The King even placed two large rocking-horses immediately outside his office door so that as he worked on his papers he could hear the thump-thump as his daughters rocked to and fro.

The park-size gardens of the Palace were a saving grace. Margaret wondered if the lake was as big as the Mediterranean Sea, which she had just encountered for the first time in Geography. By now the younger sister was joining Elizabeth for most of Miss Crawford's lessons, though the sprightly Margaret – 'a born comic' – was sometimes a disruptive influence. She always seemed to get her own way even with her serious sister, who would remark, thoughtfully, 'I really don't know what we are going to do with Margaret.' At about this time Elizabeth started going twice a week to Eton for lessons in Constitutional History with the Vice Provost, Henry Marten.[1] After the outbreak of war he used to drive up the hill to Windsor Castle in a horse-drawn carriage. Even when she was old enough to appreciate something as complex as Constitutional History Princess Margaret was always excluded from these tutorials. It rankled.

For the Coronation in May 1937 both girls wore lace frocks with small silver bows and cloaks edged in ermine. Elizabeth had a train while Margaret did not. This irritated her. The King had special light coronets made for them and they drove to Westminster in a coach with their grandmother, Queen Mary. As usual Elizabeth

---

1 Sir Henry Marten (1872–1948). Spent sixty years at Eton, mainly teaching history, but ending as Provost. Tutored Princess Elizabeth in Constitutional History.

adopted a sensible elder-sister attitude, worried that Margaret, who had a made-up seat in the carriage so that she could wave at the crowds, would disgrace everyone by falling asleep in the middle of the service. In the event, however, Elizabeth only had to nudge her once or twice because she was playing with the prayer books too loudly.

Meanwhile in the outside world – some might even say the *real* world – the threat of Nazi Germany was becoming ever more menacing. Uncle David had now well-documented fascist tendencies that were then generally unsuspected. Leaders such as Foreign Secretary Lord Halifax[1] and even Prime Minister Neville Chamberlain[2] had some trouble in taking the German leaders such as Hitler, Goering and Himmler very seriously. The Nazis were essentially figures of fun and even when they became unruly and invaded Czechoslovakia Chamberlain wrung his hands, talked sadly of conflicts 'in a far-away country between people of whom we know nothing' and came away from talks with the Chancellor waving a worthless piece of paper promising 'peace in our time'. In the nursery at Buckingham Palace life continued unchanged by outside considerations.

In 1939 the King and Queen went on a successful state visit to the United States and Canada, which had the unexpected side-effect of allowing the princesses to establish a simple and undisturbed routine of lessons, weekends at Royal Lodge and masses of unsolicited letters and photographs from North America reporting on their parents' triumphal progress. The children joined the returning King and Queen in mid-Channel, meeting the *Empress of Britain* while aboard a throbbing Royal Naval destroyer, whose captain produced a bowl of cherries, which they ate on deck. Transfer from ship to ship was by precarious ladders

---

1 Lord Halifax (1881–1959). The first Earl and best known as Foreign Secretary at the time of the Munich Treaty with Hitler but was also Viceroy of India, Ambassador to the United States and Chancellor of Oxford University.
2 Neville Chamberlain (1869–1940). Scion of wealthy Birmingham family including his half-brother Austen, but as British Prime Minister, in 1930s, the architect of appeasement and hence probably the least popular Prime Minister of the century.

and a barge. The reunion was spontaneous and joyful and Margaret, proud of having shed some puppy-fat, exclaimed, 'Look, Mummy, I am quite a good shape now, not like a football like I used to be.'

Later that summer the family travelled to Dartmouth, where the King was to inspect the Royal Naval College. There they met a good-looking blond cadet called Prince Philip of Greece, who seemed to have little time for Elizabeth but spent a lot of the visit teasing Margaret. He also ate a banana split and several plates of shrimps, thus making himself a hero in the eyes of the younger princess. The boy was to have a profound effect on the lives of both girls and, it is alleged, Princess Elizabeth fell in love at first sight.

As the year went on the atmosphere in the world at large became more and more tense. Mr Chamberlain, looking increasingly harassed, visited Buckingham Palace with increasing frequency. 'Who *is* this Hitler, spoiling everything?' Margaret wanted to know. A few weeks later, when a reluctant Chamberlain did finally declare war upon Germany and the King and Queen had to return to London in a hurry, the little girl asked her governess, 'Why had Mummy and Papa to go back, Crawfie? Do you think the Germans will come and get them?' Her elder sister took a responsible line. 'I don't think people should talk about battles and things in front of Margaret,' she said. 'We don't want to upset her.'

TWO

THE FORTIES

—

'Darling Grannie,
I thought I must write ...'

Princess Margaret soon became an iconic part of the British war effort. Early on in the hostilities the little girl is supposed to have hurled all her German textbooks on the floor and announced that she would never study the language again. She always remained unashamedly patriotic.

In 1940 a slim volume was published, for sale at 2/6d, by John Murray entitled *Our Princesses at Home*. Note the affectionate proprietorial use of 'our'. In her introduction the photographer Lisa Sheridan,[1] who worked under the umbrella name 'Studio Lisa', revealed: 'In the Spring of 1940, Her Majesty the Queen graciously gave me permission to take the photographs which comprise this book. It was suggested that the pictures should show our princesses in their home-life, away from the public eye, engaged in their lessons, their hobbies and their play.'

In other words: Look at this, Mr Hitler; you may kick our boys out of France and send your Luftwaffe to bomb us all they like, but 'our princesses' will lead the way and show that the British are not downhearted and life goes on as normal. Here at Royal Lodge in Windsor Great Park 'the King and Queen, in quiet withdrawal, find complete rest and peace in the company of their daughters during any brief week-end which can be spared from the arduous responsibilities of the present day'.

The whole book is a marvellous essay in sangfroid, a quint-

---

1 Lisa Sheridan was a leading royal and celebrity photographer in her day, which ended with her death in 1966. Also the mother of the actress Dinah Sheridan.

essential display of stiff-upper-lippery. A very posed picture of the two girls in neat kilt-like skirts and woolly jackets, leaning over a couple of garden hoes, is captioned: 'In the princesses' own garden every particle of the work has been done by their own hands. They made the paths, rolled them; found, carried and placed the bricks and white ornamental stones.

'It is a bold weed which attempts to flourish here!'

The beginning of the war was spent at Birkhall, where the two little girls conducted a well-organized regime that began with lessons at nine-thirty prompt, elevenses of biscuits and orange juice, a brisk walk with George the pony and lunch with Sir Basil Brooke, who was running the household. Mummy and Papa always phoned on the dot of six o'clock after Crawfie had conducted a slightly bowdlerized reading of the day's papers. Sometimes there was laughter, as when they read 'At a Solemn Musick' by Milton and came across the topical-sounding line, 'Blest pair of sirens, pledges of heaven's joy'; sometimes there were tears, as when the wireless gave out news of the sinking of the *Royal Oak*; and sometimes there was anger. This was particularly true of the broadcasts of Lord Haw-Haw.[1] The princesses usually laughed at the traitorous Irish-born propagandist with the oddly strangulated voice but sometimes grew so incensed that they threw cushions and books at the wireless and it had to be turned off.

Elizabeth continued her history lessons with Sir Henry Marten, sending regular essays by post to Eton and getting his corrections by return. Her younger sister did not participate in this, but the two girls shared French lessons with the popular Mrs Montaudon-Smith, also known as 'Monty'. Monty was keen on singing and taught the princesses French duets.

Every week Alah hosted a 'sewing party', where local women were given tea, sandwiches, drop scones with jam and fruitcake. The princesses handed these round and played gramophone records

---

[1] 'Lord Haw-Haw', real name William Joyce (1906–1946). Funny-voiced traitor who broadcast on behalf of Germans during World War II and was subsequently executed.

on an ancient machine with a horn that had to be damped down with headscarves. Margaret's particular favourite was Gigli singing 'Your Tiny Hand is Frozen' – not inappropriate, as the autumn was cold and the sewing room was heated by a single small 'cosy stove'.

After a while evacuees arrived to stay in Craigowan, a large house on the Balmoral estate that the King opened up for their use. Both girls joined the local Girl Guide troop, which met in the village hall. Alah took the princesses to the dentist; Crawfie took them shopping in Aberdeen. It was bitterly cold and the water froze in the unheated bedrooms at Birkhall. So did the little girls' sponges and face flannels. They didn't seem to care.

Princess Elizabeth seems to have been an exemplary little girl even to the point of sounding a bit of a 'goody-goody'. Margaret, on the other hand, was witty, sharp and even frightening to some of the old men who so adored her sister. Her governess thought her 'great gifts', amounting in her view to genius, would always be 'uncomfortable at court'. Old buffers feared that they would be caricatured by the spiky little girl. It was sometimes felt that she could have become famous as an artist, singer or dancer but that, by implication, she was not necessarily cut out to be a princess. With the benefit of hindsight one can't help wondering whether too much was sometimes made of Margaret's artistic attributes. Conversely she was never really encouraged to cultivate royal attributes in the way that her sister was. She was often indulged if not actually spoiled.

One elderly man from the Crathie village on the edge of the Balmoral estate used to bring up a film projector and show old Chaplin and Laurel and Hardy films. Afterwards Margaret would refuse to go to bed and the long-suffering Alah would chase her round the chairs and tables until Crawfie, who, by her own account, was more of a disciplinarian, took the younger princess by the arm, fixed her with a 'certain stony look' and walked her to the door with a stiff 'Go to bed!' which normally did the trick. The governess obviously liked her and said that underneath the 'pranks and tricks' she had 'the softest heart'. Crawfie continued with a charitable but perceptive verdict: 'It was to be her misfortune that the ordinary exploits of adolescence, the natural life of a healthy and vivacious girl, in her case made newspaper paragraphs, instead of being dismissed with a laugh.'

Later, when the princesses returned to England, the war-time routine was that the King and Queen spent the working week based at Buckingham Palace, accompanied by two corgi puppies, Carol and Crackers. The girls spent their week in Windsor with the two older corgis, Dookie and Jane. 'The royal dogs', says one of the captions in the Lisa Sheridan book, 'are treated with coercion rather than command by our princesses.'

After a childhood full of corgis and Labradors, Princess Margaret enjoyed a less obviously doggy adulthood than either her mother Queen Elizabeth or her sister the Queen. Her favourite was a King Charles spaniel called Rowley, who was once painted dressed as a seventeenth-century cavalier. Her final dog was a dachshund called Pipkin, who distinguished himself by having intercourse in the bushes with one of the Queen's corgis, thus generating the first in a line of 'dorgis' that survives to this day.

The picture painted by Lisa Sheridan is, of course, idealized to the point of being fey and whimsical. Yet it is interesting, because this is the way in which 'our princesses' were perceived: they are not quite real because they are characters in a fairy tale.

'Here are seen the values which Queen Elizabeth most desires for her children,' we are told. And in a way and up to a point this is probably true. More importantly these are the values that the country expected of '*our* princesses'. They are actually so bland that almost anyone would find them unexceptionable.

First and foremost, they should be perfectly natural children, surrounded by affection and happiness, and offering to all they meet in return that kindness and sympathetic insight which they have been accustomed to expect. The ease and informality of this unaffected home life is deepened by the constantly charming manners which the Queen sets as an example and an ideal. Delightfully, this quiet graciousness, and lack of fussiness, embraces even the management of the royal dogs! They are accustomed to respond to no stronger reproofs than: 'O! *please*,

Jane,' when Jane walks on the flowerbeds, or '*Invite* Dookie to go away altogether,' as a final word! One pictures our princesses in their younger, more rebellious, days also responding happily to this determined but kindly dignity.

No family, not even this one, can have possessed such irreproachable manners and sunniness of disposition. We know that the King had a filthy temper, which manifested itself in periodic outbursts. We know that Princess Margaret, even then, was viewed by her grandmother as often spoiled. However, Queen Elizabeth and her daughter Queen Elizabeth the Second always, in public at least, seemed to exhibit the almost eerie self-control and perfect good manners exemplified by this curious little collection of photographs.

Not that there aren't lessons to be derived from what superficially seems to be a two-dimensional piece of no-warts-at-all hagiography. There is one picture of Princess Margaret at an upright piano, sitting on a stool and smiling a touch insipidly at the camera. She is wearing a neat patterned frock and ankle socks with sensible shoes, which I bet are a pair of Start-rites. Start-rites of Norwich are descended from a leather merchant who, in the eighteenth century, was the first man in England to make shoes on lasts. Their children's shoes date from the 1920s, since when they have regularly held the Royal Warrant.

The caption to this picture says: 'When this photograph of Princess Margaret Rose was being taken she was asked whether she would not prefer to have music on the piano. She replied that she seldom used a music-book and preferred playing without.

'Since she was quite a baby she has shown exceptional musical memory which the years have in no measure diminished.'

This is true. She enjoyed playing the piano and singing from a very early age; she was always at least reasonably accomplished; and she seldom if ever read music but always performed by ear.

Another photograph shows 'our princess' concentrating on a painting. She is using a thin brush and what looks like one of those old-fashioned standard issue Winsor and Newton paint boxes. The caption says: 'Princess Margaret Rose, having heard a great deal about Canada from her mother, is painting a picture. In the artist's own words the water-colour shows "a Canadian lady in a canoe shooting the rapids. There is a fox watching her between the fir-trees on the bank."'

Again 'our princess' looks as if butter wouldn't melt in her mouth and it seems as if she is colouring in one of those painting-by-numbers books. This suggests a lack of spontaneous creativity and destroys any possibility of suggesting that there might be some sort of interesting Freudian subtext involving the fox watching the lady in the canoe. It sounds as if there should be.

One example that definitely suggests an interesting puzzle below the surface is of the two girls, in the same outfits as they wore for their piano-playing, seated on low hassocks and playing a lettered card game which looks much like a primitive form of Scrabble. The caption reads: 'Princess Margaret Rose has just found that the word "PEG" will rid her of one more card, but this will not compensate her as yet for Princess Elizabeth's long word "POISON".' Note that at this time Princess Margaret is always given her full name: Margaret Rose; also that she was never, as far as I know, called 'Peg', which was a name reserved for their relative-by-marriage 'Princess Peg', more formally known as Princess Margaret von Hesse und bei Rhein.[1]

Although this revealing little book usually treats the two girls as if they were an indissoluble team and sometimes as if they were almost identical twins, it is obvious that Elizabeth is the elder and already the more serious. It is noticeable that when she is sitting alone at the piano she has sheets of music in front of her, unlike her younger sister; and although there are pictures of Margaret reading and painting, it is Elizabeth who is shown 'studying' above such captions as: 'Princess Elizabeth is studying a book on English literature', or 'She has to work much harder than most girls of her age and has a larger variety of essential subjects to study. History and geography of course play a large part in her

---

[1] Princess Margaret von Hesse und bei Rhein (née Geddes) (1913–1997). Related to British Royal Family through marriage to Prince Louis of Hesse. Indefatigable patron of the arts, including Aldeburgh Festival.

curriculum.' Of course. She is to be 'our queen' and her sister is not.

The apparent favouritism led to a certain resentment. Margaret was already arguably the sharper of the two girls and was always the more intellectually curious. Yet when Sir Henry Marten came driving up the hill to conduct tutorials with Princess Elizabeth, Princess Margaret Rose was still not allowed to sit in on them. This always irritated her. The King was so grateful to Marten, who had been an Eton 'beak' all his life, that he knighted him at the end of the war in the courtyard outside the famous chapel in front of the entire school.

Returning to Windsor after months in Scotland the girls rejoined the local Girl Guides, now augmented by cockney evacuees. There was some talk of the princesses being evacuated themselves – perhaps, like many British children, especially those with money, to Canada. The Queen soon put a stop to any such notion by declaring that the children could not possibly go without her and she could not possibly abandon the King. So that debate was abandoned before it began. Not that the war could be entirely banished. At weekends when the family were gathered together at Royal Lodge or Windsor Castle there was always much to-ing and fro-ing. Once a particularly threatening long black car came hurtling into the courtyard as Princess Margaret and Crawfie gazed down.

'Boiling lead was a pretty good idea,' said the Princess thoughtfully.

During air raids the princesses together with Alah and Crawfie would descend to the dungeons, where Margaret would sleep on her governess's knee. Eventually they were kitted out in siren suits and headed off to the dungeons at seven every evening carrying small suitcases. Before long there were daytime raids too and they sheltered in summerhouses or the curious cave excavated in the hill at one side of the castle by King George III. Margaret liked to run ahead of Elizabeth and Crawfie, hide and then jump out with a loud 'Boo!' After a while a company of Grenadiers was assigned to guard duty and the girls would play hostess at meal times. Margaret, though still very young, revelled in male company.

She made everyone laugh and 'had a gay little way with her that won everybody's heart in that gloomy old Castle'.

In 1940 Lilibet made her first BBC broadcast, addressing it to her fellow children, and concluding with a piece of teamwork when she invited her sister to say goodnight to the nation. This she did, in a small, clear, slightly pompous voice, saying simply, 'Goodnight, children.'

The Queen Mary presents were not always one-way. In 1940 Margaret sent a card with 'roses for a very happy birthday'. The envelope was sealed with black wax and a distinctive, slightly spidery 'M' surmounted by a coronet. This was to remain her cipher for the rest of her life.

In 1940 'Mummy said that it would probably be a very warlike birthday with only a few presents but I think it was the nicest birthday I've ever had.' Her presents from Queen Mary were a 'sweet little walnut shell work basket and a lovely silver kettle'. That Christmas she was given 'lovely silver bowls'. Thanking the Queen on Boxing Day she wrote from Windsor, 'We decorated our own Xmas tree for the first time. The soldiers had a ball last night I think which they enjoyed very much. We gave all the servants their presents which took a long time. Mummy, Papa and Lilibet had a funny sick feeling on Xmas Eve. It went off yesterday but Papa didn't feel too good. Wasn't his speech good?'

At ten she suddenly started being given books. Her grandmother sent 'a lovely book about Grandpapa' and the little girl responded with remarkable tact and grace, 'I remember him so well and I am sure I will enjoy reading it.' For her birthday she was given books about Marco Polo and Vasco da Gama, while her sister 'gave [her] lots of books and some gramophone records'. She did particularly well that year – a great surprise in wartime – for her grandmother came up with silver spoons and sugar tongs, while her father gave her a red handbag with her initial on it, and on top of the improving books from her mother came a brooch of diamonds and aquamarines as well as a box of chocolates. In addition 'all the dogs gave me presents. Ching, my little Tibetan dog, gave me a little brooch of ivory elephants, Carol and Jane gave me a napkin ring, and Crackers gave me another little brooch.

Alah gave me a little china ornament.' At this point she realized that this recitation might be becoming tedious, so she finished, 'I am afraid you must be getting tired with this long list so I'll stop.'

There were more silver spoons and tongs from grandmother that Christmas, which 'was very dull without you and we miss you very much. We also miss Sandringham with all the presents and the Xmas tree.' However, at Windsor 'We laughed an awful lot, we pulled crackers and we had a little tree which we decorated ourselves. We broke a lot of the glass bulbs I'm afraid but we had enough to do it nicely.'

Before Christmas the girls starred in a pantomime written by Hubert Tanner, a master at the Royal School in the Great Park. 'It was very good really,' wrote Margaret. 'It was Cinderella. I was her and Lilibet was Prince Florizel. Our friends were in it too, who are really the dancing class. The two ugly sisters were very good, Dandini was quite good and Mr. Tanner was Baron Blimp. It went off quite well only the costumes which were very nice cost an awful lot and we were only left with £50 out of £72 ...'

The previous year the princesses had performed a Christmas play with Elizabeth as one of the Kings and Margaret as the Little Child in the Shepherds' hut. *Aladdin* was altogether more ambitious and clearly fired Princess Margaret's enthusiasm. 'She produced drawings of Aladdin. She arranged all the parts. She talked pantomime constantly.'

Princess Elizabeth sailed through the pantomime with predictable sangfroid; her little sister in stark contrast woke up 'absolutely pea-green' and was still in bed ten minutes before the curtain went up. Despite this she got up, had make-up slapped on and came through with flying colours.

Meanwhile the socially acceptable Grenadiers continued to mount guard and many servicemen visited the castle from home and abroad. Margaret was assured and welcoming, often observed slipping her tiny hand into a large masculine one and asking the owner if he had seen the horses or would like to look at the gardens. She was particularly taken with the Americans. All seemed to begin their conversation by remarking that they had a little girl back home just the same age. Margaret was incredulous. 'The children there must be in America,' she whispered once, 'all our age. *Billions* of them!'

That summer of 1942 saw the completion of Margaret's tea set with a cream jug and a mother-of-pearl carriage clock from her grandmother. Everything was carefully packed away 'underground' for the duration of the war. Her parents gave her a garnet suite consisting of a necklace, a brooch, a bracelet and two little hair ornaments on combs. Lilibet gave her a small brooch with owls as well as the now customary 'lots of books'.

The following year, when she sent her grandmother the traditional birthday greeting in May, she told her, 'I am working for my needlewoman's badge. I have done hemming, gathers, a button hole, over-sewing and a darn. Then I have to do a patch on flannel and make a useful garment.'

This workaday Girl Guide stuff was in dramatic contrast to next summer's sapphire necklace in August and bracelet and sachet at Christmas.

The weather was often 'a bore' and there were few deviations from the routine of Buckingham Palace, Windsor Castle and Balmoral. In 1944 there was a weekend at Badminton. 'Nice seeing Master and Mary again,' she wrote, referring to the Duke and Duchess of Beaufort. The Duke was not only master of his eponymous hunt but also His Majesty's Master of the Horse. Hence the nickname.

Equestrian and outdoor life was important. 'We are practising very hard for the show and are driving every day,' she wrote. 'Tomorrow we are getting some soldiers to cheer and clap us to get the ponies used to it.' The following August, 'We went out shooting for the first time and it was very cold and there weren't any birds, but it was great fun.'

That year the manned German bombers were replaced by V1s – pilotless flying bombs – one of which hit the Guards' Chapel at Wellington Barracks in London during matins one Sunday. More than a hundred were killed. The tragedy was particularly disturbing for the Royal Family. The chapel was just down the road from Buckingham Palace and the Guards themselves were 'Household' troops with a special place in royal affections and mythology.

Margaret herself had a relatively narrow escape in Windsor Great Park. She was cooking sausages with the Girl Guides when they heard a 'doodle-bug' approaching. All the guides flung themselves flat on the grass and the bomb passed overhead, cutting out and exploding on Windsor Racecourse a few miles further on. Until then the guides had frequently slept out – Lilibet in a summerhouse, Margaret in her own flea-bag under the stars. Occasionally the Chief Guide would upbraid Margaret and her friends for making a noise; silence would briefly ensue, only to be broken by peals of girlish laughter as Margaret gave an imitation of the Chief Guide's lecture. Even then she was an effective mimic with a subversive sense of humour. The advent of the flying bombs drove the girls back indoors, but Margaret was obviously very naughty.

She was also precocious. In December 1943 Mark Bonham Carter[1] twice danced with her at a ball at Windsor where the food was 'exquisite', the band 'marvellous' and the champagne flowed in 'rivers'. Wartime rationing was always said to extend to the Royal Family as well as everyone else, but it sounds as if there were exceptions. Bonham Carter reported to his mother, the formidable Lady Violet,[2] that Princess Margaret was 'full of character and very "tart" in her criticisms'.

A photograph of 1945 shows a picnic scene somewhere in the hills above Balmoral. There are a dozen or so in the party and Margaret, although petite as she always was, looks well developed, pert and grown-up in her kilt and cardigan. Even more significantly, only three of the group are smoking cigarettes: Lady Victoria 'Tor Tor' Gilmour, wife of the baronet and mother of the later *Spectator* proprietor and Tory grandee Lord (Ian) Gilmour,

---

1 Mark Bonham Carter (1922–1994). Balliol graduate and Grenadier Guards officer, famous Liberal victor in Torrington by-election of 1958 and created life peer.

2 Lady Violet Bonham Carter (1887–1969). Well-connected grande dame of Liberal Party, daughter of Prime Minister H. H. Asquith, mother of Mark (above) and prolific diarist.

Princess Margaret and her father the King. In an age when new legislation has made it illegal for anyone under eighteen to purchase tobacco the sight of a fifteen-year-old girl precociously drawing on a cigarette in the Highlands is surprising, almost shocking. In the 1940s it was quite usual. Princess Margaret smoked from a very early age and was certainly not discouraged by her devoted and adored papa. In the long run it became a hallmark habit and one that was, inevitably, detrimental to her health.

Her grandmother was meanwhile anxious to ensure that her more cerebral pursuits were not being ignored. The birthday of 1944 thank-you was for a 'perfectly lovely set of Dickens books' and the Christmas one was for 'the lovely set of Chaucer books and also for the book on Queen Victoria'. Two years later 'Grannie' gave her 'simply lovely book-plates' for her expanding library.

The girls were growing up. Crawfie later told some stories about Princess Elizabeth joining a Voluntary Aid Detachment mess near Camberley with officers smoking, drinking sherry and painting their nails in the mess. Another exotic Crawfie-ism had Princess Elizabeth driving a Red Cross van solo up the Great West Road. Both were accompanied by supposed younger-sisterly amusement and frustration. Both are said to be pure fabrication, though the wide circulation of the Crawfie book meant that many people believed the stories.

In January 1945 Princess Elizabeth *did* join the ATS – the Auxiliary Training Service – which was, in effect, the women's army. This meant abandoning her tutorials with Sir Henry Marten and devoting all her time to the war effort. She was almost twenty. In May the war with Germany was over. On the night of 8 May victory was celebrated by huge crowds in London and the King and Queen allowed their daughters to join the throng outside the Palace, escorted by protective young Guards officers including Henry Porchester,[1] later the Queen's racing manager. 'Porchie' recalled walking along Whitehall and Piccadilly and even

---

1 Lord (Henry) Porchester, later Earl of Carnarvon (1924–2001). Racing manager and close friend of Queen Elizabeth II.

calling into the Ritz Hotel without once being recognized.

The crowds sang old favourites such as 'Roll Out the Barrel' and 'Hang Out Your Washing on the Siegfried Line'. Back outside the Palace they stood with the rest of the crowd and called, successfully, for Mummy and Papa to appear triumphantly on the Palace balcony.

The Guards, particularly the Grenadiers, played an important part in the lives of the teenage princesses. One Grenadier, Lord Montagu of Beaulieu,[1] was of the same generation as Princess Elizabeth and Princess Margaret – he was born in 1926. Montagu recalls that when stationed either at Victoria Barracks in Windsor or Wellington Barracks close to Buckingham Palace he and his contemporaries were often asked to make up numbers at royal meals. Young Grenadiers were useful for cards, dancing, charades or even singing madrigals under the direction of Dr Harris, the choirmaster of St George's Chapel, Windsor.

Later, Montagu took Princess Margaret to the theatre. He remembers buying her chocolate mints and, years later, still treasured her handwritten thank-you letter. On one occasion at dinner in the private dining room at Buckingham Palace with the Royal Family he was surprised when a uniformed footman came in with an occasional table and a Roberts radio. As they ate they listened to the comedy programme *Much Binding in the Marsh* starring Kenneth Horne and Richard Murdoch. The show was a particular favourite of the King's.

At Christmas that year their nanny, Alah, the redoubtable Mrs Knight, died unexpectedly from meningitis at Sandringham. Her younger charge was just fifteen years old and rebellious about still having to spend her days in the schoolroom while her elder sister was a grown-up in military uniform. 'I was born too late,' she protested.

There were not only street parties to celebrate the end of the war but a solemn service of thanksgiving at which Princess

---

1 Lord Montagu of Beaulieu (1926–). Grenadier Guards officer, stately home owner, imprisoned after celebrated law-changing homosexuality trial and founder of National Motor Museum.

Margaret wore dove grey. Despite continuing austerity there were more parties and Princess Margaret joined in eagerly and vivaciously. The Bonham Carters, for instance, gave a supper at their house in Gloucester Square. Their son Mark invited both princesses. The senior Bonham Carters did not join in supper but could hear much laughter and then Princess Margaret singing 'The Bonnie Earl of Moray' at the top of her voice. 'Then', wrote Lady Violet, 'they all came up and we played games ... they were wildly keen, amused and unblasé – so that it was real fun to play with them. They stayed till 1.30 and then rolled home – after a most successful and amusing evening.'

In 1947 the nuclear Royal Family of Papa, Mummy, Lilibet and Margaret undertook a unique foreign tour. Later in the year Lilibet was married. The King, already unwell, was dead within five years. This was the only time that the 'family firm' operated together as a tight, cosy unit on a prolonged royal duty. Royal Family life for George VI and his wife and daughters was never the same again.

The visit was to South Africa, designed by the King's private secretary 'Tommy' Lascelles[1] in part to thank Field Marshal Smuts[2] and his countrymen for their support in the war. Although still part of the British Empire, South Africa was a country divided not only between black and white but between British and Boer. A full, official account of the trip was written by Dermot Morrah,[3] a *Times* leader writer and Arundel Herald Extraordinary, who always liked to have the words 'Late Fellow of All Souls College, Oxford' prominently displayed after his name. He was perfectly entitled to this but, whatever his merits, you would never describe Morrah as hard-hitting, let alone investigative. Smuts, who wrote

---

1 Sir Alan ('Tommy') Lascelles (1887–1991). Traditionalist courtier who served three kings, most notably as King George VI's private secretary, and was private secretary to his daughter, Queen Elizabeth II, for the first year of her reign.

2 Field Marshal Jan Smuts (1870–1950). South African Prime Minister and international statesman who opposed apartheid and was author of the preamble to United Nations Charter.

3 Dermot Morrah (1896–1974). Leader writer for *The Times* and *Daily Telegraph*, Herald Extraordinary, academic and monarchist.

the foreword, described Morrah's account as 'fair and delightful', which speaks for itself.

Nevertheless, by the time of writing Morrah had become the prime, though not the only, source of information about the trip. By 2006 Her Majesty the Queen and Sir Edmund Grove, sometime Chief Accountant of the Privy Purse, were the only two survivors of the tour.

The royal party sailed to South Africa aboard HMS *Vanguard*, the ninth Royal Naval ship to bear the name since the first had fought against the Spanish Armada in 1588. There was no royal yacht in the immediate aftermath of World War II, but *Vanguard*, the last battleship in the Navy, was a stirring sight, commanded by a rear-admiral called Agnew[1] who came from the picture-dealing family in Bond Street who were also, for a time, the publishers of *Punch* magazine. This made him just about 'one of us' and he presided over a wardroom of a hundred nice and similarly acceptable officers.

It was very rough crossing the Bay of Biscay, but the midshipmen gave a cocktail party in the Gun Room, Tommy Lascelles read Trollope and later, when the weather grew hot and sticky, they crossed the equator and fireworks were let off. The two princesses, 'crossing the line' for the first time, were initiated in the traditional manner along with about a thousand members of the ship's company. Actually the princesses were only given a token initiation accompanied by elaborate certificates before retiring when the remaining 'initiates' became boisterous and began ducking one another more or less indiscriminately.

One day an enjoyable treasure hunt was organized for the midshipmen and the princesses, but generally the days passed with deckchairs, deck games, dinner with a handful of officers followed by a film or dancing. It was all very agreeable – so much so that for years afterwards the surviving members of the Wardroom and the royal party used to meet for an annual commemorative lunch in London.

---

1 Rear-Admiral, later Vice-Admiral Agnew (1896–1974). Career naval officer and member of Bond Street art-dealing family.

The royal party arrived off Cape Town on 17 February. Morrah described Table Mountain as 'clean-cut as a painting by Canaletto' and wrote that 'the grey and silver bulk of the greatest of British battleships, HMS *Vanguard*, the gaiety of her bunting contrasting with the grimness of her mighty guns, lay motionless on a shimmering sea'.

For three and a half days 'us four' and their entourage enjoyed what sounds like a euphoric reception in Cape Town, which included a ball where Princess Elizabeth danced with the Mayor and Princess Margaret with the Minister of Economic Development. The Cape party culminated in the State Opening of Parliament and the visitors then set off across the Union in the special White Train of eight English carriages and six South African a third of a mile long. This was to be home for 6,944 miles and thirty-five nights. Half an hour ahead of the White Train went another pilot train containing the King's barber, a florist and the ladies and gentlemen of the press, including Dermot Morrah. There was also a back-up train ('the Ghost Train'), a fleet of thirteen or fourteen large limousines and four Viking aircraft of the King's Flight. Royalty travelled heavy in those days.

'Long thought and contrivance', wrote Morrah, 'in two countries had gone to rendering this mechanized caravan as perfect for the arduous functions required of it and as comfortable for its exalted passengers as the engineer, the architect and the decorator could make it.' The White Train was the longest and heaviest ever to travel across South Africa.

Princess Margaret wrote two long letters home to her grandmother Queen Mary. The first of them, from the White Train, was dated 10 March.

'Darling Grannie,' she wrote,

I thought I must write and tell you how we are getting on in this lovely country. We have been here three weeks today and it is extraordinary to think how much ground we have covered and how many new experiences we have had since leaving England.

We are now in the Free state and we stayed two days in the charming new house they have built for the Governor-General at

Blomfontein. While we were there I had my first trip by aeroplane, which was very exciting. I went with Papa in one and Lilibet with Mummy in the other. Paying no attention to what the rest of my family said about flying I enjoyed every minute of it. The sensation of leaving the ground and feeling completely away from everything and everybody was wonderful.

We find it very difficult to take any exercise being on the train, but Lilibet and I have managed to ride quite a lot, on horses lent by people who happen to be near the train. And at Port Elizabeth the train was drawn up on the beach so that it was very easy to just rush down to the sea and have a swim in between functions and drives.

The heat luckily is not too great; and considering that I have never been in a hot climate, I don't feel it too much. Your parasols have saved my life more than once. Our hat maker being horribly fashionable refused to give us brims on our hats, so a sunshade is the only thing. Today we visited Kronstad and Bethlehem and tomorrow we get into Basutoland which we are all looking forward to very much. The natives are such fascinating people and they must be much more interesting living in their natural state.

The Royal Archives have asked me not to transcribe the remainder of this letter, not on the grounds of its content but because I am 'not writing an official biography'. It continues for a further twenty-six lines in print and is written in much the same vein as the earlier part. The Princess says that the family has been having an interesting time, although some of the local officials have been lacking in imagination and seem perfectly happy for their royal visitors simply to drive around, meet the town council, see the town hall, present an address and depart. The royal party have, however, been curious and discovered some things for themselves – notably a vine at Cyraff-Reinet which was even bigger than the one at Hampton Court.

In East London Princess Elizabeth opened a new dock and made a speech which her family thought quite good. They had a recording which Princess Margaret offered to play for her grandmother on her return.

The Princess admits that she had previously no experience of black people and had been apprehensive, even frightened, about meeting them. After her time in South Africa, however, she had come to like them very much. She particularly warmed to their enthusiasm and their singing. Her father, the King, so liked their national anthem that he was organizing a special recording to take home.

The weather remained hot and Princess Margaret was concerned about the cold back home and felt it was unfair that her grandmother was forced to endure it. The Princess ends by asking Queen Mary to let her know what she would like to hear about – always supposing that the old lady did write a letter. In that way she could provide more interesting information. She signed off, simply, with the one name, 'Margaret' and sent her 'best love'.

When she wrote about the daily morning ride with her sister, she failed to mention the chaperones who regularly rode out with them. These were a young naval officer called Peter Ashmore,[1] who was an extra-equerry to the King and was later to become a knight, a vice-admiral and, in the seventies and eighties, Comptroller of the Royal Household. It was Ashmore's job to look after Princess Elizabeth. The younger princess was left in the charge of the senior of these two young men, Group Captain Peter Townsend. One morning Lascelles himself got up at 6.45 in the morning and rode out with the princesses and 'the boys'. It was the first time he had been on a horse for over ten years and he was afraid he might be stiff the following day. It was rare, however, for the little quartet to be accompanied. Most often they rode out alone.

'We sped in the cool air, along the sands or across the veldt,' recalled Townsend thirty years later. 'Those were the most glorious moments of the day.'

Just four days later Margaret was writing to her grandmother again, this time from Natal, where the family and their entourage were staying at the National Park Hostel at Mont-aux-Sources. The flimsy air-mail paper has a picture of the rather functional

---

1 Vice-Admiral Peter Ashmore (1921–2002). Master of the Royal Household from 1973 to 1987.

bungaloid main building at the top and at the bottom of the page a line which boasts: 'BOATING, HIKING, RIDING, SWIMMING, TENNIS, CINEMA EVERY WEEK, DANCING'.

'Darling Grannie', she wrote,

> I wrote my last letter at a very inopportune moment as we were just about to go into Basutoland. Therefore I told you nothing about what it was like.
>
> We had visited Ladybrand in the morning and motored from there, over the bridge into Basutoland. There we were welcomed by the High Commissioner, Sir Evelyn Baring.[1] I can't tell you how extraordinary it was, but we all had the feeling that we were in a kind of England overseas. The atmosphere had changed in one hour since we had crossed the bridge.
>
> We drove in two cars from the border to the Residency two miles away. Lilibet and I were fascinated as the whole way there the road was lined by native horsemen. We had never seen so many mounted people in our lives. The whole of Basutoland had rolled into Maseru. Luckily they are not too civilised and wear blankets with wonderful head-dresses made of high feathers on their heads.
>
> The Residency had a swimming pool which we were allowed to use which was great fun. We also rode some Basuto ponies the next morning.
>
> After riding we went to the Pitsu which was the native gathering of everybody. Then the High Commissioner, Papa and the Paramount Chief, who is a woman, made speeches.
>
> It was an amazing sight, the whole population of Basutoland was a vast silent staring crowd, completely covering the hillside where we were.
>
> Unfortunately we only stayed two days so that we really didn't have time to see very much but all the same we were very sad to leave so soon.

Once more the Royal Archives have asked me to stop quoting

---

1 Evelyn Baring (1903–1973). British proconsul and scion of the great banking house; later Governor of Kenya during the Mau Mau rebellion. Became 1st Baron Howick of Glendale in 1960.

verbatim at this point, though the rest of the letter continues charmingly and harmlessly. The young Princess thought Natal lovely and apologises for the writing paper although she thought her grandmother might be amused by it, not least because of the information it conveyed. The mountain which almost surrounded the place was called 'The Amphitheatre' and the camp-site, which is what the hotel most resembled, was made up of a dozen bungalows. The Princesses had one and the ladies and gentlemen were segregated into others which were called 'Rondovels'. It was all thoroughly enjoyable except for the frequent thunderstorms which sometimes led to one being marooned, umbrella-less, in one's room. Many people asked after the girls' aunt and uncle, the Earl and Countess of Athlone[1] and hoped they would return for a visit to the country of which Uncle Alge had once been Governor-General. They had obviously been popular. This time the Princess asked her grandmother to pass on her love to the rest of the family and signed off as her 'very loving Margaret'.

On 2 April Peter Townsend featured, by his own account, in one of the oddest and perhaps most significant moments of the entire visit. King George VI was notorious for his sudden violent outbursts of temper. One occurred in South Africa when he discovered that there had been severe flooding at Windsor and no one had told him. He and the Queen had experienced misgivings about sunning themselves in South Africa while their British subjects starved and froze at home. Rationing that year was at its most severe. One commentator (Paul Addison, quoted in Peter Hennessy) remarked that the images that evoke that time are

> of hardship and high endeavour. They conjure up a land in which it was usually winter and people were digging themselves out of snowdrifts. The middle classes had disappeared and the male population, driven on by the exhortations of the government, were all digging coal or building ships. The women, meanwhile, were queuing for offal at the butcher's. In such spare time as they

---

1 The Earl of Athlone (1874–1957); Countess of Athlone (1883–1981). She was a granddaughter of Queen Victoria; he was Queen Mary's youngest brother and Governor General of South Africa 1924–31.

had left the people were grappling with social problems and were either squatting or looking forward to a set of NHS dentures.

For the King, the Windsor flooding was the last straw and he came to Lascelles' office to remonstrate almost incoherent with rage.

The Townsend incident was more dramatic and certainly more dangerous. It happened on 2 April in an open Daimler driving the 120 miles from Pretoria to Johannesburg. We only have Townsend's word for what actually took place and he recalled the incident in his memoirs, *Time and Chance*, thirty years after the event.

The King was under huge pressure throughout the tour. At times he still suffered from stage fright and he was never truly relaxed when confronted with large crowds. Even the light-hearted moments were often the result of interventions by others. There was, for example, one jolly moment when an elderly man in the crowd removed his hat in a royal salute and released the best part of a swarm of bees from underneath. They had been attracted by the sticky brilliantine with which the man had smarmed down his hair. Quick as a flash Tommy Lascelles whispered to the King that it was better to have bees in your bonnet than ants in your pants. The remark was picked up by the monarch and relayed to the crowd, who roared with mirth. Consequently King George acquired something of a reputation as a relaxed, laid-back wag. This, however, was an illusion. Already thin to the point of gauntness he lost a whole stone on that South African visit. He was worried about the trip itself and deeply concerned about the troubles of 'his' people back home in England fighting hard against the horrible weather and the privations of a rationing system that still, two years after the end of the war, only allowed each adult a weekly diet of a single egg, one loaf of bread and meat to the value of one shilling and two pence.

The King was always on edge and his family and immediate entourage were permanently terrified that his ever-tense condition would teeter over the edge into one of his uncontrollable 'gnashes'.

This is what happened on 2 April. The route lay through the

Reef towns of Waterkloof, Zesfontein, Putfontein, Geduld Mine
and on through Springs and Brakpan. 'Hundreds of thousands of
sweating, screaming, frenzied blacks', recalled Townsend, 'lined
the route, pressed about the car, waved frantically and hollered
their ecstatic joy at the sight of this little family of four, so fresh
and white and – apparently – demure, seated in the back of the
open royal Daimler.'

Townsend, as equerry, was up front alongside the chauffeur.
The Royal Family were behind and the King decided to take up
back-seat driving. This took the form, eventually, of an 'incessant
tirade'. The Queen tried to soothe her husband; the princesses
tried to make light of it all; Townsend chatted encouragingly to
the driver. But the situation became worse and worse and the
chauffeur became seriously rattled. Eventually Townsend decided
there was only one thing for it. He did the unforgivable; he turned
round and shouted angrily at his sovereign: 'For Heaven's sake,
shut up, or there's going to be an accident.'

They were just coming into Benoni where a year later Denis
Compton hit a triple century in one minute over three hours.
Suddenly Townsend saw a policeman with a 'terrible determined
look in his eyes' come running at the car. Behind them a thin
black man was running frantically towards the Daimler clutching
something in his hands and shouting dementedly. With great
presence of mind the Queen whacked him several times with her
parasol before he was beaten senseless by the police and dragged
away. Only later did they discover that the man was a loyal
subject, that he was calling out 'My King! My King!' and that the
object in his hand was a ten-shilling note that he intended as a
present for Princess Elizabeth.

That evening Townsend had a long heart-to-heart with Lascelles
in which he talked of his 'remorse and disgust', of the 'lamentable'
scene and even of tendering his resignation. Much later, just before
midnight, the King summoned him.

'All he said, very simply and with complete sincerity,' recalled
Townsend, 'was: "I am sorry about today. I was very tired."'
Townsend's verdict on this was: 'More than ever before, I realised
how lovable the man was.'

Dermot Morrah, in his contemporary official account, had part of the story but far from the whole truth. He did not enjoy Townsend's privileged view and he was shackled by writing something authorized in the entirely different world of the 1940s. This is what he wrote:

> It was during the morning's tour of the East Rand that there occurred the only incident of the entire tour of the Union which for a moment seemed to be the expression of disloyal or unfriendly feeling. An excited Zulu came charging out of the ranks and bore straight down upon the royal car, which owing to the pressure of the crowds was moving at a slow walking pace. He looked as if he was bent upon attack, and the Queen with a smile on her lips, but determination in her eye, had to fend him off with the point of her sunshade. On inquiry, however, it turned out that this apparent rebel was yet another devoted patriot, whose only desire was to press a ten-shilling note into the hand of the object of his particular adoration, Princess Elizabeth.

Throughout this tour the Queen was a tower of strength and Princess Elizabeth was felt to have grown enormously in stature. The King got through, but at a cost. Of Princess Margaret, Townsend wrote: '[She] played a relatively thankless role for, beside her sister, heir to the throne, she cut a less prominent figure in the eyes of the public. She was not yet seventeen. Yet, throughout the daily round of civic ceremonies, that pretty and highly personable young princess held her own.'

Throughout 1947 she signed herself plain 'Margaret' and was referred to as such. In earlier years she had always been known by the two names with which she was christened: Margaret Rose. However she always hated the name 'Rose' and in 1947 she became, of her own volition, plain 'Margaret'. 'I dropped the Rose when I was seventeen', she used to say later, with quiet satisfaction.

The engagement of Princess Elizabeth and Prince Philip was announced after the family's return and that summer at Balmoral Margaret reported to her grandmother that the weather was 'too good to be true' so that 'Philip spends his entire time in the river or the loch'. That year's grand-maternal present was a 'beautiful brooch', which 'everyone agrees is the most lovely thing they have ever seen'. For a fortnight Margaret seems to have been alone, 'doing nothing very much except go for picnics, expeditions and feel very happy'.

As always in Margaret's life, however, there was room for a cultural dimension. In early September her mother whisked her off to the Edinburgh Festival for concerts and plays as well as a somewhat dire-sounding celebration of Scottishness called 'Enterprise Scotland'.

In 1948 the young Princess was beginning to undertake official duties. They were not always glamorous or exciting. Royal duties were ever thus. In February she reported to Queen Mary: 'The opening of the pumping station went very well in spite of the gale that was blowing. I am afraid that one photographer rather overdid things by taking a picture of me with my eyes shut.' Pumping stations and photographers represent the downside of royal duties: tedium and intrusion. These are two constants in the life of a member of the Royal Family and there are fewer compensations for a minor than for a major royal.

That year Princess Margaret represented the King, her father, abroad for the first time when she went to Holland for the formal abdication of Queen Wilhelmina[1] and the accession of her daughter, Juliana.[2] She was 'so glad that Uncle Alge and Aunt Alice are to be there'. She seems to have been fond of the Athlones, whose continuing popularity had been so evident in South Africa the previous year. She needn't have worried about her own performance, for she was an uncomplicated and unaffected success.

At eighteen she was beautiful, sexy, seemingly self-assured – the drop-dead gorgeous personification of everything a princess was supposed to be. 'It always sounds so old', she wrote, 'when other people have eighteenth birthdays and yet when it comes to oneself one doesn't feel any older at all.'

---

1 Queen Wilhelmina of the Netherlands (1880–1962). Symbol of Dutch independence and resistance to Germans in World War II.

2 Queen Juliana of the Netherlands (1909–2004). Like mother, symbol of robust bicycling Dutch independence but sometimes overshadowed by domineering German husband, Bernhard.

This first solo foreign assignment was a royal occasion that carried implicit messages for the House of Windsor and the way it perceived its role. Queen Wilhelmina had been on the Dutch throne for more than half a century, succeeding her father William III in 1890 when she was only ten years old. Forced to flee to Britain after the Germans invaded her country in World War II she spent the conflict in Great Britain, where she was a constant symbol of Dutch resistance and a resolute example to her beleaguered subjects. She, and the rest of her family, remained immensely popular in Holland, where they ruled by common consent rather than divine right – not like the House of Windsor.

Traditional monarchists in Great Britain always derided the style of the House of Orange which, compared with the pomp and circumstance of its British counterpart, was secular, egalitarian and unostentatious – the archetypal bicycling monarchy. Those, particularly the British, who believed that if you were going to do royalty then you should do it royally, felt the Dutch rather let the side down.

The decision of the elderly Queen Wilhelmina to abdicate voluntarily in favour of her daughter Juliana was an example of this almost republican attitude to the role of kings and queens. With the terrible exception of the Duke of Windsor the British don't do abdication – least of all Elizabeth the Second.

Not so Wilhelmina. After fifty-eight years she had had enough. She decided to abdicate on the Friday. Her daughter Juliana would be invested as queen the following Monday. The ceremony would be held in the Nieuwe Kerk but would be secular. It was not even a coronation. The Dutch crown together with such ancillary symbols as the orb and sceptre remained on a table in front of the monarch, who was certainly not to be anointed with holy oil as is the historic custom for British monarchs.

'What do you think, Crawfie?' Margaret exclaimed to her governess. 'I am going to represent Papa and Mummy at Juliana's coronation!' Crawfie commented, 'It was her first big undertaking, and probably I was not the only person in the Palace who felt a little apprehensive for her. We had great fun getting her clothes together, and on that occasion I played the governess's part thoroughly and gave her a lot of good advice.'

Margaret did not leave for Amsterdam until the evening of Friday 3 September. She drove – 'motored' was the journalistic argot of the day – from Balmoral to Aberdeen, where she boarded a special sleeping car attached to the 6.45 night express for King's Cross. The party was small but sufficiently senior to command respect. The other members of Her Royal Highness's suite were the Countess of Halifax[1] and the Duke of Beaufort. In support were Margaret Egerton[2] as lady-in-waiting and Peter Townsend. 'All details of transport and administration should be fixed by Wing-Commander Townsend in liaison with our Ambassador,' wrote Tom Harvey in a memorandum on 28 July.

The areas of responsibility between the sexes were sharply defined along predictable lines. 'Michael' (presumably Adeane),[3] wrote lady-in-waiting Delia Peel to 'Dearest Dorothy' (Lady Halifax), 'has just laid it upon me to let you know that Princess Margaret is proposing to wear the new tiara given her by Queen Mary for Her Birthday on some occasion in Holland. I was to say that Michael thought it was more my affair than his to convey this news to you. I apologise for "butting in" as they say.'

But, of course, she wasn't butting in.

Men did motor-cars and aircraft. Tiaras were girls' stuff.

The night express was two hours late because of flooding north of Newcastle. It was Saturday morning when they arrived at King's Cross but it was reported in London that 'People on their way to work cheered as she drove from the station to Buckingham Palace.'

The royal party later flew to Schipol airport in two Vikings of the King's Flight, the principals supported by three ladies' maids,

---

1 The Countess of Halifax, née Onslow (1885–1976). Much-loved matriarch who met her husband in the refreshment room at Berwick-on-Tweed railway station en route to a ball in Kelso.

2 Margaret Egerton (1918–2004). Lady-in-waiting to Queen Elizabeth, the Queen Mother. Wife of ubiquitous *éminence grise* Sir John ('Jock') Colville.

3 Lord (Michael) Adeane (1910–1984). Private secretary to Queen Elizabeth II from 1953 to 1972.

one manservant for Beaufort, a footman and a detective. In Amsterdam they checked into the Amstel Hotel, where Margaret was welcomed with real red roses from the hotel's board of directors and artificial ones from a Mr A. P. Porte, who got one of those charming but archaically worded letters of thanks from the lady-in-waiting: 'I am desired by the Princess Margaret to reply to your letter of the 8th September and to convey to you Her Royal Highness' most sincere thanks for the charming bunch of artificial roses which you so kindly sent to the Amstel Hotel and which the Princess had great pleasure in accepting.'

This sort of sonorous formality was pervasive though tinged with some characteristic Dutch simplicity. At the ceremonial abdication the anonymous *Times* correspondent noted that the momentous transition of authority from mother to daughter was stoically witnessed until the family element became so pronounced that it 'brought the handkerchiefs at last from reticent Dutch pockets'.

The British Ambassador, Sir Philip Nicholls, in his dispatch to his boss, Foreign Secretary Ernest Bevin,[1] on holiday at Mullion Cove in Cornwall, was acute and observant. 'It was noticeable', he wrote of Wilhelmina, 'that she looked happy if not jubilant on this occasion whereas the new Queen looked grave and pre-occupied. One was renouncing, the other assuming, the burdens of office.' Juliana herself said, '[The event] fills me with melancholy but at least I can do something for my Mother, for her to whom together with that good man my Father, I owe my life and all else.'

Margaret herself was not, of course, centre stage. In the *Times* report of 'The solemn enthronement of Her Royal Highness Princess Juliana as Queen of the Netherlands' Margaret does not even get a mention until paragraph six, after a detailed description of the main business and of Juliana's deportment ('calm and queenly').

---

1 Ernest Bevin (1881–1951). General Secretary of the Transport and General Workers Union which he helped create; a Somerset orphan who left school early but went on to be powerful and popular Foreign Secretary in post-war Labour government.

It's a classic piece of hushed-voice royal reportage, typical of the period and the essentially deferential, Establishment tone of the nation's self-appointed 'paper of record': 'Then, capping all in brilliance, and arriving only after all others were seated, there came the royal guests from abroad. Among these was Princess Margaret, a small but stately figure in a long gown of pale pink moiré, and wearing a white satin bonnet embellished with pink ostrich feathers, who walked with assurance to her place between Lady Halifax and the Duke of Beaufort.'

'Small but stately' sounds less than ecstatic but the 'pale pink moiré and ostrich feathers' are nice touches, and even though Margaret had only to walk to her place in church she managed it without mishap.

This was the main event, but there were others involving the Princess. She was presented with the Grand Cross of the Order of the Netherlands Lion, which is the highest honour in Dutch chivalry. Beaufort and Townsend were honoured too, though less ostentatiously. There was a splendid dinner at the Dam Palace, a return lunch at the British Embassy in The Hague and a military tattoo ('Well carried out except that the troops were kept too long at attention, a point which did not escape the expert eye of Lord Athlone'). The Canadian Ambassador also gave a luncheon, the Concertgebouw Orchestra played Beethoven's Fifth and there was a small, informal 'dancing party' at the Amstel Hotel, where Margaret danced with Prince Bernhard and with Townsend. The Ambassador reported: 'Queen Juliana herself danced and the party was both gay and informal.' Margaret and her group also visited a flower market at Aalmseer and managed a drive through the surrounding countryside, which included brief visits to Utrecht and Hilversum. The flight home made a special detour, at her request, so that she could view the battlefield of Arnhem and she finally got back to Balmoral in time to catch her parents' account of Friday's Braemar Gathering before they set off for the State Opening of Parliament, making a stop at Doncaster to take in the St Leger.

It was an impressive debut for the young Princess. It was true, perhaps, that she didn't have to do a great deal. Being herself was more than enough. She obviously looked far more beautiful and fairy-princess-like than that bald journalistic 'small but stately' phrase suggested. One or two members of the public wrote in enthusiastically along the lines of a local Save the Children worker (Kathleen Freeman), who said that 'Of all the Royal Guests your little Princess Margaret Rose was most cheered. The English King could never have sent a better Ambassador.'

But the most telling comments came from the Ambassador himself. In his dispatch to Ernie Bevan Sir Philip Nicholls wrote,

> As I have already reported by telegram the visit of Her Royal Highness was an unqualified success from the start to the finish. It is quite certain that the Dutch public have taken more interest in Princess Margaret than any other of their Royal guests and the attention devoted by the Dutch Press to Her Royal Highness was second only to that accorded to the House of Orange itself.
>
> Her public appearances both in Amsterdam and in the countryside were greeted with great enthusiasm and I, and all the members of my staff, have received tributes to her good looks, dignified bearing and unaffected charm. The impression made on the members of the students' guard, which she inspected on arrival at the Dam Palace for the State Dinner on September 6th, was so marked that on the following evening these students serenaded her with flowers from a boat on the River Amstel beneath her hotel.

If the Ambassador had been dishing out marks he would surely have given the Princess an alpha. 'The manner in which Her Royal Highness carried out her duties has been very widely recognised and commended,' he concluded, ending with quiet satisfaction that the whole visit was 'most useful in emphasising and cementing Anglo-Dutch friendship'.

Margaret was still in her teens but, at a time when royal ambassadors were thin on the ground and not always imbued with genuine glamour and star quality, her arrival was a real plus. Already she was beginning to look like a useful member of the family firm.

On her return she was met at the airport by Jock Colville[1] and Crawfie, who told her that everyone was very proud of her.

'She gave me that mischievous side glance of hers, half laughter, half solemn.

'"Well, I have to behave myself now, Crawfie, don't I? There is no Lilibet around, to keep me in my place with a sisterly poke."'

It was the first of a number of such tasks that she carried out throughout her life. All were different but similar. It was what being a member of the British Royal Family was all about: ritual rites of passage in foreign monarchies, independence-grantings, or just foreign visits involving flag-waving, tree-planting, smiling and waving and acting out a very particular role. Margaret pulled off an impressive debut and enjoyed a number of subsequent successes. At other times her attention wandered, the smile faded and she didn't always wave.

The following May she visited Italy for the first time and began a passionate affaire with the country that was to last the rest of her life. As soon as she arrived at the Gritti Palace Hotel in Venice, after a seven-hour drive from Florence, she sat down and penned a letter for her darling Grannie. She was having 'a lovely time', she wrote and continued, 'Travelled up from the South to Rome where we spent a week trying to see everything which was impossible, then to Florence, also for a week and your list was a great boon and we managed to see everything you suggested. The only difficulty about seeing so many churches and picture galleries and museums on top of each other is that one can't remember what was in which place'. She made lists but they didn't really help. She also lunched with Gitta and Tim Aosta in their house, which was entirely covered with red roses.

She was in love with almost everything but there was just one small blot. Until now she had enjoyed a charmed relationship with a gentle and deferential British press, which was respectful and kind about royalty in general and about her in particular. Italy was different. Italy was abroad. Italy was republican. Italy was

---

1 Sir John ('Jock') Colville (1915–1987). Private secretary to Winston Churchill, courtier, diarist and universal *éminence grise*.

the birthplace of the paparazzi. For Margaret the foreign press came as an unwelcome shock.

'I do hope you didn't believe a word in any of the papers about the visit to Capri,' she wrote to the famously regal Queen Mary. 'I am afraid that they really rather overdid everything and wrote some rather vulgar and unnecessary things all of which were perfectly untrue.'

America's *Time* magazine in a long article suggested that the thirty-five-day holiday, which also included a postscript in Paris, had not been much fun. The magazine claimed that the Princess had been nagging her parents for more than a year to let her go on her own to the Continent but, in no time at all, 'Whitehall, the Queen, the embassies of two foreign capitals and a clutch of palace aides were all involved.' By the time she actually embarked on one of her father's aeroplanes the holiday had become a royal tour, chaperoned by the Queen's private secretary, Major Tom Harvey, and his wife. *Time* reported that she showed no disappointment but repeated her alleged remark on arriving in South Africa in 1947. 'Isn't it a pity', she was supposed to have said to the King, 'that we have to travel with royalty?'

Despite being chaperoned by Major and Mrs Harvey she did manage to cut loose in Capri, taking a dip in the Mediterranean wearing what was decorously described as a 'two piece bathing costume'. Paparazzi took photographs. They were published around the world. The idea may seem perfectly normal more than half a century later but at the time the idea of royalty being photographed in swimming gear was amazing. No wonder she was afraid Granny might be shocked.

Time magazine reported:

One Dip. No Hips. Hounded by newshawks, plagued by photographers, dogged by detectives and ringed around by protocol, prudence and propriety, the little (5ft) princess had not had what could be described as a rip-roaring time. Many an evening during her holiday, when the stars twinkled over Capri or the lights of Montmartre beckoned, Margaret had sat primly in a hotel room chatting with a palace aide, Major Thomas Harvey, and his wife.

When she did go to a Paris nightclub, she sat out all the rumbas to avoid undignified hip-waving. A simple dip she took in the surf at a private estate on the Bay of Naples filled the world's press with bootleg photographs of royalty in a two-piece bathing suit and set editors snarling at one another over problems of journalistic good taste.

The magazine also outlined her social calendar and wrote: 'With sister Elizabeth safely settled in matronhood, Margaret is the most eligible partygoer in Britain ... it is Princess Margaret's particular task to extend her hand to passée old Dame Society, and to make it seem that everyone is having a ripping time at her parties.'

The British press did not yet write about royalty like that, much less repeat an anecdote that would certainly have upset Queen Mary. It ran like this.

'Look into my eyes,' Princess Margaret ordered a startled dancing partner not long ago. 'I am looking into them, Ma'am,' he stammered. 'Well,' said Margaret, 'you're looking into the most beautiful eyes in England. The Duchess of Kent has the most beautiful nose. The Duchess of Windsor has the most beautiful chin. And I have the most beautiful eyes. Surely,' she added, with an impish gleam in her eye, as her flustered partner groped for a suitable answer, 'you believe what you read in the papers.'

Prince Charles was born in the autumn of 1948, moving Margaret a step further away from any possible succession. Not that she mentioned this to her grandmother or seemed to exhibit anything other than genuine affection for her new nephew. 'Darling Charles has been with us for a fortnight,' she wrote in August 1949 at Balmoral, 'and is standing holding on to things at only nine months.' Later, around the time of her twenty-first birthday, she wrote of Charles and Anne, 'The children get more and more angelic every day.' One afternoon in Scotland, after hearing her sister's Canadian pipers – the Argylls – piping, they all had tea together and 'Charles put on one of the huge feather bonnets the drummers wear! He completely disappeared.'

With her elder sister married and, early in 1948, pregnant, Margaret became in a sense an only child. She was still only seventeen, a single teenager, racketing around that gloomy great Palace at the end of the Mall, with no very obvious purpose in life and, for the first time, no companion of roughly her own age. All her life she and Elizabeth had been a sort of duet. Even though her sister was the future queen and she was destined to be for ever a princess they had been an item, the two apparently inseparable children in a happy but small nuclear family. The change was sudden and dramatic.

Part of the solution was for Margaret to take on more public duties – more pumping stations and photographers. In 1948 she carried out thirty-five public engagements, and while some of these were actually private dances where she was among friends and acquaintances, others were genuine public occasions on which she had a royal duty to perform.

The first that year was the opening of the Sandringham Company Girl Guides' Hut on 31 January. 'Dear Lady Delia Peel,' wrote Diana Musselwhite, the boss of the local guides, from her home at Wolferton Rectory near King's Lynn, 'You may know that the King has graciously given the Guides a hut ... I hesitate to ask but I wonder if a member of the Royal Family would kindly perform this little ceremony.' Princess Margaret duly obliged. The last of her royal engagements that year was a visit to the Tate Gallery on 31 December. In between there were Mrs Douglas's cocktail party on 12 February (she was the wife of the American Ambassador and her daughter Sharman[1] was a glamorous contemporary and friend); Lady Kemsley's[2] dance on 9 June, a celebration for her son Tony's twenty-first that had been postponed

---

1 Sharman Douglas (1928–1996). Daughter of Lewis Douglas, American Ambassador to London in late 1940s, close to Princess Margaret and rumoured, baselessly, to be more than just good friend.
2 Lady Kemsley, wife of first Viscount (Gomer Berry), famous for complaining about photograph of bull's testicles in the *Sunday Graphic* which led to their removal by airbrush and a successful law-suit by the owner.

on account of Tony's military service; the Guards' Boat Club Ball (this soon became a regular fixture), and a dance preceded by a small private dinner given by Lady Joan Peake. Other engagements sound less fun, but they all demanded a surprising amount of detailed planning, and all of them had the Princess uncompromisingly at their centre. Outsiders are often dismissive about royal engagements and one can only guess at the demands they make. My main observation is that they are seldom as easy as they look and not often a lot of fun.

Although conscientious in fulfilling public duties, Margaret was often reluctant to make speeches. You can see why. At the opening of the Guides' Hut, for instance, her words have a presumably unconscious whiff of Joyce Grenfell at her most mischievous. 'Looking round me,' said the Princess, 'I can imagine how hard Miss Musselwhite and the company must have worked ... I do congratulate you on the charming appearance of your new meeting place. I have been in the movement ten years (doesn't that sound a long time?) as a Brownie, a Guide and now a Sea Ranger ... I have now great pleasure in declaring this hut open.' In a more innocent, more deferential age these agreeable banalities might have passed muster, but those days were already numbered.

Margaret was assisted in her pleasures and duties by a series of ladies-in-waiting and by her mother and her mother's staff. Of these the most noticeable were Major Tom Harvey the affable holder of a Distinguished Service Order, and Wing Commander, later Group Captain, Peter Townsend, who was even more extensively decorated, with a DSO and a couple of DFCs. Harvey was well connected, reliable and universally acknowledged as a safe pair of hands. People liked him. Townsend was young, good-looking, a fighter ace, unhappily married and a particular favourite of the King. He was also, alas, a particular favourite of his younger daughter's.

George VI liked young warriors. He was fond of Prince Philip, who had been mentioned in dispatches at the Battle of Matapan, and of his dapper Australian private secretary, Lieutenant

Commander Mike Parker,[1] who had also fought with distinction during the war. That war was a vividly recent memory. The world was dominated by old and bold commanders and peopled by their young and dashing subordinates. The forties and fifties were the legacy of conflict.

The ladies-in-waiting, mostly a few years older than the Princess, were the sort of young women you'd expect to find at the front of *Country Life* in twinset and pearls: Alice Wemyss, Delia Peel,[2] Meg Egerton, later to marry Sir John 'Jock' Colville, Jean Rankin,[3] Jennifer Bevan.[4] Although their notes and memoranda to their boss always began with the deferential words 'With my humble duty', they do not sound as if they were in the least overawed by royal surroundings. If not titled, they were certainly aristocratic and used to mixing in grand surroundings with grand landowners. One splendid letter from the Duchess of Buccleuch begins, 'Dear Jennifer', on the grounds that she cannot address someone as 'Miss Bevan' when she remembers her so well as a little girl. Crawfie described Jennifer Bevan as 'a charming little person with pretty manners'. She became a close friend.

Margaret's distaste for public speaking was understandable. She was, after all, only seventeen and she had been brought up and educated privately in a privileged and protected cocoon. Nevertheless, when required to do so she would say a few words, writing them out neatly in pen or ink beforehand with occasional deletions and changes and odd spelling mistakes, such as not always managing 'i before e except after c'.

The stock photographs of the period were those taken by

---

1 Lt. Cdr. Mike Parker (1920–2002). Breezy Australian who served as Prince Philip's private secretary before being forced into early retirement by highly-publicised divorce.

2 Dame Delia Peel (1881–1981). Great-aunt of Diana, Princess of Wales, and long-serving courtier.

3 Lady Jean Rankin (1903–2001). Long-standing friend and lady-in-waiting to Queen Elizabeth, the Queen Mother.

4 Jennifer Bevan, m. Sir John Lowther, later Lord Lieutenant Northamptonshire 1952. Early lady-in-waiting and friend of Princess Margaret.

Dorothy Wilding[1] of Bond Street. Whenever an organization asked for permission to use a picture in a brochure or programme they were referred to the Wilding studio, which provided a standard photograph of a very pretty girl, looking slightly stern and in a full-skirted outfit nipped in to a tiny waist. Gloves. Hat. She looked older than her years and the pictures were too formal to offer more than a suggestion of the charm and sheer sexiness that she so evidently exuded.

She was issued with her first regiment that year when she was appointed Colonel-in-Chief of the Highland Light Infantry and was present in Glasgow when they received the freedom of the city on 16 March.

This was her first meeting with the regiment's colonel, a splendid-sounding Major-General named Alec Telfer-Smollett CB, CBE, DSO, MC. In the regular correspondence that ensued between 'My dear Harvey' and 'My dear general' it became abundantly clear that Telfer-Smollett, like many of the senior officers of the day, was much smitten with the Princess.

Her first regimental function was a dinner at the Central Hotel with an enormous number of Scottish 'baillies'. Margaret made a speech in which she mentioned Palestine, where the regiment saw active service, and expressed the hope that 'in the near future peace will come to that unhappy land'. The BBC recorded the speech and sent her a record with the warning: 'As this disc is unprocessed it is liable to wear out quickly and should be played only on the King's personal radiogram which has a light-weight pick-up.' Afterwards Major Harvey wrote a long letter of thanks to the Lord Provost, concluding: 'Finally would you please congratulate your chauffeur, who did splendidly.'

Not all her engagements were publicized. When she went to hear the Fleet Street Choir sing Thomas Wood's *Chanticleer*, preceded by a recitation from Nevill Coghill[2] who had translated

---

1 Dorothy Wilding (1892–1976). Old-fashioned court and society photographer whose posed and rather wooden style was superseded by the innovative informality of later rivals such as Cecil Beaton.
2 Nevill Coghill (1899–1980). Oxford professor of English best known for his modern version of Chaucer's *Canterbury Tales*.

Chaucer's 'Nun's Priest's Tale' on which it was based, Sir Arthur Penn[1] instructed the choir's conductor, T. B. Lawrence that there should be no publicity but that he might 'tell the choir and friends what [was] anticipated'. On the other hand, a little later Harvey told Commander Colville,[2] the Queen's press secretary, 'There is no objection to television on the arrival of Princess Margaret at Lady Crosfield's tennis party on 8 June.'

The Bath Festival was a success thanks largely to another admiring senior officer, Somerset's Lord Lieutenant, Admiral of the Fleet Sir James Somerville[3] – father of Julia, the television newscaster of the last quarter of the twentieth century. To him Harvey wrote, 'I know very well that a good deal of the enjoyment she herself derived, and of the ease with which she took her fences, was due to the support which your presence gave her.'

The Admiral himself, who had promised to 'do [his] best to see that the poor Princess does not have too ghastly a time', was able to report: 'HRH was magnificent and scored a tremendous personal success: she looked charming and was charming through-out a long day which for her must have been very tedious at times. If good fortune brings her to Somerset again she can be sure of a *very* warm welcome.'

Not for the first time the top brass at the Palace and elsewhere were concerned that those who, unlike them, did not really understand the ropes might mess things up. Harvey wrote tetchily to the Mayor, when additions to the draft programme were proposed, to say that the day was already quite long enough and that 'the request that she should attend a Civic Ball on the night of Friday April 30th has been turned down and I hope that it will not be revived'. Admiral Somerville offered to intervene on HRH's

---

1 Sir Arthur Penn (1886–1960). Lifelong courtier, close friend of Queen Elizabeth, the Queen Mother and uncle of (Sir) Eric.

2 Commander Richard Colville (1907–1975). Palace press secretary from 1947 to 1968, widely considered to dislike journalists and publicity though this view is disputed by erstwhile friends and colleagues.

3 Admiral-of-the-Fleet Sir James Somerville (1882–1949). One of most prom-inent British naval commanders of World War II and responsible for con-troversial sinking of French Fleet off North Africa.

behalf: 'The Mayor of Bath is a very good type of an old Labour lad and I can easily slip in a word if necessary.' It is interesting to observe how senior ranks were often very fond of such 'Old Labour' stalwarts who, at a guess, reminded them of the regimental sergeant majors and chief petty officers of their service days. It may seem a rather patronizing regard, but it is nonetheless genuine and often reciprocated. Patrician, landowning Tory stalwarts respected non-commissioned Labour men who might have been their tenants or batmen. It was a feudal affection, founded on old-fashioned class values, and has little or no echo in the relatively egalitarian world of the twenty-first century.

Generally speaking the organizers of events were under-standably protective or overprotective of the Princess. An extreme example was M. Bera of the Institut Français, who failed to put out his beloved visitors' book when Margaret came for a piano recital in aid of the Scottish Fund for the Children of Greece on the grounds that 'he had been afraid to ask the Princess to sign it in case of soiling her gloves'. It was brought round to the Palace after the event and duly signed in private.

She was obviously keen on all things musical and these interests were reflected in her programme and her responses. There was the Thomas Wood choral evening with the Fleet Street Choir, the piano recital at the Institut Français – 'Her Royal Highness,' wrote her lady-in-waiting, 'who is as you know a keen pianist, was most impressed by Mademoiselle Darre's skilled performance.'

After the Victoria League Ball in the Assembly Rooms in Edinburgh Jean Rankin wrote to the organizer, Lady Wallace saying, 'I do not have to tell you the extent to which Princess Margaret enjoys Scottish dances and how much she appreciated the opportunity of doing them with good dancers in ideal sur-roundings.' The evening included two sixteensomes and five country dances as well as a rumba and samba and a polka and a galop. The first sixteensome was danced with officers of the Cameron Highlanders and their partners, and her partners in 'Speed the Plough', the 'Duke of Perth', 'Strip the Willow', the '51st Divisional Reel' and 'Hamilton House' were David Scott-Moncrieff, Captain the Master of Erskine, Guy Grant, Lieutenant

Neil Wimberley and Gavin Younger. This was the sort of Scottish society into which she had been born at Glamis.

She also visited Glyndebourne for a performance of the 'Jupiter' Symphony and a lecture by Sir Thomas Beecham.[1] John Christie,[2] owner of Glyndebourne, drove her to and from Lewes station, doing so with the breezy instruction that he would take the wheel 'unless she want[ed] to drive herself'.

One of her earliest patronages was that of the English Folk Dance and Song Society. The director, Douglas Kennedy, asked if she'd like to bring some friends to accompany her in dancing, but she said she would be perfectly happy to dance with the members. 'I know that it would be wonderful if you could manage to dance a little,' Jennifer Bevan urged her. 'Apparently all the dances are frightfully easy and I think that a short demonstration of each dance will be given beforehand.' Kennedy's son arranged a special set called 'The Princess Margaret's Fancy' and she joined in dancing it. Kennedy wrote an enthusiastic thank-you. 'What delighted everyone was the charming way in which Her Royal Highness entered into everything and especially her kindness in taking a place in the set for "The Princess Margaret's Fancy".'

Matters of protocol, closely allied to class and politics, were pervasive. Shortly after Margaret ricked her neck and had to cancel engagements the Town Clerk of Wanstead and Woodford telephoned 'to ask if we could tell him whether or not it is desired that the Mayor should attend in civic robes accompanied by the Mace Bearer'. The answer was yes. A child sent in an autograph book and Margaret scrawled a note to the lady-in-waiting saying, 'I suppose we'd better send this back.' Protocol dictated that royalty never signed autographs, even for children.

All this was time-consuming and, in a sense, trivial; yet such events and all that went with them were regarded as the woof

---

1 Sir Thomas Beecham (1879–1961). Dashing and much loved founder and conductor of orchestras, famous for 'Lollipops' and bons mots such as the remark to a lady cellist that she had, between her legs, 'an instrument capable of giving pleasure to thousands, yet all you can do is to scratch it'.

2 John Christie (1882–1962). Sussex landowner who transformed his country house into the home of the Glyndebourne Festival Opera.

and warp of royal life. Like others of her generation and the ones immediately before her Princess Margaret, at this time, had a strongly developed sense of duty. This was encouraged by everyone at court and by those who asked favours of her. Events were, mostly, conducted in a traditional, old-fashioned way with great regard for convention and protocol. It seems, now, a stuffy world, but it was the way it was.

People could seem ludicrously sensitive. For example, when Margaret was to name a new ship after John Williams, a missionary martyred and eaten in the New Hebrides in 1839, there was trouble between the Lord Mayor of London and the Mayor of Stepney. This was resolved by the Reverend Cecil Northcott of the London Missionary Society deciding that 'The Princess should be received outside the Port of London Authority's Building which is within the City boundary.' You can almost hear Mr Northcott's relief at smoothing ruffled mayoral feathers. 'I hope you will agree to this suggested revision,' he wrote to the Palace, 'as it gets us all out of a very real difficulty.' The relative dignity of the Lord Mayor and his Stepney counterpart obviously knew few bounds.

Politics were bound to be tricky from time to time. Although the Attlee government was genuinely supportive of the Royal Family, most courtiers, members of the family and their friends and associates were Tory. Whatever affection may have existed between them there were also quite fundamental political differences. We have already seen the Lord Lieutenant of Somerset explaining patiently that the Mayor of Bath was perfectly nice given that he was a socialist. Time and again we find the great and the good doing the same. Lady Spencer, for example, wrote from Althorp to 'darling Katherine' (Seymour – a lady-in-waiting) about one of her minions at Doctor Barnardo's: 'She [Anne Tyson] is nice, clever and Labour.' A few months later no less a person than Geoffrey Fisher,[1] Archbishop of Canterbury, wrote to say

---

1 Geoffrey Fisher, Archbishop of Canterbury (1887–1972). Conservative Archbishop from 1944 to 1961 who advised, vainly, against the choice of his former Repton pupil Michael Ramsey as his successor, only to be rebuked by Churchill who told him, 'You may have been Dr Ramsey's headmaster but you were not mine.'

why he thought it inappropriate for his dean at Canterbury to be invited to lunch with Her Royal Highness and the royal party. The cleric in question was Hewlett Johnson,[1] universally known as 'the Red Dean'. In a letter to Jennifer Bevan, Fisher wrote that Johnson was actually a perfectly nice chap except for his politics, which were dangerously left-wing.

The naming of ships is almost a ceremonial cliché for female members of the Royal Family. Margaret had already made her relatively low-key debut with the naming of the *John Williams* missionary ship when Buckingham Palace received a letter from Sir William Fraser, the boss of the Anglo-Iranian Oil Company. The previous year, Fraser recalled, Princess Elizabeth had christened *British Princess* on the Tyne, and this year was to see the launching of her sister ship, the 12,250-ton *British Mariner* on the Clyde. It seemed only appropriate for Elizabeth's sister to do the honours this time. 'It would be a source of tremendous encouragement to the men who build the ships, the men who sail in them and, indeed, to all the members of our world-wide organisation.'

Hector McNeil, the Lord Provost of Glasgow, whom the Princess had already encountered when the Highland Light Infantry received the freedom of the city, was able to assure Her Royal Highness of a 'very cordial welcome' and also offered her, once again, his splendid official limousine and his even more splendid chauffeur. Major Harvey was able to approve a ruby-centred brooch offered by a fellow Major (Mackay) on behalf of the oil company as a thank-you, and after some incredibly convoluted letters from British Rail (Midland) at Euston concerning the relative merits of a special train from Ballater as against a motorcar to Perth it was agreed that a special saloon should be attached to the 5.30 Aberdeen to Glasgow Buchanan Street, which would be 'tripped' for overnight 'stabling' at Whitecrags. The return journey would be in the same saloon, leaving Glasgow at five and arriving in Aberdeen at 8.58. The royal party would consist of

1 Dr Hewlett Johnson (1876–1966). 'Red' Dean of Canterbury so-called because of his exuberant support for the Soviet Union.

Her Royal Highness, Lady Mary Strachey (lady-in-waiting), Wing Commander (as he then was) Townsend, a lady's maid, a footman and a policeman. Two of the Princess's friends, Lady Caroline Scott[1] and the Earl of Dalkeith[2] (children of the Duke and Duchess of Buccleuch), would join the train for the return journey to Balmoral.

Not everyone could be relied upon. The chairman of Harland and Wolff was a case in point, as evidenced in a letter from Major Mackay to Major Harvey.

'I shall arrange to let you have either a copy of what Sir Frederick Rebbick will say, or the gist thereof. I understand, however, that this will not be too easy as apparently Sir Frederick does not prepare his speech until shortly before the occasion and even then cannot be relied upon to stick to his original words!'

Everything did not always go according to plan. That October, at her first event as President of Doctor Barnardo's homes in succession to Stanley Baldwin, she spent a happy time talking to 'toddlers' in Kent, but when Frederick Potter, Barnardo's secretary, sent a commemorative film he had to admit: 'Unfortunately the film does not contain any photographs of Her Royal Highness with the children, for our photographers did not know of Her Royal Highness's intention to go down on to the lawn towards the end of the visit and the camera ran out of film soon after Her Royal Highness reached the lawn.' On another occasion the impresario Emil 'Prince' Littler[3] caused offence by entering the royal box unannounced and uninvited. 'Without sanction' were the words actually used in the official rebuke. And there was a serious diplomatic incident at Sadler's Wells in 1949 when the main speaker, Jimmy Smith, completely forgot to mention Sir

---

1 Lady Caroline Scott (1927–2004). Daughter of 8th Duke of Buccleuch, married to Sir Ian (later Lord) Gilmour, Conservative Cabinet minister and *Spectator* magazine proprietor.
2 The Earl of Dalkeith (1923–). Conservative politician, leading member of Princess Margaret set and touted as possible suitor until marriage to Jane McNeil in 1953. Succeeded as 9th Duke of Buccleuch in 1973.
3 Emile Littler (1903–1985). Theatrical impresario married to one of his own stars, Cora Collis.

Bronson Albery,[1] who had been a distinguished general manager of the company for many years. 'I fear', wrote Smith apologetically, 'that Sir Bronson was, very naturally, extremely hurt.'

All went well at the launching on the Clyde. Ladies-in-waiting inspected and approved the ruby-centred brooch; Lord Plunket[2] chose menus 'A' and 'C' for dinner on the train and in her speech Margaret said of the *British Mariner*, 'All of us know how much we depend on his efforts: the flow of imports and exports are as vital as pulse-beats, and we do well to recall that in our present struggle for solvency, the British mariner plays a leading part.'

Some things change but others do not. 1948's Australian cricket team were christened 'The Invincibles' and were possibly the best ever. Two days later Margaret was back at Balmoral to welcome them to tea. 'The King and Queen and the Princesses', it was reported, 'conversed with everybody in turn.' *The Times*, which had earlier carried a picture of Margaret shaking hands with a Harland and Wolff apprentice at the ship-christening, this time depicted a distinctly stubbly Aussie captain, Bradman,[3] chatting with the Princess and her mother. They look a lot more relaxed than did the little couple on Clydeside two days earlier. Bradman caused offence by being pictured walking across the lawn next to the King with his hands in his pockets. The offence was not, however, taken by George VI, who said that had he not been wearing a pocketless kilt he too would have had his hands in his pockets.

Most of the time Margaret seems to have worn feathery hats and full dresses, tightly nipped in at the waist. In some of her roles, however, she had to dress in uniform. On 26 August the Chief Commissioner of the St John Ambulance, Lieutenant General

1 Sir Bronson Albery (1981–1971). Theatrical manager after whom the New Theatre in London's St Martin's Lane was re-named in 1973, only to be rechristened the Noël Coward in 2006.
2 Lord (Patrick) Plunket (1923–1975). A particular favourite of Queen Elizabeth II who served as her equerry and Deputy Master of the Household from 1954 until his death.
3 Sir Donald Bradman (1908–2001). Australian cricketer, nicknamed 'The Don' and generally accepted as the best batsman ever.

Sir Henry Pownall,[1] was getting agitated about his new Commandant-in-Chief not yet having the appropriate uniform. Apart from anything else he wanted a uniformed photograph for the *Cadet* magazine.

At Margaret's suggestion Major Harvey wrote to the Brigade's Superintendent-in-Chief of Nursing, who fortuitously was the fabulously chic Edwina Mountbatten.[2] 'It is time Her Royal Highness was photographed in her uniform which must clearly be very well cut ... She has suggested that I should write to you to ask for particulars of a good tailor.'

Lady Mountbatten's reply was entirely characteristic:

I personally always go to the tailoring department of Messrs Hawes and Curtis at 43 Dover Street. The head cutter, and I believe now the part owner of the business, is Mr. E. H. Watson. He has made my husband's clothes for years, and came out in charge of the Headquarters Tailoring Department in South East Asia where he made the uniforms for the officers of all the women as well as the men's services.

He has always made my uniforms admirably. I believe he used to make clothes for both the Prince of Wales and the Duke of Kent in the old days and is an extremely competent and pleasant man.

Mr Watson duly made the uniform, Margaret was photographed in it – though there was almost a disaster when the organization's stores department supplied the 'wrong' hat badge – delivered a prepared speech ('We found it a little difficult to frame such a speech without appearing to be extremely self-satisfied') and presented the annual prizes to general satisfaction. Lord

---

1 Lt. Gen. Sir Henry Pownall (1887–1961). Allied Commander in Far East at time of fall of Singapore.
2 Edwina, Countess Mountbatten of Burma (1901–1960). Heiress to vast fortune of grandfather, Sir Ernest Cassell, glamorous Vicereine of India who enjoyed intimate friendship with premier Nehru – he sent two Indian warships as escort when she was buried at sea after early death in Borneo.

Wakehurst,[1] the Prior, tactfully remarked: 'It was with special pleasure that we saw Her Royal Highness in her uniform as Commandant-in-Chief of the cadets.' Delia Peel replied with equal tact: 'Your reference to Her Royal Highness's uniform is greatly appreciated!'

A morale-boosting 'pageant' in Sheffield almost came unstuck and was obviously viewed with some ambivalence at court. For some reason the city's original request for a royal presence was fielded by Edward Ford,[2] one of the King's assistant private secretaries, who unaccountably failed to respond, so that the slack was taken up by Tommy Lascelles himself. Lascelles seemed uncertain and took soundings from the Earl of Scarbrough,[3] Yorkshire's Lord Lieutenant. Scarbrough lived at Sandbeck House near Rotherham and offered to have Margaret to stay. Of the pageant itself he said, with cautious tact, 'There is no doubt it is rather a unique occasion.' Tom Harvey seemed disconcerted to find that 'dinner' was scheduled for 6 p.m. and was even more bothered by a memo from the pageant producer Dr du Garde Peach,[4] with the rider: 'I still hope it will be quite a good pageant.' 'Thank you for sending me du Garde Peach's blurb,' replied Harvey, 'which I can hardly bear to read. I am afraid the principal characters of the Pageant look like being Jolly Jack Girder, Good Queen Bessemer and the Big Bad End. However I am sure it will be most enjoyable.'

He doesn't sound at all sure and when he explained to the Town Clerk that HRH would only make an opening speech of twenty words the response sounds distinctly stuffy. Once again

---

1 Lord Wakehurst (1895–1970). Conservative MP who succeeded to the title in 1935 and was Governor of New South Wales and of Northern Ireland.

2 Sir Edward Ford (1910–2006). An assistant private secretary to the sovereign from 1945 to 1967, he was responsible for the phrase 'annus horribilis' used in a speech at the Guildhall by Queen Elizabeth II to describe the unpleasant fortieth year of her reign.

3 Lawrence, 11th Earl of Scarbrough (1896–1969). Tory MP who served as Lord Chamberlain from 1952 to 1963.

4 L(awrence) du Garde Peach (1890–1974). Prolific humorist, writer of plays and children's books, and producer of pageants.

the tension between the fancy-hat courtier-patrician camp and the cloth-capped workers can be put down to differences of class and politics. For example, Sheffield said that their menfolk wished to wear morning dress. Harvey explained, 'They feel it would be the right thing to do and not allow anyone to suggest that because they are a Labour controlled council they lower the standards.'

Two relatively minor comments in Harvey's lengthy memorandum to the Town Clerk are of more than passing interest. One apropos the loyal toast said simply and baldly: 'Her Royal Highness does not smoke.' Another said: 'It is suggested that press, police and chauffeur should all dine together.' There are those who argue that Commander Colville's attitude to journalists was friendly and enlightened but others continue to believe that it was at best paternalist. By the time Colville made way, in the 1960s, for the quite different Bill, later Sir William, Heseltine[1] relations between press and Palace had become distinctly frosty. Colville did give the impression that the hacks definitely belonged well below the salt along with the police and the drivers. It was not, on the whole, a good way to guarantee a favourable press. As for smoking, it is abundantly clear that Princess Margaret was a smoker and had been one for several years with the full knowledge and support of her father and, presumably, her mother.

The inference must be that the habit was not something to be indulged in public. This has often been the case with royalty: that what is acceptable in private is not done in public.

In the event the whole visit seems to have passed off more happily than was expected. The Town Clerk wrote to the lady-in-waiting Jean Rankin to say that she and Margaret had made his task a very easy one. He added: 'The crowds exceeded all expectation and she did make an extemporary speech.' He also appreciated 'many acts of kindness and consideration in a programme which was performed with a charm, simplicity and dignity which it would be difficult to surpass'.

---

1 Sir William Heseltine (1930–). Relaxed and informal Australian who became press secretary to Her Majesty the Queen, transferred to the secretariat and served as private secretary in the late 1980s.

At a concert at the London Casino for Denville Hall, the nursing home for retired actors, Mrs Attlee, the Prime Minister's wife, was a late-announced guest, which caused a bit of a shock. There was apprehension about the entrance and a message from the Casino said, 'May I prepare Her Royal Highness for a very cramped entrance to the Royal Box; it is like a narrow passageway direct from the street.' Jennifer Bevan replied, 'I have warned Princess Margaret of the cramped entrance to the Royal Box.'

So what conclusions do we draw at the end of year one? The most obvious and up-beat is that she did what she did well. Everyone seemed to be genuinely bowled over. She looked fantastic but, just as important, she dazzled them with her smile and her interest, and the interest appeared to be more than superficial and also directed at quite ordinary people – especially quite ordinary people. The level of preparation was painstaking and meticulous – a point one can't emphasize too much. Moreover, when someone appeared a bit ramshackle or lazy or unpredictable the Palace picked up very fast. The ladies-in-waiting were cheerful and efficient (especially Jennifer Bevan) and wonderfully high-spirited. Political complexion was a matter of permanent concern, especially as the government was Labour. Margaret was already showing a serious interest in music and the arts, unlike her elder sister, who seemed well disposed but indifferent.

Perhaps most important, precedents had been set and patterns established. Her popularity, so strikingly evident in these early years, might wane, though those closest to her would remain resolute and loyal, but the calendar would remain relatively unchanged. Regiments would amalgamate or disappear, responsibilities diminish, organizations vanish or – very rarely – simply be dropped. Foreign countries would often be novelties, though the formulae when visiting them would invariably be similar. The pencilled amendments to speeches and menus would continue for half a century; ladies-in-waiting and private secretaries would lay invitations before her and do so with their 'humble duty'. From now on it would be a case of change but no change, of '*Plus ça change, plus c'est la même chose'* – especially in public and the semi-privacy of office life.

The whole period from 1948 to the Coronation was a sort of honeymoon in which Margaret embarked on public life, established connections with organizations such as the Folk Song and Dance people or the St John Ambulance that lasted all her life. During this period she could seemingly do little or no wrong.

On 19 February 1948 Duff Cooper[1] and his wife Lady Diana[2] had lunch with the King and Queen and the two princesses. Cooper was a significant figure in his day, most of all as British Ambassador to Paris. He was also, as his diaries reveal, a compulsive philanderer. 'We enjoyed it enormously,' he recorded of this lunch. 'Conversation never flagged and was really amusing. Margaret Rose is a most attractive girl – lovely eyes, lovely mouth, very sure of herself and full of humour. She might get into trouble before she's finished. The Duchess of Edinburgh will probably make a better Queen.'

Cooper was a shrewd and prescient judge but had apparently failed to pick up on the fact that the Princess had 'dropped the Rose'. She was now simply Margaret.

The first half of 1949 had a slightly ad hoc appearance because Margaret was supposed to go on a long tour of Australia with her parents, but the King's serious illness and subsequent operation put the kybosh on that. So Margaret's actual programme for this period was necessarily something of an improvization.

The first thing she attended was a Not Forgotten Association tea party in the Royal Mews. Cabaret included the famous Coco the Clown (by kind permission of Cyril and Bernard Mills[3]),

---

1 Duff Cooper, 1st Viscount Norwich (1890–1954). Ebullient Conservative MP and Cabinet minister who served as post-war Ambassador to Paris, wrote self-revelatory diaries (published in 2005) and a memoir, *Old Men Forget* (1953).
2 Lady Diana Cooper (1892–1986). Wife of above; beautiful and stylish daughter of Duke of Rutland, brilliant hostess and friend of royalty.
3 Cyril and Bernard Mills (1902–1991). Circus-owning sons of founder of eponymous Bertram Mills organization.

Peter Brough[1] (the name associated with the ventriloquist's show *Educating Archie*), Anona Winn,[2] Eric Barker and Pearl Hackney.[3] All were household names of the day. Afterwards Louis Greig[4] (grandfather of Geordie, editor of the *Tatler* in the early years of the twenty-first century) from Thatched House Lodge, Richmond Park, wrote, 'I hope Princess Margaret was none the worse for her gloriously long stay at yesterday's party ... The men were enthralled at Princess Margaret's kindness and interest and may I say it, quite glorious appearance ... The singing of "She's a Jolly Good Fellow" was unexpected and entirely on the men's own. It has never been sung before on similar occasions and they all adored singing it.'

Greig then wrote again quoting a Scottish paper, which read, 'The nicest thing we've ever heard said about anybody was said last week by Sir Louis Greig about Princess Margaret. He told her at a Not Forgotten Association event: 'You do give a little glamour and gaiety to a drab world.' If your friends can say the same about you, then you haven't much to worry about.

Greig added: 'It strikes the note I tried to strike, namely how much we all love and admire Princess Margaret in *all* her manifold duties.' He sounds, like many senior citizens of those years, both smitten and sycophantic. This is not written unkindly. The first was genuine and the second routine.

She and Jennifer Bevan went on their own to a concert of Festival Music at St Paul's Cathedral. A 'delicious tea' at the Citizens' Advice Bureau (founded in 1939) was primarily educational. Sample enquiries provided for the Princess included: 'The laundry has lost my shirt. How can I claim compensation and

---

1 Peter Brough (1906–1999). Ventriloquist, best known for series of *Educating Archie* in which he was bullied by striped-blazer-wearing, revolving-eyed dummy called Archie Andrews.
2 Anona Winn (1907–1994). Australian singer and comedienne.
3 Eric Barker (1911–1990) and Pearl Hackney (1916–). Husband and wife team of comedians, principally on radio but also in films.
4 Group Captain Sir Louis Greig (1880–1953). Friend of King George VI and Comptroller of his household when Duke of York. Played tennis with him at Wimbledon.

had not been properly consulted about the contentious visit. He was given to understand that the Princess 'perfectly understands about your engagements and would hate you even to consider not going'. She could be conciliatory and understanding on occasions, especially when someone was, like the Duke, an old family friend, who had incidentally hosted Margaret's grandmother Queen Mary throughout the war.

Princess Margaret cut the ribbon to open the school and got to keep the scissors. The school, thanking her, said that the event had 'already had an effect on recruitment of nurses. We have received numerous applications from as far away as Northern Ireland and we can only attribute it to the visit of Her Royal Highness.

'We were suffering from an acute shortage of nurses and the events of last Monday have given us fresh enthusiasm for the cause of recruitment.' Aneurin Bevan had chosen his iconic royal wisely if cynically.

Afterwards the BBC sent a recording which 'is playable on an ordinary gramophone just like an ordinary record', to which Jennifer Bevan responded, 'The record fits Princess Margaret's gramophone perfectly.'

On 8 March the Princess visited Basil Henriques[1] at his East London Juvenile Court. Henriques was a charismatic figure with a high profile, especially for a London magistrate.

'It was a veritable delight to have there someone who was so extraordinarily understanding of what took place and who was so quick in grasping the difficult problems with which the court had to deal,' he wrote afterwards. 'I especially want the Princess to know how much pleasure she gave to all the probation officers. Their work is very disheartening and difficult, and the way in which Her Royal Highness discussed with them the work which they do, was an encouragement such as they will never forget.'

---

1 Basil Henriques (1890–1961). Jewish philanthropist and author who devoted himself to services for young people, especially Boys' Clubs, in East End of London.

The Princess's life then was already an extraordinary roller-coaster of contrast. One minute she was undertaking apparently mundane public duties that even the obsequious press of the day did not bother to report; the next she was tripping the light fantastic among social swells in a way that a later generation of journalists was to find curiously reprehensible. So, almost immediately after the workaday visit to Henriques' Juvenile Court in East London the Duchess of Buccleuch wrote to Jennifer Bevan: 'Caroline is collecting some friends for the weekend – unfortunately it is not very easy for the Oxford and Cambridge boys to get away so if you can think of any (acceptable!) young men, will you let us know?' It is hardly surprising if at times Princess Margaret seemed not to be entirely clear who she was.

Geoffrey Ingram, an Australian ballet dancer, after a reception for Rhodes Scholars at the Grocers' Hall, was quoted, writing: 'As yet it is impossible to convey the true importance of such an occasion to the writer as it is indeed impossible to estimate the new depths of sentiment evoked by the event. This much I can and do say. One does not come by grace without courage nor dignity without taste for life, and that one so young should enshrine and be the very embodiment of these truths adds much to the reflections of another, a humble and fortunate witness.'

In March the Princess and her lady-in-waiting went down with flu. A letter about Bethnal Green to Brigadier Sir Wyndham Deedes CMG, DSO[1] was followed by one about another visit to the East End of London. The official programme included advertisements for 'Kelly for Jelly' – since the beginning of the century Kelly's have been associated with the eel business in this district – and 'Jim's Boot and Shoe repairs – repairers to the youth of the Borough.'

Attention to detail and especially matters of protocol loomed

---

1 Brigadier Sir Wyndham Deedes CMG, DSO (1883–1956). Civil servant in Middle East, for two years Chief Secretary in Palestine; subsequently devoted himself to good works in Bethnal Green and East End of London, assisted for a time by his nephew, Bill, later Lord Deedes, editor of the *Daily Telegraph* and the 'Dear Bill' of *Private Eye*.

large. Major Harvey wrote to the Mayor of Ramsgate: 'I think that people should stand up when Her Royal Highness is about to speak and she will no doubt invite them to be seated.'

Competition for the Princess's favours was often fierce. Lena Prescott from Aneurin Bevan's Ministry of Health wrote yet again to say,

> Quite frankly we feel puzzled that the Mayor should have initiated the invitation without previous reference to the Chairman of the Regional Hospital Board who would then, of course, have consulted my Minister as to the propriety of the approach.
>
> My Minister's advisers feel that it is a pity that this rather minor project should be singled out for such an exceptional honour; there are indeed many new developments in the National Hospital Service which we feel would be more worthy of Royal notice.

Harvey seems embarrassed by having acceded to the Mayor of Ramsgate's request for a visit, though he was doubtless irritated by this further Bevanite presumption. He pleaded 'the geographical factor', meaning that the Princess was in Kent anyway.

In an internal memorandum to the Princess he then suggested: 'If your Royal Highness wished to emphasise the importance of Hospitals by preceding your visit with a visit to a coal mine nearby this could easily be arranged.' (In the margin the Princess pencilled 'No' without explanation). In all conscience it is difficult to see why a visit to a coal mine should have emphasized the importance of hospitals.

Then the Lord Lieutenant of Kent, Lord Cornwallis,[1] steamed into action in a manner that seems characteristic of Lords Lieutenant at the time. He sounds peppery and easily put out.

'I am rather angry with Ramsgate,' he wrote; 'they have evidently approached you without my knowledge, and they have been spoilt.' Lord Cornwallis would much have preferred a royal visit to Margate, which was, in his opinion, a more deserving case. He added petulantly: 'I have not been asked by the Mayor

---

1 Lord Cornwallis (1892–1982). Lord Lieutenant of Kent from 1944 to 1972.

to lunch but suppose I can "gate crash" ... I hope Her Royal Highness will have a happy visit to my family home, Linton Park, which I had to sell to Olaf Hambro[1] to pay Death Duties.'

For the Mayor of Ramsgate to be caught in a pincer movement between Lord Cornwallis and Nye Bevan suggests an almost cavalier lack of political commitment.

Meanwhile the Archbishop of Canterbury, Geoffrey Fisher, continued to be very closely involved in the visit to Canterbury with a final 'The Princess did write herself, putting me to shame by doing so before I had been able to write and thank her. I hope she will forgive me for the belatedness of my letter.'

The ever-peppery Lord Cornwallis wrote to Jennifer Bevan: 'I have sent a reprimand to Ramsgate ... I am a bit worried about Royal Visits in general ...' He told her that the Chairman of the Regional Hospital Board, Reverend Harcourt Samuel, 'was a very violent left-winger,' though he conceded: 'I think he has mellowed a little.'

Jennifer Bevan for her part was unhappy with the headmaster of St Edmund's. 'He seems to be remarkably vague about everything. His writing is so bad I do not even know his name.' She gets round this by writing: 'Her Royal Highness desires me to ask, first of all, whether we could arrange this with somebody else, instead of troubling you. The Princess was touched by your personal interest but feels that it must surely be taking up too much of your time.'

The Archbishop on the other hand continued to take a detailed interest, which seems surprising for such a busy and important figure. 'It will be noted', he wrote to Jennifer Bevan, 'that I have not included the Dean of Canterbury but I am perfectly ready to include him if the Princess would desire it. The reasons for not including him are sufficiently obvious. As you may know, apart from his opinions he is a most charming person.'

As it happened Hewlett Johnson managed, diplomatically, to be out of town when the Princess came calling.

---

1 Olaf Hambro (1919–1994). Financier who was eating oysters at the bar in Wilton's Restaurant in St James's, London, when a bomb fell nearby, after which he casually asked for the restaurant to be added to his bill. It was.

Nevertheless Jenny Bevan wrote to the Archbishop saying, 'I agree with you that there is no necessity to include the Dean of Canterbury,' and followed this up with a memo to Harvey saying, 'Secondly, as I threatened, here comes Portsmouth for you.' The Commander-in-Chief Portsmouth was Admiral of the Fleet Sir Algernon Willis,[1] who was evidently well satisfied with the way things turned out when Princess Margaret came to inspect the fleet. He wrote afterwards to Jenny Bevan: 'If an old Admiral may presume to say so the Princess won over all our hearts by her charm, her composure, and the lively interest she took in the people she met and in all she saw.'

Already, so early in her official life, the routine was there; already there is a feeling of repetition, of going through necessary motions. Always behind the smiling, waving façade there was a private personality. Sometimes this showed and sometimes it didn't.

The marriage of Princess Elizabeth was a watershed, for Margaret was now the only Princess at the Palace. 'More and more parties,' observed Crawfie with governessy disapproval, 'more and more friends, and less and less work.' She loved music. She danced an exuberant cancan at a ball at the American Ambassador's with Jenny Bevan, the Ambassador's daughter (her then friend, Sharman Douglas) and three other girls. She was already the party animal that she remained for most of the rest of her life. Cecil Beaton photographed her for her nineteenth birthday in August 1949. He found it hard work as his subject 'had been out at a night-club until 5.30 the morning before and got a bit tired after two hours posing'. All the same Beaton, who grew cattier with age, seemed to approve of her. 'She is witty', he wrote, 'and seems quite kindly disposed towards humanity.' Later he was a great deal less charitable towards the Princess but he invariably took some of the most attractive pictures of her, including the one that appears on the cover of this book. That session is unrecorded in his diaries. According to her son, Viscount Linley, it was taken in the loo,

---

1 Admiral of the Fleet Sir Algernon Willis (1889–1976). Second Sea Lord from 1944 to 1946.

just off the hall in the apartment in Kensington Palace. The light in there was particularly good but she would not have taken kindly to being asked to pose on the seat. She looks cross; it shows. But it works. Beaton, ever a professional, obviously realized.

She regularly danced the night away with the rest of the Princess Margaret set led by Billy Wallace, Domi Elliot, the Earl of Dalkeith, Mark Bonham Carter, the Marquis of Blandford and sundry now-forgotten Guardsmen. And she loved to sing. She sang in the back of the car with Jenny Bevan; she sang at the piano with the Earl of Minto's son Domi Eliot. She sang songs from all the latest shows; she sang classics like 'Old Man River' and Dorothy Shay.[1]

Shay was an American nightclub singer, famous in the forties and fifties when she was known as 'the Park Avenue Hillbilly'. Like the Princess she liked to sing with a drink and a cigarette in a long black holder and her words were clever and brittle and somewhat risqué: 'Finishing school was the finish of me ... Them Hillbillies are Mountain Williams now ... Don't learn your lesson from Dad's Smith and Wesson.'

Shay's best-known number was 'Feudin' and Fightin'', which began:

> Daughter, baby daughter
> Poisoned all the neighbors' chickens
> Daughter shouldn't oughter
> Least till she could run like the dickens.

The song continued with references to feuding, to fighting, to fussing and cursing, all rendered in spoof-hillbilly accents so that 'fussin'' and 'cussin'' came to rhyme with each other; the baby daughter was hit with a shovel and then provided with a pistol, despite only being four years old, then she accompanied her elders on another round of feuding and fighting.

---

1 Dorothy Shay (1921–1978). American singer and comedienne who starred in Abbott and Costello film *Comin' Round the Mountain* and performed at President Eisenhower's inaugural ball in 1953.

Very Princess Margaret – or to be more accurate, very much one side of Princess Margaret. One can just see her at the piano in the small hours of the morning, accompanied by Domi Elliot, long black cigarette holder close at hand, glass of Famous Grouse at her elbow, a group of laughing friends gathered round, as she tinkles the ivories. It would be a mildly decadent gathering, men in black or even white ties, women in long dresses – sophisticated, private and unreported.

All 'feudin' and a fightin' and a fussin'', but also friends together helping Her Majesty the Queen's younger sister let her hair down. It is a seductive image and light years from the Girl Guides.

THREE

THE FIFTIES

———

'A gross outrage and very cruel'

As she approached her twenty-first birthday in 1951 Princess Margaret was exhibiting unmistakable star quality. That she was a pocket Venus made her alluring, but her royal status and her consequent occupancy of centre stage made her incontestably special. Her sister, Princess Elizabeth, was now a young naval wife, the mother of two children born in 1948 and 1950, who were ranked ahead of their aunt in order of succession. However, while the King still reigned this succession seemed remote and in a way Margaret, who continued to live with her parents, seemed almost closer to the throne than her married sister. Princess Elizabeth was, for a brief period, as close to being a 'normal' young married naval wife as was possible for the heir to the throne. Her sister, on the other hand, single, nubile, attractive and much-photographed, was still living at home with her parents the King and Queen.

She celebrated her twenty-first birthday at Balmoral, where she usually spent her birthdays and where the family traditionally gathered for shooting, stalking and fishing – none of which particularly appealed to her – as well as for picnics, long walks and Highland reels – all of which definitely did. It was, obviously, a special occasion.

> In the evening we went outside [she told her grandmother in the south] and I lit a torch which was carried, running, across the lawn and through the garden and then in relays up the hill where it was used to light a huge bonfire which blazed up and which could be seen for miles.

During all this the pipers were playing so we suddenly thought what a good idea to dance a reel. So we did! Just in front of the front door in and out of the puddles and by the light of the fire way up on the hill-side.

It was too moving for words and we all felt rather chokey by the end of the evening.

The Princess at that time seemed an almost impossibly glamorous figure. Photographs of the day show her in an enormous number of different situations with a dressing-up cupboard of wasp-waisted outfits to match. Hats, bouquets, handbags are all apparently permanent fixtures, as is a wide seductive smile. She is almost always pictured on her own, often with an elderly gentleman or two in attendance – clerics, mayors, veteran morris dancers. All wear an expression of obvious adulation and the Princess gives every indication of much enjoying centre stage. Surviving ladies-in-waiting are keen to emphasize her star quality and the rapture and enthusiasm with which she was received wherever she went. The crowds were always huge and they waved and smiled as happily as she did herself. Survivors of that period invariably make comparisons with Princess Diana. Those who remember the fifties usually find in favour of Charles's Aunt Margaret rather than his later ill-fated bride.

Already, however, it was clear that her future was going to be very different from that of the sister with whom she had hitherto shared so much. One contemporary publication (*The Pitkin Princess Margaret's Nineteenth Birthday Book*) said presciently if prosaically that in adulthood the two girls 'must now follow different paths'.

There were two Orders in Council that highlighted these differences. The first allowed Princess Elizabeth to serve on a Council of State from the age of eighteen onwards. This meant that as a counsellor she could, in effect, stand in for her father the King when he was away. No such rule applied to Princess Margaret. She had to wait until she was twenty-one, just like other members of the Royal Family. The difference may seem trivial but it drew attention to the fact that Elizabeth was to be queen while Margaret, however glamorous and popular she might appear, was fated to be just 'another member of the Royal Family'.

Another even more significant Order in Council decreed that the ruling on Royal Style and Titles decided on by King George V in 1917 should be altered so that they should no longer pass to descendants through the male line but automatically pass to the children of Princess Elizabeth by dint of her position as heiress presumptive. No such change was made for Princess Margaret, so that although she was, at the time of the alteration, third in line to the throne, she was destined not only to move further and further away from the Crown herself but also to watch any descendants of hers do the same. For someone who had been brought up believing that she was a major royal figure this was a harsh decision.

Eventually, it was thought at the time, Princess Margaret would become more like the Princess Royal in the late forties and fifties. She would, in other words, be an essentially private figure with a public function. At this time, however, she remained the sovereign's only unmarried daughter, a figure of stunning beauty, the cynosure of all eyes, and a key figure in a very small Royal Family. It was difficult to understand that she would in due course be known mainly, if at all, as 'Charlie's aunt', an ageing figure on the periphery of royal life. This ultimate fate seemed infinitely removed from the life she was leading in the very early fifties, but the future was already written. It is unfair that women, more than men, should be thought to become less attractive as they get older; but that is woman's lot and Margaret was to suffer the inevitable problems of ageing much as all other women. At the same time it was her personal sadness to become, especially as far as the outside world was concerned, progressively less and less royal as time passed. The corollary was that as she faded away her elder sister seemed to pass from one regal strength to another. The impressive and dutiful reign of the one accentuated the relative fall from grace of the other.

Although she had many friends such as Domi Elliot, Billy Wallace, Johnny Dalkeith, Sonny Blandford and Mark Bonham Carter who more or less conformed to the social stereotyping of the times and formed the core of the Princess Margaret set, she also enjoyed friendships in quite different quarters. Ann Fleming,[1] married at the time to the newspaper heir Esmond Harmsworth,[2] later Lord Rothermere, and subsequently to Ian Fleming, author of the James Bond books, expressed herself as becoming 'increasingly interested in Princess Margaret' and introduced her to the choreographer Freddy Ashton,[3] the actor Alec Guinness[4] and the eye surgeon Patrick Trevor-Roper,[5] brother of the historian Hugh. The Princess herself 'collected' the actor-director Orson Welles,[6] whom she apparently enjoyed alternating with other friends such as the painter Lucien Freud[7] and the publisher-politician Mark Bonham Carter, who, being both clever and aristocratic, was able to straddle both worlds.

An era was already coming to an end. Her sister's marriage in 1947, the birth of her nephew in 1948 and niece in 1950 and her own coming of age in 1951 were symptoms of optimism for Margaret, but her father's health was giving serious cause for anxiety. In February 1952, days after cheerily saying goodbye to

---

1 Ann Fleming (1913–1981). Unkindly dubbed Tugboat Annie because of her habit of moving from 'peer to peer', she was a lively letter-writer and hostess.
2 Esmond Harmsworth, 2nd Viscount Rothermere (1898–1978). Conservative MP and press magnate who ran *Daily Mail*.
3 Sir Frederick Ashton (1904–1988). Became legendary choreographer with Royal Ballet, after life-changing experience of seeing Pavlova in Peru when he was only thirteen.
4 Sir Alec Guinness (1914–2000). Chameleon-like actor who spanned decades from youthful Ealing Comedy classics such as *Kind Hearts and Coronets* to Smiley in TV version of John le Carré spy series. Won Oscar for portrayal of Colonel Nicholson in *Bridge on the River Kwai* and was also distinguished theatrical actor and diarist.
5 Patrick Trevor-Roper (1916–2004). Brilliant and popular eye-surgeon brother of Oxford historian Hugh, author of *The World Through Blunted Sight* who wrote his own obituary for the *British Medical Journal*, claiming to be 'a diffident bachelor of moderate erudition and talent'.
6 Orson Welles (1915–1985). Larger-than-life American polymath actor/writer/director and creator of *Citizen Kane* and star of *The Third Man*.
7 Lucien Freud (1922–). Painter of lifelike nudes of sometimes portly males and sylphlike females including Kate Moss as well as – uncharacteristically – portrait painter of Her Majesty Queen Elizabeth II.

Elizabeth and Philip as they flew off to East Africa on the first leg of an arduous and extensive tour, George VI enjoyed a happy day's shooting at Sandringham and then died in the night. He was just fifty-six years old.

More than half a century after the event the King's death has, inevitably, taken on an aura of inevitability, but at the time it came as a shock. Mike Parker, private secretary to Prince Philip, was adamant that had the King's elder daughter and husband suspected that the King was in imminent danger they would never have embarked on a long foreign tour. In photographs of the farewell scenes at London's Heathrow airport the King looks emaciated and glum, but Parker always insisted that in real life he seemed perfectly healthy and was bounding around, smiling and telling jokes. The day before his death he was happily shooting hares in the traditional cull of the animals conducted every year by local Sandringham residents. He showed no signs of ill health that day nor in the evening before he retired to bed. No one expected him to make old bones, but his death that February night was not only premature but wholly unexpected.

For several months afterwards Margaret's letters were fringed in mourning black even though there was a stiff-upper-lipped attempt at carrying on as if all were well. The court went into mourning, or 'half-mourning', for a total of six months. Full mourning involved funereal black but 'half-mourning' allowed black, white, grey or even mauve. A pretty and imaginative young lady-in-waiting could do a lot with mauve, but it imposed a severe burden on private purses, for the average lady-in-waiting received only five hundred pounds to deal with every eventuality. Days after the King's death Margaret wrote to Queen Mary: 'I am sending all Papa's and my Christmas cards for you as usual.' This was presumably a way of letting the old Queen keep in vicarious touch with her son and granddaughter's contacts.

'After the King's death there was an awful sense of being in a black hole,' she told the Queen's biographer Ben Pimlott. 'I remember feeling tunnel-visioned and didn't really notice things.' Her sister, the Queen, had a necessarily busy life in which to immerse herself; Princess Margaret had no such consolation. She took little solace in the company of her old friends and took refuge in private early-morning visits to churches unannounced and accompanied only by a lady-in-waiting. She always found consolation in religion.

The following month Queen Mary ventured out despite the bitterness of a harsh winter for the confirmation of her grandson the Duke of Kent in Eton College Chapel. The following day Margaret wrote to the old lady telling her: 'It was so nice you were able to come yesterday snow, or no snow. It has always meant a lot to your grandchildren if you are with them when important things happen in their lives.'

Within a year Queen Mary was dead. She did not survive to see one grandchild crowned but she had lived to see one son abdicate and another die in a wartime flying accident. Now her second son, King George VI, had died early and the nation welcomed a second Elizabethan age with a genuine and spontaneous enthusiasm. Queen Mary symbolized the past.

In later years it was alleged by several who wrote about her that Princess Margaret 'couldn't stand' her grandmother. People who knew the Princess have said that she used to proclaim truculently that whereas her grandmother was royal only by the accident of marriage she, Margaret, was a king's daughter and therefore royal by virtue of the blood that ran through her veins. The old Queen is supposed to have commented tartly on the fact that Margaret was not only spoiled but also vertically challenged. Mary was not only stately but rather tall; Margaret was decidedly short – not much more than five foot tall. Legend, possibly fostered by Princess Margaret herself in later years, has it that she resented these judgements and did not much care for her grandmother. This view is disputed and sometimes dismissed as 'gossip', but there is no doubt in my mind that in later life Princess Margaret let several people know that she had not cared for her grandmother.

It seems different in their letters. However, the passing of the old Queen was not in any way as traumatic for Princess Margaret as the death of her father had been. This was not only an occasion for deep personal sorrow; it also marked a definitive turning point in her life. Had he survived even for another few months Princess

Margaret's life might have been very different and it is at least conceivable that what came to be known as 'the Townsend affair' might have turned out quite differently. Not only was the romance hastened if not precipitated by the sudden death of the King, it was also allowed to spiral out of control in a way that would have been unlikely if not impossible had he been around to control events.

At the time of the King's death Townsend had been at court for the best part of a decade. For much of that time he had been very close to Princess Margaret. He had gone riding with her most mornings in South Africa on the 1947 tour. He had been the official in charge on her first solo official visit – to the Netherlands for Queen Juliana's accession. He had been, in effect, a constant presence since the Princess was only fourteen years old.

For years his remained the only detailed account of the relationship between the two of them. He went public with his memoir *Time and Chance* published by William Collins in 1978, the year of Princess Margaret's divorce from Lord Snowdon. This remained for more than a quarter of a century the only full version of the affair by someone in a position to know what really happened. Townsend's elder son Giles still regards it as gospel. In 2006, however, Sir Alan ('Tommy') Lascelles' diaries were published together with a full memorandum of 'the Townsend affair', to which, as the Queen's private secretary, he had been a crucial and possibly decisive witness.

Princess Margaret herself never spoke of the relationship in public apart from putting her name to the statement, at the time of the crisis, to the effect that she and the Group Captain would not be marrying.

Townsend's book is, naturally, partisan. It is also only partially revealing and in some respects quite misleading. He begins his section on Princess Margaret with the simple sentence: 'During 1952 Princess Margaret and I found increasing solace in one another's company.' Both were disturbed and bereft. Townsend's deteriorating marriage finally collapsed in June that year and in November he was awarded a decree nisi with legal custody of his two sons, though they remained in the care of their mother

Rosemary. Two months later Rosemary married John de Laszlo, son of the portrait painter Philip.

Meanwhile Margaret was grieving for her father and despite adoring her mother she was finding life with her in Clarence House lonely and boring. The change in her circumstances was brutally abrupt. One minute she was at Buckingham Palace basking in the affection of her father the King, a glamorous figure at the very centre of British life. The next moment she was exiled to Clarence House, along with a distraught mother who had lost a husband and a role in one swift blow. Margaret herself was suddenly and totally eclipsed by her sister Lilibet, the new young Queen, supported by her glamorous and heroic naval husband and their two more or less angelic children. Nearly everyone was too busy adjusting to the dawn of the new second Elizabethan Age to give much thought to the little sister. Margaret was marginalized and despite brief moments of attention and notoriety, that was how she was to remain, increasingly, for the rest of her life.

Group Captain Townsend was similarly cast aside. He had always been the King's man and although the new Queen was perfectly well disposed towards him he was not part of her own team, which was composed of men such as Martin Charteris,[1] later to become her private secretary, and Prince Philip's old friend and colleague Mike Parker. She inherited another, older and more experienced group of courtiers from her father. This was headed by Sir Alan 'Tommy' Lascelles, his and now her private secretary. The Group Captain had no place in this outfit either. In fact, although Townsend maintained that he had always enjoyed a friendly and uncomplicated relationship with Lascelles, Tommy seems to have had more of a soft spot for Townsend's wife and also had a low opinion of Townsend's abilities. In a letter to his friend John Gore, Lascelles confided that he thought Townsend

---

1 Lord (Martin) Charteris (1913–1999). Gnomic, sometimes outspoken, private secretary to Queen Elizabeth II from 1972 to 1975 and subsequently Provost of Eton College, he once described the Duchess of York as 'vulgar, vulgar, vulgar' and Queen Elizabeth, the Queen Mother, as 'a bit of an ostrich'.

'a devilish bad equerry: one could not depend on him to order the motor-car at the right time of day, but we always made allowances for his having been three times shot down into the drink in our defence'.

Townsend does not give specific dates in his account of the affair, but he obviously wants us to believe that the couple first discovered their love for each other in February 1953. He says that at Sandringham he and Princess Margaret 'rediscovered one another' – a curiously ambiguous turn of phrase since he never tells us quite what the original (lost) discovery consisted of. He does, however, tell us that a year had passed since Princess Margaret had kissed her father before he went to bed for the last time. That was 5 February 1952.

Then, some time later – Princess Margaret's authorized biographer puts it as late as April 1953 – Townsend and Margaret found themselves alone at Windsor Castle in the red drawing room, where they talked together 'for hours'.

This was, according to Townsend, the crucial moment. 'It was then that we made the mutual discovery of how much we meant to one another. She listened, without uttering a word, as I told her, very quietly, of my feelings. Then she simply said: "That is exactly how I feel too." It was, to us both, an immensely gladdening disclosure, but one which sorely troubled us.'

This suggests that the relationship between the Group Captain and the Princess only became a serious romantic entanglement in early February 1953. Yet according to Lascelles himself, Townsend had visited him in September the previous year. Townsend had wanted to discuss a routine matter, but once this had been dealt with Lascelles gave the younger man an avuncular warning. Tongues, he told him, were wagging. It was being commonly and widely alleged that the Group Captain was seeing too much of the Princess. Lascelles felt it incumbent on him to remind Townsend that 'in our profession there was one cardinal and inviolable rule of royal service: that under no circumstances ought any member of a Royal Household to give cause for such talk'. This was especially so if the member of the Household was a married man – which Townsend still was – and if the member of the

Royal Family was the sovereign's sister, which Princess Margaret was.

This may, in less ordered, more liberal times, seem unduly rigid, but the Lascelles view would have been widely if not universally accepted in the early 1950s. The powers that be would have had little sympathy with Townsend's starry-eyed view, which was astonishingly naïve given that he was a much-decorated war veteran and a father of two who who was pushing forty. He was born in 1914, sixteen years before the Princess.

Yet still he describes the situation in words almost worthy of Barbara Cartland. 'Our love,' he writes, 'for such it was, took no heed of wealth and rank and all the other worldly, conventional barriers which separated us. We really hardly noticed them; all we saw was one another, man and woman, and what we saw pleased us.'

One doesn't have to be a particularly dry or uncharitable old stick to understand why Tommy Lascelles, Winston Churchill, the Archbishop of Canterbury or even Prince Philip might have found this slightly exasperating.

Apparently Townsend said nothing at all in response to Lascelles' lecture about a courtier's duty. Instead he left the room without replying. If so, this was not the only time the Group Captain evaded giving an answer by simply ignoring the question. The practice, often also attributed to members of the Royal Family itself, is known as 'ostriching'.

The received wisdom is that, when he did eventually write his memoir and included his own version of the love affair with Princess Margaret, she was perfectly happy about it. Philip Ziegler,[1] the royal biographer, was then an editor at William Collins, the publisher, and he looked after Townsend's book. Like almost everyone else who knew the Group Captain, Ziegler liked him very much and said that the basic propriety of writing the book was never in question. According to Ziegler, Princess Mar-

---

1 Philip Ziegler (1929–). Urbane Eton- and Oxford-educated book editor with publisher William Collins, who later became respected royal biographer and author of authoritative biographies of Lord Mountbatten and King Edward VIII.

garet seemed quite happy, made no protest of any kind. As proof Ziegler cited a luncheon at Kensington Palace many years later when the Princess and Townsend sat next to each other and talked long and intimately and in perfect amity.

When I mentioned this to Lady Penn she became quite indignant. She told me that Princess Margaret had been so upset by the publication of the book that she had asked her old friend Prue to take the matter up with Townsend, who was a close friend of the Penns. Lady Penn accordingly wrote to Townsend in France saying that Margaret was most upset and wanted some sort of explanation. Lady Penn never received a reply. Townsend simply ignored her letter.

This apparent pretence was what seems to have happened after Lascelles' original lecture. Townsend does not refer to it in his memoir. According to Townsend, the first time the matter was raised at a meeting between him and Lascelles was when, on an unspecified date, Townsend went, at his own request and of his own volition, to tell the Queen's private secretary that he and Princess Margaret were in love.

Townsend says that he 'very quietly' told Lascelles the facts. When he had done so Lascelles, who had been looking at him 'very darkly', was 'visibly shaken', as well he might be. Then, again according to Townsend, 'All that Tommy could say was: "You must be either mad or bad."' Townsend comments: 'I confess that I had hoped for a more helpful reaction.'

Lascelles himself says that this meeting actually took place before Christmas the previous year and that Townsend told him that he and the Princess wished to marry because 'they were deeply in love with each other'. Townsend, in his memoir, however, insists that, even in February 1953, 'Marriage ... seemed the least likely solution; and anyway, at the prospect of my becoming a member of the Royal Family the imagination boggled, most of all my own. Neither the Princess nor I had the faintest idea how it might be possible for us to share our lives.'

Lascelles made no mention of the 'mad or bad' outburst but says that his only comment was that, 'as Townsend must realise, there were obviously several formidable obstacles to be overcome before the marriage could take place'. He is absolutely adamant that Townsend said that he and the Princess wished to marry. His account, though undated, was probably written within a year or two of the events described. Townsend's did not appear until a quarter of a century after the Coronation.

What seems to be common ground is that the Queen and Prince Philip were the first to be told. The meeting between Lascelles and Townsend is not in dispute, but the date is. According to Townsend he, Princess Margaret, the Queen and Prince Philip had enjoyed a happy evening together. Prince Philip evidently saw the funny side of it all and cracked a joke or two. Townsend was much impressed by 'the Queen's movingly simple and sympathetic acceptance of the disturbing fact of her sister's love for me'. He doesn't, significantly, say anything about the question of marriage, whether it was raised that evening nor what the Queen's reaction to the idea might have been.

It seems to be agreed, however, that Lascelles consulted Her Majesty the Queen the day after Townsend's revelations to him – whether that was in December 1952 or February (or later) the following year. At this meeting Lascelles gave his boss an outline of the provisions of the Royal Marriages Act of 1772. The most important fact was that, according to this, the Queen's consent would be required for any marriage of Margaret's before she was twenty-five. After that she would still need permission from the British Parliament as well as from those of the Empire and Commonwealth.

Throughout the early months of 1953 Lascelles continued to discuss the affair with the Queen and Prince Philip and Princess Margaret, though not, as far as one can see, with either Queen Elizabeth the Queen Mother or Townsend. Despite this, Lascelles wrote, 'no definite conclusions were reached'.

The death of Queen Mary on 25 March 1953 and preparations for the Queen's Coronation on 2 June preoccupied most of the main players at court during the spring, but there was disturbing evidence that sooner or later the romance between the Group Captain and the Princess would become a matter of press comment on both sides of the Atlantic.

The Coronation of Queen Elizabeth the Second was an event which, fifty years after it took place, seems virtually incredible. Much of it, though not the most solemn moment, was captured on live television, but this was a foggy, flickering affair, far removed from the digitally enhanced, flat-screen vision of the early twenty-first century. The primitive television pictures enhance the historical differences, emphasizing the fact that monarchy in the 1950s was a solemn, even holy, institution tinged with mystery as well as romance.

Jan Morris,[1] as James Morris, was the *Times* correspondent on John Hunt's expedition to Mount Everest that successfully planted two men – the New Zealand apiarist Edmund Hillary and the Sherpa Tenzing on the peak of the world's highest mountain a few days earlier. Thanks to Morris's journalistic ingenuity news of this British and Commonwealth success arrived in London on the very morning of the Coronation. Years later Morris wrote a short memoir entitled *Coronation Everest*. Paradoxically he is not only a passionate Welsh nationalist and republican but also one of the most lyrical celebrants of Britishness in general and monarchy in particular.

'Thousands will no doubt still stand agog, if ever another English monarch is crowned at Westminster Abbey,' he wrote, 'but not with the same mysterious depth of pride and latent superstition that animated them in 1953.' This judgement was all the more convincing for coming from one who 'always stood outside these sources of inspiration'. There was a magical quality about the Coronation in 1953 and a magical quality that translated itself into other aspects of monarchy as well. Morris saw that, even though he was not a believer himself. He also believed that in the ensuing years that magic has vanished as the British Royal Family 'has come to feel more like mere fodder for the tabloids'.

Yet for the Queen's younger sister the Coronation was a reminder not only that her beloved father was dead but also that

---

1 Jan Morris (1926–). Originally journalist, historian and travel-writer James, the writer changed sex after surgery in Casablanca, re-emerging with considerable authorial qualities mercifully intact.

she was no longer central to the national ritual. She herself had a walk-on part, sitting on one side of little Prince Charles while her mother, the little boy's widowed grandmother, sat on the other. The whole rich ceremonial was focused on the image of the young Queen making her vows and pledging her life. Margaret was little more than just another spectator.

One tiny vignette illustrates quite cruelly the new distance between the two sisters. Both young women naturally had formal gowns with trains. Queen Elizabeth's was borne by her Mistress of the Robes, the Dowager Duchess of Devonshire,[1] and no less than six maids of honour, all of them the daughters of dukes, earls or marquesses. They were headed by Lady Anne Coke,[2] the Earl of Leicester's daughter, later a favourite lady-in-waiting of Princess Margaret. Princess Margaret herself had an impressive train like her sister but she had just the one attendant to carry it – her lady-in-waiting, the Hon. Iris Peake,[3] understandably terrified of committing some ceremonial gaffe or solecism not least because there would be nobody else to pick up the metaphorical pieces. The contrast reflects the sisters' relative status in a way that was inevitable but is nonetheless revealing

It was at the Coronation that Townsend and the Princess finally let their guard slip and gave the world's press the opportunity they had been waiting for with increasing impatience. It was an innocent enough gesture but one that conveyed an apparently revealing sense of intimacy. Somehow Townsend had acquired a piece of fluff – he later joked that it was probably a bit of some dowager's fur coat that had rubbed off on him in the abbey – and this had attached itself to his Royal Air Force uniform. Margaret, seeing it, flicked it off with a finger. The foreign press, followed

---

1 Deborah, Dowager Duchess of Devonshire (1920–). Last of the celebrated Mitford sisters, and for years chatelaine and public face of Chatsworth, the family pile in Derbyshire.
2 Lady (Anne) Glenconner (née Coke) (1932–). Daughter of the Earl of Leicester who married Colin Tennant, later Lord Glenconner, and became lady-in-waiting to Princess Margaret as well as close friend.
3 Hon. Iris Peake, later Mrs Dawnay (1923–). Lady-in-waiting to Princess Margaret who had early ill-starred liaison with secret agent George Blake.

by the British, took this as a signal that the relationship was fair game and could be discussed in print. This they then started to do, though Townsend – surely naïvely – claims not to have known anything about it and even goes so far as to accuse Lascelles of concealing the fact from him.

Ten days after the Coronation, on Friday, 12 June, the Queen's press secretary Commander Richard Colville showed Lascelles a copy of an article about the affair between Princess Margaret and Peter Townsend that was to appear the following Sunday in *The People*. This would give chapter and verse concerning the whole relationship.

The time had clearly come to tell the Prime Minister what was going on. The following day Lascelles drove down to Chartwell and told Winston Churchill what was happening. 'A pretty kettle of fish,' observed 'Jock' Colville, Churchill's private secretary, who sat in on the session. Lascelles had hardly started when Churchill observed that Princess Margaret was only a single 'motor accident' away from the throne. Churchill didn't seem particularly bothered by the religious angle – the great man always had a pragmatic attitude to Christianity – but he *was* bothered about the Commonwealth. Commonwealth countries might not have a problem with Margaret marrying a commoner and a divorcee but they might well take exception to having the child of such a union foisted upon them as head of state.

After Lascelles had left, clear in his own mind that Churchill would only countenance a Margaret–Townsend marriage if she renounced all rights to the throne, the Prime Minister grew maudlin and said something about letting the path of true love take its course. He was rather given to this sort of thing, but his wife Clementine snapped at him and told him not to be so stupid. He had made just that mistake when he had supported Edward VIII before his abdication. Churchill also asked Lascelles if he might tell two of his senior Cabinet colleagues – Lord Salisbury and 'Rab' Butler; his Foreign Secretary and eventual successor Anthony Eden was then abroad. The Queen demurred, reasoning that this was still a family affair and the fewer people who were involved the better. Before the end of the month Churchill suffered a severe and debilitating stroke that was concealed from practically everyone while, temporarily, the country was run by Colville and Churchill's son-in-law Christopher Soames.[1]

Lascelles suggested at the meeting with the Prime Minister that Townsend should be sent abroad. Churchill agreed. So did the Queen. And so, apparently, at a subsequent meeting attended by Lascelles' successor Sir Michael Adeane, did Townsend himself. After consultation with Lord de Lisle and Dudley, the Secretary of State for Air,[2] it was suggested that jobs could be found for the Group Captain in Singapore, South Africa or Brussels. In the event Brussels was chosen, on the grounds that he couldn't possibly look after his two young sons from as far away as South Africa or Singapore, and Townsend left for the less than arduous position of Air Attaché at our embassy in Belgium. His closest colleague was the Military Attaché Colonel Robin Drummond-Wolff of the Black Watch, who may, as Townsend later wrote, have been 'a formidable giant' but was hardly the acme of military accomplishment. In truth Brussels was a backwater and the job a sinecure.

This option, thought Lascelles, was agreed between the Queen, Princess Margaret and Townsend. It was a classic Establishment stitch-up. The Queen was naturally sympathetic to her younger sister and she liked Townsend, but she was still a crucial part of the exercise.

Townsend felt 'bounced', particularly with regard to the timing. He claimed that he was promised an opportunity to say a proper farewell to Margaret but that this was denied. He was, unexpectedly, ordered to leave before Margaret and her mother returned from an official visit to Rhodesia.

Many, some of them senior and not without influence, were

---

1 Lord (Christopher) Soames (1920–1987). Son-in-law of Winston Churchill, Conservative MP and minister, Ambassador to Paris and last Governor of Southern Rhodesia.
2 Viscount de Lisle and Dudley VC (1909–1991). Won Victoria Cross at Anzio in World War II and was Governor General of Australia during government of Sir Robert Menzies in the 1960s.

sympathetic to Townsend and the Princess. Lady Violet Bonham Carter, for instance, wrote:

> A horrible campaign has been raging in the Press during the last fortnight – led by *The People* – hotly followed by the *Daily Mirror* and the *Sunday Express* about Princess Margaret and Peter Townsend who has been posted to Brussels. The decent papers like the *News Chronicle* have alas limped – or scurried – as the case may be – after the indecent ones. It is a gross outrage and very cruel. What she must be feeling like on her Rhodesian tour I shudder to think. Mark says the Palace have behaved very clumsily. The thing started abroad – in USA, Canada and Europe. He says that PT told him that posting him to Brussels wld produce the explosion of gossip, rumour, speculation etc. which has in fact followed.

Later Princess Margaret told friends and close staff that Lascelles personally had 'ruined her life'. To her private secretary, Lord Napier, she referred to him as 'that snake'. Yet long after the event and even after her eventual marriage she remained on apparently cordial terms with Lascelles, who subsequently became her neighbour at Kensington Palace. Years later, in May 1962, Lascelles was digging his compost heap at Kensington Palace when the Princess appeared pushing a pram containing her infant son David. 'Talked amicably for ten minutes,' recorded Lascelles.

It has been said, too, that she harboured a grudge against Geoffrey Fisher, the Archbishop of Canterbury, who had rashly and uncharacteristically referred to the Townsend affair as 'a stunt'. Fisher was understandably adamant in his and the Church's opposition and never made any secret of this. Princess Margaret, who was religious even if in a mildly unconventional way, accepted this and, as with Lascelles, never appeared to bear a grudge but continued to enjoy perfectly amicable relations with him – at least in public.

It is the attitude of those closest of all to her that remains complicated and perhaps ultimately contrary. Both Queen Elizabeth the Queen Mother and Her Majesty the Queen seem to have been genuinely fond of Group Captain Townsend. They remembered his close and loyal relationship with the late King and they were appreciative of his years of dedicated service at court. He was in a real sense a friend. However, that did not mean that Queen Elizabeth thought it appropriate that he either could or should marry Princess Margaret. All the evidence suggests that Princess Margaret's mother failed to confront the issue and avoided discussing it with her daughter. Several close observers say that Princess Margaret often disagreed with her mother, sometimes to the point of being positively, even embarrassingly, rude. When this happened the Queen Mother seldom if ever remonstrated or answered back. In the words of one old friend, 'She took it on the chin.' There is no evidence of the Queen ever having expressed her personal opinions on the possible match. There would have been no need. It would have been more than enough to hide behind the advice of her archbishop and the Church and of her prime minister and the Cabinet. Both were unequivocal.

It was Townsend, apparently, who chose Brussels and he did so because of his two young sons Giles and Hugo, aged eleven and eight, of whom (as already mentioned) he had legal custody. It was, he reckoned, Hobson's choice. The Queen was loyal and asked him to accompany herself and Prince Philip on one last visit to Belfast. Meanwhile Princess Margaret went off to Rhodesia with her mother and the hope and intention was that she and Townsend would have one final farewell meeting after her return before he went to Brussels.

It was not to be. His departure was accelerated and it was in 1955, over a year later, that the two lovers met again. Townsend was obviously embittered and felt as if he had been sent into a medieval exile. 'It was, in truth', he wrote, 'an unnatural move to an obsolescent post in which my RAF career was to end.'

Princess Margaret was clearly devastated.

Years later Lord Snowdon, who was her only husband, said to me, 'I never really thought the Townsend business was all that it was cracked up to be, did you?'

Jane Bown,[1] the *Observer* photographer, who in her wonderful but almost defiantly un-showy way was the *Observer*'s answer to the *Sunday Times*' Snowdon, photographed the Princess at Clarence House around this time. Mrs Bown said to her editor, David Astor, that the paper had no photographs of the Princess and this was a dreadful gap. Astor told her to see if she could get one and Bown was amazed to find that her request to visit Clarence House was met with an entirely positive response. She went round and spent some time photographing Princess Margaret in a downstairs drawing room that had windows looking out on the garden. She remembers the Princess's wonderful eyes, like twin pools, bottomless and beautiful. She also remembers that the Princess seemed both bored and lonely and how as she stared gloomily out of the window she said, 'You know I seem to spend most of my days like this.'

The *People* article which appeared, as threatened, on Sunday, 14 July certainly meant that a taboo subject suddenly became common gossip. *The People* itself adopted the off-putting tone of the popular press in one of its moods of righteous indignation. 'It is high time for the British public to be made aware of the fact that newspapers in Europe and America are openly asserting that the Princess is in love with a divorced man and that she wishes to marry him.'

The subsequent debate led *The Times*, on 24 July, to react in a pompous-sounding manner that was almost as repellent. 'It is a pity', opined the Thunderer, 'that these royal and remarkable weeks have been personally saddened for the Queen by the bandying about of her sister's name in public gossip.'

Townsend's exile did not silence the gossip. The *Mirror* ran a mischievous article based on a report from their Brussels correspondent who, on enquiry instigated by Churchill himself, turned out to be 'well known to them [the British Embassy in Brussels] as an irresponsible and dangerous person'. Another private report

---

1 Jane Bown (1925–). Unshowy but brilliant *Observer* photographer whose pictures adorned the paper from the 1950s to the first decade of the twenty-first century.

reached Lascelles and Colville to the effect that Townsend was canvassing support among political contacts. In a private note Colville advised the Palace: 'This matter is not one which in its present stage requires Ministerial advice. It has never come before the cabinet. It might be hoped that in a personal matter of this kind, the feelings of those concerned would be respected by everybody and the present deplorable speculation and gossip brought to an end.'

Lascelles considered holding a press conference but was dissuaded. In the post-Coronation euphoria and amid talk of a new Elizabethan Age, criticism was muted. *Tribune* wrote of the Cabinet agreeing with the Church that there could be no Townsend–Margaret marriage and ranted on, with impressive indignation: 'This intolerable piece of interference with a girl's private life is all part of the absurd myth about the Royal Family which has been so sedulously built up by interested parties in recent years.' This was exceptional.

Years later the journalist Alastair Forbes wrote a characteristically well-informed and acerbic review of Townsend's memoir, which he thought self-serving. Forbes, who knew Group Captain and Mrs Townsend as well as the Princess, agrees with Rosemary Townsend that 'Peter seemed to have gone off his chump'. When he writes that his mind 'boggled' at the thought of becoming a member of the Royal Family, Forbes comments waspishly: 'Boggled perhaps, but no more than it had been Mittyishly boggling away on the back burner for years.'

As for Townsend's disappointment when Lascelles told him he must either be mad or bad, Forbes's response was: 'Then more fool or knave, he. And more fool or knave he for not knowing, as he quite incredibly asserts he did not, what scandal he was creating during Coronation year in the foreign press and elsewhere for the family which had shown him such kindness.'

Forbes, up to a point, forgave the Princess. She was, after all, still in her early twenties and had in Thoreau's words, quoted by Forbes, had an upbringing that was 'worse than provincial, it was parochial'. Forbes adds, 'Poor Princess Margaret, with no intellectual or other reserves to fall back on, was stunned by genuine grief at the loss of her beloved father and found it hard to adjust to her now very different life.' Townsend, on the other hand, was the father of two sons, almost forty years old and a man of the world. He should have known better.

Anne Glenconner, who not only remains loyal to the Princess but knew her better than most, believes that her eventual decision not to marry Townsend was not based, as many suggested, on the subsequent loss of money or status, but because of her deep and genuine religious beliefs. Kenneth Rose said, 'Her faith was built on granite but ringed by qualifications.' To many more conventional Christians her religion seemed strange, but it was nonetheless real and Anne Glenconner strongly believes that it was the Church's teaching on divorce that persuaded Princess Margaret that she should not marry Townsend.

To the watching press, marriage still seemed a possibility when Townsend returned to England in 1955, by which time the Princess had passed her twenty-fifth birthday and technically no longer required her sister's consent to marry, under the terms of the Royal Marriage Act.

It was not to be, however, and the couple drafted a solemn statement saying that their relationship was over. This was composed at the London flat of the Princess's old lady-in-waiting Jenny Bevan, now married to a Northamptonshire landowner called John Lowther. It was broadcast on 31 October 1955 and signed by Margaret alone. The crucial message was: 'I have decided not to marry Group Captain Townsend,' and the most important reason was that, 'mindful of the Church's teaching that Christian marriage is indissoluble, and conscious of my duty to the Commonwealth, I have resolved to put these considerations before others'.

Lady Violet Bonham Carter, who had been fending off marauding journalists who got wind of the fact that Townsend and Princess Margaret were dining with her son Mark, heard the news early in the morning on leaving the Savoy Hotel with her brother, the film producer Anthony ('Puffin') Asquith. They had been dining together after a royal command performance of Hitchcock's

To Catch a Thief. There were banner headlines in the early editions of the morning's papers and underneath, verbatim, the statement from the lovers. 'A most poignant statement, perfectly expressed,' thought Lady Violet, 'basing their decision on the Church's teaching of the indissolubility of marriage and her duty to the Commonwealth. It is a heroic decision and rends one's heart. She is so vital, human, warm and gay – made for happiness. And what she must be suffering doesn't bear thinking of.'

Years later, Theo Aronson, the South African writer who specialized in books about royalty and wrote an unauthorized biography of the Princess (*Royal Subjects*), wrote that the more he delved into the Townsend affair – and he delved assiduously – the more he was convinced that the public perception was wrong and the official statement misleading. 'The Princess's choice was not between love and duty but between her life as a princess and life as Mrs Peter Townsend.' The judgement was harsh but not implausible. In the end the answer was that too many powerful interests were opposed to the match and they didn't love each other enough.

The decision was painful, all the more so for being so public. In the ensuing months various other suitors were rumoured: the Marquess of Blandford, heir to the Duke of Marlborough; the Earl of Dalkeith, heir to the Duke of Buccleuch; Domi Elliot, son of the Earl of Minto. The most plausible was the Hon. Billy Wallace,[1] almost the only member of her eponymous set still to be unmarried. In fact, Wallace did propose to Margaret on a more or less regular basis and she, just as regularly and routinely, turned him down. Eventually, however, she said 'yes', though no one now seems to believe that either party seriously intended going through with the marriage. In the event Wallace confessed to an ill-advised sexual liaison elsewhere and the Princess used his admission as a pretext for breaking off their engagement. Another candidate for marriage was rumoured to be her old and close friend Colin Tennant, later Lord Glenconner. In August 1954 the

---

1 Hon. Billy Wallace (1927–1977). Son of a Minister of Transport, educated at Eton and Oxford, married daughter of Lord Inchyra.

'yellow press' (Ann Fleming's description) 'were full of rumours of an impending engagement between the two. Tennant even travelled under the pseudonym Archie Gordon on the train from Balmoral, where he had been helping celebrate the Princess's birthday. The Princess's friend Judy Montagu, who was about to go off to Venice with Tennant, thought nothing would come of it. Ann Fleming was not so sure and thought Tennant 'would enjoy being a Prince Consort'. Judy Montagu was right. Nothing came of it. Despite various rumours, usually involving foreign royalty, no other serious candidate for her hand presented itself for several years.

John Moynihan, the journalist son of the painter Rodrigo, was a columnist specializing in nightclub duties with the London *Evening Standard* at this time. He wrote, years later, in the *Oldie* (January 2007) of how he witnessed the Princess's 'zest for whisky at various nightclubs'. He made the point that although Princess Margaret's capacity for hard liquor was prodigious, he never saw her remotely the worse for wear. Instead, he remembered, 'Her eyes became as hard as coins as she dragged on her long cigarette holder. But no assistance was needed as she rose imperiously for the drive back to Buck House escorted by a number of doting male friends, including Billy Wallace.'

It is not a particularly attractive picture. Moynihan, looking back, remembered balls at Cliveden – later notorious as the setting for the John Profumo scandal involving Christine Keeler and a Russian KGB member called Ivanov – and the Hurlingham Club. There were gulls' eggs and lobster at the former and at the latter she danced energetically in 'a floating dress of red spotted white tulle and a diamond necklace'. Those in attendance included Dominic Eliot, Lord Plunket, Lord Patrick Beresford[1] and Prince Aly Khan,[2] playboy brother of the Aga. At a Curzon cinema

---

1 Lord Patrick Beresford (1934–). Polo-playing son of Marquis of Waterford, once romantically linked with Princess Margaret and prominent member of her eponymous set.
2 Prince Aly Khan (1911–1960). Son of 3rd Aga Khan and father of 4th, international playboy, racehorse owner and briefly UN Ambassador for Pakistan.

première Billy Wallace was in the party and Moynihan noticed that he was acquiring 'pudding cheeks'.

The 'Princess Margaret set' had a regular stamping-ground of West End nightclubs. These were dominated by the 400, Les Ambassadeurs, the Milroy and the Casanova Club. Although regularly observed by such lowering presences as the journalist John Moynihan the Princess and her friends were, on the whole, able to disport themselves relatively undisturbed, unreported and unphotographed. If serious eating was involved the favoured restaurants were the Mirabelle in Curzon Street, generally regarded as London's most fashionable eating place, or Quaglino's in Bury Street.

Quaglino's was the regular haunt of 'Hutch', the black singer whose full name was Leslie Hutchinson. 'Hutch' used to croon such standards as 'A Nightingale Sang in Berkeley Square' and the Princess would sit as close as possible to his trademark white grand piano. When he wasn't playing and singing, 'Hutch' would chat to the Princess and sometimes dance with her. For a big man he was remarkably light on his feet.

After he had finished at Quaglino's 'Hutch' would move on to the Colony Room in Berkeley Square, well known as the London plaything of the Hollywood actor and alleged Mafioso George Raft. The Princess would move to the Colony as well and continue to watch, listen, chat and dance. Before long, however, 'Hutch' fell on hard times. His familiar drophead Bentley was no longer seen in Mayfair streets and he seems to have frittered away his fortune, probably on the serious gambling to which he was addicted. He died, virtually destitute, at the Royal Free Hospital in Hampstead in 1969. He was just sixty-nine years old.

It was not all nightclubs, however. In 1958, for instance, she presented the Duff Cooper Memorial Prize to the poet John Betjeman[1] for his collected works. Duff Cooper's son John Julius,

---

1 Sir John Betjeman (1906–1984). Poet Laureate much loved for his uncomplicated rhyming English verse and his passion for traditional English architecture and teddy bears, all of which masked a complex and uneasy character.

the second Viscount Norwich, was technically one of the judges but was abroad with the Foreign Office for the first five or six years of the prize's existence and was usually informed of the result by Maurice Bowra, who was actually in charge. John Julius would thus get a telegram along the lines of: 'PROPOSE GIVE PRIZE BETJEMAN ASSUME NO OBJECTION BOWRA'.

Bowra and the other judges, Lord David Cecil[1] and Harold Nicolson,[2] seriously considered giving the award to General de Gaulle for his memoirs but decided that he had had enough honours already. On the day of the presentation at the London home of Lady Jones, aka the playwright Enid Bagnold,[3] the *Evening Standard* reported the event and revealed that 'Betjeman's house in Cloth Fair had recently been swept by fire' and that 'the poet, 52' was 'sleeping in a room in Rotherhithe lent to him by photographer Tony Armstrong-Jones'.

Lady Diana Cooper, Duff's widow, thought the Princess looked like 'a jewelled, silky bower-bird' and 'made her funny, faultless speech with art and sophistication'. The *News Chronicle* explained: 'The poet first met the Princess five or six years ago. He has taken her to look at some of the old churches about which he is so enthusiastic.' She got a laugh from a deft allusion to Betjeman's poem on social graces that began with the line 'Phone for the fish knives, Norman ...' 'Anyone who has studied John Betjeman's poems closely will have learned not only about England's lovely old churches,' she said, 'but also how to move in society with confidence.'

The poet was so overcome that he burst into tears and forgot to give the Princess a specially bound copy of his poems. He had

---

1 Lord David Cecil (1902–1986). Academic son of Marquess of Salisbury who was Oxford Professor of English from 1948 to 1970 and was famous for machine-gun-speed delivery of his lectures.
2 Harold Nicolson (1886–1968). Bisexual husband of Vita Sackville-West, politician, author, diarist and, with wife, creator of great garden at Sissinghurst Castle, Kent.
3 Lady Jones (Enid Bagnold) (1889–1981). Writer whose 1935 novel, *National Velvet*, was filmed with Elizabeth Taylor and who wrote the play, *The Chalk Garden*.

to slip it to her later under the table, only to have it returned so that he could pen a suitable inscription inside. Finally the host, Sir Roderick Jones, head of the Reuters news agency and Bagnold's husband, described by the feline Lady Diana Cooper as 'the only living man shorter than the Princess', offended Bowra by referring to him as Sir Horace rather than Sir Maurice.

Betjeman, who remained married but was in a long-term partnership with Princess Margaret's lady-in-waiting Lady Elizabeth Cavendish, evidently took a shine to the Princess and she to him. He became a regular dinner-party guest at Kensington Palace. Bowra, Warden of Wadham College, Oxford, and a friend and contemporary of the prizewinner, wrote an ode in honour of the event and in parody of Betjeman. It ran for seven verses, the first of which was

> Green with lust and sick with shyness,
> Let me lick your lacquered toes.
> Gosh, O Gosh, your Royal Highness
> Put your finger up my nose,
> Pin my teeth upon your dress,
> Plant my head with watercress.

In May 1958 Lady Elizabeth Cavendish gave a modest dinner party at her Chelsea house. Lady Elizabeth was the sister of Andrew, the Duke of Devonshire. She was tall, aristocratic and, as we have seen, the companion of John Betjeman, the complicated architectural enthusiast and popular poet who was ultimately to become the Poet Laureate. Her interests and connections were artistic and even bohemian, which was moderately unusual in a society that was not only still class-bound but in which it was generally expected that the upper classes would be not much interested in books or ideas. Lady Elizabeth was, particularly by the standards of the time, unusual and it was both unusual and characteristic that among her guests that night should be the Queen's younger sister Princess Margaret and a raffish young photographer called Antony Armstrong-Jones.

Almost half a century later Lord Snowdon, as the young photographer had become, would speak wryly about how the

Royal Family and their associates assumed that he had come from 'the gutter' and was 'just a photographer'. This is misleading. Armstrong-Jones's parents were divorced. His father Ronald[1] was a successful barrister, Queen's Counsel, and the owner of an old manor house called Plas Dinas in North Wales. It is now a country-house hotel. A neighbour was Sir Michael Duff,[2] Lord Lieutenant of Caernarvonshire at the time of Prince Charles's investiture as Prince of Wales and godfather to the young photographer. His mother Anne[3] had remarried, as her second husband, the Earl of Rosse, who owned and lived in Birr Castle in the Irish Republic. This had sixty rooms. The Earl employed a butler, a dozen footmen, and was on Christian-name terms with Eamon de Valera, President of the Republic.

It was stretching a point, therefore, to suggest that Antony Armstrong-Jones came from the gutter. It was true that the double-barrelled name had only been invented by his grandfather, a successful doctor called Jones who had been one of the founders of Somerville College, Oxford. Enemies suggested that grandfather Jones was a jumped-up quack who had made a fortune out of inventing dubious patent medicines and was known in his home neighbourhood as 'Jones the pill-pusher'. Nevertheless, young Armstrong-Jones had had a nanny, been educated at Sandroyd – a posh-ish preparatory school in Wiltshire – and at Eton and Jesus College, Cambridge. From there he had come down without a degree but had coxed the 1950 Cambridge rowing eight to a three-and-a-half-length victory over Oxford. It was the first ever University Boat Race to be televised and a blue, at least in those days, was considered of infinitely greater value than a mere degree.

The defining event in Armstrong-Jones's life before meeting

---

1 Ronald Armstrong-Jones QC (1899–1966). Father of Antony Armstrong-Jones.
2 Sir Michael Duff (1907–1980). Witty Welsh aristocrat, great favourite with Royal Family, who was godfather to Antony Armstrong-Jones. The family estate at Vaynol in North Wales was sold soon after his death.
3 Anne, Countess of Rosse (1902–1992). Mother of Antony Armstrong-Jones by marriage to Ronald, the QC, and keen costumier who presented Messel Collection to Brighton Museum.

Princess Margaret was being struck down by polio when he was just sixteen years old. He was at home in North Wales trying to kick-start his BSA motor-bike. He failed and then experienced a stabbing pain in his leg that didn't go away. He was rushed to hospital in Liverpool and spent a year away from school, part of it in an iron lung. When he returned, one leg was shorter than the other and although he was able to enjoy an active adult life, including the 1950 Boat Race, the disease returned in old age with crippling effect. For someone who led an active life despite his diminutive physique – he was just 8 stone 8 pounds when he coxed the Cambridge boat – this was particularly distressing.

By the time he met Princess Margaret he had achieved considerable success as a photographer. He was much in demand by 'society' for weddings such as that of Colin Tennant and Lady Anne Coke, but he had also started to specialize in theatrical portraits after having been introduced to stage circles by his uncle, the famous designer Oliver Messel.[1] Already he had photographed the great Laurence Olivier himself and embarked on what was to be a lifelong friendship.

He was also, despite his Etonian background and affluent parentage, a somewhat bohemian if not exactly iconoclastic figure. He had served an apprenticeship with the photographer Baron,[2] who was not only a brilliant photographer but also enjoyed a slightly louche reputation. Through Baron the young Armstrong-Jones had experienced an early near miss with royalty. Baron was a friend of Prince Philip and was slated to join the Queen's husband on the controversial world cruise he was to make in the Royal Yacht *Britannia* in 1956. Alas, Baron went in for what should have been routine surgery and died under the knife. Mike Parker, Prince Philip's breezy Australian private secretary, was sent down to Baron's studio to check out his young assistant and

1 Oliver Messel (1904–1978). Brother of Countess of Rosse, uncle of Antony Armstrong-Jones, celebrated designer starting with Diaghilev masks and proceeding via Hollywood to eponymous suite at the Dorchester Hotel.
2 Sterling Nahum (1906–1956). Under the pseudonym Baron, was successful society photographer and friend of Prince Philip.

see if he might make a suitable substitute. He returned shaking his head and saying that Armstrong-Jones was definitely not an appropriate choice. Four years later Prince Philip took some pleasure in telling Parker that the young man whom he had rejected was about to become his brother-in-law.

There is some dispute about when exactly the relationship between the photographer and the Princess began in earnest and even Snowdon himself now seems uncertain. One version is that the affair began soon after the Cavendish dinner and was prompted by this particular meeting. Another is that the dinner led to nothing directly and it wasn't until Armstrong-Jones was assigned to take a new batch of photographs of the Princess that the affair took fire.

It is said that the actual engagement was a direct response to Townsend's unexpected engagement to a Belgian girl half his age. Marie-Luce Jamagne[1] looked strikingly like Princess Margaret, was to bear him three children and remain happily married to him until his death in 1995. Princess Margaret took the news of the engagement badly. Her dismay was conveyed in a personal letter to Townsend and she felt it was a betrayal of what they had agreed, namely that they would never marry anyone else. She wrote passionately to Townsend upbraiding him for what he had done and I have been in touch with at least one person who saw the letter.

She became engaged to Armstrong-Jones in the immediate aftermath of the news that her old beau Peter Townsend was marrying his new nineteen-year-old Belgian sweetheart, thus inevitably provoking rumours that she got engaged 'on the rebound' and that it was she who proposed. Armstrong-Jones, now Snowdon, is, by contrast, sceptical about the importance of Peter Townsend in the life of his wife. He queried the significance of 'the Townsend business' more than once in conversations with me. He should, of course, know far better than I whether or not it was crucial or merely a passing fling.

---

1 Marie-Luce Jamagne. Married, as his second wife, Group-Captain Peter Townsend.

The Princess and Antony Armstrong-Jones were in many ways well suited. Both had a strong streak of irreverence, though this was perhaps more pronounced in him than in her. She was naturally cheeky, prone to mockery and mimicry, but at the end of the day she was a king's daughter and a queen's sister, which she seldom forgot and then not for long. Any rebelliousness was always, in her case, qualified. He, on the other hand, was in many ways an outsider and, as a popular photographer, doubly so. Friends were aware that he had misgivings. John Moynihan says that in the days before the marriage he and Armstrong-Jones shared a girlfriend and 'she told me that he wept on her bare breasts when he revealed that he was dreading getting engaged to "Royalty"'.

Almost fifty years later the seventy-six-year-old Lord Snowdon recalled a game that he and the Princess used to play together. They called it 'the bread game' and it was all about clichés.

I asked him to explain.

'OK,' he said, 'I'll say "Ireland". How would you respond?'

I still didn't understand.

'All right,' he said, exasperated, 'you'd say "Ireland's all very well but you wouldn't want to live there". That's a cliché. So as soon as you hear it you tear a piece of bread off your roll' – and he did just that – 'and put it in the middle of the table.'

The person with the most bits of bread in the middle at the end of the meal was the winner.

Part of the magic of the game, of course, was that no one else even realized that it was being played. It was Princess Margaret's and Antony Armstrong-Jones's private way of cocking a snook at the rest of the world without the rest of the world knowing.

FOUR

THE SIXTIES

'Her Royal Highness would very much like to
see Mr Armstrong-Jones turn a pot.'

In her thirtieth year Princess Margaret still had star quality and desirability. The camera, held by expert photographers such as Cecil Beaton and Antony Armstrong-Jones, loved her. In conversation she was lively, flirtatious, irreverent and, as far as her admirers were concerned, an accomplished mimic. She was still a fairy princess.

And yet ... She was widely perceived as a tragic figure, denied the opportunity to marry the man she loved, eclipsed by her elder sister the monarch and by her beatific-seeming mother, who was carving out a special niche in the nation's affections. Even republicans such as Frances Partridge,[1] a leading member of the left-leaning Bloomsbury set, regretted the public spectacle of the Princess's efforts to resolve her involvement with Peter Townsend. 'It is morally wrong to keep our Royal Family like animals in cages, unable to lead their private lives,' thought Partridge. 'It is degrading to us who allow it, like Capital Punishment.' The Princess was still, in her prime, the object of intense public scrutiny and many felt sorry about it. Her very private tragedy had been played out in public. Those who regretted it, however, were still absorbed by the Princess's life and loves in a way that sometimes seemed quite ghoulish.

Then, on 26 February 1960, Queen Elizabeth the Queen Mother announced the engagement of her 'beloved daughter',

---

1 Frances Partridge (1900–2004). Last surviving member of the Bloomsbury set, this strikingly beautiful woman came, in her seventies, to be its chronicler through many volumes of her published memoirs and diaries.

Margaret Rose, to Antony Armstrong-Jones. The news came as a surprise to almost everyone.

Public reaction was, as far as one can see, favourable to enthusiastic. The public were pleased that the pretty, smiley Princess was not going to be left on the shelf. There were exceptions. One of the groom's oldest friends from Eton and Cambridge, the Hulton heir Jocelyn Stevens, cabled to say, 'Never has there been a more ill-fated assignment.' Mind you, Stevens, who incidentally told me that he wanted nothing whatever to do with this book, was not a model of consistency. His *Queen* magazine diary writer, the formidable if anodyne Betty Kenward,[1] was staying on Lyford Cay, where Stevens had a house. Hearing the news she phoned to tell her boss. 'Splendid,' said Stevens. 'I like my staff to marry well.' At the cocktail party later that day Mrs Kenward said, 'There were many happy toasts to the newly engaged pair.' Armstrong-Jones, incidentally, couldn't stand Mrs Kenward. 'She was a monster,' he said, later. 'I remember going up to her at a party once and she said, "Don't you dare address me. I don't talk to photographers." Then, after the engagement, she phoned me for a quotation and I had great pleasure in saying that I didn't think I could help her as she didn't speak to photographers.'

Noël Coward,[2] lunching with Marina, Duchess of Kent, and her daughter Princess Alexandra, detected a *'froideur'* when the subject came up. There was a decided *'froideur'* too from the photographer Cecil Beaton. 'Oh ma'am,' said Beaton, to the bride, 'thank you for ridding me of a rival.' When he'd first heard, however, he'd exclaimed to his house guest John Sutro, 'Not even a good photographer!' When he phoned his neighbour, the Earl of Pembroke, he was pleased to hear him say that if the news were true he would go and live in Tibet. Later, when it transpired

---

1 Betty Kenward (née Kemp-Welch) (1906–2000). Immaculately coiffed and implacably snobbish, she was for more than half a century the author of Jennifer's Diary in *The Tatler* and later *Queen* and *Harper's & Queen* magazines.
2 Noël Coward (1899–1973). Witty, gay playwright, song-writer and epi-grammatist well known for inimitably clipped delivery of own work.

that Armstrong-Jones had no intention of giving up photography, Beaton was unamused.

Another grumpy old man who greeted the engagement with scorn was the writer Kingsley Amis,[1] who sneeringly mocked the 'loyal British', who were so 'terribly thrilled' by the marriage. Amis obviously felt he spoke for *bien pensants* everywhere when he fumed:

> Such a symbol of the age we live in, when a royal princess, famed for her devotion to all that is most vapid and mindless in the world of entertainment, her habit of reminding people of her status whenever they venture to disagree with her in conversation, and her appalling taste in clothes, is united with a dog-faced tight-jeaned fotog of fruitarian tastes such as can be found in dozens in any pseudo-arty drinking cellar in fashionable-unfashionable London. They're made for each other.

By and large, however, the engagement was welcomed. The bride's mother seemed particularly ecstatic, greeting her charming future son-in-law with apparently open arms, not least, one suspects, because the engagement meant an awkward problem solved – at least for the time being. There was a widespread relief that the lucky man was not from the old Princess Margaret set. The beginning of the 'swinging sixties' was no time for the likes of 'Johnny' Dalkeith (later the Duke of Buccleuch), 'Sonny' Blandford (later the Duke of Marlborough) and, perhaps least of all, the Princess's chinless former fiancé Billy Wallace.

The new groom had been educated at Eton but he was also a feisty little battler and a successful photographer, which was, at the beginning of that socially transforming decade, a smart thing to be – much smarter than being an aristocrat. Most importantly, however, the young couple were very obviously in love. There seemed absolutely no suggestion of 'convenience' or 'arrangement'. To observers they seemed besotted with each other.

*

1 Kingsley Amis (1922–1995). Splenetic novelist, poet and bon viveur as well as father of equally famous novelist Martin.

John Timbers,[1] later a successful photographer in his own right, worked as an assistant in the studio of Antony Armstrong-Jones.

'I'd studied at the Regent Street School of Photography,' said Timbers, 'and then I was out on the street. I rang Tony and pitched up at the ground floor flat at 20 Pimlico Road. The door that he put in is still there. It was lunch time and he gave me avocado vinaigrette, the first time I'd ever had it. He said, "Can you start tomorrow?" and I thought, Christ, well why the fuck not? I was completely mesmerized by him. He had something. I don't know what it was but he was special. We got a lot of theatre work through Oliver Messel. That was his passion. He revolutionized theatre photography. And he photographed a lot of girls. A lot of girls. And we did grand weddings. Very grand.'

At just such a wedding the Princess had first come across Armstrong-Jones. This was at Holkham Hall in Norfolk, when the Earl of Leicester's daughter Anne had married the Hon. Colin Tennant. However, the meeting had had little or no significance because Armstrong-Jones had been there in a professional capacity and the Princess simply hadn't noticed him. She wouldn't. To the Royal Family, and even more so their acolytes, his attendance as a photographer at Holkham would have marked him down firmly as 'trade', and not, therefore, worthy of attention. Old Etonian 'trade' Oxbridge 'trade', but especially, as far as lords, ladies and members of the Royal Family were concerned, 'trade'.

The first proper meeting between the glamorous Princess and the stylish photographer was at the dinner party given by Lady Elizabeth Cavendish. Within three weeks the Princess had taken Armstrong-Jones home to Clarence House to meet her mother, Queen Elizabeth.

One of the first public signs of Armstrong-Jones's involvement with the Princess came, quaintly, in a correspondence between her

---

1 John Timbers (1933–2006). Photographer who began professional life as assistant to Antony Armstrong-Jones but later became successful in own right, notably as best of all photographers of Dame Judi Dench.

private office and Harold Partington, the Town Clerk of Bootle in Lancashire. He wanted a photograph for the Mayor and instead of being referred, as was usually the case, to the Dorothy Wilding studio, he wrote to Princess Margaret's office: 'The photographs will be obtained by me, as instructed, from Mr. Armstrong-Jones of 20 Pimlico Road, London SW1.' Princess Margaret visited Bootle shortly afterwards and was greeted with a programme including the new photograph of her by her future husband.

John Timbers remembered that no one knew what was going to happen until the very last moment. Then one afternoon everyone in the little Pimlico office was summoned into the Armstrong-Jones presence and he announced that the organization was being wound up with immediate effect. 'He moved into Buckingham Palace next morning,' said Timbers. Modern courtiers think this unlikely but Lord Snowdon says that the Palace insisted. 'It was for protection,' he says; 'they didn't think Pimlico was secure.'

Iris Peake, a lady-in-waiting at the time, recalled that the public announcement was imminent and the Prime Minister was informed. Then Lady Mountbatten died unexpectedly in India and the official announcement was postponed until after the period of official mourning was finished. Prime Minister Harold Macmillan had, however, already been told. Her Royal Highness's household was terrified that one of his cabinet ministers – or more probably one of their wives – would let the secret out. Miraculously, however, no one talked. Or if they did, no one listened.

The wedding took place at Westminster Abbey on 6 May 1960. The many thousands of sightseers along the wedding route caused what was described as 'Britain's biggest traffic jam' and many were reported to have fainted in the Mall. *The Times*, with the sort of smug, self-congratulatory tone that the British mass media adopt on such occasions reported: 'Only here in London could a ceremony of such traditional splendour be staged,' and their special correspondent described it as a 'Cinderella-like occasion'. Cecil Beaton was the official photographer.

At the Queen's reception before the ceremony Beaton was a characteristic mixture of the condescending and the kind. On the one hand he thought the groom 'extremely nondescript, biscuit-complexioned, ratty and untidy', 'of little standing' and 'not worthy of this strange fluke fortune or misfortune'. On the other hand part of Beaton liked his rival, prompting him to add the codicil: 'Because he is likeable and may become unhappy makes one all the sorrier.'

Armstrong-Jones, who relished the role of impresario – a craving which found fruition a few years later when he effectively master-minded the Prince of Wales's investiture at Caernarvon Castle – did his best to keep the occasion simple. It was he who reined in the royal dressmaker Norman Hartnell,[1] who was fond of elaborate grand gowns. Under the groom's direction Hartnell produced a wedding dress that was 'spectacularly plain' even though it involved the use of thirty yards of white silk organza. Virginia Graham, a friend of the designer Victor Stiebel, who was doing a roaring trade in wedding-day ball-gowns for duchesses, reported to her friend the actress and wit Joyce Grenfell, 'Poor Hartnell is having a truly ghastly time, as the bridegroom is having "ideas". Sequins or anything glittery are definitely out, and that for Hartnell is a major disaster.'

The bride also wore her 'Poltimore tiara', which made her seem taller than she really was. This not especially attractive piece of headgear was originally made by the Royal Jeweller, Garrard, for the wife of the second Baron Poltimore in 1870. It had been bought at auction for £5,000 precisely for its height-enhancing qualities. After her death it was one of the most prominent items in the Christie's sale of her effects. Estimated at between £150,000 and £200,000, it actually fetched £926,400. The purchaser lived in Shanghai. The original owner had been the daughter of the playwright Sheridan. Her husband, the second Baron, had been a hunting and shooting Cornishman who was briefly Treasurer to the Royal Household.

At her wedding the Princess looked 'serenely happy'. People in

---

1 Norman Hartnell (1901–1979). Dress designer best known for his 'White wardrobe' for Queen Elizabeth the Queen Mother in 1938 and his wedding and coronation gowns for Queen Elizabeth II in 1947 and 1953.

the crowd called out 'Isn't she lovely?' and 'How beautiful!' An American from Missouri said, improbably, that he wouldn't have missed it for 'all the presidents in China' and 'a small stout woman submerged behind a Guards band sounded more plausible when she was quoted as saying, 'I didn't see much and I couldn't tell which was which, but God bless them all.'

The best man was Doctor Roger Gilliatt,[1] not a particularly close friend of the groom and not the first choice. Doctor Gilliatt's wife, the writer Penelope, was, however, a very close friend. Originally the honour had fallen to Jeremy Fry[2] who really was close to Armstrong-Jones. Gossips said too close, but this was never substantiated. Although he worked for an engineering company, Fry was interested in all aspects of the arts, particularly theatre, ballet and architecture. He was a little older than the groom but they shared many interests. These included Fry's wife, who was an ex-girlfriend of Tony's. Rumours of an indiscreet homosexual past surfaced in the run-up to the event and Fry stood down. In fact he had once been fined £2 at Marlborough Street Magistrates' Court on a charge of importuning. Trivial, but damaging.

There was a noticeable absence of foreign royalty and some observers thought the Queen looked frosty. On the whole, however, the nation did what it always does at great royal events even if they are weddings between dangerously mismatched individuals. It suspended disbelief and indulged in a day of happy, if possibly self-deluding, euphoria. An exchange between the publisher Rupert Hart-Davis[3] and his friend the Eton beak George Lyttelton[4] summed up both points of view. 'We all loved it,' wrote

---

1 Roger Gilliatt (1922–1991). Brilliant neurologist, married first to film critic Penelope.
2 Jeremy Fry (1924–2005). Inventor, engineer and patron of the arts best known for almost single-handedly saving the Theatre Royal, Bath.
3 Sir Rupert Hart-Davis (1907–1999). Eponymous publisher, editor of the letters of Oscar Wilde (among others) and his Eton housemaster, George Lyttelton; biographer of Hugh Walpole.
4 George Lyttelton (1883–1962). Cricketer, shot-putter, cellist who was archetypal Mr Chips and spent almost entire life at Eton as boy and beak. Father of jazzman and broadcaster Humphrey.

Lyttelton, who had hired a television set specially. 'As you see, I grow more militantly Royalist daily.'

A day or so later Hart-Davis replied, remarking that his friend had failed to comment on 'the countless rumours about and against the poor young photographer'. He also said, 'Everyone hereabouts has commented on the black depression on the Queen's face, and the rustic mind likes to invent the causes of it as jealousy, snobbery etc. But how can you rely on a photograph? Probably she had left the bath-tap running.'

Hart-Davis added, more seriously, 'Like her grandma, when she isn't smiling, she does look over-serious.'

The honeymoon was spent on *Britannia*. The Royal Yacht had been attracting mounting criticism. This was based on her apparent luxury and the millions of pounds a year she cost to run. She was increasingly regarded as an unjustifiable extravagance, particularly when the once all-conquering Royal Navy was being consistently cut back, and by the early sixties was manned by a mere 45,000 men. The wedding had already cost £26,000. The Royal Yacht apparently cost £10,000 a week. The honeymoon was scheduled to last for six whole weeks.

Britannia's crew were not told that they would be manning the vessel for Princess Margaret's honeymoon cruise until 23 March. They had steamed 62,495 miles in 1959 and 1960 and they were due for leave. Now they were unexpectedly told that leave was cancelled and they were to return to the West Indies with the Princess and her new husband. Their discontent was manifested through the 'Canteen Committee', which refused to make a contribution to *Britannia*'s wedding present on the grounds that the cancellation of leave and return voyage to the Caribbean was gift enough in itself.

The beginnings were not auspicious. On the morning of the wedding the yacht managed to fly the Union Flag upside down – a signal of distress – because the dockyard had inadvertently sewn the toggle on the wrong end of the flag. Then a *Daily Sketch* photographer bluffed his way on board with a jovial letter of goodwill from his editor. He was sent packing and the editor undertook not to publish any pictures he might have taken.

Commander Richard Colville RN, the Queen's press secretary, known aboard *Britannia* as 'the Court Jester', told the crew they should have confiscated the camera, which as they knew perfectly well would have ensured the worst possible publicity.

At 17.30 the royal party embarked with the Princess in a yellow suit and yellow turban hat. She stayed on the bridge waving to crowds until dusk. The Royal Marine band disembarked at Southend along with a stoker on compassionate leave because his father was dying.

On 17 May the yacht anchored off Tobago. Things were not going well. A young cook was rude to a petty officer in the galley and would have to be sacked; the mail was sent to Grenada by mistake; the new rubber swimming pool collapsed and couldn't be repaired; a signalman and a steward barged into the royal presence unannounced and unwanted; a 'moronic' signal arrived for 'the Master HM Yacht *Britannia*' demanding to know exactly where the yacht was and when it would arrive at its destination. It was signed: 'Watkins and Hopkins, *Daily Mirror* and *Daily Express*'.

In Tobago the lights failed just as the Princess was returning from a visit to the Governor General and when the royal party went off to an idyllic beach at Le Petit Rameau they found that three rather drunk French fishermen from Martinique had got there first. *Britannia* then sailed twenty miles to Mustique, famously owned by Princess Margaret's old friend Colin Tennant, who had bought it, as a virtual wilderness, for next to nothing. Tennant offered the Princess a plot of land as a wedding present. More than four decades on Lord Snowdon could barely bring himself to hear the name Tennant – or Lord Glenconner, as he had become. 'That shit,' he said, with feeling. Tennant gave the land to Princess Margaret alone, not to the pair of them together. 'Odd, don't you think?' said Snowdon. He never visited the island again. Princess Margaret built a house there called Les Jolies Eaux. It became her favourite place and a valued escape. Not for her husband, however.

From Mustique the Royal Yacht proceeded to Dominica, where the honeymoon couple drove across the island and were picked up on the other side before carrying on to Antigua. The plan was to disembark the royal couple there. However, after a confused day the Admiral was informed, for the first time, that the *Britannia* was to stay in Antigua for an extra six days.

Despite opportunities to go ashore, to swim and to picnic, the mood among the crew remained, in the words of one officer on board, 'glum'. Some members of the crew never went ashore at all. Finally the Wardroom organized a barbecue with a steel band on a beach opposite the ship. It ended when several officers were thrown into the water. Then the same fate befell Major John Griffin,[1] the popular equerry. He thought it was funny. The Princess did not. The barge was summoned and every officer 'felt that he had two left feet'.

Two days before the ship docked at Portsmouth the royal couple at last went round the ship to meet everyone. Years later Lord Snowdon said that one of the attractive aspects of the honeymoon was that the couple had been housed in private quarters and had no need to meet people. They were, for the most part, able to be on their own. This was ideal for the honeymooners but not entirely tactful when it came to relations with the ship's company. This was the first time that many of the crew had seen the Princess and her new husband.

In the ship's company galley the chief cook tried to explain the gastronomic delights of ox hearts. 'You know, ma'am,' he said, beating his chest in exasperation, 'In 'ere. Cows' hearts.'

'I follow,' said the Princess, sounding equally exasperated, 'but I think all innards are awful, don't you?'

The ship docked at Portsmouth in heavy fog on 18 June. The three senior officers received souvenir photographs; the barge's crew got a pencil apiece and the Wardroom was given a piece of coral picked off the beach in Antigua. Forty-six years later the Edward VII silver inkstand that bears the legend 'Presented to Her Royal Highness Princess Margaret on the occasion of her

---

1 Major (Sir) John Griffin (1924–). Long-serving courtier who occasionally undertook public relations duties for Queen Elizabeth, the Queen Mother and for Princess Margaret.

marriage 6th May 1960 by the Admiral, Officers and Royal Yachtsmen' was sold at auction for £4,560.

The beginnings were not therefore entirely auspicious and perhaps the most ominous aspect of the new deal was that neither of the principals seemed to be aware that they were not making an entirely wonderful impression. There is nothing to suggest that the honeymooners thought they were sailing in an unhappy ship. If they did understand, they seemed not to be concerned.

The subsequent marriage of Princess Margaret and Antony Armstrong-Jones was never easy or straightforward. A staff long accustomed to dealing with a single mistress found it hard to get used to an extra person they regarded, in effect, as a male interloper. It seemed not to matter that the new man at Kensington Palace was the Princess's husband; they still talked about him 'raiding the larder' or 'making off with the car' as if he was not entitled to help himself to food and drink in his own house or to drive the automobile parked in his own garage.

Snowdon had particular problems with the autocratic Ruby MacDonald,[1] the bossy termagant who was the Princess's dresser and whose sister, Bobo, performed a similar service for Her Majesty the Queen. It was Ruby's custom to bring up an early-morning tray for her royal mistress and she continued to do this after the Princess married Armstrong-Jones. More than forty years on he looked back on what happened with disbelief. The tray kept on coming and on it was just a single cup for tea and a single glass of orange juice. There was nothing for the new master of the house. He found Ruby's attitude and position intolerable; there was a battle of wills and this time Armstrong-Jones won. Ruby was dismissed.

There was another sort of difficulty with his wife's official support team. He had his own office, his own dark room, his own career and his own secretary, Dorothy – or 'Dotty' – Everard. His

---

1 Ruby MacDonald. Sister of Bobo; after working throughout Princess's childhood became integral part of adult Princess's household but fell foul of Lord Snowdon and was dismissed.

wife's private secretary was not *his* private secretary and her ladies-in-waiting were not *his* ladies-in-waiting. The latter soon discovered that they could do nothing right in Princess Margaret's husband's eyes. One complained that he had a habit of summoning her to his office and pointing to a letter or memorandum on his desk and demanding angrily, 'What is the meaning of this?'

The document would remain on his desk, unexplained and from the lady-in-waiting's point of view upside down. He would take an apparent delight in leaving her to guess what it might be and what she had done wrong. He also seemed to make a point of prevaricating over the many joint invitations involving himself and the Princess. No matter what, the ladies-in-waiting always got it wrong. If they said, 'Yes, Mr Armstrong-Jones would be pleased to accept your kind invitation,' he would ask the wretched lady-in-waiting what on earth made her think he could possibly want to accept an invitation such as this. If, on the other hand, a lady-in-waiting declined on his behalf she would be greeted with a 'What on earth made you think I wouldn't want to accompany Her Royal Highness? Of course I do. Nothing would give me greater pleasure.'

Then there was the family. As we have seen, there was much merriment in 1960 when Commander Mike Parker called in at Buckingham Palace to see his old boss and naval colleague Prince Philip. 'Who do you think is going to be my new brother-in-law?' the Prince asked a discomfited commander. Parker was embarrassed, if amused, to learn that it was the raffish young man he had rejected four years earlier when he had been proposed as a candidate to take Baron's place as photographer on board the Royal Yacht during her round-the-world voyage in 1956. Now the tables were turned, but only up to a point. Armstrong-Jones might have married into the family but that didn't make him any the more 'suitable', or any the less an outsider.

In conversation with Lord Snowdon years later that word 'gutter' seemed to crop up quite often. It was an extreme way of describing the gulf that seemed to exist between him and his new in-laws, but it is the word he used, and used with feeling. At the beginning of the sixties, photography, despite the success of people such as Baron and Beaton, was not the fashionable calling it later became. And there was a definite feeling that Princess Margaret was marrying 'beneath herself'. Hence the Duke of Gloucester's reported dismay when he greeted the Prime Minister at Sandringham with the words: 'Thank Heavens you've come, Prime Minister. The Queen's in a terrible state; there's a fellow called Jones in the billiard room who wants to marry her sister. And Prince Philip's in the library wanting to change the family name to Mountbatten.' The words are those of Harold Macmillan, who was not above embellishment in order to improve a good story. Even if the anecdote is Macmillanized, however, it gives an acute idea of what some people felt about Armstrong-Jones, and, perhaps as importantly, what he sensed that they felt. It wasn't so much the members of the family itself that he felt patronized by as those who surrounded them.

The question of the family name was arcane but troubling, especially for the Mountbatten side of the family. It tended to take precedence over any concerns there might have been over the desirability of the Princess's marriage, which seems not to have been seriously questioned. For those most intimately concerned – Princess Margaret's elder sister the Queen, and her mother Queen Elizabeth – it meant the removal of an increasingly tiresome irritant. At last, perhaps, and God willing, Margaret could go away and live happily ever after.

Armstrong-Jones's background would have been considered by most people even in the early 1960s as upper-class or at worst upper-middle. Those were still impossibly snobbish times and it was less than a decade since Nancy Mitford had helped coin the terms 'U' and 'non-U' and John Betjeman, Lady Elizabeth Cavendish's lover, had written the poem 'How to Get On in Society' with its mockery of people who used fish knives and switched on logs in the grate.

Armstrong-Jones had been educated at Eton, had been invalided out when struck down with polio, at the age of sixteen, and confined to an iron-lung. Despite suffering a permanent disability as a result of this illness and being forced to give up boxing, at which he excelled, he had gone on to cox the winning Cambridge boat in the University Boat Race, as mentioned earlier. His father was a Queen's Counsel and a deputy lieutenant and his mother married, second time round, the Earl of Rosse and was therefore a countess. By average standards Armstrong-Jones was almost grand. Royalty and a certain sort of aristocratic courtier, however, sneered at his relatively newly double-barrelled name, his supposedly common Welsh ancestry and his lowly occupation. In the early twenty-first century such attitudes seem prehistoric, but they were still very much around in Britain in the fifties and sixties.

'They hated the fact that where I'd been brought up was rather nice,' he said later. And they scoffed that, for instance, he had no idea about how to deal with 'servants' or 'staff' such as Ruby MacDonald because he had never had any of his own. Such condescension, based on falsehoods or ignorance, annoyed him and his resentment was particularly provoked when he visited Balmoral for the first time. He didn't fish and the family didn't particularly hold this against him, for what would a mere photographer be doing with fishing? He was given a rod and line and told by the Duke of Edinburgh to sit on a stool in the middle of the lawn and practise his casting. It began to rain. The Prince of Wales came by and asked him what he was doing. Armstrong-Jones told him he'd been instructed to sit in the middle of the lawn by Prince Philip. Prince Charles said that he was being silly and would get wet. He should go and practise indoors in the cinema. Armstrong-Jones did as he was told and with his very first cast managed to snag the screen.

Shooting was worse. Again the assumption was that the photographer wouldn't shoot and these suspicions were entirely correct. This didn't particularly concern the men, who only felt confirmed in their prejudices about photography and gutters. However, Armstrong-Jones was a competitive little man, as evinced by his boxing and coxing, and when he returned south he enrolled at the shooting school run by the gunmakers Holland and Holland in Ruislip a few miles outside London. When he next returned to Balmoral he was able to shoot rather better than most members of the royal party. 'They hated that even more than my not being able to shoot at all,' he remembered with a pleasurable smile.

The landed, moustached, tweedy old-timers who were most suspicious of Armstrong-Jones seemed to think him chippy and cocky and he himself found it difficult to conform. They – meaning the court and those connected with it – did not always make his life easy. Time and again institutions of one sort and another that had enjoyed a happy association with Princess Margaret as their friend, patron or colonel-in-chief, seemed to find it difficult to come to terms with the new man in her life.

The University College of North Staffordshire at Keele was a case in point. The college was founded in 1951 on the initiative of 'Sandy', Lord Lindsay of Birker,[1] formerly Master of Balliol College, Oxford, and a pioneer in the field of extending university education beyond the privileged few. The college's initial reputation was radical and egalitarian so it is a little surprising that it should have had a royal patron in Queen Elizabeth the Queen Mother and a royal President in Princess Margaret. It is perhaps even more surprising that, after a visit to the foundry where a specially commissioned Epstein bronze of Margaret was being cast, in January 1960, Keele's Principal, Sir George Barnes,[2] was moved to write to her private secretary, 'I fall more deeply in love with Princess Margaret every time I see her.'

The Princess seems to have had a problem with the Epstein bronze, for Francis Legh, her private secretary, wrote rather cryptically to Sir George, 'I gather also, that the Princess is writing to you herself about the Epstein announcement on which she has, I think, certain views of her own.' She communicated these views to the photographer Cecil Beaton over lunch one day, complaining that she had been 'Epsteined'. The sculptor had, she complained, given her 'eyes as large as goggles, very cadaverous cheeks and a long Jewish nose'.

1 Lord ('Sandy') Lindsay of Birker (1879–1952). For twenty-five years Master of Balliol College, Oxford, and subsequently, in effect, the founder of Keele University.
2 Sir George Barnes (1904–1960). Long-standing BBC figure who ended up as Director of Television (1950–1956) before moving into academe.

Despite her views on the Epstein bronze she was conscientious about her visits to Keele and seemed to be interested, knowledgeable and supportive. For example, she consented to attend the degree ceremony on 29 June 1960, almost immediately after returning from honeymoon, though it was not clear whether Armstrong-Jones would accompany her. On 6 April Francis Legh[1] wrote to Sir George, saying, 'I cannot yet say whether Mr. Armstrong-Jones will be accompanying the Princess.' Such uncertainty was typical of these early months after the engagement was announced, to the extent that one feels it was a device of Armstrong-Jones, a way of flexing his muscles and telling his wife's associates not to start taking him for granted.

It was clearly irritating to those who had to issue formal printed invitations and programmes, draw up seating plans and generally tiptoe through the minefield of protocol implicit in anything to do with royalty. Some of the reactions to Armstrong-Jones seem almost calculated to irritate. When it finally seemed that he might agree to go to Keele for the degree ceremony the Registrar sent a note concerning 'The proper place for Mr. Armstrong-Jones at this ceremony'. The Registrar thought that there were just two alternatives: 'Either on the gangway seat of the first row of the arena or on Her Royal Highness's left on the platform.'

Faced with this barely concealed sigh about what on earth to do with this new commoner-appendage, it's not perhaps surprising that Armstrong-Jones eventually declined. He did, however, attend the Final of the Gentlemen's Singles at Wimbledon a few days later. A Wimbledon Final was a lot more fun and in the Royal Box at the All-England Club he could seem to have equal billing with his bride-to-be.

That December the Princess returned to Keele, this time accompanied by her husband to attend a ball. Her admirer Sir George Barnes had died and the new acting principal, Professor W. A. C.

---

1 The Hon. Francis Legh (1919–1994). HRH Princess Margaret's first private secretary.

Stewart,[1] suggested that the couple and their entourage might like to stay in the as yet unoccupied new hall of residence. 'It may be', he wrote mischievously, 'that for the President and her husband the suggestion may even have a little piquancy.' The invitation was accepted and in his thank-you letter Francis Legh wrote that 'the entire party was blissfully happy in such extremely attractive and comfortable quarters'.

Music was provided by Johnny Dankworth[2] and his wife, the singer Cleo Laine, who were to become lifelong friends of the Princess. Legh, on behalf of the royal party, considered that 'the Dance was a tremendous success'. It was 'a most happy visit' and 'the entire evening delightfully gay and entertaining'.

This may have been so, but it is not how one other guest remembers it. An officer of the National Union of Students was invited, by Keele's Student Union President Colin Thomas and his Vice-President Jocelyn Rider-Smith, to come down for the night. Over forty years on, this man remembered the occasion somewhat differently. It seemed to him that the royal couple would rather have been almost anywhere else on earth and found the students callow and uninteresting. The students thought the Princess unexpectedly sexy but she, her husband and their friends weren't interested in fraternizing. When the man concerned confided his memories to me, he asked not to be identified, which in itself makes me a shade suspicious. Defenders of the Princess would allege that to relay anonymous memories such as this is merely to pass on malicious gossip. Maybe so. Maybe the memory is false, and the perceptions prejudiced. However, the allegations are typical of the sort of thing that was often said of the Princess. Throughout her life observers thought she was snobbish and offhand and seemed to take a delight in conveying the impression to others. My informant may have been wrong but he felt

---

1 Stewart, William Alexander Campbell (b. 1915) joined Keele as Professor of Education in 1950, appointed Vice-Chancellor in 1967, serving as such until his retirement in 1979.
2 Johnny Dankworth (1927–). Jazz musician married to Dame Cleo Laine (1927–).

Princess Margaret and her party were snubbing him and his friends. In a sense whether he was right or wrong is immaterial. It is the fact that this was what he felt and this is what he said that is significant.

For whatever reason, the Princess often managed to give the impression that she was standoffish and aloof. The impression may have been unfair and the apparent hauteur unintended, but that doesn't make the perception less real.

On 2 May the following year Keele celebrated its tenth anniversary with a visit from the patron and the President together. Both made charming short speeches, the Princess gently suggesting that 'her' university was superior in many ways to London, where Queen Elizabeth was Chancellor. Professor Stewart, now permanently ensconced as Principal, was so overcome by the occasion that he left the only existing copy of the Keele development plan in the Queen Mother's Daimler, from which it was retrieved and handed in to Chief Inspector Crocker, the Royal Police Protection Officer, who was mistakenly told that it was for the Chief Inspector's own personal use.

In the morning while his wife toured her college Mr Armstrong-Jones went off to Stoke nearby to fulfil duties on behalf of the Council for Industrial Design, for whom he was now working part-time. Another modest gesture of independence.

The following day the couple toured the Wedgwood porcelain factory, where further snubs, intentional or not, were delivered. Her Royal Highness was asked if she would like to 'turn a pot'. She declined on the grounds that 'she ha[d] not the happiest memories of a previous experience of this nature when things apparently went sadly awry and pieces flew in every direction'. On the other hand, 'Her Royal Highness would very much like to see Mr Armstrong-Jones turn a pot.' You can almost hear the Wedgwood exasperation. 'No doubt this can be arranged,' came the reply, 'Mr Armstrong-Jones would go round the factory perhaps a dozen yards behind in the wake of Her Royal Highness ... He would join the Princess in the Ornamenting Shop temporarily in order to turn the Black Pot.' He would then return to his position a dozen yards in her wake where, we infer, he belonged. At the end of the visit the Princess was presented with a twelve-setting dinner service. Mr Armstrong-Jones got a 'Boat Race Bowl'. The difference in present clearly demonstrates the perceived difference in status.

On the weekend of 22 July 1960 the Princess and Tony flew down to Devon where, at the invitation of her cousin Margaret Elphinstone, who was then married to Denys Rhodes, she unveiled a statue of St Boniface in Crediton. The presiding clergy were the Bishops of Exeter and Crediton, Robert Mortimer[1] and Wilfrid Westall,[2] well known as a mutually supportive ecclesiastical double act in the diocese. This time Tony found himself at lunch sitting next to the Bishop of Exeter's wife. 'You will find Mrs Mortimer a delightful person,' opined the Reverend Sir Patrick Ferguson-Davie, who acted as a sort of unofficial master of ceremonies for the Exeter diocese. The whole occasion seems to have been agreeably relaxed and convivial in a mildly Wodehousian way. It was followed by the passing-out parade at the Royal Naval College in Dartmouth on Devon's south coast some miles away.

The only person apparently unamused was another of those peppery Lord Lieutenants, this time Lord Roborough,[3] who complained to Francis Legh, 'There has been considerable publicity of Princess Margaret's visit to Devon in the papers, but the Lieutenancy has received no information whatever, and apart from what the papers have said and local gossip, I am completely ignorant.

'It would be a great help to me if I could be informed of any Royal visit *before* it appears in the papers. This procedure has always been adopted when other members of the Royal Family have visited Devon.'

---

1 Robert Mortimer (1902–1976). Craggy and deceptively austere academic who was Bishop of Exeter from 1949 to 1973.
2 Wilfrid Westall (1900–1982). Bishop of Crediton from 1954 until 1974. He was not only a popular figure in Devon but also nationally known for his radio appearances, most notably on *Any Questions*.
3 Lord Roborough, 2nd Baron (Massey Henry Edgcumbe Lopes) (b. 1903); Eton, Christ Church, Royal Scots Greys (twice wounded in WWII), Lord Lieutenant and Custos Rotulorum Devon 1958–78.

The righteous indignation of Lord Lieutenants was a recurring feature of Princess Margaret's life. They tended to be prickly and very aware of their position. Princess Margaret, characteristically, was friendly and courteous to those she knew and liked but sometimes less so to others.

Despite her apparent raciness, her liking for late nights, a glass and a cigarette at hand, and plenty of song and dance, she was also genuinely religious and particularly enjoyed the company of the grander sort of cleric, such as Mortimer and Westall. Among her own contemporaries she seemed especially fond of Nicholas Stacey and Simon Phipps. Launcelot Fleming[1] was a true friend and mentor. She was also close to John Bickersteth,[2] Clerk of the Closet to the Queen. Another clerical favourite was the flamboyant Bishop of Southwark, Mervyn Stockwood.[3] On Sunday, 25 September 1960 Princess Margaret attended one of his ordination services and after she accepted the invitation the Bishop wrote to her private secretary to say, 'After Ordination Services at Southwark Cathedral I usually lunch at the interesting old Southwark Inn – the George. I wonder whether Her Royal Highness, Mr. Armstrong-Jones and the Lady-in-waiting would care to join me and my chaplain for luncheon at the George.'

The reply was sent by return: 'Her Royal Highness would be delighted.'

---

1 Fleming, the Right Reverend (William) Launcelot (Scott) (1906–1990), polar explorer who was chaplain and geologist on the British Graham Land Expedition to the Antarctic 1934–7, was fellow and chaplain of his old college, Trinity Hall, Cambridge, and then Bishop of Portsmouth and of Norwich before ending his career with five years as Dean of Windsor until his retirement in 1976.

2 Bickersteth, the Right Reverend John Monier (1921–), a member of one of the most distinguished ecclesiastical family dynasties in the Church of England; Bishop of Warrington 1970–75; Bishop of Bath and Wells 1975–87. Claimed to be only bishop to have shot with the Duke of Edinburgh at Sandringham.

3 Stockwood, the Right Reverend (Arthur) Mervyn (1913–1995). Vicar of the University Church, Cambridge, before becoming Bishop of Southwark in 1959, where he remained until retirement in 1980. Famous for his snobbery and love of wine, he kept a cellar in which wine was graded in separate racks as appropriate for laity, vicars, bishops and members of the Royal Family.

This was the sort of company and the sort of occasion that the Princess and her fiancé most relished. Later that year there was another small gathering that almost perfectly encapsulated Margaret's liking for the smart and sophisticated. This was a dinner at the zoo given by Sir Solly Zuckerman.[1] The other guests were the Mark Bonham Carters, the Hugh Frasers, the John Wyndhams, the Duke of Devonshire, Mrs John Astor and Michael and Lady Ann Tree.[2]

These were recurring names and, although the cast list changed over the years as friends died off or fell out of favour and new relationships were formed, one gets a definite sense that the Princess felt most at ease within a relatively small group of the tried and trusted. These came to include the occasional wild card or maverick, but they tended to be what one might loosely describe as the well-connected, arguably well-bred chattering classes. She was most at home with people who had an interest in the arts, a predisposition that had been there from early days but was reinforced by marriage. She and her husband tended to enjoy the company of the same sort of people.

The devil during many of the royal visits is in the detail. Even the most routine such events involved an inordinate amount of planning and hard work, often of apparently mind-blowing tedium. Lord Derby suggested that a local school be named after her but Francis Legh wrote back, after 'private investigation' to say, 'I wonder therefore if this question could be quietly dropped.' It was and the school was named after Derby's wife. Notwithstanding

---

1 Zuckerman, Solly (1904–1993). Born in South African, became a polymath pillar of the British Establishment with the Order of Merit, a life peerage and much else besides. Chief Scientific Adviser to Harold Wilson's government from 1964 to 1971. Hon. Sec. of the Zoological Society of London from 1955 to 1977 and its Chairman thereafter until 1984. Wrote an autobiography called *Monkeys, Men and Missiles* (1988).
2 John Wyndham, created Baron Egremont in 1963, lived in the magnificent family home at Petworth in Sussex; the Trees had a less grand but still elegant house in Wiltshire. She was a Cavendish. Mrs Astor was, of course, an Astor. They were all smart and landed and had an appeal for someone such as Princess Margaret.

this, the school suggested giving the Princess a brooch with the Bootle arms on it. The long-suffering Legh wrote back to say, 'Princess Margaret also feels that it really would be unnecessary for the school to give her a present, particularly with the Borough coat of arms, which she would not be very likely to wear much afterwards. Would not a handsome bouquet of flowers (not wired) do the trick?'

An invitation to the Grand National was declined on the grounds that 'I think her last visit to Aintree left rather sad and indelible memories' (a reference presumably to the later-than-last-ditch defeat of her mother's horse Devon Loch, in the 1956 Grand National. The horse was ridden by Dick Francis,[1] later a celebrated writer of mainly equine whodunnits). An anonymous letter complained that a church service attended by the Princess was confined only to 'monied people'. Sir Cuthbert Ackroyd, who had helped organize it, wrote that this was 'a case where whispering tongues can poison truth'.

The chairman of a telephone manufacturing company, Sir Thomas Eades, said his firm would like to 'present a coloured telephone instrument of the latest British Post Office design to HRH Princess Margaret if this would be appropriate'. The reply was rather surprising: 'Princess Margaret has always wished to design a telephone instrument herself to her own specifications and needs.' This sounds like Antony Armstrong-Jones to me. He seems infinitely more likely to have harboured unfulfilled ambitions to do with the design of telephones! The answer came back that they'd be delighted, though it might take time.

Lord Leverhulme[2] declined an invitation to the Jodrell Bank Observatory as, he wrote, 'unfortunately, I broke my leg in a hunting accident some three weeks ago.'

Lord Woolton, Chancellor of the University of Manchester wrote, 'If by any chance Princess Margaret would care to add Mr.

---

1 Dick Francis (1920–). Successful steeplechase jockey who became *Sunday Express* columnist and best-selling author of equine thrillers.
2 Lord Leverhulme, 3rd Viscount (1915–2000). National Hunt and Jockey Club steward.

Armstrong-Jones to her party at Jodrell Bank of course he would be very welcome.'

The reply from Legh was: 'I am afraid he has other commitments which will unfortunately prevent this.' Yet again, one can almost feel the hidden agenda.

On 23 March the Princess went to a Palace Theatre preview of *Flower Drum Song* without her fiancé. This was the last musical composed by Rodgers and Hammerstein. On 28 March, however, Armstrong-Jones *did* accompany her to the Victoria League.

A not untypical letter of the time says, 'I seem to remember that Princess Margaret likes Chesterfield Cigarettes and VAT 69. Do you mind refreshing my memory?' To which the answer was: 'I think that Princess Margaret would like a Gin and Tonic before lunch and you are quite right about Chesterfield Cigarettes ... no particular dislikes in food except that she never eats oysters or caviar.' It is amazing how much time and trouble is devoted to such mundane matters as alcohol, tobacco and food. As so often, there is an apparent inconsistency. One minute she seems to care passionately about such things and at others not at all.

They both went to *Once More with Feeling*, with Rex Harrison and his then wife Kay Kendall, in aid of an arthritis charity at the Leicester Square Theatre on 31 March and to the Boat Race in the Cambridge launch. (They were invited by Oxford as well but understandably opted for the Cambridge invitation.)

On 24 June she opened a school in Stamford – 'As you know, my husband and I have just got back from our honeymoon in the beautiful West Indies' – and talked of 'Christian virtues which alone can give any real meaning to happiness and success'. She went alone with Jenny Bevan. Her husband was, however, with her at the Royal Tournament on 28 June.

On 6 July she visited the Air Navigation School on Thorney Island and there was another of those peppery letters from a Lord Lieutenant, this time the Duke of Wellington:[1]

---

1 Arthur, 8th Duke of Wellington (1915–). Soldier and owner of family home of Stratfield Saye – named Arthur after ancestor, the victor of Waterloo and Victorian Prime Minister.

You may perhaps have thought that I was showing a certain reluctance to meet Princess Margaret at Thorney Island on July 6. This was far from being the case but I know from past experience that sometimes service units resent the appearance of Lord Lieutenants and Mayors on such occasions. I have known this pushed to the point of real rudeness.

However in this case nothing of this kind can arise as far as I am concerned for I am assured that the whole of Thorney Island and the Air Force Station is in Sussex and not Hampshire.

Yours sincerely,

Wellington.

Legh replied: 'I am still somewhat mystified ... but naturally I must take your word for it. I am so sorry to have troubled you but the Air Ministry told me that the address was Hampshire.'

Even curiouser was when the Duke of Norfolk replied from Arundel that 'the Station Commander had already informed me'.

There is no sign of her husband at this event.

On 8 July there was a farewell parade for the disbanding of the 3rd Battalion Grenadiers. This time Armstrong-Jones went along and the couple had lunch afterwards in Wellington Barracks.

He didn't do the St John Ambulance at York but did a Buckingham Palace Garden Party and a Guides Gala at Wembley Pool (he sat between Miss Gibbs and Lady Burnham).

He wasn't at the Princess Margaret Rose School in Windsor when the vicar, the Reverend Cyprian Dymoke-Marr said, 'I think we are most grateful for the relaxed atmosphere she creates when she comes,' but he did go to Glasgow for the presentation of colours to the Highland Light Infantry (in September 1960).

Major-General Ronnie Bramwell-Davis (the Colonel) suggested a message for the 1st Battalion, which was about to leave for Aden. The Princess scribbled in the margin of his letter: 'Please write a *nice* message.' A note was sent from her office to the Lord Provost's office: 'Mr. Armstrong-Jones will be accompanying Princess Margaret throughout the day; could someone be detailed to look after him and make presentations – not possible to have one person for both Her Royal Highness and Mr. Armstrong-Jones.'

Later Legh wrote to the Lord Provost, saying, 'I need hardly tell you that Princess Margaret (and indeed Mr. Armstrong-Jones) was delighted with everything.' Perhaps one is being unduly paranoid in observing that 'Mr. Armstrong-Jones' is once again relegated to an afterthought in parentheses. This would surely grate on anyone's nerves, particularly those of a young man in an obvious hurry and with an evident talent to exploit. He had his own life and no need to lead a vicarious one, confined to brackets around a subordinate clause behind his wife.

At the film première of *The Alamo* she was presented, by the equally diminutive American actor John Wayne,[1] with a Texan saddle. Wayne produced and directed the film as well as starring in it. It had been supposed by the organizers and by her staff that she would rather have almost anything else. On the contrary. 'I'd love a Texan saddle please, M,' she scrawled on an internal memo to her private secretary. It is characteristic that when her staff and others tried to second-guess her requirements she proved them wrong. It may not have been deliberate, but one senses that she enjoyed doing so.

At Lincoln's Inn, where she was a bencher, she was accompanied by her husband who, as the son of an eminent Queen's Counsel, might be expected to have a prejudice in favour of one of the famous Inns of Court. The evening was, as were all her evenings among the Law, a great success. The 'bread-and-butter-letter' from her private office said, 'Her only criticism – if such there could be – was that the time fled by all too quickly.' Rightly or wrongly you learn, after a time studying such documents, to distinguish between the heartfelt thanks and the genteel hypocrisy. This response seems to belong in the former camp.

Occasionally other members of the family pulled rank. Thus Lord Mountbatten who wrote, 'Dearest Margaret, Would you and Tony please attend a concert being held at the Festival Hall on

---

1 John Wayne (1907–1979). Born Marion Robert Morrison and invariably known as 'the Duke'. Wayne, an iconic Oscar-winning actor with distinctive voice and gait, was one of the great all-American stars of the celluloid Wild West.

9th November in aid of the Edwina Mountbatten Trust. Do come, Much love, Dickie.'

They did. Legh wrote to her to say that the star was 'Mr. Yfrah Neaman. He is, I believe, a well known violinist but I must admit that I have never heard of him.' Neaman was indeed a well-known violinist who had, in the 1950s, given the first performances in Britain of violin concertos by Walter Piston and Roberto Gerhard.

On 11 December she visited HMNZS *Otago*, which she had launched in 1958, the first of her sister's – or 'Her Majesty's – ships she had christened. A Haka party greeted her with a traditional Maori challenge from Able Seaman Tito and a fern on the deck, which she subsequently had to pick up. She was given a greenstone paper knife.

She later made a short speech to the Friends of the Elderly and Gentlefolks Help. It is interesting to note the changes that she made to the original draft. 'Thank you very much' became 'I am so touched'. This seems gratuitous but suggests idle hands, as if she had nothing better to do than fiddle with phrases.

Early in 1961 Antonia Fraser[1] asked her to a charity performance of the musical *King Kong* as chairman of the Première Committee for the African Music and Drama Trust. There was a note from Brian Gilmore at the Commonwealth Relations Office, worried about another Sharpeville. He said the risk was 'not very great, and if Her Royal Highness accepted the invitation and in fact there were troubles between now and the occasion, I suppose it would not be suggesting too much for her to plead a cold.' She accepted and did not have to invent a diplomatic cold.

Such engagements came to a temporary end in 1961 when the Princess became pregnant for the first time. Many engagements were perhaps necessary but many were, perhaps inevitably, boring and possibly trivial. Being a figurehead is wearing but not often

---

1 Lady Antonia Fraser (née Pakenham) (1930–). Daughter of Lord and Lady Longford, wife of Conservative Sir Hugh Fraser and then playwright Harold Pinter; crime-writer, historian, hostess, political activist, known to early gossip columnists as 'Hot-Lips Pakenham'.

rewarding. For her husband, who had notionally abandoned his professional career, such royal waving and smiling was no substitute, particularly if his own position was a subordinate, often irritating one. He had his job as a consultant at the Design Centre to stave off boredom. He also designed a 'birdcage' for London Zoo and he busied himself with the refurbishment of the apartment at Kensington Palace which was to become the couple's principal home. This was not enough. The day-to-day programme of quasi-ceremonial happenings which were bread and butter to his wife did little more than rankle as far as Armstrong-Jones was concerned. The crumbs of part-time employment and interest were no more than crumbs. He was simply not cut out to be a conventional royal consort.

Early in 1962 he was appointed to a permanent position with the new *Sunday Times* colour magazine, edited by his old Cambridge friend, the suave and talented Mark Boxer.[1] Before taking the job he had to ask permission from his sister-in-law, Her Majesty the Queen. This was granted, though she was concerned that there might be criticism. In this she was justified. The rival *Observer* took the appointment particularly badly, observing that the Thomson Organisation, which owned the *Sunday Times*, might just as well have hired Princess Margaret herself.

The beginning of married life was spent at Clarence House, where Lord Linley was born by Caesarean section on 3 November 1961. The Caesarean was not carried out on medical grounds but because Princess Margaret did not approve of natural childbirth and believed that infants who were born 'naturally' emerged into the world looking imperfect. One could say, unkindly, that she was one of the pioneers of the 'too posh to push' school. The

---

1 Mark Boxer (1931–1988). Core member of a Cambridge mafia which included Antony Armstrong-Jones and Jocelyn Stevens, Boxer was beguiling, urbane, iconoclastic yet simultaneously disarming. He was the first and defining editor of the *Sunday Times* colour magazine, a deft pocket cartoonist and caricaturist (as 'Marc'), who ended an all-too-short career as editor of the glossy *Tatler*.

Caesarean was not publicized at the time but was recorded by later writers.

The baby's father had been created Earl of Snowdon a month earlier and the infant assumed the subsidiary title of Viscount Linley of Nymans. Nymans was once a Messel family home in Sussex and later Snowdon renovated a cottage nearby. This was to be his own private bolt hole, from which his wife was effectively excluded. It was, in a way, his equivalent, perhaps even his riposte, to her house on Mustique.

When the Princess gave birth for the second time, on 1 May 1964, this time to a daughter, Lady Sarah, she again had a Caesarean. This second birth was at Kensington Palace and once more the reasons for the Caesarean section were essentially cosmetic rather than medical. Once more the operation was not publicized.

Clarence House had been home for Princess Margaret since the death of her father in 1952, but it was accepted that the newly married couple should move into Apartment 1A at Kensington Palace. At one time 'Apartment One' at the palace had been undivided, but part of it was lived in by the widowed Princess Marina, Duchess of Kent, and her three children. For years the Kents spent much of their time at Coppins, in Buckinghamshire. Despite having the use of the Kensington apartment this remained the case until 1973, when the Duke found it too expensive to maintain and instead leased a country house at Anmer on the Sandringham estate.

1A had been empty for many years and the Snowdons made it their first and only home. Indeed Princess Margaret lived there for the rest of her life. In the latter half of the twentieth century 'KP', as it was affectionately known, was famously and quite accurately known within the Royal Family as 'the Aunt Heap'. Princess Margaret and her elder sister certainly called it that, at least since they took tea there with their great-great-aunt Princess Louise. It was ironic that years later Margaret herself should graduate from being a young niece to being an old aunt and part of 'the Heap' herself. Prince Charles always referred to the palace by that facetious and irreverent name and was widely though inaccurately credited with having invented the name himself.

The Snowdons' part of the palace had previously been occupied by two members of the Royal Family – Queen Victoria's uncle, the Duke of Sussex, and, much later, Victoria's daughter Princess Louise. Both, like Princess Margaret, enjoyed a reputation for being unusual, artistic and sometimes almost dangerously difficult.

Prince Augustus, Duke of Sussex, popularly thought of as just one of Queen Victoria's 'wicked uncles', was actually a much more interesting and complex figure than that suggests. He infuriated his father, George III, by marrying Lady Augusta Murray and did it again with a second marriage to the widow of Sir George Buggin. ('Buggin's turn', the system of giving jobs by rote rather than on merit, may have been named after him, but the origin of the phrase is unknown and its first use is accepted as having been by Admiral of the Fleet Lord Fisher in 1901.) Buggin's widow was Cecilia, ninth daughter of the Earl of Arran. Augustus was an advocate of electoral reform, the abolition of slavery and female emancipation. He was President of the Society of Arts and of the Royal Society as well as being Grand Master of British Freemasons. In the apartment at Kensington Palace he created a magnificent library, bookshelves from which survived long enough to be items in the 2006 sale of Princess Margaret's possessions at Christie's of London. Yet, like Princess Margaret, he was, in the words of his biographer, 'too exalted for ordinary employment and not useful enough for the adequate allowance that would enable him to maintain the princely state expected of him.'

The Duke was granted the apartments at Kensington Palace in December 1804 and he lived there until his death in 1843. They were originally furnished, in haste, with furniture from Hampton Court and new wallpaper for just one room. When his widow, who had been given the title of Duchess of Inverness, stayed on in the apartments, it was said that 'The decoration and furniture of the suite of apartments were very old-fashioned, the small dining room was fitted up like a tent and was very stuffy. The large dining room was a fine spacious room.'

The Duke himself was noted for his informality and yet he was always aware that he was royal and he had a sharp eye for

breaches of etiquette. His great library eventually ran to fifty
thousand volumes, the purchase of which helped to ensure that
he was almost permanently in debt. Unlike Princess Margaret,
who regularly weeded out unwanted books with the help of her
friend and biographer Christopher Warwick and sold them
off, the Duke of Sussex never seems to have got rid of a single
volume.

He was relentlessly convivial and gregarious. Thomas Moore
writes of an evening in 1830 when, having just ordered dinner at
Brooks's Club, he was tempted to join a party at Kensington
Palace by a man called Stephenson, 'who had been commissioned
by the Duke of Sussex to throw his dragnet at Brooks's for any
stray guests he could catch for an impromptu at Kensington'.
Moore thoroughly enjoyed himself, recording, 'The day most
royally odd, and (to do it justice) *un*royally easy and amusing.'
The *Morning Chronicle* almost presaged the evening enter-
tainments hosted by Princess Margaret over a century later when
it wrote, 'Nothing could be more delightful than the evenings
when Kensington Palace was thrown open by His Royal Highness
to the public. At his soirees were to be seen all that was dis-
tinguishable in science, art and literature, natives and foreigners –
men of all particular opinions.'

When he died in 1843, twenty thousand people came to
Kensington to see his body lying in state. His diminutive widow
lived on in the apartment until her death in 1873. She was buried
alongside the Duke under a huge granite block in Kensal Green
Cemetery. Two years later Queen Victoria decided that her daughter Louise should move into 1 Kensington Palace and a new era
began.

Princess Louise and her husband Lorne, Marquess of that name
and subsequently Duke of Argyll, thus took up residence in their
new home in 1875. The Princess was the first member of the
Royal Family to marry a 'commoner' for more than 350 years,
since Henry VII's daughter Mary had married the Duke of Suffolk.
You could plausibly argue that neither the Duke of Suffolk nor
the future Duke of Argyll were 'common' in the usual sense of
the word, and certainly not in quite the same way as the untitled

Antony Armstrong-Jones, who was the next husband of a royal princess to live in these rooms.

In later life Louise's Lorne developed some eccentric habits and rumour had it that he was in the habit of letting himself out of the French windows at Kensington Palace in order to conduct assignations with young Guardsmen in Hyde Park. This may be a calumny: it seems just as likely that Lorne was suffering from some form of dementia and just given to wandering around at night. In any event the window was blocked up and was still like that when the Snowdons moved in at the beginning of the 1960s. Princess Margaret had it unblocked and asked the housekeeper why it had been bricked up in the first place. The answer was that Princess Louise had done it to keep her husband inside, but there was no explanation as to why he had been trying to escape.

Louise was of an artistic bent and was, unusually for any woman in her time, an accomplished sculptress. Her best-known work was a depiction of Queen Victoria at her coronation as a girl of nineteen. The Princess was also rumoured to have conducted some extramarital liaisons and it was even said that the distinguished sculptor Sir Edgar Boehm had died in her arms while making love. This was, needless to say, never confirmed, but it was widely believed and talked about. Although she had the common touch and was particularly popular with her mother's subjects in North America when her husband was Governor General in Canada, she was also subject to sudden unexpected bouts of imperiousness. On one famous occasion she was asked at a children's party: 'Is your mother well?' Her reply, delivered with Lady Bracknell hauteur, was: '*Her Majesty* is very well, thank you.' The story is almost exactly the same as the popular anecdote involving Princess Margaret. When asked how 'her sister' was, Princess Margaret was said, invariably, to ask the questioner whether she meant 'Her Majesty the Queen'. Perhaps she learned the put-down from Princess Louise.

Louise was also given to writing prayers including one to the Archbishop of Canterbury during the General Strike of 1926 and another that cheered up Neville Chamberlain on the outbreak of World War II. Her final defiance of convention was giving orders that after her death she was to be cremated. Elizabeth Longford wrote of her: 'She finished as a remarkable and fascinating woman, who was no longer frustrated by her joint royal and artistic roles.'

It seems a strange coincidence that Princess Margaret, whose contrary and sometimes unconventional style echoed so much of Princess Louise's, should have lived the last forty years or so of her life in the same rooms in the same palace. Both women were cremated and both wrote prayers. Neither practice would usually be considered royal.

That the two princesses should have been preceded by the Duke of Sussex is even odder. Just the three royal inhabitants in the course of a couple of centuries and all three, in their different ways, mavericks if not exactly black sheep.

Number 1A sounds modest or even poky, but this is misleading. Anywhere else it would be considered a grand London house. In the Snowdons' day it had a dog-washing room, a sun-bed room and even a Christmas-present-wrapping room. (I'm not aware that there was a birthday-present-wrapping room.) When I walked round in the spring of 2005 I didn't count every single room but, if not precisely cavernous, it seemed far from modest. The office staff had separate quarters on the other side of the courtyard, at Apartment 5, so although it was only about half the size of the accommodation enjoyed by the Duke of Sussex and Princess Louise it was still substantial.

Quite how dilapidated it had become when the Snowdons took it on is a matter of some dispute. Certainly the rooms had not been inhabited since Princess Louise had died there in 1940. There were rumours that it suffered from enemy bombing during the war. Part of the roof had never been properly repaired and was just covered in corrugated iron.

When I saw it in the course of researching this book, the main impression was one of rather bleak emptiness. I remembered it from my only visit during Princess Margaret's life as cluttered and dark, a bit like one of those antique showrooms in Honiton with the blinds drawn. This was confirmed later when many of the Princess's possessions were sold at auction. Even for a royal princess she seemed to have an enormous number of 'things' and the sale did not include, for example, her huge collection of seashells.

One of the curators of Historic Royal Palaces actually described the agency's inheritance as 'a shambles. A real "old lady's house"'.

In the early 1960s, when the apartment was extensively renovated, there was much ill feeling, both in public, where the expense was questioned in parliament, and privately. The work was done largely at the taxpayers' expense and led to considerable tensions between the Snowdons on the one hand and Harold Yexley, the architect from the Ministry of Works, on the other. There was bitterness in official circles that 'misleading claims' had led to the needless destruction of priceless original Christopher Wren interiors. Historic Royal Palaces considered their substitution by the Snowdons in the early sixties ephemeral vandalism.

All this was disputed then and now. Harold Yexley's posthumous account – he died in 2003 – is illuminating and sometimes highly entertaining though not deliberately so. Some of those who worked on the refurbishment, including Yexley, found the Princess's swings from childlike levity to stiff formality difficult to predict or understand. When, for example, she first saw the new bath in the centre of the Gothick Bathroom with its unusual hexagonal towel rail, she lay down in the bath laughing as if she were playing charades. The workers were enchanted by this informality but later, when she thanked them all for the efforts they had made, she treated the whole thing with the formal solemnity of a Buckingham Palace investiture. Outsiders were perplexed.

The Snowdons always maintained that when they took over the apartment it was empty and neglected, riddled with dry rot and damp from leaks in the roof. According to the Christie's catalogue for the 2006 sale, which included much of the contents of Princess Margaret's former home, they were faced with an 'uphill task' but one for which they were 'uniquely well-suited'. According to this version of history, 'It was Armstrong-Jones who succeeded in transforming 1A into the modern family home they desired.' In this he was assisted by the well-known designer Carl Toms, who had worked as an architectural assistant to

Tony's uncle Oliver Messel and who became a close friend.

Christie's furniture expert, Orlando Rock, paints a heart-warming picture of the young couple battling against bureaucracy and rising damp: 'Thankfully the new incumbents could not have been more hands-on and thus whilst Lord Snowdon laid out the slate and marble chequerboard floor in the Entrance Hall, the Princess herself was gluing on the mahogany veneer to the doors of the Dining and Drawing Rooms and "dragging" the turquoise glaze to the wallpaper in the Drawing Room.'

A hole was knocked through the wall between the drawing room and the library so that a built-in projection unit could be installed for showing movies. Two lifts, one for people and one for luggage, were installed along with a grey-and-white plastic telephone and intercom system. The basement was converted into a workshop and dark room and the couples' offices were kitted out with modernist furniture by the Dane Ole Wanscher, some of which was auctioned off after the Princess's death.

There is no mention of the long-suffering Ministry of Works architect Harold Yexley in this version of events and yet, for some, it is he who was the hero of the hour. Luckily his papers survive. It is clear from these that relations between the Snowdons and himself were seldom easy. When his name came up in conversation with Lord Snowdon more than forty years later, the rolling of eyes needed no verbal addition. Yexley's notes are often terse but they are nearly always revealing.

On 7 March 1962, for example, Yexley, the Princess and Lord Snowdon walked round the entire apartment and 'Lord Snowdon instructed that the following items shall be done.' Not much suggestion of friendly discussion or give-and-take. A fortnight later the three travelled by car to Allied Ironfounders in Brook Street to meet Mrs Adams of Adamses and choose baths. Lord Snowdon had his own shower but no thermostatic control. Princess Margaret also wanted something done about the water closet in a commode chair that had arrived and was sitting in the Kensington Palace chapel. This meeting apparently lasted from ten to three in the afternoon until ten at night. On 25 March Princess Margaret was shown samples of taps but came to no conclusion until Lord

Snowdon had also had a chance to look at them. Later there were problems finding mahogany doors; a drawing of a fireplace by Yexley was humorously 'beautified' by the Snowdons and a mermaid given a black-and-white Campaign for Nuclear Disarmament badge. As late as October that year Lord Snowdon was reported to be asking for further samples of a sealer that might be applied to softwood floors 'to give a light gold colour'. The attention to detail is impressive. So is the time taken. Official patience, meanwhile, was obviously wearing thin.

Mr Yexley was the Ministry of Works architect on site, but in the background was the memorably named Mr P. H. Ogle-Skan, Assistant Secretary at the Ministry of Works. From his office in Lambeth Bridge House one can still imagine the pursing of the Ogle-Skan lips and the drumming of the Ogle-Skan fingers as the young Snowdons argue over 'fibrous plaster cornices' and 'hand hair shampoo units', and the budget and the time schedule both veer further and further off course.

On 8 March 1962 Harold Yexley wrote a minute by hand. It concluded,

> I have informed Mr. Ogle-Skan that Lord Snowdon gave orders that I was to be informed he required certain extra works to be carried out immediately during his visit to site with Mr. Watkins on 7/3/62. I am following instructions to obtain estimates of the cost of these items and submitting them for your approval before instructing the site. Lord Snowdon appears to be unaware of the financial restrictions under which I am working and his ideas will generally tend to increase the cost of the job rather than help to economise.

Over the next couple of months the situation must have improved, for on 18 May Yexley reported: 'We are getting decisions from Lord Snowdon rather more quickly now, but he is inclined to change his mind. This has caused no difficulty at present and he is aware of the need for economy.'

Yexley still sounds tetchy and the relationship between him and the Snowdons does not seem to have been particularly harmonious. Nevertheless there is no disputing Snowdon's invent-

than Margaret. Ideal. 'She was *so* pretty,' said Lady Antonia, looking wistfully at the young Princess doing a Balinese dance with all the gestures, flirting outrageously with the camera, 'and *what* a show-off!'

The Snowdons, the Devonshires and the Frasers would have made an exotic half-dozen passengers on that BOAC plane to Jamaica. In the early twenty-first century they seem almost quaint, but at the time they were at the cutting edge of upper-class sophistication, the acme of the aristocracy.

'I remember nodding off to sleep,' recalled Lady Antonia more than forty years later, 'and suddenly the curtain to my bunk was pulled aside and a royal voice said, "I'm terribly sorry but Tony and I were playing a game and I'm afraid our ball has rolled under your bunk."' The Snowdons' main quarters were just aft of where Lady Antonia and 'Debo' Devonshire were sleeping. Everybody else, apart from the royal couple and the two ladies, had to make do with chairs.

In retrospect the British High Commissioner thought it rather a mistake for the Frasers and Devonshires to travel in the royal plane, as they became unduly overshadowed by the royal couple. 'Despite the efforts of my information officer,' he wrote, 'we were not able to obtain as much publicity for Mr. Fraser and the Duke of Devonshire as I could have wished.'

'My chief memory', said Lady Antonia, 'was the determination of the Jamaicans to treat Andrew and Debo as senior to Hugh and myself. I do see their point. I mean a duke's a duke. Andrew was, of course, extremely embarrassed and kept trying to push forward Hugh. Debo rather less so ... We both borrowed hats from Drue Heinz.' The Duchess of Devonshire apologized in 2006 because, she said, 'my memory is hazy'. However, she did add: 'All I do remember is the long, long journey in the plane and relentless rain.'

Not for the first time people seem to have had trouble with the idea of the Earl of Snowdon and of his place in the hierarchy. At one point the Americans, led by a notably truculent Vice President Lyndon Johnson, had to be told crisply that as the husband of the Queen's sister and an earl into the bargain

Snowdon most certainly took precedence over LBJ. However, when the first draft of the programme was submitted to Kensington Palace Princess Margaret had to go through the whole thing inserting 'E of S' at appropriate intervals and rescuing him from a metaphorical seat in the upper circle in order to place him next to her in the Royal Box, where she, not unreasonably, felt he belonged.

At home he was evidently playing a dominant role within the marriage. When a new independent airline called Cunard Eagle offered the couple the use of the entire first-class section of one of their aircraft it was Snowdon who dealt with the matter. The Snowdons were feeling bruised by regular accusations of extravagance, most notably over the refurbishment of their Kensington Palace apartment. They did not want to appear to be spending unnecessary sums on their visit to the Caribbean. It didn't help either that the Queen Mother had recently flown to Canada on a scheduled flight. On the other hand Margaret *was* representing the monarch and the Jamaicans might not have taken kindly to the sight of the Princess coming down the steps of her aeroplane along with a whole load of ordinary fare-paying passengers.

A 'Dear Tony' letter from Michael Adeane, the Queen's private secretary, offered avuncular advice on how such a difficult problem should be resolved.

> I can quite see Princess Margaret's and your difficulty [he wrote]. The press-reading public may see little difference in the two ventures and they may even decide to think the Caribbean the more attractive; you will be criticised for not being as economical as Queen Elizabeth. And so on. It is not easy. Nevertheless if it was for me to decide (which it is not) I feel pretty sure that I should say that it ought to be a charter plane ... Would it not be a good thing to talk it over with the Government Department concerned?

Adeane's advice was that Snowdon could eventually – through Richard Colville – make it clear that it's Government policy. The advice was followed and, in the event, there was little or no fuss.

The premier of Jamaica was the tall, flamboyant Sir Edward Bustamente, the leader of the opposition the radical and charismatic Michael Manley. 'Everyone was very excited by Manley,' recalled Lady Antonia Fraser. 'There were all sorts of rumours about what he would do, none of which he did do.'

It was LBJ, not Manley, who made a nuisance of himself, as the witheringly mandarin report of the High Commissioner, A. F. Morley, made abundantly clear. 'Vice President Lyndon Johnson's efforts to steal the thunder considerably irritated the local authorities,' he wrote. 'His attempts to obtain for himself special treatment were, at least to the Jamaican official world and among the upper classes, distinctly counter-productive.' Morley was outraged at the Texan's attempts to 'steal Princess Margaret's show', at his 'bad manners arriving late and after prayers at the opening of parliament and his failure to keep his promise to leave the building before Her Royal Highness arrived.

'The powers above appeared to share the Jamaican view ... it rained hard and continuously throughout his reception and the occasion became a shambles.'

There was obviously not a lot of love lost there. Almost the worst American crime was their mounting a helicopter reconnaissance without consulting the British or the Jamaicans and trying to commandeer one of the Half Moon Hotel cottages that had been earmarked for royal use. An exasperated Governor, Sir Kenneth Blackburne, wrote home to say, 'I have been subjected to heavy pressure from American representation here ... the arguments are that Anglo-American relations will be impaired if special treatment is not accorded to the vice-president.'

Duncan Sandys, the Colonial Secretary, wrote back to say, 'We have been told by U.S. Embassy that vice-president is suffering from exhaustion.'

It was not a happy moment in Anglo-American relations but the High Commissioner did not allow this to diminish his optimism about the future and his overall satisfaction with the way in which the Independence celebrations were conducted.

As the final icing on the Princess's cake she received a typically mandarin thank-you from the Prime Minister, Harold Macmillan.

'In spite of the somewhat unconventional behaviour of certain other representatives on this occasion, Your Royal Highness's presence invested the Ceremonies of Independence with a dignity, spontaneity, and charm which they could not otherwise have achieved. I therefore write to offer my humble congratulations on what was a considerable personal triumph.'

* It is characteristic that he does not mention LBJ by name, though Supermac's effortlessly superior Eton, Balliol and Grenadier tones clearly imply that he thinks the Vice-President an uncouth Texan. It is also interesting that, although the visit was very much a joint effort, he fails to mention Lord Snowdon. This must have been galling but continued to be common. Everyone was used to dealing with Princess Margaret on her own and there was a widespread feeling, especially among old-fashioned snobbish elements, that the Princess's husband was not quite 'one of us'.

In 1963, the following year, the Snowdons visited the United States together. They stayed twenty days, fourteen of which were entirely taken up by public engagements of which there were more than sixty. One or two people wrote to the Foreign Office to complain that the government was footing the bill, but the American reaction was generally favourable. The *Herald Tribune* described the couple as 'engaging and popular' and said that they represented the British Crown with 'a fine combination of majesty and zest' and the *Washington Post* pointed out that 'she [was] a salaried employee', adding that 'if there were a union for princesses she could claim time and a half for overtime'. A doctor from Greenwich, Connecticut, sent the British Embassy a cheque for ten dollars to cover the Snowdons' expenses, though it is difficult to see whether the gesture was ironic or genuine. In any event the cheque was returned.

That same year, perhaps prompted by this public adulation, Cynthia Gladwyn wrote an altogether more hostile account of the Princess's behaviour abroad. Lady Gladwyn was the wife of Sir Gladwyn Jebb, who was British Ambassador in Paris during the 1950s. In 1963 the Gladwyns were living in Suffolk and we simply don't know what suddenly moved her ladyship to recall

With fashion icon Yves St. Laurent at Blenheim Palace, Oxfordshire. 'Sonny', Marquess of Blandford and heir to the Marlborough dukedom as well as ownership of the palace, is in the background. He was, before his marriage, a leading member of the Princess Margaret Set.

Princess Margaret meets the Italian-born, Paris-influenced designer Valentino who also designed for Jacqueline Onassis and Elizabeth Taylor. When he introduced the Princess to his mother, the signora clipped her boy round the head and exclaimed proudly, 'My son is good'.

1959 and the last official birthday portrait before her marriage to the man who took the picture – the raffish and controversial Antony Armstrong-Jones.

One of the best of the many emblematic Cecil Beaton portraits. This one, a mirror image of the famous Annigoni portrait in the background, was taken in 1958.

The groom as snapper. Antony Armstrong-Jones takes Cecil Beaton's place as photographer on his wedding day in 1960. The balcony is the famous one at Buckingham Palace.

A happy family snap of the Snowdons and their two children in the courtyard at Kensington Palace taken by Cecil Beaton.

the time that Princess Margaret came to stay. Recall it she did, however, telling her diary that 'the impression that still remains very clear after four years is the flagrant behaviour of Princess Margaret'. This obviously made a considerable impression on the Ambassador's wife.

At first the Jebbs, as they then were, anticipated a visit from the Queen Mother on her own. She was to open a big international flower show on her way home from Rome. Then came a letter announcing that she hoped to bring Princess Margaret with her as well. Lady Jebb was not pleased. She would have to think of things to amuse her and people who would not bore her. 'Her reputation when staying in embassies and government houses, was not an encouraging one,' she wrote. 'To make matters even worse it seemed the only reasons for Princess Margaret wishing to come to Paris were to get her hair done by Alexandre, and to fit a Dior dress.'

At Orly, where the Jebbs met mother and daughter, Queen Elizabeth was radiant and Princess Margaret was not. Evidently the Princess had been gallivanting around Rome with Judy Montagu and some friends and had had little or no sleep. The two women brought a retinue of eleven, which was, as Lady Jebb pointed out, 'quite a number of people to arrange for'.

No fault could be found with the Queen Mother, who was her usual 'sparkling and delightful' self. Not, alas, her daughter.

Lady Jebb wrote:

Princess Margaret seems to fall between two stools. She wishes to convey that she is very much the Princess, but at the same time she is not prepared to stick to the rules if they bore or annoy her, such as being polite to people. She is quick, bright in repartee, wanting to be amused, all the more so if it is at someone else's expense. This is the most disagreeable side to her character. She is very small, but somehow not nearly as exquisite or pretty as the Queen, despite beautiful eyes.

There was uncertainty about whether ladies should wear long or short dresses for dinner and the Princess went for a short one which Lady Jebb wrote, cattily, one Frenchman commented 'began too late and ended too soon'.

After dinner, which seems to have passed off without incident, everyone adjourned to the ballroom for a cabaret given by a quartet of *chansonniers* called Les Frères Jacques. Princess Margaret, unlike her mother, was miffed because the French audience failed to stand at the royal entrance. She refused to stick to the seating plan, insisting that she sat next to Jean Cocteau. 'She took such a fancy to him that she would hardly talk to anybody else the whole evening.' This is a frequent complaint. If she took a shine to someone she would, apparently, monopolize them to the exclusion of everyone else. This could be embarrassing, particularly for a host or hostess who had gone to some trouble to arrange appropriate conversation partners. Lady Jebb tried to get her to speak to the former French Ambassador to London, but failed utterly and gave up.

Sunday was even worse. After church the plan was to change into country clothes and make a couple of visits where groups of suitable and enthusiastic young people had been arranged. 'So', wrote a visibly exasperated Lady Jebb, 'it was upsetting when, as we entered the Embassy, the Princess came towards me and told me she had a cold and therefore could not come with us. Simultaneously she began clearing her throat, cooked up a few coughs, and said that her voice was going.'

The Queen Mother apologized; Iris Peake, Princess Margaret's lady-in-waiting, seemed disappointed; and as Lady Jebb was changing, her old maid Berthe announced triumphantly that she had been able to arrange, as requested, that the famous Alexandre could call round after lunch to do the Princess's hair. 'Clearly', wrote Lady Jebb, 'Princess Margaret's cold was a fake.'

The Ambassador's wife was now clearly enraged. She confided in the Queen Mother's lady-in-waiting, who shrugged and was unsurprised. Her boss would be unfazed. Lady Jebb thought it might be better 'if her husband had been disturbed, and that Princess Margaret had been firmly dealt with.' She obviously thought the Princess was a spoiled brat.

Only when she was persuaded that the guests at dinner were

sufficiently distinguished did the Princess deign to appear at dinner. 'Difficult girl,' wrote Lady Jebb, adding that 'the farce of the cold was still kept up'. She gave her some credit for 'being a good actress', though she felt the mask slipped from time to time and ultimately 'what was really remarkable was her lack of desire to please'.

The next day Lady Jebb was accompanying the Queen Mother to the flower show and Princess Margaret was flying home early after the Dior fitting. At 10 a.m. Lady Jebb called to say goodbye. The Princess said she was feeling much better. 'As I curtseyed,' wrote Lady Jebb, 'I could not resist remarking, "I'm so glad, ma'am, that having your hair shampooed did not make your cold worse."'

Not, by the sound of it, a resounding success. Years later, Iris Peake, by then the Hon. Mrs Dawnay, recalled slightly ruefully that Lady Jebb and the Princess had not exactly hit it off. However, she made the point that the French people whom she was supposed to have stood up were no part of any official business and had been set up entirely on Lady Jebb's own personal initiative. Even so it does not sound like a happy occasion and there can be no doubt that the Princess made a bad and lasting impression.

Lady Jebb obviously very much disliked Princess Margaret and the feelings seem to have extended to Lord Snowdon. At a party given in aid of the Hertford Hospital in Paris, hosted by Gladwyn and Hugh, the Marquess of Hertford,[1] the Queen Mother and the Snowdons were guests of honour. The Queen Mother, as usual, could do no wrong, and Lady Gladwyn conceded that Princess Margaret not only looked 'very pretty' but was also 'fortunately in a good mood'. Snowdon, however, was chastised for a 'sun-lamp burnt brown complexion' and hair that had been tinted 'a curious new colour'. Afterwards she obviously discussed it with Sacheverell Sitwell,[2] who described it as peach. Lady Gladwyn

---

1 Hugh, 8th Marquess of Hertford (1930–1997). Water-skiing owner of historic family pile, Ragley Hall, Worcestershire, and leading member of stately-home-owning lobby.

2 Sir Sacheverell Sitwell, 6th Bt. (1897–1988). Eccentric and prolific writer; brother of Osbert, to whose family title he succeeded in 1973, and Edith.

thought it more apricot. Five years later she sat behind Tony at a performance of two Neapolitan plays at the Aldwych. This time Snowdon's hair was 'auburn' and dressed in two handsome waves, 'which seemed to preoccupy him very much'. This time, after dinner at the Italian Embassy, Princess Margaret refused to leave. 'All just to tease and annoy,' wrote Lady Gladwyn.

This condescending and catty attitude to the Snowdons was typical of a certain old guard. They tended to be the same sort of people who had been disdainful about Prince Philip when he had first arrived on the royal scene. Snowdon was a much easier target and there was also a sense in which the Queen's younger sister was fair game whereas her mother and Her Majesty were, by comparison, off limits. When people such as Lord Altrincham[1] (better known, after renouncing his title, as plain Mr John Grigg) criticized the Queen it was considered bad form and a betrayal of his class. That wouldn't have mattered if he had been rude about Princess Margaret and Lord Snowdon.

Partly because she was 'only the sister' and partly because her behaviour sometimes encouraged it, people sometimes treated her with a familiarity bordering on contempt. This was particularly true abroad, where the almost religious respect the British still had for their monarchy was much less in evidence. There was one such occasion in 1966 at the Cannes Film Festival when she arrived late for a performance of *Modesty Blaise*, a Dirk Bogarde[2] vehicle that the star enthusiastically disliked. She was noisily heckled. The British Ambassador, Sir Patrick Reilly,[3] wrote to the

---

1 John Grigg (Lord Altrincham) (1925–2001). Peer who renounced title and attacked monarchy albeit in a manner that would have been considered almost feeble in later years; remained, in fact, paid-up member of Establishment whose last job was Obituaries Editor at *The Times*.
2 Dirk Bogarde (real name Derek van den Bogaerde) (1921–1999). Matinee idol who successfully metamorphosed into serious actor and stylish novelist, memoirist and book reviewer.
3 Sir Patrick Reilly (1909–1999). Career diplomat who was Ambassador in Moscow and Paris before having diplomatic career cut short by controversial Foreign Secretary, George Brown.

Foreign Secretary, Michael Stewart,[1] to say, 'It was all the more unfortunate that a part of the audience at the Film Festival at Cannes which consisted principally of International Film Critics should have given Her Royal Highness so impatient a welcome and have unjustly accused her of being more than a very few minutes late. Whatever the rights and wrongs of this matter may be Her Royal Highness's presence at Cannes provided most valuable support to the British participation.'

In a certain sort of smart, bohemian world the Snowdons were much sought after. One superficially unlikely Margaret groupie was the writer and *Sunday Times* book critic Cyril Connolly,[2] whose 'liberal sympathies were', in his biographer's opinion, 'perfectly compatible with royal infatuation'. Despite being pop-eyed and bald Connolly was not only a thorough-going snob but also a compulsive lady's man. He was wildly flattered when the Princess sought him out at a party in aid of some Snowdon photographs in 1966 and 'felt like a large dog trying to amuse someone who may not be a dog-lover'. He subsequently dreamed that Princess Margaret had given him a castle and was beside himself a year later when, while staying with his friend the Oxford don Maurice Bowra at Ann Fleming's house in Sardinia, he discovered that the Snowdons and the Aga Khan had come to stay nearby.

'Cyril made fearfully restless by vicinity of Snowdons,' complained his hostess, in a letter to her friend Debo, née Mitford, the Duchess of Devonshire, 'saying not to meet them was like being in Garden of Eden without seeing God.' Eventually an invitation was arranged and, better still, Ann Fleming invited the Snowdons back. Connolly's excitement rose 'to fever pitch'.

Ann Fleming recorded: 'Next morning Cyril rises at 11.30 and asks what I have ordered special for lunch, I say nothing since I

---

1 The Rt. Hon. Michael Stewart, Baron Stewart of Fulham (1906–1990). Labour politician and MP who served as Foreign Secretary in Wilson government.

2 Cyril Connolly (1903–1974). Unattractive, snobbish writer and book reviewer of distinction whose best-known work *Enemies of Promise* carried unacknowledged autobiographical undertones.

can only communicate with Italians in deaf and dumb language, he scowls and says did I notice what the Princess drank last night, I say no, he says it was white wine and martinis and may he go to the hotel for the right stuff. I say yes, and have to pay enormous bill.'

Lunch went well. Afterwards Bowra sang songs from World War I, in which he had served with the Royal Flying Corps, and the Princess and Connolly adjourned to the pool, 'Cyril looking like a blissful hippo!' Anticlimax followed the Snowdons' departure and Connolly moped around complaining about the mosquitoes, the food and the climate and only wanting royalty and money. 'Now he has met the Snowdons,' said Ann Fleming waspishly, 'he dreams of being invited on the Aga's yacht saying wistfully, "But if I was, I might be expected to act charades on water-skis!"' His biographer writes that Connolly was not the only one to succumb to 'Princess Margaret mania' at this time, but that it 'seems to have struck down even the most cynical and level-headed'.

In the summer of 1969 the Snowdons visited Japan, where they were looked after by the affably Pickwickian Ambassador Sir John Pilcher[1] and his wife. Sir John was known as a peerless raconteur and wit. He also suffered from haemorrhoids and acquired a moment of posthumous fame as the man who finally persuaded parsimonious bureaucrats at the Foreign Office to abandon cheap abrasive 'Bronco' lavatory paper in favour of softer more user-friendly tissues. At the time he was also having to act as mentor to Prince William of Gloucester,[2] who was on a brief stint with the Foreign Office and was posted to Tokyo. Sir John used to complain, 'I am not at all Hanoverian-minded, but nevertheless here I am, stuck with Sweet William.'

Princess Margaret called on William during this visit but Sir John soon whisked the Snowdons off to Kyoto, which he adored,

1 Sir John Pilcher (1912–1990). Career diplomat who was Ambassador to Japan from 1967 to 1972 and was described as 'the last of the scholar-diplomats'.
2 Prince William of Gloucester (1941–1972). Heir to the Duke of Gloucester who was killed in a flying accident near Wolverhampton.

particularly because he had lived there in a Zen temple while studying Japanese in the thirties. The director of the newish British Council Centre in the city was Peter Martin,[1] who also wrote a successful series of Japanese detective stories under the alias of James Melville. Martin lived above the shop with his wife Joan and their two young sons, Adam and James, and was gratified when told that the Princess and her husband would be calling at his centre for a twenty-five-minute visit to meet the Japanese staff, look round, sign the visitors' book and as Martin recalled, 'generally act in a benignly affable manner' until their escorts from Japan's Imperial Household agency whisked them away.

It promised to be a routine, and for some of those concerned, frankly boring occasion, and so it turned out until the Snowdons asked the Martins where they lived.

'When we told them that we dwelt, actually, er, upstairs, the royal couple asked eagerly if they might have a look at our quarters. So up the four of us trooped, to the evident consternation of their Japanese minders, who had to remain below agitatedly reporting this unheard of initiative to their masters through their personal radios.'

It is a characteristic of royal occasions that changes of plan are often what turns them from being unmemorable to something far more effective and enjoyable. Informal deviations, however, are not usually built into the schedule and they give organizers palpitations. So it was on this occasion. It would have been bad enough in many places but much worse in Japan.

'Margaret', recalled Peter Martin, 'won the boys' hearts by first asking if she could see their bedroom, allowed herself to be towed there, sat on one of their beds, took out a long holder, inserted a cigarette and lit it. James appointed himself Ash-tray Bearer in Waiting and followed her around the domestic quarters as she examined their goldfish swimming around in their bowl, their toys and their modest clothes cupboard and quizzed them gently about their lives for fully a quarter of an hour.'

---

1 Peter Martin (James Melville) (1931–). British Council official and author of *Otari* series of crime novels beginning with *The Wages of Zen* in 1979.

Eventually the Snowdons thanked everyone and left, half an hour behind schedule, and the Martins settled down with Fujikawa-san, their widowed 'resident treasure'. A quiet recuperative evening *en famille* was what they anticipated, but an hour later the phone went and one of the royal entourage said that the Snowdons had much enjoyed their visit and hoped that Peter and Joan would come round for a drink at the Old Imperial Palace at 7 p.m.

The group when they arrived was small: the Pilchers, the Consul General from Osaka and his wife, a lady-in-waiting and a personal bodyguard whose name was not mentioned but whom Martin privately named after the *Private Eye* policeman of the day – Inspector Knacker.

Peter Martin takes over the story:

I didn't notice what Joan had, but considering I'd earned it, I chose whisky and water having spotted a bottle of Johnnie Walker Black Label along with other imported beverages on a side table. Then, somewhat to my surprise, Margaret came over and said 'Come and sit beside me, Mr. Martin, and tell me more about living in Kyoto,' indicating an overstuffed sofa, sinking down in it and patting the space beside her. It was a very warm evening and she was wearing a simple cotton frock.

So I did as I was bidden, and like to think that we got on famously. Until I became enthralled with the sound of my own voice, made an expansive gesture with the hand holding my glass, and tipped its contents in the royal lap. Gibbering apologies for what seemed like an eternity but was probably only the few seconds it took for Margaret to stand up and be led out of the room by her lady-in-waiting. I was then left in stunned silence, while the Ambassador, the Consul-General, their ladies, Inspector Knacker, Joan and even the Japanese flunkies all glared at me in outrage at my act of *lèse majesté*. Lord Snowdon was the one exception, stifling a grin as he took the scene in.

In less than five minutes Margaret was back in a different summer frock. She smiled at me sympathetically, sat down again on the sofa beside which I was now standing, dazed, and briskly said 'Do sit down again, Mr. Martin ... you were saying?' Relief flooded my very soul as I sank down at her side and accepted a fresh glass of Johnnie Walker. It seemed that I was forgiven, and I gradually relaxed. So much so that within a very few minutes, with another airy gesture, *I did it again.*

I gazed at my royal victim in misery as the lady-in-waiting bustled forward to do her stuff and moaned 'Oh God, you'll have my head cut off now.' 'No', the amazing woman replied, 'but when I come back next time I think I shall sit somewhere else.'

And she did.

When I repeated this story to her old friend and lady-in-waiting, Anne Glenconner, she said, 'He was very lucky,' and paused. 'It could easily have gone the other way.'

British Council reports involving incidents such as this should be a rich source of history if only because so many Council Reps were observant and literate, quite a few becoming, like Peter Martin, published novelists. However, many such reports fell victim to the Great Purge known as Operation SHIVA mounted by Goths and vandals in the seventies and eighties. SHIVA stood for 'Stop hoarding irrelevant and valueless archives'. This resulted in pages of priceless prose being shredded and burned.

Another incident that never found its way into the official records also took place in Japan. This was when the Princess found herself partnering one of the imperial princes at a ball. The Prince had little English and the Ambassador, Sir John Pilcher again, acted as interpreter. As the royal couple contemplated the floor the Princess enquired politely whether His Royal Highness enjoyed dancing. Quick as a flash the Japanese prince replied, 'No, I prefer my balls on ice.' Before the Princess could register shock or disapproval the Ambassador hastily intervened. 'I think', he said, 'that His Imperial Highness means that he prefers skating to dancing.'

That year – 1969 – the musicians Johnny Dankworth and Cleo Laine started a (charitable) music scheme based on the stables of their home near Milton Keynes. Princess Margaret came down frequently, unaccompanied, and once even stayed the night. She opened a new wing, with a hundred seats, and years later she came down and opened another new £5 million development.

Dankworth and Laine first came into contact with Princess Margaret at the dance at Keele in 1960 but they can't remember if they actually met, even though they were performing. They first met properly when Dankworth wrote a Lysistrata opera with libretto by Benny Green. Ted Leather,[1] the Canadian-born MP, later Governor of Bermuda, was much involved and gave a big party at which the Snowdons were present. After a while the Dankworths started to play and sing and the Snowdons came and leaned on the piano to watch and listen. The Dankworths hadn't realized any royal was interested in music so they were impressed. Later the Bishop of Bath and Wells took to the drums!

Subsequently they got invited to Kensington Palace from time to time. 'I'm not really sure why,' says Dankworth, 'but I think there was always a hope that we'd sing for our supper.'

Angela Huth,[2] who was married to Quentin Crewe at the time, came to live nearby and Dankworth and Laine found themselves often being invited over for 'old-fashioned Victorian house parties'. There was 'nothing outlandish, but lots of laughs, informal games and a chance to see a side of royal behaviour that you don't usually see'. Incidentally, says Dankworth,

> It's said that Princess Margaret used to smoke thirty a day. Well as far as I was concerned I reckon she smoked about one cigarette every four hours ...
>
> I heard her sing but never play the piano, which makes me think that whatever she did wasn't terribly serious even though I'd always heard she did things on the piano. We have an open field at the back of the building, which means that potentially we could have an apron stage opening out on to it and could stage events outside. She was very keen on that and took music and the

---

1 Sir Edwin ('Ted') Leather (1919–2005). Canadian-born broadcaster and Conservative one-nation politician who was MP for North Somerset from 1945 to 1964 and was appointed Governor of Bermuda after the murder of Sir Richard Sharples in 1973.

2 Angela Huth (1938–). Author friend of Princess Margaret, married to Quentin Crewe and then to Oxford don, James Howard-Johnston.

arts very seriously. We have a lot of handwritten letters from her, which we treasure. She even flew to New York City for Cleo's seventieth-birthday concert. You didn't have to treat her as a princess but you did – just to be on the safe side. I suppose the English are like that.

On one occasion Dankworth went to Kensington Palace to show her the plans for a proposed new theatre. They were so large that he had to spread them out on the floor. Princess Margaret summoned tea with cakes and, although she was standing, he knelt down to get a closer look and in doing so knelt straight into a squishy cream cake, which exploded all over his shoe. For ten minutes the Princess dabbed and polished away at his shoe with a cloth she got from the kitchen. She tried to make him feel completely at ease. A little later they met again and Dankworth confessed that he'd related the incident to a number of different people. 'Oh,' she said, 'I've dined out on that story too.'

On another occasion she got a mutual friend, Laurie Holloway, then married to the singer Marion Montgomery[1] and a fine musician in his own right, to combine with Richard Cawston,[2] the BBC man who'd produced a number of royal broadcasts, to make a disc of Princess Margaret and her sister reciting the nursery rhymes they had learned in childhood as a birthday present for their mother.

Later Dankworth asked how it had gone. The Princess replied that all had gone well but that her sister was ... and she couldn't think of a word so Dankworth suggested 'klutz', which the Princess seemed to think was about right.

Evidently as soon as Laurie sent round the finished tapes Margaret phoned the Palace and went round to play them to her sister. When she arrived, however, the Queen said it was a bit of a problem because 'we haven't got anything to play it on'. Then she had a brain-wave. 'Oh,' she said, 'we've got a machine in the

---

1 Marion Montgomery (1934–2002). American-born jazz singer married to British pianist and arranger, Laurie Holloway.
2 Richard Cawston (1923–1986). TV documentary-maker who specialized in films involving the monarchy.

car.' So she rang down to the Mews and asked them to send a Rolls round, greatly to the excitement of the sightseers outside. The car duly arrived and the royal sisters tripped down the stairs and solemnly sat in the motionless car listening to the tape recording of nursery rhymes.

When they had finished they went indoors and the phone rang. It was Prince Charles, and his mother told him to come round quickly and listen to the tape. When he got there his mother said she'd phone down for the car once more. Whereupon Charles asked why, and on being told said, 'Oh don't be ridiculous!' and went to a corner of the room where, behind a curtain or screen, he found a perfectly serviceable state-of-the-art tape recorder!

Princess Margaret was always very generous with her time when it came to fund-raising for the Dankworths. On one occasion at dinner in the Banqueting House she lit up, contrary to all the fire regulations. She was sitting between Dankworth and Ned Sherrin. Dankworth says he funked telling her she must put the cigarette out but people around were extremely agitated. He thinks perhaps Ned eventually plucked up the courage to do it!

Sherrin was exactly the sort of spiky, witty, entertaining showbiz personality that the Princess enjoyed. Their paths had first crossed earlier in the decade at a party given by the writer Quentin Crewe, first husband of Angela Huth. Sherrin was then producing the satirical TV programme, *That Was the Week That Was* fronted by the young, then iconoclastic David Frost. At the party the Princess, admitting to being a fan of the programme, asked why it didn't do something about the absurdly deferential way in which 'we' were reported. Frost remembered a sketch written by Ian Lang, later a peer and Tory cabinet minister, which had the sinking of the royal barge described by a BBC commentator doing a Dimbleby and recounting the whole accident in typically hushed tones, including the phrase 'The Queen, smiling radiantly, is swimming for her life.' The sketch was resurrected with Frost in the Dimbleby role. It was a huge and irreverent success.

Sherrin's judgement of the Princess was that she was 'often quotable'. Once in the Banqueting House in Whitehall at a lunch to raise money for the Dankworths' Wavendon All Music Plan (possibly the occasion when she smoked against the regulations!) she pointed out the window from which 'poor King Charles' had walked to his execution. Sherrin was duly interested, even more so when she added, 'At Windsor we still have the shirt he was wearing.'

At a cocktail party given by the film-maker Derek Hart[1] the Princess asked Sherrin to accompany her to dinner at the Ritz. Sherrin declined because he had to see his friend and collaborator Caryl Brahms,[2] who was ill. 'How old *is* Caryl?' When Sherrin told her, she replied, 'My God! She's nearly as old as Mummy! You'd better go straight away. You may never see her again.'

Nevertheless she was not, could not, ever be truly relaxing company. Sherrin remembered her coming to see his production of *Side by Side by Sondheim* at London's Mermaid Theatre. She enjoyed the show and made the fact clear, but 'half the house inevitably spent the evening craning necks to check on the royal reaction'. As he said, such divided attention 'diminishes audience response dramatically'.

But even with someone whose company she obviously enjoyed and even when there was no one else watching or listening, she could behave with a disconcerting regal hauteur. Once, giving the Princess a lift home from yet another Dankworth–Laine production, this time at Ronnie Scott's jazz club in Soho, Sherrin was driving them down the Fulham Road and she pointed to a derelict shop. 'Fortunately that has closed,' she said. 'They used to sell dresses. It was called the Countess of Snowdon. People thought I was selling my old clothes. I was going to sue them; now they've gone bankrupt I don't have to.'

Sherrin's response was flip, clever and on his own admission a touch unwise. 'It must have been very difficult for you,' he said.

---

1 Derek Hart. BBC TV personality who found fame as a presenter on Cliff Michelmore's BBC *Tonight* programme and later became a producer of documentary films.
2 Caryl Brahms (Doris Abrahams) (1901–1982). Collaborated with S. J. Simon on a series of comic novels including *No Bed For Bacon*, later adapted for stage with Ned Sherrin and the basis – at first unacknowledged – for the film *Shakespeare in Love*.

'After all, you've got that restaurant at the back of your house called the Maggie Jones.'

Had she not been sitting in the passenger seat of Sherrin's car the Princess would have drawn herself to her full if diminutive height. 'Ned,' she said, 'I *am* the Countess of Snowdon. I have *never* been called Maggie Jones.'

The remark was made humorously – well, half-humorously. She was being good-natured – up to a point. But she was still delivering a rebuke and reminding Sherrin that he was a commoner while she was the Queen's sister. Sherrin was chastened, though not to the point where he did not repeat the story.

Another sparky, acerbic conversationalist was Roy Strong,[1] then the Director of the National Portrait Gallery and later of the Victoria and Albert Museum. She enjoyed the company and talk of witty, garrulous, intelligent men and women such as Sherrin, Dankworth and Strong and, on the whole, paid little or no attention if they sometimes appeared to flout royal convention and become what in others she might have found worthy of rebuke. On 27 November 1969 she attended the gala opening of *The Elizabethan Image*, curated by Strong at the Tate. In his diary Strong recorded: 'Princess Margaret is a strange lady, pretty, tough, disillusioned and spoilt. To cope with her I decided one had to slap back which I did and survived.'

Strong doesn't explain the precise nature of his 'slap back' although this was a high-risk policy. On this occasion it seems to have paid off for the Princess evidently asked Strong back home after the event. Somehow, however, he 'forgot' and wound up at home with friends instead. On another later occasion Lord Napier told me that she cancelled some boring daytime engagements on the grounds of some more or less illusory illness – shades of the Princess's charades while staying at the British Embassy in Paris with Sir Gladwyn and Lady Jebb. This time she made as if to go

---

1 Sir Roy Strong (1935–). Museum director, aesthete, gardener and diarist who transformed the antediluvian National Portrait Gallery before becoming the youngest ever director of the Victoria and Albert Museum which he ran from 1973 to 1987.

out for a Strong event at the V&A that evening. Napier, bravely, told her she couldn't because she had told the world she was ill. She demurred. 'Tell them I've made a miraculous recovery,' she said and tried to go out. This time Napier was adamant and forcefully told her it was out of the question. 'If the world found out what had happened the result would be quite ghastly. She knew I was right.' So she acquiesced, but a compromise was effected whereby Strong and friends came round for drinks at the palace after the event.

All was not well in the marriage. Tony's old Cambridge contemporary Jocelyn Stevens, editor and proprietor of the glossy magazine *Queen*, noted that it was like a showbiz liaison – a roller-coaster of a relationship, which was idyllic when going well and poisonous when not. 'Tony and she were both very determined and highly individual,' commented her cousin Margaret Rhodes.

'They both behaved badly,' said Tony's former assistant John Timbers. Timbers remembered the eccentric atmosphere at KP. He was invited for tea by his former boss, just the once, and went along with his wife. After a while, when they were sitting drinking tea and indulging in light small talk, Princess Margaret entered, sat down at the piano and began to play and sing. 'She could certainly belt it out,' said Timbers. There were no introductions. The Princess played and sang for about twenty minutes, then stood up and walked out of the room. No words were exchanged. Nothing was said. Timbers thought it odd, but it seemed quite usual.

On another occasion Lieutenant Colonel 'Johnny' Johnston,[1] an old friend and sometime Comptroller of the Lord Chamberlain's Office, was asked to dinner at Kensington Palace.

It was just before one of her shoots in the Great Park. The Queen gave her a day or two in November. Linley's taken it over since she died. That year they were due to shoot on a Monday and she asked me to come to dinner on the Saturday before. She said

---

1 Lt. Col. Sir 'Johnny' Johnston (1922–2006). Grenadier Guards officer and Comptroller of Lord Chamberlain's Office from 1981 to 1987.

there'd be one or two others but when I turned up everyone else had cried off because of the weather and the only others there were Tony and Sarah.

After dinner Tony disappeared and I thought the sooner I get off the better so I said, 'Please may I go to bed?' 'It's a bit early,' she said. But she agreed and we went off for me to say goodnight to Tony. When we went into his room he was on the phone. 'Tony, Johnny's just going,' she said.

But it was obvious that Snowdon had been caught in the telephonic equivalent of *in flagrante delicto* and was talking to someone he shouldn't have been.

Next morning Lord Napier rang to ask what had gone wrong. Johnston told him. Evidently the situation had deteriorated after his departure. Words had been exchanged, objects thrown. The marriage was obviously in disarray.

An element of deterioration had entered the relationship some time in the mid-1960s. Snowdon was often away on photographic business and indulged in a series of casual liaisons. In 1966 Margaret had a brief fling with Snowdon's old Cambridge friend Anthony Barton.[1] Barton was a godfather to the Snowdons' daughter, Lady Sarah Armstrong-Jones, so the affair was practically a family one. She later confessed, tearfully, to Barton's wife Eva, which was probably ill-advised. A year or so later she had a brief but passionate liaison with the society photographer Robin Douglas-Home,[2] who subsequently committed suicide. In 1969 Snowdon embarked on a serious affaire with Lady Jacqueline Rufus-Isaacs,[3] daughter of the Marquess of Reading.

The couple enjoyed the company of interesting but – as far as

---

1 Anthony Barton (1930–). Owner of famous family vineyards, producing Leoville-Barton and Barton-Langoa clarets, friend of Lord Snowdon and lover of Princess Margaret.

2 Robin Douglas-Home (1932–1968). Nightclub pianist, nephew of Prime Minister Sir Alec, husband of fashion model Sandra Paul (later Mrs Michael Howard), and lover of Princess Margaret.

3 Lady Jacqueline Rufus-Isaacs. Daughter of Marquess of Reading and lover of Lord Snowdon.

royalty was concerned – unlikely friends. They often dined together and dinners sometimes assumed a positively surreal character. One such occasion, in 1967, was described by the theatre critic Kenneth Tynan as 'one of the oddest occasions of my life'. The Tynans' guests were the comedian Peter Cook[1] and his wife, the playwright Harold Pinter and his first wife, Vivien Merchant, and the Snowdons.

The evening got off to a bad start when Mrs Pinter was introduced to the Princess and 'merely extended a vague hand' while continuing her conversation with Cook and remaining seated. At dinner Mrs Pinter sat next to Snowdon, who had just taken a picture of her as Lady Macbeth. She was playing in 'the Scottish play' opposite Paul Scofield at Stratford. After a while Tynan heard her say, 'The only reason we *artistes* let you take our pictures is because of *her*.' At this point she jabbed a finger at Princess Margaret. Everyone heard, including the Princess, who, according to Tynan, 'was awkwardly unruffled, but every word had registered on that watchful little psyche'. Everyone now started to drink 'steadily'.

Tynan, famous for being the first person to use the word 'fuck' on television, had decided to show blue films after dinner. He had warned Snowdon, who apparently retorted that it would do his wife good. The first blue movies produced little or no effect but 'the atmosphere began to freeze' when the programme moved to a Genet film about convicts in love with one another. It was full of penises intercut with lyrical fantasies set in vernal undergrowth. 'Silence became gelid in the room; no one was laughing now,' recalled Tynan. Mercifully Peter Cook came to the rescue by supplying an impro-vised commentary in the style of a Cadbury's Flake Milk Chocolate commercial to the otherwise silent film. 'Within five minutes we were all helplessly rocking with laughter, Princess M included,' wrote Tynan. Afterwards Pinter fell down the stairs and Tynan gave Cook a big hug for saving an awkward situation.

---

1 Peter Cook (1937–1995). Comic actor who made his name in ground-breaking revue *Beyond the Fringe*, helped found *Private Eye* magazine and starred in TV comedy show with Dudley Moore.

This was all very sophisticated and sixties, but it was also dangerous.

Nevertheless the Snowdons remained a proper functioning part of the Royal Family. Princess Margaret always enjoyed the title Countess of Snowdon – unlike the hated second name, Rose. Had they maintained a hypocritical façade and continued to carry out royal duties in public while going their separate ways in private they would have created no precedent.

In July 1969 the Princess's husband enjoyed perhaps his most satisfactory moment as a new member of the family firm. Her Majesty the Queen made him Constable of Caernarvon Castle, a particularly appropriate honour for someone who came from that part of the world. In this capacity he was largely responsible for staging the investiture of Prince Charles as Prince of Wales. The Constable designed an original uniform for himself, and his friend, the designer Carl Toms,[1] was responsible for much of the 'set', including a very sixties take on the traditional royal-occasion chair – a functional scarlet-painted wooden seat with gold Prince of Wales' feathers embossed on the back. Several of these can still be found in Lord Snowdon's present London house. He enjoyed particularly good relations with the hereditary Earl Marshal, Bernard, Duke of Norfolk. Norfolk was well known for such pithy responses as: 'We'll all get bloody wet,' when asked what would happen if it rained. He allowed Snowdon an invigoratingly free hand and would often merely shrug when Snowdon made a suggestion and tell him to go away and get on with it. Snowdon's relations with Sir Anthony Wagner,[2] Garter King of Arms, were less cordial. 'Oh Garter, darling,' Snowdon exclaimed on one occasion, 'couldn't you be a little more elastic?'

Some continued to be unswervingly hostile to both Snowdons.

---

1 Carl Toms (1927–1999). Designed theatrical productions in London from 1957 onwards as well as films, opera, ballet and at Edinburgh, Chichester, Glyndebourne; responsible for world première of Benjamin Britten's *Midsummer Night's Dream* at Aldeburgh in 1960.

2 Sir Anthony Wagner (1908–1995). Garter Principal King of Arms enjoyed a deserved reputation as tight-lipped traditionalist and opponent of innovation and informality.

Shortly before the investiture the film *Royal Family*, directed by Richard Cawston, was shown on television. Despite being, in effect, a piece of royal propaganda, it was ground-breakingly revelatory and comparatively revealing if not actually intrusive. One or two eyebrows were raised when Lord Snowdon was shown addressing his mother-in-law as 'ma'am'. Generally it made a good impression and though, with the benefit of hindsight, some critics thought it the thin end of a quasi-republican wedge, it was well received in public.

Privately some were more hostile. The feline Cecil Beaton commented in his diary, 'Princess Margaret mature and vulgar, Snowdon common beyond belief.' His jealousy of Snowdon knew few bounds but, despite the undoubted whiff of sour grapes, his harsh verdict was not confined to himself alone.

FIVE

THE SEVENTIES

'It would of course be very easy to fill
every hour of her stay with visits ...'

By 1970 the Snowdon marriage was damaged beyond repair. Andrew Duncan[1] published a ground-breaking book that year called *The Reality of Monarchy*, which was the first 'royal' book to break the mould of Dermot Morrah, Helen Cathcart,[2] Hector Bolitho[3] and their ilk. In a breezy, determinedly non-forelock-tugging style Duncan interviewed the Snowdons, described them as he saw and heard them and wrote, 'Endless rumours circulate about Tony and Meg, setting the cocktail party circuits of the world alive – if anyone is still interested. When is Tony going to leave? Or vice versa. Whose car was parked outside Kensington Palace, and why? Why? Where? What? How? When? God, is *that* true? I tell you, she was *seen*.'

Duncan thought the Princess was 'fabulous'. He saw her twice at Kensington Palace because something went wrong with his tape recorder and the interview with her was obliterated. When he told her, she just laughed and suggested he came round and did it again. Then, when it worked second time round, he sent her a printed text and she came to his house in Hampstead. 'It was a risk,' he says, 'but in the end she added more than she took out. I thought she was sexy and charming and indiscreet and lots of fun. Finally she wrote me a letter just saying that she hoped I'd

1 Andrew Duncan (1942–). Author and freelance journalist.
2 Helen Cathcart, fictitious royal biographer concealing the identity of an unknown writer named Harold Albert.
3 Hector Bolitho (1897–1974). New Zealand-born author of royal potboilers as well as the official biography of Mohammed Jinnah, founder of Pakistan, for which he was recommended by the author Beverley Nichols.

make her sound more "interesting" than usual.' He liked Snowdon as well but recalls that he was much more snobbish than his wife. It was always he who corrected such social solecisms as 'lounge', insisting that the word should be changed to 'drawing room'.

Duncan's verdict on the state of the marriage was, in the end, surprisingly charitable – or gullible. 'A middle-aged couple whose previous affairs have been widely and inaccurately enough publicized to give a credence to any supposition,' he opined. 'They are no more nor less happy than many others.'

Insiders were more sceptical. 'It was open warfare,' said one of her ladies-in-waiting, 'like *Who's Afraid of Virginia Woolf?*'

Lord Snowdon's campaign extended to the staff. Ladies-in-waiting continued to complain about crucial letters being left on his desk without their being able to read them, about his prevarications over invitations, about a general sense that he was not playing on the same team as themselves and the Princess, who was, after all, their boss and employer. As one insider put it succinctly: 'Tony may have been the head of the house, but he was not the head of the household.' It was not a happy home.

One particular victim of this marital strife was Lieutenant Colonel Freddy Burnaby-Atkins, who succeeded Francis Legh as private secretary in 1970. Burnaby-Atkins was recruited by another colonel, Sir Martin Gilliat, who joined Queen Elizabeth the Queen Mother as her private secretary in 1956. The two colonels were from different regiments: Burnaby-Atkins was commissioned into the Black Watch and Gilliat was from the King's Royal Rifle Corps. However, they had both been taken prisoner at Dunkirk and had become firm friends as prisoners of war. After the war Burnaby-Atkins had become ADC to Lord Wavell[1] in India, continuing in the same position when Wavell had been succeeded by Lord Mountbatten. Gilliat had also served in Delhi as Deputy Military Secretary.

This kind of military friendship was often crucial in the immediate post-war period, particularly when it came to

---

1 Field Marshal Lord Wavell (1883–1950). Viceroy of India and unexpected compiler of poetry anthology, *Other Men's Flowers*.

appointments at court. In the early years of the twenty-first century that may seem preposterous, but it was true. For years Britain was run by men who had served together in World War II.

The well-connected Burnaby-Atkins was an obvious candidate for a job working for the Queen's sister. Not only had he been aide-de-camp to Wavell and Mountbatten, he had also acted as chief of staff to Sir Bernard Fergusson, later Lord Ballantrae,[1] when he was Governor General of New Zealand and had served as Defence Attaché in Morocco. Fergusson was also a Black Watch officer. Although Burnaby-Atkins had not then met Princess Margaret, he had one characteristic story involving his boss, the notoriously laconic Wavell, and the young Princess. Wavell found himself seated next to the Princess at the palace one lunch-time and, trying to be polite, asked if she liked *Alice in Wonderland*. 'No,' she replied. And that was that.

Some time in 1970 Burnaby-Atkins and his wife Jean, sister to the amateur jockey John Lawrence, later Lord Oaksey,[2] were introduced to the Snowdons over a drink at Gilliat's flat. Everyone seemed to get on well and it was agreed, almost by osmosis, that Burnaby-Atkins would take over from Legh.

Burnaby-Atkins had a period of working alongside Legh and later said that, although he found his predecessor utterly charming, they were very different sorts of people. For a start he thought Legh 'delightfully idle'. In the handover period, when the two men worked side by side at Kensington Palace, a speech needed drafting for the Princess and Burnaby-Atkins undertook the task with a zeal and enthusiasm that the languid Legh found almost incomprehensible. Others say that Legh was not so much 'delightfully idle' as 'effortlessly superior'. He had a very good brain and could knock out a deft speech in far less time than it would take his successor. He evidently had great charm and was much liked by his boss. It did not hinder their relationship that he was the Hon.

---

1 Lord Ballantrae (Sir Bernard Fergusson) (1911–1980). Scottish soldier who became Governor General of New Zealand.
2 Lord Oaksey (John Lawrence) (1929–). Champion jockey who became journalist for the *Daily Telegraph* and author of several books.

Sir Francis Legh, son of Lord Newton. The Princess was always predisposed in favour of the peerage.

Contemporary documents confirm that the appointment of Burnaby-Atkins was at first a success. In April 1971 Bernard Fergusson and his wife dined at Windsor Castle and he reported Princess Margaret's verdict to a friend, Bill Cochrane, who had been a Black Watch padre. Fergusson said, 'She was telling me how lucky she thought she was to have him.'

Either the Princess was being less than honest with Fergusson or she and Burnaby-Atkins were still enjoying a honeymoon period, which was not destined to last. Ladies-in-waiting remember Burnaby-Atkins as a genial but ineffectual presence. I heard stories that he and his boss never really hit it off, that his drafting of speeches was not appreciated and his organizational abilities were not well regarded.

Years later this seemed to be the general verdict, but on 9 August 2006 he wrote to me firmly disabusing me of this idea. 'No,' he said, 'I did not have an unhappy time with her. As Private Secretary for two and a half years I got on very well with Princess Margaret. Tony Snowdon was the trouble for many diverse reasons which I can easily and simply explain to you.'

The office memoranda seem to support him. For a start it is obvious that Burnaby-Atkins knew and was liked by those that mattered, such as Patrick (Lord) Plunket, the popular equerry to the Queen who always wrote to him as 'Dear Freddy' and signed off as 'Yours, Patrick'. Burnaby-Atkins later said that it helped that so many of his Etonian contemporaries were by 1970 serving as Lord Lieutenants of various counties. It was therefore easy for him to use the old boy network to approach friends and enquire whether they might like to have the Princess and her entourage to stay for a few days, as she was anxious to see their part of the world.

The Princess herself was, as always, finicky about menus, changing haricots verts to Brussels sprouts and fussing about a Keele University diced chicken salad with egg whites and gherkins. This must have seemed tiresome, but exchanges with the private secretary sound genial and breezy. Thus Burnaby-Atkins writes,

'The Bishop of Southwark has now got in on the act with a luncheon invitation,' to which the Princess responds, 'Yes, I see. I'm just checking trains. Hold it. M.'

So far so good. There is evidence, however, that relations with Lord Snowdon were not so relaxed. In April 1972 Burnaby-Atkins wrote to Princess Margaret about a gala performance at the Theatre Royal, Windsor: 'They want to know who else Your Royal Highness would like to bring. Tony cannot go.' That same month Burnaby-Atkins wrote: 'After dinner, Lord Snowdon and Miss Hoyer Miller (lady-in-waiting) will be dropped at Kensington Palace and Her Royal Highness will drive to Windsor Castle.' Later in 1972 Burnaby-Atkins wrote to Geoffrey Hardy-Roberts,[1] Master of the Queen's Household from 1967 to 1973, and said, apropos the twentieth anniversary of the Queen's accession in 1972, 'Lord Snowdon is still away and I cannot yet say whether or not he will be able to accompany Princess Margaret on this occasion.'

I detect a note of exasperation in these communications and when I met him at his home in Wiltshire the Colonel confirmed this. Relations between the staff at Kensington Palace and Lord Snowdon were often strained and those between Burnaby-Atkins and the boss's husband were as bad as any.

The private secretary found life most difficult when the Princess was away on holiday on Mustique, where she invariably went alone, without her husband. In her absence Burnaby-Atkins often had to represent her on official occasions but felt that his position was undermined by Lord Snowdon, who would use the official car to visit his girlfriend Jacqueline Rufus-Isaacs, taking food from the palace larder without consultation and – according to Burnaby-Atkins – generally upsetting the staff. They complained to him, but he felt unable to do anything about it.

Matters came to a head one Monday morning when Burnaby-Atkins was due to attend a memorial service for a distinguished judge who, like Princess Margaret, was a bencher at Lincoln's Inn.

---

1 Geoffrey Hardy-Roberts (1907–1997). Master of the Household from 1967 to 1973.

An hour or so before the scheduled departure time the chauffeur, Mr Larkin, went to Burnaby-Atkins and asked him to come and inspect the Rolls-Royce. When the private secretary did so he found the car parked 'obviously by Snowdon and all skew-whiff'. It was covered in mud and in such a filthy state that it could not possibly be used to convey Her Royal Highness's private secretary to St Paul's Cathedral. He took a taxi instead and was embarrassed to have to get out of a London cab to be received by the Dean and Chapter on the cathedral steps. Furious, he later penned a stroppy note to Lord Snowdon, telling him that his behaviour was completely out of order, made it impossible for him to do his job properly and compromised the dignity of the Princess. It was the first of a number of such notes.

Relations with the Princess continued to be, on the whole, spirited but amicable. On one occasion, for instance, the Princess was asked to open a new airport in the Seychelles. At that time Princess Margaret was the only senior member of the Royal Family who had never been to Australia. She was keen to go and when Burnaby-Atkins consulted his atlas he discovered that the Seychelles were within a reasonable distance of Western Australia. The previous year the Queen had made a tour of Australia and visited most of the country with the notable exception of Western Australia. This seemed a good opportunity of killing two birds on a single outing. The Princess would be able to see Australia for the first time and Western Australia could have a royal visit like everyone else in Australia. The private secretary therefore wrote to the Lieutenant Governor of the state, who was a retired general and former England rugby international called Joe Kendrew.[1] Like almost everyone else of any significance in that world Kendrew was an old friend of Burnaby-Atkins.

A reply soon came – rather pompously phrased – to the effect that Kendrew and his government would be delighted to welcome the Princess. Time was too short to allow the usual reconnaissance

---

[1] Major-General Sir 'Douglas' Kendrew (1910–1989). Better known as 'Colonel Joe', played for England at rugby ten times and captained the side in 1935. Governor of Western Australia.

trip, but Kendrew did phone with a word of warning. The previous year the Duke of Kent[1] had been to Western Australia and failed to make the expected speech. As a result he had been roundly booed. Kendrew was worried that the same thing might happen if Princess Margaret also remained silent.

Burnaby-Atkins told the Princess, but she was unimpressed. 'I do so hate the sound of my own voice,' she said. And despite all attempts at persuasion she refused to budge. She would make no speech. She was adamant. Nevertheless the private secretary drafted an anodyne and emollient little utterance saying how happy she was to be in Australia for the first time, how much she was enjoying everyone's welcome and how she very much hoped to be able to come back one day. Princess Margaret read this but said, yet again, that she would not be making this or any other speech.

They started off in the Seychelles, where Burnaby-Atkins said they had 'a whoopsy time'. The airport was opened without undue incident and there was an enjoyable moment when the plumbing at Government House failed and Lord Snowdon gamely took his trousers off, got into the cistern and wrestled with a recalcitrant ballcock – alas to no avail. The Governor, 'marvellous chap called Sir Bruce Greatbatch,'[2] said he would summon the Minister for Works, which he did. The minister duly arrived and turned out to be a qualified plumber. He fixed the problem in a few moments.

Australia was also 'whoopsy', though Burnaby-Atkins was in an increasing depression about his short speech. The Princess showed no signs of changing her mind. She vowed to remain speechless. One evening the Kendrews and the Snowdons and their entourages went to floodlit trotting races. The four principals sat in a front row with their noses pressed to a plate-glass window while their aides sat behind. Colonel Burnaby-Atkins was clutching

---

1 Field Marshal HRH the 2nd Duke of Kent (1935–). Cousin of Princess Margaret and Queen Elizabeth II. After regular military service was for many years a hard-working globe-trotting representative of British trade and industry.
2 Sir Bruce Greatbatch (1917–1989). British Governor of the Seychelles from 1969 to 1973.

his typed-up speech and decided to have one last go at persuading his boss to deliver it. Tiptoeing up to the front row, he tapped Lord Snowdon on the shoulder, handed him the speech and asked him to have one final attempt at persuading the Princess to say a few words. He watched as Snowdon said something to his wife, but it looked to him as if she was refusing yet again and he watched with horror when, a few seconds later, the glass parted and General Kendrew led the royal visitor out on to the track and down to a microphone on a dais.

The lights shone on the Princess, the crowd held its collective breath, Burnaby-Atkins prepared himself for the boos and then the Princess, in a firm, well-rehearsed voice, read out the felicitous words exactly as he had written them. The crowd applauded politely and the Kendrews and Snowdons went back up the steps. Just before resuming her seat Princess Margaret gave Burnaby-Atkins a huge wink and said, in a stage whisper, 'You didn't think I was going to do that, did you?'

His departure was a matter of regret for the Colonel. He was very fond of his boss and felt he was doing a good job. One day, however, Sir Martin Gilliat called from Clarence House and said he needed to come round for a chat. When he arrived he told Burnaby-Atkins that it was all over and he would have to go. There had been too many notes of remonstrance to Lord Snowdon and it was all too obvious that the two men were not getting on. In the circumstances Burnaby-Atkins would have to resign. 'So Martin hired me and Martin fired me,' said Colonel Burnaby-Atkins, sadly. The *Daily Telegraph* got wind of the story and sent a photographer and reporter to whom the Colonel said that he had been in the Army for thirty years and the average posting was about three. He had served Her Royal Highness for just about that amount of time, so he felt he should move on.

This was untrue. As Burnaby-Atkins put it laconically, 'Tony didn't like the little notes.'

Burnaby-Atkins never spoke to Her Royal Highness again. However, as London boss of the Black Watch Association, he saw Queen Elizabeth the Queen Mother on a regular basis and he and his wife were often invited for meals with Queen Elizabeth at

Clarence House. On these occasions they discussed the Princess's children and their growing up in a relaxed and friendly way as if nothing had happened. 'Such a shame,' said Burnaby-Atkins; 'if only one had been working for a happy loving couple and been able to watch them bringing their children up together. But it wasn't like that.'

In May 1972 the Snowdons were invited to the Badminton horse trials by the Duke and Duchess of Beaufort in whose grounds the event was staged. At first Lord Snowdon refused with the excuse that horse trials bored him. The Beauforts were rather pleased by this but less so when, just two days before the trials were due to begin, he changed his mind and said he'd come after all. When he turned up he infuriated the Duke by saying that hunting was cruel. The Duke denied this, but Lord Snowdon then went on to say that the competitors at Badminton must be terrified. 'Equestrians are never terrified,' said the Duke angrily. 'Only cissies are terrified.' At this point the Duke started to take it out on the fire with a poker and the Princess, anxious to calm him down, said, 'Tony doesn't mean terrified – he means nervous.' 'No,' said Snowdon, 'I mean terrified.' This really infuriated the Duke, who banged away at the fireplace, bending the poker in the process and shouting out, 'Damn this fire, I tell you. Damn it, damn it!'

Lord Snowdon left that afternoon without saying goodbye.

The following month, on 28 June 1972, James Lees-Milne attended a private dinner party for ten at Rules' restaurant in London's Maiden Lane. The Snowdons were of the party as was the Prince of Wales. 'I hardly spoke a word to the royals,' Lees-Milne confided to his diary. 'Prince Charles is very charming, and very polite, shook hands with us all and smiled. P.M. is far from charming, is cross, exacting, too sophisticated, and sharp. She is physically attractive in a bun-like way, with trussed-up bosom, and hair like two cottage-loaves, one balancing on the other. She wore a beautiful sapphire and diamond brooch. She smoked continuously from a long holder.'

At one point Lady Elizabeth Cavendish kicked off her shoes and went downstairs barefoot to bid Prince Charles goodbye. In her absence the Princess put Lady Elizabeth's shoes on her plate. Lord Snowdon found this unfunny and said so, whereupon his wife transferred them to a chair and went to sulk by a window. Eventually the remnants of the party were invited back to Kensington Palace, where Lord Snowdon explained the architecture. 'P.M. more gracious to me in her own house,' recorded Lees-Milne, 'but I did not find conversation very easy or agreeable.'

Despite the obviously failing relationship the couple kept up appearances and continued to perform public duties as a couple. Otherwise they led separate lives and had separate friends. This was quite distinct from sex. From that point of view neither was blameless, but the extent to which they led different existences in what one might describe as 'respectable' life was quite unusual.

At a dinner given by Anouska Hempel,[1] the New Zealand born actress turned hotelier and designer, married to the entrepreneur Sir Mark Weinberg, the Princess found herself sitting next to an affable and roguish Irishman who had a stall in the Portobello Road market. His name was Ned Ryan[2] and he told the Princess about his antiques business and how he used to go very early in the mornings to Bermondsey Market in the East End of London, where he would seek out bargains. The Princess listened. 'She was fascinated,' said Ryan later, 'and asked if she could come with me one morning. I said it would mean my calling for her at five-thirty in the morning and she still said she'd love to come. So one morning we went down to Bermondsey with a mutual friend and that's how our friendship started. We became chums.'

The mutual friend was Elizabeth Vyvyan,[3] one of the Princess's ladies-in-waiting. Her version of events is slightly different. Her recollection is that Her Royal Highness was not so easily seduced.

---

1 Anouska Hempel (Lady Weinberg) (1941–). New Zealand-born actress who became Princess Margaret's couturier, friend and designer of her Garden of Remembrance in Oxford.
2 Ned Ryan. Tipperary-born antiques dealer, property magnate and man-about-town, who became friend of Princess Margaret and regular 'walker'.
3 Elizabeth Vyvyan (née Paget) (1950–). Wife of Major-General Charles Vyvyan, friend and lady-in-waiting to Princess Margaret.

She was not, after all, an early-morning person and Ryan was, when all was said and done, an Irish street trader. Still, he had charm and he was persistent. Mrs Vyvyan's recollection is that he spent a lot of time trying to persuade her to remind her boss of the conversation at Anouska Hempel's dinner. For a while she demurred but eventually Ryan's persistence or charm, or a mixture of both, won the day and the excursion was agreed. Liz Vyvyan went along as the lady-in-waiting and, as always, there was a discreet police presence.

It was supposed to be a private occasion but, largely because of Ryan's behaviour, clowning around and pretending to do a Sir Walter Raleigh act – flinging his cloak over a puddle so that his Queen Elizabeth didn't have to get her feet wet – the people in the market cottoned on to who their visitor was. Photographs were taken. The visit was reported in the press, the cover blown. Princess Margaret, however, seemed not to care and Ryan did indeed become a friend. The two remained close.

In November 1972 the house on Mustique, designed by Lord Snowdon's uncle Oliver Messel and built by the island's owner, Princess Margaret's great friend and Snowdon's bitter enemy Colin Tennant, was finally completed. Annabel Hoyer Miller, later Whitehead, packed for her in London and unpacked for her in the West Indies. Life there was relaxed, mildly bohemian, very informal and quite intimate. The island's occupants all knew each other and they moved to and from one another's houses rather as if life was one long get-together. 'There were only fifteen houses on the island and everyone knew everyone else,' recalled Mrs Whitehead. 'Someone would have a house party one day and the next day someone else would have the whole island to lunch.' Tennant, as owner-impresario, orchestrated the whole performance and was on terms of easy familiarity with the Princess that hardly anyone else approached. 'He got away with murder all his life,' said one observer enviously.

Mustique enjoyed a reputation for being a hedonistic playground for the rich and aristocratic. It was the antithesis of the misty feudal Scottishness of Balmorality that was the preferred holiday place of Princess Margaret's sister the Queen. And it was always off limits to Lord Snowdon, who, in any case, seemed to prefer Sussex. My favourite image of the island is a photograph in Lady Penn's album. It shows her husband, Sir Eric,[1] the tall ramrod-straight, magnificently moustached Etonian Guardsman who was Comptroller of the Royal Household. He is standing on the beach, holding forth, as if commanding a military parade. Opposite him is the perspiring figure of Sir John ('Jack') Plumb,[2] the distinguished Cambridge historian, who was, for four years, Master of Christ's College. He looks attentive but mildly ill at ease, like an undergraduate at an early-morning lecture. Beside them is the tiny Princess. She is the only one of the trio who looks at home.

The island was certainly relaxing as far as she was concerned. It also attracted some doubtful characters. Perhaps the least appealing of these was one called John Bindon,[3] who was best known for a party trick that involved hanging beer tankards from his erect penis. Bindon, who died of cancer aged fifty in 1992 (or thereabouts), was a small-time gangster and hoodlum who had a long-standing relationship with the model Vicky Hodge and was eventually charged with murder after another petty hood called John Darke was stabbed to death in a dive called the Ranelagh Yacht Club under the arches in West London.

Bindon claimed to have had a physical relationship with Princess Margaret and to have procured cocaine for her. He seems to have talked about the relationship to all and sundry while claiming to have been utterly loyal and discreet. He also claimed to have been warned off at least once by spooks from MI5. Photographs of him with Princess Margaret are alleged to have been taken from private photo albums belonging to various friends of Bindon.

---

1 Lt. Col. Sir Eric Penn (1916–1993). Comptroller of the Lord Chamberlain's Office from 1960 to 1981; was in effect brought up by his uncle, the courtier and friend of Queen Elizabeth, Sir Arthur Penn, after his parents' death.
2 Sir 'Jack' Plumb (1911–2001). Cambridge historian and authority on 'the long eighteenth century', briefly Master of Christ's College and memorably skewered in novels by C. P. Snow and William Cooper.
3 John Bindon (1943–1992). Violent criminal of exhibitionist disposition who visited Mustique and claimed to have had an affaire with Princess Margaret.

Bindon was certainly on Mustique on at least one occasion and behaved in a characteristic fashion witnessed by a number of onlookers including the Princess. That seems to have been it, but Bindon traded on the encounter by implying all while proving nothing. His posthumous biographer certainly gives credence to the idea of a relationship. He obviously knew Princess Margaret, though not, perhaps, as intimately as he liked everyone to think.

Rumours such as this dogged the Princess and often involved Mustique, not least because the island was remote and essentially private. What happened there was unreported except as gossip. Those who knew the Princess well, in London and elsewhere, gave scant credence to such rumours. 'I frankly do not believe a word of the suggestion that there was any form of sexual relationship,' said one long-standing observer, commenting on Bindon. 'Knowing her as I did she totally abhorred anything that was even faintly "seedy" or vulgar. I consider the story to be media invented.' She herself once confided to Cecil Beaton that she loathed squalor, which was why she so hated Tennessee Williams.

Mud, however, if that is what it was, stuck. Even in 2006 a book review of her old adversary Tommy Lascelles's diaries by Michael Bloch, himself the author of no less than six books about the Duke of Windsor, casually and without even a suspicion of evidence referred to Margaret as 'the nymphomaniac Princess'.

Late in 1973 Burnaby-Atkins was gone from the private secretaryship and replaced by another protégé of Sir Martin Gilliat – Major the Lord Napier and Ettrick, formerly of the Scots Guards. Lord Napier was regarded as a safe pair of hands and had already experienced royal life as equerry to the Queen's uncle, the Duke of Gloucester, between 1958 and 1960. He stayed for a quarter of a century and, had he realized that the Princess was nearing the end of her life, would never have retired when he did.

That year Princess Margaret's niece, Princess Anne, married a handsome young cavalry officer and horseman, Captain Mark

Phillips.[1] There was a ball before the wedding and Cecil Beaton, in his diary, reported a sighting of the Princess with even more than his usual waspishness. 'Gosh the shock,' he wrote. 'She has become a little pocket monster – Queen Victoria.'

Beaton produced a strange cocktail of pity and bile including a passing reference to the absence of 'the horrid husband'. He took evident relish in describing the Princess's outfit, surmounted by the Poltimore tiara and so bulky that she kept being knocked around by other guests and even a waiter passing by with a tray of champagne glasses. 'Poor brute,' wrote Beaton, 'I do feel sorry for her. She was not very nice in the days when she was so pretty and attractive. She snubbed and ignored friends. But my God has she been paid out! Her eyes seem to have lost their vigour, her complexion is now a dirty negligee pink satin. The sort of thing one sees in a disbanded dyer's shop window.' Even allowing for Beaton's spleen she sounds sad.

In 1974 the Snowdons visited the United States and Canada. Despite their increasingly separate lives and the widespread reports of rifts and fights they remained a public item. On 7 May that year they arrived in New York and were told that the Duchess of Windsor[2] was staying in a suite on the fourth floor. Despite her supposed and highly publicized antipathy to the Duchess, the Princess suggested a meeting and even that photographers should be allowed to record it. They stayed for a quarter of an hour and, though they never met again, the Snowdons sent the Duchess photographs of their two young children – the Duchess's great-nephew and great-niece.

The range of the Princess's acquaintance and her apparent lack of self-awareness continually amaze. On 26 January 1975 she

---

1 Captain Mark Phillips (1948–). Equestrian cavalry officer, unkindly known as 'Fog', who married Princess Anne in 1973; they divorced twenty years later.
2 Wallis Simpson, Duchess of Windsor (1896–1986). American divorcee whose relationship with the uncrowned King Edward VIII precipitated the 1937 abdication crisis.

watched Peter Hall's[1] film adaptation of Ronald Blythe's[2] *Aken-field*, a classic book about rural East Anglia. She phoned the following day to congratulate Hall personally. Hall said that she was perplexed by some critics' inability to understand the regional accents. 'Though, of course,' she said, 'one did grow up there, in Norfolk at any rate.' She presumably meant the Sandringham estate, which may have been Norfolk but was hardly what Blythe was writing about in *Akenfield*.

Later that year the Snowdons were invited to visit Australia. Relations between the couple were now extremely strained. In fact they were barely speaking. Nevertheless on 11 March Martin Charteris, Her Majesty the Queen's private secretary, wrote to the Australian High Commission saying: 'Her Majesty is glad to approve that the Princess Margaret and Lord Snowdon should be invited to visit Australia.' He noted that, now this had been done, an official invitation would be issued by Canberra. This duly came and almost as an afterthought contained a sort of postscript, which ran: 'In all of that I have not mentioned Lord Snowdon. If he were to accompany you it would give us added pleasure.'

Alas, the presence of Lord Snowdon could no longer be guaranteed to give added pleasure to his wife. Lord Napier accordingly wrote to Sir John Bunting,[3] the newly arrived Australian High Commissioner in London. 'It is a little difficult', he explained, 'to know whether it will be possible for Lord Snowdon to accompany Princess Margaret over this period because of his professional commitments, but I will endeavour to let you have his decision as soon as possible.'

Arrangements went ahead on this basis. It was suggested that the Princess might like dinner one night in a private house 'with lots of young'; it was explained that she found the paintings of

---

1 Peter Hall (1930–). Theatre director who ran first the Royal Shakespeare Company 1960–1968, then the National Theatre from 1973 to 1988.
2 Ronald Blythe (1922–). East Anglian author with acute and sensitive sense of place.
3 Sir John Bunting (1918–1995). Influential civil servant who was Cabinet Secretary during the 1970s.

Sir Sidney Nolan[1] 'fascinating'; Russell Drysdale[2] the painter, Patrick White[3] the Nobel Prize-winning novelist and David Williamson[4] the playwright were all invited to lunch at the Sydney Opera House; the Princess said she did not want a woman soldier from the Women's Royal Australian Army Corps – of which she had been Colonel-in-Chief since June 1953 – as her equerry. She preferred a man.

Then Lord Napier was summoned to his mistress's presence and asked if Lord Snowdon was intending to visit Australia with her. Lord Napier replied that he wasn't entirely certain but thought he was. Her Royal Highness was not pleased. Icily she commanded her private secretary to go to her husband and tell him that if he insisted on going ahead with his plans to visit Australia she would cancel the trip. She was intent on making the trip on her own or not at all.

This was a tricky task but, being a consummate courtier, Lord Napier duly presented himself at Lord Snowdon's office and told him what Princess Margaret had said. There was a silence, which must have been fairly ugly. It was eventually broken by Lord Snowdon, who asked if he was right in thinking that the invitation had been extended by the Australian government to both of them. Lord Napier confirmed that this was the case. Then, argued Snowdon, he was perfectly entitled to go. Indeed he was, answered Lord Napier, but if he decided to go Princess Margaret would cancel. In the event Lord Snowdon withdrew and those 'professional commitments' mentioned earlier were called in evidence to justify the decision.

Privately, however, it was a low moment in the already fraught atmosphere at Kensington Palace. There were some high spots on

---

1 Sir Sidney Nolan (1917–1992). Australian painter, notably of the notorious outlaw Ned Kelly in his trademark home-made iron mask.
2 Russell Drysdale (1912–1981). Australian landscape artist best known for his gum-tree-filled evocations of the outback.
3 Patrick White (1912–1990). Australian Nobel prize-winning author best known for his novel, *Voss*.
4 David Williamson (1942–). Prolific Australian playwright with controversial take on such seminal topics as his country's participation in the Vietnam War.

the tour when it did actually take place. The Princess enjoyed the performance of *The Two Pigeons* by the Australian Ballet and the Chief Protocol Officer of the Moonee Valley Racing Club praised her 'dedication and co-operation' under what he described as 'appalling conditions'. There was also a ticklish occasion when the Princess mulishly told Anne Tennant, her lady-in-waiting, that she was not, as scheduled, going to step on to Bondi Beach, meet the lifeguards and see them demonstrate traditional and modern methods of life-saving. Lady Anne, who had been prepared for trouble, said that she really felt she should because Bondi Beach enjoyed an iconic importance in Australian culture and to be seen to be snubbing the lifeguards could be construed as a dreadful insult to the Australian nation.

The Princess insisted and explained that she had the wrong sort of shoes and, as her lady-in-waiting knew, the one thing she couldn't stand was getting sand between her toes. With an air of triumph Lady Anne said that she had foreseen this and just happened to have a more appropriate pair of flat shoes in a bag with her in the limo. Princess Margaret looked at her, smiled ruefully, conceded defeat and stepped on to the beach to meet the lifeguards.

The journey home also sounds fraught. The Princess would not alight in Bahrain. The Australian Consul General came aboard when the plane landed, but the Princess was lying down and no one was told; they couldn't stay with the High Commissioner in Singapore because he was too busy packing to go home; Princess Margaret ordered special shirts and a message came through to say that they had been delivered and 'Ah Chum is about to start work on Lord Snowdon's pyjamas' – which makes one wonder if there had been at least a marginal reconciliation. On balance the Princess was glad to be home.

Later in the autumn of 1975 there was an encounter in France with Roy Strong. Strong was delivering a lecture and Princess Margaret was just back from Australia, which she told him she 'hated'. She complained that there had been no crowds and the traffic lights had been left on. During this meeting, according to Strong's account, she 'smoked non-stop'.

She turned up with Colin Tennant and was 'in beaming mood, slimmer and wearing a weight of make-up, her thin hair heavily back-combed.' In his diary entry of 25 November Strong was very hostile. 'She is, as we all know, tiresome, spoilt, idle and irritating,' he wrote; 'she has no direction, no overriding interest. All she now likes is la jeunesse dorée and young men.'

Next day, 'HRH in purring mood, wrapped in mink.' (One wonders what the difference is between 'beaming mood' and 'purring mood' – they sound similarly happy.) Strong went on: 'After dinner we sat and sat and sat. HRH and Colin wanted to go dancing but nothing in the end happened. All the time HRH slugged through the whisky and sodas. She loved her house in Mustique, she told me. Then she had a rave about Snowdon and how awful he was in various ways – alienating the chauffeur and going off at weekends without telling her where or with whom.'

Nevertheless Strong compared her favourably with Princess Anne whom Strong heard make a turgid and defensive speech. In his opinion, 'Anne has nothing like the sweeping *de haut en bas* of her Aunt Margaret who rightly has the knack or nerve to sail on, indifferent to criticism.'

Comparisons with her niece, Princess Anne, were inevitable and frequent. The apparent inconsistencies in the behaviour of these prominent princesses were matched in the reactions of press and public. One minute people were friendly, the next hostile. It was just so with Roy Strong and the Princess. One minute Strong is waspish and critical, the next he is friendly and deferential.

There were some other revealing encounters that year. Before a visit to Venezuela Lord Napier told the High Commissioner: 'About twenty minutes spent talking informally with the members of the press over a drink can often be rewarding.' On the visit itself Napier caught his boss looking abstracted and sad. She was stroking the chamois-leather pouch containing her cigarette case. When Napier subsequently said, 'I noticed, ma'am, that during that tedious speech you were stroking something, why was that?' She looked at him wanly, and said, 'It was a gift from my father.' It was sold at Christie's after her death.

On another occasion Sir Edwin Leather, the Canadian-born

Governor of Bermuda, former Tory MP and well-known broadcaster, wrote a letter which, for sheer breezy *understanding*, must have been music to royal ears.

> Frankly [he wrote], it would *not* be my intention to encourage Ministers to do anything to fill up the day on Wednesday, unless Her Royal Highness specifically wished me to do so. It would of course be very easy to fill every hour of her stay with visits to hospitals, old people's homes, schools, inspecting Girl Guides etc. etc. If there is anything Her Royal Highness would particularly like to do we shall be happy to arrange it. But, I have two particular reasons for not encouraging such ventures which I hope might appeal: one, I think all members of the Royal Family must get more of this junket than any reasonable person could wish for; and two, I cherish a very great desire to demonstrate to them that Bermuda is not only the most lovely place in the Commonwealth to visit, but just about the only place where they can come and expect to relax and enjoy all the delights we have to offer. I hope that is not lèse majesté.

Princess Margaret reacted as one might hope by scribbling 'Very nice' underneath the Governor's proposed – and very relaxed – programme, though it has to be conceded that Sir Edwin marginally let himself down by adding, 'I take it Princess Margaret would be agreeable to planting a tree in Government House grounds on the Wednesday morning.' She was, and the tree was duly planted.

The National Theatre was opened that year and the Princess attended as the guest of Peter Hall, the first director. That occasion – *Hamlet* – passed off well, but a subsequent visit to the Cottesloe for *Bow Down*, a musical concoction by Harrison Birtwistle[1] and Tony Harrison,[2] was less successful. 'A fairly disastrous evening,' reported Hall. 'Princess Margaret was very affronted by the whole thing, and afterwards said she didn't think she should have been invited. This surprised me, though *Bow Down* is certainly strong, cruel and somewhat upsetting.'

---

1 Sir Harrison Birtwistle (1934–). Avant-garde composer and academic.
2 Tony Harrison (1937–). Avant-garde poet and playwright.

She could sometimes appear gratuitously ill-tempered. Professor Richard Cobb,[1] the eminent Oxford historian of the French Revolution, a somewhat unlikely guest at a Buckingham Palace banquet, observed in a private letter that the Princess, whom he did not know, looked distinctly 'grumpy'. On 11 April 1976 James Lees-Milne saw her at a Sunday-morning church service at Badminton when she was staying as a house guest of the Duke and Duchess of Beaufort. Lees-Milne thought she looked 'miserable, trussed up like a broody hen, pigeon-breasted and discontented'.

The Princess's reaction to the Birtwistle–Harrison musical was not forgotten. The following year, on 20 July, Hall encountered her at the Queen's Buckingham Palace Jubilee party. As they chatted the band of the Coldstream Guards played pieces from Gilbert and Sullivan. The Princess asked Hall if he'd like to choose their next piece, so he mischievously suggested something by Birtwistle. The Princess was not amused. 'She didn't find that funny and went into a long pout about her evening at Harry's *Bow Down*. I, with enormous smiles, told her what frightful trouble her dislike of the production had caused us because what she thought had so disturbed the chairman (Sir Max Rayne).[2] I then moved further through the crush and met Max Rayne. He asked me if I'd seen *her*. "Who?" I asked. "The Princess," he said; "I'm keeping well away from *her*."'

In 1973 Anne and Colin Tennant had introduced the Princess to Roddy Llewellyn, the twenty-six-year-old son of Sir Harry Llewellyn, the showjumper, who, riding a famous horse called Foxhunter, had won Britain's only gold medal in the 1952 Helsinki Olympic Games. This first meeting was at lunch in Edinburgh. Llewellyn was seventeen years younger than the Princess, but when he subsequently made up the numbers at a house party given by

---

1 Professor Richard Cobb (1917–1996). Oxford University professor, letter-writer, autobiographical essayist and cult-inspiring Francophile expert on all things French, particularly the Revolution.
2 Max Rayne, Baron Rayne of Prince's Meadow (1918–2003). Rich property developer and philanthropist who was Chairman of the National Theatre Board from 1971 to 1988.

the Tennants at the ancestral home, Glen, near Innerleithen, they had got on spectacularly well. Roddy was good-looking in a slightly androgynous way – not, as onlookers observed, unlike a younger Snowdon. After the stay at Glen he told his hostess that the Princess had the most beautiful eyes. Lady Anne told the young man to tell the Princess herself. He did and the following February she invited him as her guest on Mustique.

By 1975 the relationship with Llewellyn was universally acknowledged and widely accepted, but the Princess continued to undertake official engagements on her own. Her own family was not keen on the idea of an only moderately successful landscape-gardener toy boy and the Princess seemed keen to continue with a social life where she was the sole centre of attention. She particularly enjoyed staying in Cambridge with 'Jack' Plumb, and in Oxford with the novelist Angela Huth and her historian husband James Howard-Johnston.

Angela Huth remarked much later that royalty, including Princess Margaret, had a disturbing effect even on the most sophisticated and worldly-wise, including those whose sympathies were almost certainly not royalist. One who seemed to be affected in this way was the aristocratic writer Jonathan Gathorne-Hardy, author of successful books on, among other subjects, nannies, public schools and the sexologist Dr Kinsey.

Early in 1976 Gathorne-Hardy was bidden to dinner at his friend Angela's because Princess Margaret apparently wanted to meet some 'new writers'. When Gathorne-Hardy arrived in his hand-me-down dinner jacket he found only one other guest: Martin Amis. Amis rather surprisingly explained royal etiquette to Gathorne-Hardy and that he should always address Princess Margaret as 'ma'am'. Gathorne-Hardy was surprised by this. 'What?' he asked. 'Even "Did you come, ma'am?"' Amis hesitated for a moment and then answered, unequivocally, 'Yes.'

Eventually the other 'new writers' arrived, though they seem to have been an eclectic bunch of scribblers to whom the epithet 'new' was not appropriate. The Derek Marlowes were there, and the Bamber Gascoignes, Bryan Forbes and Nanette Newman. When the Princess arrived, Gathorne-Hardy remembered: 'Like all of us, I was immediately engulfed by a wave, a tsunami, of sycophancy and showing off.'

His own chance did not come until after dinner. 'Princess Margaret', he wrote, 'had somehow become stuck playing Angie's upright piano – rather well, in fact, with a large tumbler of whisky precariously balanced on it like Fats Waller – but stuck.' Eventually the hostess prised her away from the piano and took her over to the sofa, where Gathorne-Hardy was sitting, 'fairly drunk by now'. The writer was immediately sobered up by what he called 'the adrenaline of royalty', but royalty herself had had her glass 'generously replenished'.

They talked of this and that until Gathorne-Hardy said he had just seen Lady Sarah at Bedales, where she was at school. He thought her beautiful and said so, whereupon her mother leaned against him rather heavily and said, 'I don't live with my husband any more, you know.'

Gathorne-Hardy now felt alerted and sensed that the word 'ma'am' no longer seemed quite appropriate.

'Well, I'm divorced,' he said, 'or rather divorcing. It is an extremely upsetting process.'

At this point the Princess was momentarily distracted by Bryan Forbes saying loudly and not for the first time that the life of a writer was very lonely. To restore the Princess's attention, Gathorne-Hardy said, 'I met your husband once. It was years before he met you.'

'Really?' she said.

'Yes. I was a copywriter then. We did a campaign together advertising the *Queen*.'

'Advertising my *sister*?' she said, astonished.

After he explained that he was talking about the magazine not the monarch she leaned against him again and said *sotto voce*: 'As a matter of fact I'm going to leave him. It's going to be announced in a few weeks.' Evidently she thought better of this almost at once for she added, 'Please tell no one.'

To which he replied, 'Of course not, ma'am.'

The subject changed then and the Princess confessed to keeping a diary. Gathorne-Hardy urged her to be indiscreet when writing in it and subsequently wondered, as many of us do, whether or not it still exists. Then the Princess got up to talk to other 'new writers', but later, as she was leaving, she came back to Gathorne-Hardy and repeated, 'Don't tell anyone.'

And he didn't. There had been much media speculation already and had it not been for other 'more legitimate sources in the offing', he might have been tempted. Who knows, he thought, it could have netted him up to, say, £50,000. But he did as the Princess asked and told no one.

In February 1976 the Snowdons finally did split up. The ostensible cause was a photograph that appeared in the *News of the World* of Princess Margaret and Roddy Llewellyn on Mustique. The quality of the picture was poor, but the Princess was in a bikini and Roddy in swimming costume. It was 'intimate' enough to appear 'compromising'. *Private Eye*, typically, improved on the picture in a later edition with a cover of the Princess's and Llewellyn's heads superimposed on near naked 'me-Tarzan-you-Jane' bodies with the caption: 'Margaret and Roddy. The Picture they tried to ban. Eye Exclusive'. Inside a story about the Glenconners' son Charlie Tennant stealing more pictures of Roddy and Margaret referred to the Princess as 'the Royal Midget'.

The Monday after the *News of the World* published its fuzzy snap, Snowdon summoned his wife's private secretary, Lord Napier, to his office and demanded an explanation. What was the meaning of it?

An exasperated Napier told Snowdon not to be ridiculous. He knew perfectly well what the meaning was. The relationship between his wife and Llewellyn had been going on for ages and Snowdon himself had been conducting an affair that would eventually lead to marriage with Lucy Lindsay-Hogg. Snowdon listened and then buzzed his own secretary, Dorothy Everard. When she arrived, her boss said crisply: 'Dotty. We're leaving,' and then, turning to Napier, told him, 'We'll be out by the end of the week.'

Privately Napier was elated. His problem, however, was passing the news on to Princess Margaret on Mustique. Communications with Les Jolies Eaux were relatively primitive and there was no secure line. Napier was reluctant to conduct this particular conversation *en clair*, fearing, with reason, that if he did the contents were likely to find their way into the *News of the World* or similar. Then, in fine melodramatic mode, he hit on a simple way of sending a coded message.

When he finally made contact with the Princess at home in the Caribbean Napier said, 'Ma'am, I have been talking to Robert and he has given in his notice. He will be leaving by the end of the week.'

There was a pause. Then the Princess spoke.

'I'm sorry, Nigel. Have you taken leave of your senses? What exactly did you say?'

Very slowly, like a secret agent in a black-and-white movie, Napier repeated, 'Robert has given notice. He will be out by the end of the week.'

There was a pause. Only then did the Princess evidently remember that her husband's third Christian name was Robert.

'Oh I see,' she said. 'Thank you, Nigel. I think that's the best news you've ever given me.'

True to his word, Snowdon was gone by the following Friday and on 19 March an official release was sent to the press announcing their separation.

Roy Strong wrote:

At last the HRH Margaret separation came. Not a divorce. She said that put the papers down a bit as it eliminated the Archbishop of Canterbury. Frankly we're all relieved, although the hideous coverage really tarnishes. She looks better. At the French Embassy soirée for *Fashion* she complained bitterly about the press (on the day Anne Tennant's nanny had rung her and said don't come back to the house as it was besieged by photographers and reporters). She complained that Tony never stopped talking, and when I said that I had noticed on a newspaper billboard that someone had slashed Tony's pictures in his Australian exhibition she replied, 'Good'. In spite of all the efforts to shrink she looks very Hanoverian. Her dress was white trimmed with turquoise-blue embroidery and beading and totally uninteresting.

A few days later *Private Eye* had another of its waspish stories alleging Llewellyn's pleasure at the number of column inches he had garnered in the popular press and carried a wounding postscript. 'Colonel Harry Llewellyn, father of the amorous brothers Roddy and Dai, was asked what he thought of Yvonne, after Roddy had taken the royal dwarf to visit him.

'You mean Roddy's new friend?' barked the Colonel. 'Well, it makes a change from his usual Italian waiters.'

The *Eye* remarked, 'I am baffled by this observation.'

The relationship continued for some years though not without its ups and downs. On one occasion Llewellyn apparently lost the plot altogether and fled to Turkey, confessing to a complete stranger on the plane to Istanbul that he was having an affair with a married woman and that the question of sex had become a problem. Roddy's father was not the only person to suggest that his sexual interests were not entirely heterosexual and it was always alleged that the Princess's own sexual appetite was voracious. Age was not the only difference between the two. On the occasion of the Turkish flight Llewellyn's whereabouts were completely unknown for three weeks or so. Princess Margaret was so distraught that she took an overdose.

'She did take an overdose,' said one confidant (Napier, letter and talk, 23 August 2005), 'although how much it was done to create a drama I shall never know. Remember she was a great actress.' A number of close relations came round to be at her bedside and it took a long time to bring her round. Nevertheless she survived.

On 13 February 1978 Strong was at a Kensington Palace dinner for Sybil Cholmondeley.[1] 'Her Royal Highness', he wrote, 'is an extremely good hostess and moves people around so that everybody speaks with everybody including her. Her dress was virtually topless, apart from two thin shoulder-straps and the top was entirely made of glitter beads.' Strong felt Roddy was on the

---

1 Sybil, Marquess of Cholmondeley (née Sassoon) (1894–1989). Wife of the 5th Marquess and painted, twice, by John Singer Sargent.

make ('purely selfish'). He much preferred the film-maker Derek Hart – 'Would that she'd marry him!' Instead,

> She seems to have thrown all discretion to the winds. He [Llewellyn] apparently stays at The Royal Lodge and shortly afterwards he flew off quite publicly with HRH to Mustique, where he was carried off to hospital due to internal bleeding and HRH rushed to his bedside. It is all rather sad and pathetic and deeply embarrassing for the Queen surely? During this period Peter Townsend published his memoirs of their attachment, an act in the worst taste. Derek Hart said that she never did love him. One does feel rather sorry for her but she does so very little to help herself.

Strong was an astute occasional observer of the Princess in the 1970s. At the end of May 1978, for instance, he wrote a sad little follow-up to the news of the Snowdons' separation: 'Poor HRH Margaret was carted off to hospital with hepatitis. What a tragedy it has all been and needlessly. And now the divorce with Snowdon is announced. How little people will understand the agonies which she has gone through as a practising Anglican to let the divorce happen. How silly but understandable to fall for Roddy and what an inevitable end. The loneliness of it all for her must be terrible.'

Earlier, at a State Banquet for Valéry Giscard d'Estaing on 22 June 1976, he had recorded: 'Princess Margaret, relaxed and tanned, was off the cigarettes for once and zoomed us round to show off this and that room.' Sir Nicholas Henderson,[1] sometime British Ambassador in Paris and Washington, was also present. He observed that the Queen, who sat on the President's right, got on like a house on fire. He made no comment about Princess Margaret, who sat on Giscard's left.

Later that same year Strong was at the opening of the National Theatre, where he wrote, 'The Queen collected her sister, who had been bored by the play but more by the fact that when she

---

1 Sir Nicholas Henderson (1919–). Career diplomat who served as Ambassador in Warsaw, Bonn and Paris before being recalled by Mrs. Thatcher to serve as Ambassador in Washington. Elegant diaries published under title *Mandarin*.

sat down the wall in front of her in the circle was so high that she couldn't see over it. Thus opened our long-awaited National Theatre.'

The following year he was at Kensington Palace and enjoyed a first sighting of Roddy Llewellyn: 'Usual scene. HRH in plummy red with a gold belt, smoking and drinking whisky, in good form surrounded by a motley crowd ...' Of Llewellyn he wrote, 'He was like Tony round again, thirty-ish, rather dapper, but very polite and assigned to a kind of "host" role getting drinks and ferrying them to people. HRH showed no overt interest in him, although he would spring up and actively join in anything that she wanted.' Roy asked the Princess what he called 'the million-dollar question – 'Does Roddy stay here?' 'Yes,' was the reply. His final verdict was: 'He's agreeable, not nearly as bright as Tony, rather silly and giggly, but kind, and she hasn't had much of that.'

Llewellyn himself much disliked Strong and referred to him privately as 'Ron' Strong. The Christian name seemed to Roddy to be more appropriate than 'Sir Roy'. He naturally resented Strong's strictures but even more thought it improper to publish private diaries and make money from them. He himself turned down large sums of money – hundreds of thousands – to betray confidences to the popular press and was particularly distressed when his elder brother, popularly known as 'Dirty Dai', was rumoured to have taken £50,000 from the *News of the World* to talk about the relationship between Roddy and the Princess, a rumour which was never proven.

At lunch in April 1978 he sat next to Mollie, the Duchess of Buccleuch,[1] at Bowhill, the family mansion in the Scottish lowlands. She recalled how Colin and Anne Tennant had endlessly brought Princess Margaret and Roddy to Bowhill and Drumlanrig.

Mollie and Queen Elizabeth were greatly at variance, going back to the days of the 'romance' between Johnnie [Dalkeith] and

---

1 Mollie, Duchess of Buccleuch (née Lascelles) (1900–1993). Gregarious and well-connected aristocrat actually christened Breda Mary.

HRH. For months it was touch and go but, thank heaven, it didn't happen. She then gave an hilarious description of her sister, Diana, and Princess Alice of Gloucester at Drumlanrig being confronted by HRH, Roddy and Bianca Jagger on a visit. They were all mystified. Who were these people, both ladies living an existence totally oblivious to *le monde*? HRH and Prince Philip didn't hit it off – all those jokes about the navy irritated her.

On 11 July he came across the Princess at a dance of Drue Heinz's. She was 'looking relaxed and rather marvellous in white and complaining that her summer arrangements had gone awry'. Another time she was 'in a most unbecoming orange-pink Chinese package patterned in gold, along with Roddy Llewellyn, who hid his face for most of the evening either behind opera glasses or buried in his programme'. At Windsor she was looking ill with 'red' flu but 'obviously pleased to see us amidst a bevy of people she probably regarded as "heavies"'. Evidently publicity over her and Roddy meant that there were serious questions about whether she would retire to private life.

Three of the remaining pink bits on the map were to get their independence in 1978 and 1979 and the Foreign Office duly advised Buckingham Palace that it would be appropriate if the new constitutions and instruments of independent government should be formally handed over by members of the Royal Family on behalf of Her Majesty. In due course Sir Philip Moore, the Queen's deputy private secretary, announced the results of what sounds almost like a royal raffle. The Duke of Gloucester was to do the Solomon Islands in July 1978; Princess Anne was to take care of the Gilbert Islands in early 1979 and Princess Margaret drew somewhere called Tuvalu, which turned out to be what used to be known until their partition as the Ellice part of the Gilbert and Ellice Islands.

This seemed a bit of a short straw. Margaret had set her heart on a visit to China, but although the infamous Chairman Mao was gone and there were slightly misleading signs of reform in the People's Republic, the Foreign Office's mandarins advised that it was too early for a royal visit. That year – 1978 – Sir Percy

Cradock, a lifelong sinophile and old China hand, was transferred from East Germany to Beijing. A long association with repressive dictatorships such as these had imbued Sir Percy with a more than natural caution and a desire not to cause offence or upset to his hosts. Princess Margaret would be a *gweipor*[1] too far. Tuvalu was to be her consolation.

The islands, coral atolls strung out in a remote part of the Pacific Ocean about four hundred and fifty miles from Fiji and 2,500 from Sydney, had a population of less than ten thousand and had almost been wiped out by Hurricane Bebe three or four years earlier. Government House had only one spare bedroom and no hot water or air conditioning. Nevertheless Tom Layng, the Commissioner, was buoyantly optimistic.

'Everything is very much in the Polynesian tradition,' he confided to Napier: 'dancing girls rather than police guards of honour! Open-necked bula – flowered shirts or lava-lavas and informal footwear (or none) will be the dress of the day throughout.'

The only European in the incoming government was a British lawyer called John Wilson, who later remarked that Tuvalu was much the same size as a typical English village. As he said of his two-year spell on the islands: 'Imagine drafting laws to comply with the international treaty obligations of Chipping Sodbury'.

His depiction of the contrasts of life on the islands is revealing and instructive. On the one hand he worked in an office from which he could see a white coral beach sloping down to an azure lagoon. Palms waved in the trade-wind breeze, people fished by pole or net from hand-carved outrigger canoes and on the beach dogs barked, children splashed in the surf and girls in sulus or *lava-lavas* with frangipani in their hair strolled past the Maneapa meeting house arm in arm. That was paradise.

On the other hand there were moments when documents needed to be duplicated urgently and the photocopier ran out of paper. The only other machine in the building was being repaired. The

---

1 The feminine form of *gweilo*, which is derogatory Cantonese for 'roundeye' or 'foreign devil'.

computer printer was out of ink. Communications had gone down because the crucial satellite had shifted position and suddenly the draft bill on which he had been working all week disappeared from the screen with a message saying 'unrecoverable disk error'. That evening there was a heavy tropical rainstorm, the roof leaked and next morning he came in to find most of his papers soaked through. That was not paradise.

These were the two sides of life in Tuvalu.

The formal Independence ceremony would have to start at 8 a.m. on the dot because the last flight off the island could not leave after 14.30 hours. This was because there were no runway lights at Funafuti airport and if a departing aircraft got into trouble and had to return it was impossible to land safely after dark. Also there was no room to park aircraft, so the island could only accommodate one plane at a time. Getting all the guests away swiftly was going to be a challenge.

After a lot of to-ing and fro-ing Lord Napier and Annabel Whitehead finally managed to conduct a dry run or reconnaissance, as a result of which Napier reported to his employer that Government House was quite unsuitable for a royal personage and that he was therefore asking the New Zealand government to send a ship for the royal party to use as headquarters. Ideally he would like HMNZS *Otago* which was, in a sense, the Princess's own ship for, years before, she had launched her on the Clyde. This request was granted and the New Zealanders also agreed to take over the transportation with its Andovers and Hercules aircraft. They also eventually agreed to transport a royal car from Fiji to Tuvalu, as the islands did not have a suitable vehicle nor funds to buy one. (Even if they had wanted one a Rolls-Royce was hardly top of the shopping list for a community that relied on subsistence fishing and the occasional coconut for its livelihood.)

After a while the New Zealanders seem to have taken umbrage at the avalanche of requests for assistance. Tuvalu was, after all, a British dependency, but apart from sending Princess Margaret they seemed to be doing very little apart from telling everyone else what to do. An improbable-sounding Foreign Office pair called Cortazzi[1] and Snodgrass[2] were to attend the ceremonies and were lavish with their advice. H. A. H. Cortazzi was Deputy Under-Secretary of State and J. M. O. Snodgrass was Head of the Pacific Territories Department. Snodgrass subsequently became Ambassador to Bulgaria and Cortazzi to Japan. Later they both recalled the occasion vividly and were united in their adverse reactions to the Australian representative, the Foreign Minister, Andrew Peacock.[3]

'My main memory', wrote Hugh Cortazzi, 'was of the way Andrew Peacock flirted (outrageously?) with the Princess before we ever got to Tuvalu. I found him arrogant and conceited.'

John Snodgrass was also ill-disposed towards Peacock. He remembered Peacock had a reputation as a ladies' man. 'He attached himself from the outset to the attractive lady representing the Americans. When the time came for the farewell gifts, the Tuvaluans evidently assumed she was Mr Peacock's wife. To their embarrassment, and the amusement of many of the guests, the gift for the Australians was presented to them where they were sitting together. I don't know what happened to the gift for the American Representative.'

The Fijians offered their military band and the Australians said they would send a warship and entertain the royal party to dinner on 29 September. Then they had second thoughts and issued a terse message saying: 'It would be imprudent for any major war vessel to proceed into and anchor inside the atoll. HMAS *Perth* will therefore be unable to visit Tuvalu for the Independence celebrations.' Plans for the royal dinner were hastily unscrambled, but then the order to abort was countermanded and the dinner was reinstated. The French, who, unlike

---

1 Sir Hugh Cortazzi (1924–). British career diplomat and Ambassador to Japan from 1980 to 1984.
2 John Snodgrass (1928–). British career diplomat and Ambassador to Zaire, Congo, Rwanda and Burundi (1980–1983) and to Bulgaria (1983–1986).
3 Andrew Peacock (1939–). Affluent Melbourne ladies' man who famously walked out with American film star Shirley MacLaine and was for years the 'nearly man' of Australian politics whose career ended as Ambassador to United States.

the British, were keen to remain a key player in the Pacific, muscled in by sending a gunboat called *La Dunquerquoise* with an ambassador and the senior administrator of their territories, Wallis and Futuna. The Americans trumped this by ordering up an aircraft carrier, the USS *Benjamin Stoddart*, and inviting Her Royal Highness to lunch. Lord Napier politely declined on her behalf.

From an early stage the Princess seems to have taken against the hapless Tom Layng, the colonial administrator of the islands, who had insisted on a place on the departing royal aircraft on the grounds that it would be embarrassing for the former foreign imperialist to hang around after the Union flag had been lowered and the Tuvalan standard raised. The request was obviously regarded as cheeky.

Layng wrote a draft speech for the Princess to deliver at the Independence celebration. 'What a ghastly speech,' she complained to Napier. 'I've mucked it about as best I could.'

New passages included, 'I had heard from the Prince of Wales of the infectious happiness of your life here and I got an impression from him of the joyousness of these occasions – full of dance and music that was much enjoyed by him and now at first hand by myself.'

The Queen had formally approved the naming of the state's new hospital 'The Princess Margaret', and it was therefore deemed appropriate to include a sentence that read, 'I have been most impressed by how healthy everybody looks and it is also nice to know that there are no nasty tropical diseases prevalent in Tuvalu.' This eventually proved to be an unfortunate tempting of providence.

Layng proposed that the lesson at the obligatory church service should be from St Paul's Epistle to the Galatians, chapter 5, verse 13. HRH was unamused. 'Quite unsuitable,' she scribbled to Napier. 'I shall read the Beatitudes. Better than St Paul.'

Layng's communications had a mildly facetious, irreverent air, which clearly did not find favour. 'Hats are not worn,' he wrote, 'but it is hoped Princess Margaret might consider wearing a tiara on the Saturday night.' He also seemed to have his tongue fairly firmly in cheek when instructing Kensington Palace on food drill. 'Two girls will bring in a large palm leaf covered in chicken, pork, vegetables, bananas etc. This will be on a slightly raised table to bring it level with Your Royal Highness' seat. Food is eaten in the fingers and one drinks direct from the coconut shell. A bowl is provided for washing one's fingers.'

Both Lord Napier and Anne Glenconner recall the food being extremely plentiful but not appetizing. 'I have a photograph of the initial feast on arrival', said Lord Napier, 'in the Miniaba or Meeting Place with HRH looking disgusted at the food.'

Even after almost thirty years one can feel Layng not getting it right and one can sense the *froideur* of the Princess. One has to have some sympathy with him. The verse from Galatians, for instance, reads: 'For, brethren, ye have been called unto liberty; only use not liberty for an occasion to the flesh, but by love serve one another.' This sounds rather an appropriate message for a newly independent nation, whereas Matthew, chapter 5, though sonorous, has no particular relevance to the situation. 'Blessed are the poor in spirit, for theirs is the kingdom of heaven' is a powerful sentence but not particularly apt for Independence Day.

In the event, however, Her Royal Highness never read either lesson. In the middle of the night before the Independence ceremonies the phone rang in Lord Napier's cabin. It was the Princess and she was barely audible. 'Thank heaven you're there,' she began. She was ill. Very.

The ship's doctor was summoned and gave an alarming verdict. He diagnosed probable viral pneumonia. There could be no question of Her Royal Highness carrying out any of her engagements or even of proceeding by Andover to Fiji as planned. Hong Kong and the Philippines would have to be cancelled. Possibly Japan and Princess Chichibu as well. He recommended she be flown as quickly as possible to Sydney, where she could be hospitalized and X-rayed. If gentle convalescence was all that was required Sydney would be fine, for she knew the Governor of New South Wales, Sir Roden Cutler,[1] the doughty holder of the Victoria Cross, and his wife; and she had stayed in their official residence before.

The New Zealanders immediately whistled up a Hercules aircraft for the nine-hour flight to Australia; Lord Napier handed over the instruments of Independence to Tuvalu's new Governor General and read out the Princess's speech and the Queen's Message. Mr Cortazzi of the Foreign and Commonwealth Office opened the Princess Margaret Hospital. And then the caravan departed.

On Tuvalu itself few believed that the illness was genuine. Anita Wilson, wife of the Attorney General, received the Union flag when it was lowered for the last time – the only woman, she believed, to have performed such a function in the whole history of the British Empire. When I told her that the Princess did indeed have viral pneumonia, she commented, 'That wasn't the impression any (or certainly not many) of us had.' Cynics criticized the honour given to the doctor from the *Otago*, alleging it to be a kind of hush money.

Hugh Cortazzi remarked, 'Inevitably, some of the "mauvaises voix" thought that the Princess's illness was "diplomatic", though why she should have troubled to come to this remote spot unless she intended to perform the ceremony was not explained.' Davina Woodhouse, the lady-in-waiting, was suffering from insect bites so bad that the Princess gave up her bed to her and tended the bite marks herself. There are photographs to prove it. The Princess looks solicitous, caring but, dangerously, well.

Her quiet few days with the Cutlers in Sydney seemed to have worked wonders. The X-rays at the Prince Alfred Hospital in Sydney revealed nothing untoward. The reality was less comfortable. The Princess took such a dislike to Sir Roden and Lady

---

1 Sir Roden Cutler VC (1916–2002). After winning the Victoria Cross and losing a leg in Syria during World War II, served as career diplomat and was Australian minister to Egypt during Suez Crisis of 1956 and representative at United Nations during 1960s, before becoming longest-ever serving Governor of New South Wales and finally receiving unprecedented accolade of state funeral.

Cutler that Lord Napier actually had to phone our man in Japan, Sir Michael Wilford,[1] and ask if the royal party could come early because any more time spent in Vice-Regal Lodge with the Cutlers was likely to provoke an incident. Lady Glenconner, who was now with the Princess as an official lady-in-waiting, confirmed that the Cutlers were unbelievably stuffy. She herself was not allowed to use the front stairs unless she was actually accompanying Her Royal Highness. If she was on her own she had to go up and down the back stairs – not something to which, as the daughter of an earl who had been brought up in one of the grandest houses in England, she was accustomed. Every time the Princess herself came down the front stairs Sir Roden and Lady Cutler would be standing rigidly to attention at the foot of the banisters, facing away from the royal presence. The instant the Princess's foot hit the floor they would turn to face her. The Governor would perform a courtly bow and his wife would curtsey. They would then escort their guest in to the drawing room and wait standing until she sat in the special royal chair with which she was provided. Princess Margaret could not stand it. Hence Lord Napier's desperate call to Michael Wilford in Japan.

There is some dispute about this. Lady Cutler obviously did not win favours, but Princess Margaret was impressed by Sir Roden's VC, his height and his military bearing. She specifically asked for photographs of herself with the Governor to be sent on for inclusion in her album. The Cutlers presented her with a present of a 'boomerang cover', which caused much mirth. However, 'boomerang-cover' was actually the local name for a sumptuous historic quilt made by the wives of early settlers. It was not nearly such an inappropriate present as was assumed.

Life with the Cutlers was so oppressive that one morning Lord Napier telephoned a friend of the Princess called David Wilkinson and asked if he could bring the Princess and her entourage to dinner one night in order to escape 'the excessive formality' of

---

1 Sir Michael Wilford (1922–2006). British Ambassador to Japan from 1975 to 1980 and was the Princess's host when she was recovering from the viral pneumonia which struck her down in Vanuatu.

Government House. Wilkinson had met the Princess in 1975 when she was staying with Peter and Edwina Baillieu in Bowral – famous as the birthplace of the great cricketer Sir Donald Bradman. At that first meeting Wilkinson and the Princess had enjoyed a long conversation about green issues. He thought her knowledgeable and concerned. When he said that he was interested in attending the Royal Botanical Gardens at Kew as a student she demurred and said that he would be better off with the Royal Horticultural Society at Wisley and would, if he liked, put in a word on his behalf. He agreed and she did.

In 1978 Wilkinson was a young architect – once described by Norman St John-Stevas jokingly as 'Roddy Llewellyn's replacement'; he thought his bachelor pad in Sydney was insufficiently grand and therefore asked his mother if he could use the family home in the chic suburb of Vaucluse to entertain 'some friends from London'.

This house is the iconic creation of Wilkinson's grandfather, the first professor of architecture at Sydney University. Built in Mediterranean style, in 1923, using materials from newly demolished Georgian houses in the city centre, it is a two-storey brick mansion with a Marseille terracotta tile roof and double-hung Georgian windows. It sits among native gum trees (*Angophara costata*) and has ochre-painted walls to match the tree trunks and apple-green shutters to match the leaves. The view of Sydney harbour is magnificent and the night the Princess came to dinner the hosts were amused to watch her security men climbing the gum trees in the garden.

Wilkinson still remembers the Princess winking at him that night and saying that the last few days chez Cutler had been 'like being locked up in a very formal boarding school'. Dinner consisted of the Wilkinson family and 'her gang'. They ate seafood cocktail, roast lamb and pavlova which the Wilkinsons felt was 'a good Aussie menu' and the Princess was 'really crook' because no food or drink was ordered until the Wilkinsons had confirmation that 'the antibiotics had kicked in'.

Despite this and the fact that Wilkinson's sister dropped the cauliflower on the way to the dining room (it was hastily scooped up and put on another dish) all went well. 'The Princess was in great form,' said Wilkinson. 'She asked for a list of guests and was really good about doing her homework so she could chat to all about their individual interests.'

In the event she flew on to Tokyo ahead of the original schedule and intent on fulfilling her programme, including the presentation of the GCMG to Princess Chichibu. The Ambassador, Sir Michael Wilford, was impressed and pleased. 'Despite an uncomfortable cough,' he reported, 'she seemed in very good form. Far from taking to her bed or a chair in the garden within hours she was organising a trip to the Mitsukoshi department store and asking if the Sunday could not be taken up with a visit to see Mount Fuji. Both events took place!'

Slightly half-hearted attempts were made to get Her Royal Highness to try dishes such as kabayaki – barbecued eel – or sushi, but she insisted, adamantly, 'I *don't* eat Japanese food.' Special supplies of Malvern water and her favourite lemonade had been shipped ahead, but in essence the Princess was considered a model and undemanding guest. 'Despite her busy programme,' wrote Sir Michael, 'the Princess was indefatigable. We were also so grateful that she always seemed ready to go another mile; whether it was receiving members of my staff and their wives or the household staff, we shall all have fond memories of her kindness and interest.'

Princess Chichibu, who received her honour in a blue coat and shirt specially designed to match the ribbon of the GCMG, was clearly moved by the occasion and made an eloquent speech in English. The Tokyo *Shimbun* wrote, 'With charming smiles, Princess Margaret caused "a Margaret whirlwind".' The Princess had already met Princess Chichibu in London. One of her theatrical acquaintances, Sir Peter Hall, had sat next to her at a Buckingham Palace lunch for the Japanese Princess. There were only thirty people there. 'When the plates for the main course were arranged she said, "Oh, not silver. They are too hot, they burn you. Then they go cold very quickly, and you will find your food is quickly turned into a soggy mess."'

From Tokyo Margaret and her entourage, including the

Glenconners, who had been to the Philippines, where they handed over a personal note of apology to Imelda Marcos[1] for HRH's cancellation of her visit, flew east across the Pacific. There was a brief pit stop at Raratonga in the Cook Islands where the entire cabinet formed up on the tarmac. The Princess had agreed to this presentation but insisted 'no dancing'. In the event there *was* dancing and despite the Princess's objections Lord Napier penned one of his courteous letters to the Cook Island government thanking them for its excellence.

On the way home there was a week-long visit to California. The only official duty was the 'rolling-out' of a Lockheed Tri-Star, over which the Princess cracked a bottle of champagne. Lockheed's Director of Public Relations waxed enthusiastic. 'Speaking for Lockheed's rank and file, as well as our senior management, we were terribly honoured, flattered, impressed and completely captivated by our distinguished visitor.'

Maybe so, but there is a worrying gap between the emollient, gushing public statements and formal letters and the actuality behind them. One consular official was to receive 'the usual fulsome letter' with the private proviso, 'Although we did not like ...'. Their host at the hotel in Los Angeles was dismissed as 'rather deaf and in fact not very efficient in my view'. American Airlines, which provided a flight across the States, were sent a thank-you letter, but the directive to the secretary drafting it was: 'No need to overdo it ... none of the air hostesses knew who we were when we arrived on board.' Only one member of the consular staff won a generous 'quite magnificent!'

The Californian press was mixed. The Los Angeles *Examiner* described the Princess, gratuitously, as 'the blue-blooded brat of Britain's Royal Family', and it was alleged that at a party given by Wendy Stark, wife of the powerful producer Ray Stark, timed for 6 to 8 p.m., Margaret arrived at eight to find that half the guests, including Rod Stewart and Elton John, had left. 'This could never happen in England, where the dummies would just

---

1 Imelda Marcos. Flamboyant, self-obsessed wife of Philippine President Ferdinand Marcos. Famous for her enormous collection of shoes.

stand around waiting until Her Megs decided to appear.' At another party, given by Betsy and Alf Bloomingdale, it was said that the Princess ignored star guests such as the Jimmy Stewarts and Ronald and Nancy Reagan and spent all her time talking to Bianca Jagger.

Much of this was trivial and almost certainly inaccurate. For example, there was a much-trumpeted story of how the one person Princess Margaret really wanted to meet was John Travolta but that he had snubbed her and refused to see her. However, the newly arrived Ross Benson[1] of the *Daily Express* was reported to have lunched with the Princess at the Beverly Hills Hotel and said that she had hugely enjoyed meeting Travolta.

Another person she enjoyed seeing was her old friend the drama critic Kenneth Tynan, who was just out of hospital after a hernia operation. Tynan and his wife Kathleen put on a glittering dinner party that included Joan Didion and John Gregory Dunne, Gene Kelly, Tony Richardson, Joanne Woodward and Paul Newman, Neil Simon and Marsha Mason, Sidney Poitier and his wife, Ryan and Tatum O'Neal, Roddy McDowell, David Hockney, George Cukor and 'possibly a few others'. This was the sort of gathering she enjoyed.[2]

Tynan's was an unlikely friendship, for he was not only louche and exceedingly bright – qualities that Margaret tended to enjoy – he was also a fervent republican. 'For years Ken was attacked for his friendship with royalty,' wrote his wife Kathleen (seemingly oblivious to the fact that the Princess was also similarly attacked for her friendship with Tynan). 'How could he demand its abolition while consorting with one of its members? He saw no particular

---

1 Ross Benson (1948–2005). Debonair Gordonstoun-educated Fleet Street man whose languid, old-fashioned manner concealed steely inner professionalism. A class-mate of Prince Charles at Gordonstoun he was said, jokingly, to have even more shoes than Imelda Marcos.

2 The Starks' party and the Tynans' dinner containing, as they did, household names that included an American President (Reagan), film stars such as James Stewart, Paul Newman and Sidney Poitier, rock musicians such as Elton John and even one of Britain's most famous artists, David Hockney, were indications both of the Princess's eclectic pulling power and personal taste.

contradiction: he liked Princess Margaret's appetite for the theatre, her wit and her loyalty to friends.'

This particular dinner, the last of several during their friendship, was almost a disaster. The Tynans were broke, as they so often were, and living hopelessly beyond their means. Partly to save money and partly to appear innovative they hired a new black caterer who specialized in soul food. He was so late arriving that Tynan said he was going off to the bedroom in order to kill himself. At the last minute the caterer turned up and all was well. 'It was quite a sight to see Hollywood royalty scrambling over each other's backs to get to the real royalty,' said Tynan's daughter Tracy, who was a guest that evening. 'People were literally shoving each other aside to get the Princess's attention.'

As so often, royalty had the most extraordinary effect on the least likely people. Next morning Tracy overheard her step-mother Kathleen on the phone to the previous night's guest of honour. She was as formal and deferential as any courtier. 'Yes, ma'am, I am so glad you enjoyed it, ma'am', she said. 'Thank you, ma'am.'

Another unlikely friend or acquaintance who belongs in this milieu is the author Truman Capote,[1] who even wrote a sort of *roman à clef* called *Answered Prayers*, in which he himself starred as a 'big breezy peppy broad' called Lady Coolbirth. Capote was not only as deliberately outrageous as Tynan but also flamboyantly homosexual. He obviously rather fancied himself as Lady Coolbirth and used the identity to show off his showy cast of friends and acquaintances. His biographer Gerald Clarke describes one particular chapter as a pretext for getting back at 'some of his rich friends who, for one reason or another, had offended him over the years'. The chapter was entitled 'La Côte Basque' after a restaurant of that name on East Fifty-Fifth Street in New York that Capote believed to be one of the few such places with 'established chic'. In the book 'he has transformed a table in a Manhattan restaurant into a stage on which he has placed his

---

1 Truman Capote (1924–1984). Cultish American author (*Breakfast at Tiffany's*) and socialite best known for study of real-life murder *In Cold Blood*.

own jet-set *Vanity Fair.*' One of these is Princess Margaret, who has the misfortune to be stuck with Capote's alter ego, Lady Coolbirth, at a party. Capote, naturally, has the story the other way round and maintains that it is he/Lady Coolbirth who was stuck with the Princess. 'I was about to doze off, she's such a drone,' says Lady Coolbirth.

This chapter was published in *Esquire* magazine in the seventies, understandably upsetting the many so-called friends Capote pilloried. He never finished the book, but an incomplete version was published after his death in 1984.

After the Los Angeles interlude in 1978 Margaret's recovery was further assisted by a relaxed holiday with the Glenconners in Mustique before another Independence celebration, this time in the nearby island of Dominica. This was familiar country, so much so that Margaret scribbled in an addition to her speech which said, truthfully, 'I always love coming to Dominica.'

This was an enjoyable, mildly chaotic occasion, saved from becoming out of control by the presence of the British military adviser to the Caribbean, Colonel Rodney Harms. Harms quickly judged that the actual Independence parade was in danger of becoming ludicrously unmilitary and drafted in a quartermaster sergeant from Lord Napier's old regiment, the Scots Guards. 'Without QMS Milne all might have been a shambles,' wrote Napier, adding, in a letter to Harms, 'I shudder slightly to think what might have happened had you not been there.'

A new national anthem was composed specially ('Arise! Arise! Dominicans Arise!') and Sir Louis Cool-Laitigue metamorphosed in a bat of an eye from Governor General to Interim President. He was rewarded with an official and very expensive silver salver from the Princess.

Back home the ghosts of the Tuvalu debacle were swiftly laid to rest. A woollen rug arrived as a souvenir from HMNZS *Otago* together with a relieved letter from her commander, Tony Lewis, remarking: 'Instead of a court martial I received a complimentary message from my Admiral.' Napier, in turn, thanked him for everything he and especially 'your admirable "by appointment" ship's doctor' had done to help during those 'astonishing days on your ship ... an experience that neither of us will forget in a hurry'.

The Governor General, Mr Penitala Teo,[1] had his medals specially remounted at Spinks. He had fought on the Allied side against the Japanese in World War II. 'He had quite a collection of medals,' recalled Lord Napier, 'all of which were terribly badly strung together, and his Imperial Service Order was for some strange reason stuck on its own near his right shoulder.' It was also noted that he only had a rather lowly MBE. From Fiji, the High Commissioner, Viscount Dunrossil,[2] commented drily, 'It is a pity that we do not seem to be in a position to recommend something a little grander for him.' Spinks 'court-mounted' the medals and they were returned to Tuvalu by diplomatic bag.

Finally, Tom Layng, the former colonial administrator, turned up in London. He was to receive a signed photograph of Her Royal Highness as a memento of her ill-fated visit. Lord Napier asked his boss if she might receive him in order to give him the photo in person. Her Royal Highness scrawled in the margin of Napier's note: 'No, send it to him.'

She had obviously not forgotten his draft speech nor his suggestion that she might read the 'unsuitable' verse from St Paul's Epistle to the Galatians. John Snodgrass, conceding that after so many years his memory was not perfect, remarked that he was somewhat eccentric.

Her relations with the Foreign Office were often said to be sticky and I have heard it alleged that she was so inclined to treat some ambassadorial residents as if they were private hotels that she was informally banned. One specific case in point was Italy, which she had adored since that first trip, described so graphically to her grandmother Queen Mary.

---

1 Sir Fiatau Penitala Teo (1911–1998). First Governor General of Tuvalu, serving from 1978 to 1986. He died in the Princess Margaret Hospital and was commemorated with a huge traditional feast.
2 2nd Viscount Dunrossil (1926–2000). After serving as High Commissioner to Fiji went on to Barbados and the Governorship of Bermuda before retiring to Scottish country pursuits and Lord-Lieutenancy.

Sir Alan Campbell,[1] who was British Ambassador to Italy at the end of the seventies, supplies a generous corrective.

> So far as I recall there was only one time when she was 'on duty' and that was for a fashion show and dinner in Venice when she was acting as a sort of promoter of a British firm. I thought she performed admirably and certainly the firm was very pleased. Personally I found her very agreeable, though I believe it is true that she sometimes had a sharp tongue if she was bored. However she was a thorough professional so far as royal duties were concerned. I was not myself aware of any difficulties between her and the F.O.

Part of the subtext I discern is that Princess Margaret would not have been bored by Sir Alan who, whenever I encountered him, seemed notably sharp and witty, courteous but never smarmy – just the sort of man whose company she would have enjoyed. Underneath an urbane exterior he was also quite steely. He would not have stood for any nonsense, even from a princess.

The decade ended on a controversial note when, on a private visit to raise funds for the Royal Ballet in the United States, she was alleged to have been rude about the Irish in Chicago. The main event took place in a private club called the Casino and all went well. Under the headline 'Princess Meg charmingly hobnobs with Chicagoans' one local newspaperman wrote,

> Most Casino-goers were thumbs-up for Her Royal Highness who stayed beyond midnight, enjoying champagne (a switch from earlier Scotch) and smoking cigarettes through a long black holder.
> 'How can you dislike somebody like that?' one guest said.
> In terms of image she came out far ahead of former British Prime Minister Edward Heath, star of a similar Casino affair several weeks ago.
> He picked his nose at the dinner table, offending one dinner

---

1 Sir Alan Campbell (1919–). Career diplomat and British Ambassador to Italy 1976 to 1979.

partner who said: 'In *my* house, anyone who does that goes to their room for three days.'

Her Royal Highness came unstuck, however, at a private party given by a 'society heiress' called Abra Anderson in her penthouse. The story, broken in the *Chicago Sun–Times* by a columnist called Irv Kupcinet, was that Princess Margaret had told the city's Mayor, Jane Byrne, that the Irish were 'pigs'. This was evidently in response to a remark from the Mayor that she had just returned from Lord Mountbatten's funeral in London. As Mountbatten, her brother-in-law's uncle and a senior member of the Royal Family, was assassinated by the Irish Republican Army while out boating in the sea near his Irish castle, the Princess might be forgiven a somewhat spirited response, but the loyal Napier subsequently said, 'There is no truth in the allegation whatever.' Apparently when she realized that she might have been rude the Princess said to the Mayor, 'Oh, you're Irish, aren't you?' Whereupon Ms Byrne left in a huff. Napier said that she had always been intending to leave early because she had an appointment with President Carter, who was also in town. Irv, the columnist, stuck to his guns, said he'd never had such a response to a story and insisted, 'I stand by everything I wrote. My source was impeccable.'

It seems to me much more likely that the Princess said something disobliging about the IRA in particular rather than the Irish in general. Anything is possible, of course, and in a private party, after a glass or two of Famous Grouse, reminded of Mountbatten's murder, she might well have said something tactless about the Irish. Napier was not seated at the same table so relied on his boss's word. When he asked her if what was alleged had any truth in it, she said that she would never have said anything so silly. She then smiled mischievously and said that she might have said that the Irish danced jigs. If so, the Mayor had obviously misheard her. In any event the publicity was enormous and generally hostile.

Otherwise the only consequences were minimal. Two of the Californian papers – the *Los Angeles Times* and *San Francisco Chronicle* – carried a story about increased security because of threats involving a 'high-ranking IRA assassin', but although the heightened security was entirely predictable and obvious to all, nothing actually happened beyond a feeble and poorly attended 'Friends of Ireland' demonstration at the very end of the tour. The Princess returned unscathed to the United Kingdom where, unfortunately, the alleged remark had been widely reported and the consequent implications of anti-Irish prejudice accordingly went into her file.

Even her friend Ned Ryan was worried enough to call from Dublin and express his concerns. She reassured him in typically forthright terms: 'I wouldn't have dreamed of saying that,' she assured him. As usual, however, there were plenty who believed there was no smoke without fire – especially where the Princess was concerned.

The British Ambassador to Washington, the newly appointed Sir Nicholas Henderson, who had just been plucked from an untimely retirement, was in Chicago at the time. He admired Princess Margaret and remarked, 'She has of course been deeply moved by Mountbatten's murder. It was surely very bad luck that her words were picked up and quoted. I am told that she now has to be guarded by five policemen in case some infuriated Irish-American should seek to stone her.'

It sounds to me as if the Ambassador believed that she had said what she was supposed to have said but didn't hold it against her. Whatever else, her physical courage in the circumstances was not in doubt.

SIX

THE EIGHTIES

*'As her nephews and nieces came of age
Princess Margaret was knocked off the list.'*

B y the 1980s the Princess's two children were old enough to
accompany their mother on official duties. David, born in
1961, and Sarah, born in 1964, had grown into apparently well-
balanced, sensible, loving and remarkably un-royal young adults.
Both had been educated at Bedales, a private boarding school in
Hampshire that prided itself on a mildly unconventional and
artistic outlook. David Linley's interest was furniture-making, in
which he had also been encouraged by his father, acting as his
assistant in the basement carpentry shop at Kensington Palace.
Sarah was already a keen and accomplished painter and wanted
to take up painting as a career. Neither was to become a professional royal in the same way as their mother and their cousins,
but that didn't mean that they were immune from enjoying some
of royalty's assumed perks.

In 1980, its fiftieth-anniversary year, Margaret's beloved Royal
Ballet planned a celebratory tour of North America, playing in
Toronto, New York, Boston and Washington and the Princess-
President was keen to support them. Others objected. The Foreign
and Commonwealth Office judged the political situation unduly
sensitive. Canada was riven with dissent over the 'patriation' of
the Constitution, with several provinces in a state of open revolt
against Pierre Trudeau's[1] federal Government. This was a sensitive
issue for Britain because the current Canadian Constitution was
enshrined in a series of British North America Acts so that, in

---

1 Pierre Trudeau (1919–2000). Charismatic francophone Prime Minister of
Canada, 1968–1979 and 1980–1984.

effect, important decisions relating to the Dominion still had to be taken at Westminster. Patriotic Canadians were understandably outraged by this anomaly. Tension between the French community, centred on the province of Quebec, and the rest of Canada, which was predominantly of British descent, was considerable and the situation was going through one of its cyclical bad patches. Trudeau's position as a federal prime minister of French descent and upbringing was judged by many to be ambivalent. That charismatic premier did not strike many as a natural monarchist.

It was also only a year since the assassination of Lord Mountbatten. The Foreign Office judged that if the Princess turned up in North America there would be demonstrations on behalf of Irish Republicans. The IRA had always enjoyed a large following in North America and Margaret would make an easy and attractive target.

It was also argued by those trying to raise money for the Covent Garden Opera House that the presence of Princess Margaret might harm efforts by Prince Charles, who was due to make a fundraising visit to New York shortly afterwards. The Princess's nephew was thought to be bigger box office. Besides, his arrangements were already made, whereas his aunt's were still embryonic.

In response to this opposition the Princess scribbled a note to Lord Napier saying, 'I want to go to Toronto and Washington. Ballet isn't political and I'm not going for fund-raising.' She loved ballet and she adored the company. That was it. Disingenuous, possibly; but she had a point.

In the end there was a compromise. Washington, where she was scheduled to attend the ballet's first night before spending a couple of days in Virginia with friends, was ruled out and the Concorde flight home – six seats, all in 'smoking' – was cancelled. Toronto, however, remained in place and she flew to Ontario in a Canadian Forces 707, just overlapping with her mother Queen Elizabeth, who was there the week before, mainly for horse racing. The two met briefly at the Royal York Hotel and endured a short photo opportunity.

For the first time the Princess's daughter Lady Sarah Armstrong-Jones travelled with her mother. She was seventeen and studying for her GCE A levels at Bedales. Margaret waited until the outline plan for the visit was submitted and then 'put it to her'. Sarah agreed. It was the first such occasion and a good opportunity for dipping a toe in conventional royal waters. The tour meant accompanying her mother to the ballet, to the Kid Creek Mine in the north of Ontario and to a parade and lunch put on by the Highland Fusiliers in Cambridge. She also had to go to a smart dinner at Winston's Restaurant, hosted by her mother's friend the Liberal MP John Turner,[1] where her mother sat between Turner and Conrad Black,[2] already famous in Canada but still relatively unknown in Britain. Turner was later a surprisingly unsuccessful Canadian prime minister; Black was to acquire the London *Daily* and *Sunday Telegraphs*, be awarded a controversial peerage and ultimately fall spectacularly from grace and favour to face criminal charges in a court in Chicago.

Sarah was squired to this quintessentially plutocratic dinner by Tom Heintsman, head boy of one of Canada's smartest private schools, Upper Canada College. This was the North American equivalent of a CBI dinner escorted by the President of Pop at Eton: grand but stuffy.

In addition, barbecues were arranged for her with people of her own age – mainly the sons and daughters of her mother's friends and hosts. Despite requests from Kensington Palace there was no horse-riding at the Lieutenant Governor's weekend retreat, Temple Trees on Lake Rosseau, but the weekend was relaxed and almost private except for matins to celebrate the centenary of the St James's Anglican Church at Port Carling. Several hundred people turned up to see the royal mother and daughter on this occasion. Lady Sarah also went, unaccompanied, to Niagara-on-the-Lake and to the Falls, where she stood in the bows of the

---

1 John Turner (1929–). Plutocratic Canadian Liberal politician who never fulfilled widespread expectations despite serving as short-lived Prime Minister from June to September 1984.
2 Conrad Black (1944–). Swashbuckling entrepreneur and newspaper magnate who acquired British *Telegraph* group and peerage before losing empire and facing criminal charges in North America.

famous Niagara tourist boat *Maid of the Mist*, and refused to don the usual sou'wester and waterproof mac.

It was a gruelling and public baptism of royal fire for the teenaged Bedales girl and towards the end of the visit the *Globe and Mail* commented: 'The tour is beginning to show effects on Lady Sarah. During the first three days she was bright and energetic but yesterday afternoon she appeared exhausted, especially after the mine trip.' This wasn't entirely surprising. On the night of the opera, for instance, after a long day the royal couple sat through three pieces – *Daphnis et Chloë*, *A Month in the Country* and *Gloria*. The first began at 8 p.m. and the last ended shortly before an official supper party which started, at the Royal York Hotel, at 11.30 p.m.

Sarah's presence had also caused minor challenges of protocol. Lord Napier wrote to his boss: 'Do I need to seek the Queen's formal approval that Sarah should accompany you to Canada, or is this not necessary please? This has not happened before – hence my ignorance.'

His employer replied, 'I'll ask her.'

The visit also provided some salutary examples of the sort of details that are part and parcel of royal life. 'Please', ran an early request from Canada, 'provide her foot size as the province wants to give her a pair of interesting Indian "mukluks."'

Before the ballet at Toronto's downtown O'Keefe Centre there was, as had been predicted, a pro-IRA demonstration. However, it was relatively small and subdued. Margaret studiously ignored it and earned brownie points for doing so. At other times, however, the contrast with the ever-popular and ever-effervescent Queen Elizabeth, who had preceded her on her breezy horse-racing jolly, sometimes seemed painful.

Reporting the arrival of Princess Margaret and Lady Sarah, the *Globe and Mail* commented: 'She wasted little time reviewing the troops and greeting her small reception party. She did not talk to the family members of base personnel who were allowed to view the arrival, nor did she speak to members of the guard of honour.'

On cable TV the commentary said: 'Unlike her mother, the

Queen Mum, Margaret does not go out of her way to talk to people in crowds. She'll wave but that's all.'

In the *Toronto Sun* Kathy English wrote, 'Often the controversial princess appeared sullen and downright bored.' And in the *Toronto Star* Lynda Hurst, a high-profile feature writer but not a royal regular, brought a sceptical outsider's view to bear. 'There's no joy I'm sure for royals to be trotted through aerospace plants,' she wrote, 'but I can assure them there is less joy in trying to pull a story out of it ... The discovery that a princess smokes or actually has dinner in a restaurant (just imagine!) does not clear the path to the journalism Hall of Fame! Was that boredom I saw a moment ago filming over those famous blue eyes? Am I seeing wrong in the heat or is she ignoring the crowds, not bothering to wave?'

Such irreverent questions were, obviously, painful. They did not, on the whole, get asked at home in Britain, where the press was still decently respectful if not adulatory any more. In Canada the irritation with what was perceived as royal indifference and condescension was too frequent to be empty. On the other hand there *was* pleasure and satisfaction – a royal visit was still an event and regarded as special in a country that was still broadly anglophile. The presence of a glittering tiara-ed princess in the centre of the front row at the Royal Ballet's opening night was unquestionably a boost for all present and gave the event a publicity appeal it wouldn't otherwise have enjoyed.

Fourteen years earlier she had named a fine local hospital 'The Princess Margaret'. Mystifyingly, no visit to the hospital was scheduled for her week in Ontario. She herself was upset by this and when she was told that the organizers of her tour had judged that there was no time for her to go there she suggested, plaintively, 'I might pop in before lunch the first day for a peep.'

In fact she christened the hospital's new John David Eaton Building, described as 'the most up-to-date cardiovascular unit in the world', met staff and friends and was particularly pleased to encounter Mrs Esmond Frankel, a founder and honorary 'life member' of the hospital, who had been the presiding genius on her earlier visit.

Afterwards Fred Eaton,[1] the head of one of the great philanthropic Toronto families, wrote personally to thank her for performing the task and confided: 'Personally, I will never forget the gesture you made by pausing as you were leaving to take a farewell look at the building dedicated to my father's name.'

That remark was never made public and the image that many Canadians had of the Princess was the one portrayed by the reporters from the *Globe*, *Star* and *Sun*. The press was, as so often on royal tours, treated in a perfunctory way with just one fifteen-minute session at the Royal York Hotel in which they actually had a chance to meet Princess Margaret and Lady Sarah. On many other occasions, private and not so private, they were kept at arm's length, penned into tight little corrals with no chance to ask questions or form any impression other than the remote one of any distant onlooker.

This didn't help the royal image, but the impression that the visit was a chore and a bore was neither fair nor true. There were a number of unreported Fred Eaton moments and some *were* reported. After Margaret visited a sports centre sponsored by the Variety Club, TV interviewed a disabled teenager and asked if he was impressed. He thought for a moment and then said, 'Of course I was impressed – she's a princess isn't she?'

Most of the time during the eighties, however, the Princess performed her official visits on her own except for one of the ladies-in-waiting. Her once glamorous solitude had become sad and spinsterish. Whereas her sister the Queen was so often accompanied by the morale-boosting, maligned but steadfastly loyal Duke of Edinburgh, Princess Margaret cut an increasingly lonely-looking figure. Unlike her ever-popular mother Queen Elizabeth, she often seemed uninterested and disdainful, even, as in Canada, when she had one of her loving family with her. She who, in youth, had seemed effervescent could now appear cold and haughty.

---

1 Fred Eaton (1938–). Great-grandson of Timothy Eaton, founder of Toronto-based department store, gregarious philanthropist and briefly Canadian High Commissioner to United Kingdom.

It was Jean Wills who accompanied her to Germany to see one of her regiments, the 15th/19th King's Royal Hussars. It was winter and cold. 'Went very well indeed,' said the editor of the regimental magazine, *The Tab*, 'despite the weather which was bitter.' 'Tremendously satisfactory for all of us to see that the visit was so successful,' said the Colonel. 'Like a family reunion and nothing could have been improved upon,' Lord Napier told the Commanding Officer; and, to prove it, the regimental magazine carried two whole pages of black-and-white pictures: Princess arrives by helicopter and is met by the CO; takes the salute of Guard of Honour; arrives at the Hangars to meet the Squadrons; sees equipment; views man in 'NBC dress' complete with gas mask; off to the Wives' Club; meets PT instructors; from there to the Warrant Officers' and Sergeants' Mess to meet members and wives; looks inside a Scorpion; has surveillance kit explained; kindergarten; gym, where presents volleyball awards; until 'With cheers ringing in her ears from the Regiment lining the route to her helicopter ... the Colonel says goodbye.' No pictures of lunch in the Officers' Mess but in most of the photographs the Princess, sometimes in a fur coat, sometimes something lighter but always, even in the kindergarten, in a white fur hat, is smiling radiantly. The whole visit took just two hours. Reading between the lines it sounds routine and perfunctory – a duty rather than a pleasure.

She was almost fifty now and the days when she was the same age as the dashing young officers who tripped the light fantastic in the 'Reel of the 51st Highland Division' were long gone. She was now older even than the Colonel's wife and it was said she found visiting her regiments in barracks uninspiring. Publicly, at least, all professed themselves well satisfied.

The Princess's viral pneumonia in Tuvalu had prevented her from carrying out the planned visit to the Philippines in 1978 – Anne and Colin Glenconner had gone instead; but Princess Margaret made amends in 1980. This occasion was evidently dominated by the surreal figure of Imelda Marcos, the famously shoe-loving wife of the President. Madam Marcos was a relentless hostess who fancied herself as a chanteuse and habitually travelled with as many of the Manila Symphony Orchestra as she could muster. On one occasion she burst into a private dinner of the Princess and her party, intent on giving a song recital and also taking the Princess to the airport to see a collection of shells specially assembled for her benefit and later shipped to London as an extravagant present. She also gave the Princess the distinctly Oriental-looking portrait that she so disliked and used to shake her fist at when it was hung on the wall at the Aunt Heap. It's one of the few relics to remain at the palace and was neither offered for sale at Christie's nor retained by her children.

The whole bizarre episode ended in farce when Madam Marcos came to the airport to wave the royal aeroplane goodbye. Seeing the lonely figure of her hostess standing on the tarmac, the Princess asked her private secretary to step outside and keep her company until the moment came to actually taxi away. Unfortunately the crew were not aware that Lord Napier had slipped out. Doors were closed and locked and the plane was about to move off when a panic-stricken Napier came pounding up the steps and pummelled on the aircraft door in order to be allowed in. Luckily his knocking was heeded.

Unlike her elder sister the Queen, the Princess did allow her guard to come down from time to time, revealing a self which, if not exactly 'private', was still some way removed from the iconic and apparently ruthlessly self-controlled image projected by Her Majesty. Princess Margaret even ventured into print, though the exercise was not, in many eyes, a good idea and her account of her favourite picnic, which appeared in an anthology called *The Picnic Papers* edited by the writers Susanna Johnston and Anne Tennant, was somewhat expurgated – 'mercifully', in the opinion of one acquaintance. The book appeared in 1983.

It is revealing if only for its other-worldliness and apparent lack of self-awareness. Her favourite picnic, she wrote, had taken place on a rare hot day in May 1981 in a small banqueting house overlooking the Thames at Hampton Court. 'In my opinion,' she continued, 'picnics should always be eaten up at table, sitting on a chair.' The Queen had let her take friends; Sir Oliver Millar,[1] Surveyor of the Queen's Pictures, had shown her and the friends the newly restored Mantegnas and Sir Jack Plumb, Master of Christ's College, Cambridge, had suggested the venue. She had brought her butler 'to ensure that everything would be right' and they had smoked salmon mousse 'followed by that standby of the Irish: various cold meats and beautiful and delicious salads'. Those who were still not full had then had cheese and celery. They had drunk a toast to Frederick, Prince of Wales, inspected the vine, watched some real tennis and 'wandered among the many visitors'. It doesn't sound like most people's idea of a picnic at all.

The Princess's contribution to the picnic book came up in conversation with James Lees-Milne, who had also contributed to the book. This was on 22 May 1983 at the Hollands' annual concert at Sheepridge Barn. 'Into a tent where PM, guest of the evening, was drinking whisky out of a large tumbler,' recorded Lees-Milne in his diary.

> We were presented. She, possibly distracted by meeting so many people within a small enclosed space, was not gracious and a little brash. Said to me: 'Had I known you were a contributor to the picnic book, I would not have written my piece.' How does one take this sort of remark? I smiled wryly and said, 'Oh, ma'am, but I so enjoyed yours.' 'Do you like the book?' she asked. 'I liked the jacket,' I said untruthfully. 'I hate picnics,' she said, 'but did you like the book?' – this time to A [Alvilde L-M] as much as me. That was as far as our contact went. How I hate meeting royalty. One gets absolutely nowhere.

The public image of the Princess was now becoming firmly established by pundits such as Nigel Dempster,[2] the gossip columnist of the *Daily Mail*, styled tongue-in-cheek by *Private Eye*

---

1 Sir Oliver Millar (1923–). Surveyor of the Queen's Pictures from 1972 to 1988.
2 Nigel Dempster (1942–). Suave gossip columnist on William Hickey column of *Daily Express* and for many years thereafter author/editor of eponymous column in *Daily Mail*. Retired on health grounds.

as 'the Greatest Living Englishman'. Dempster, one of several biographers of the Princess, was an acquaintance of hers and, by dint of his marriage to a daughter of the Duke of Leeds, a member of the aristocracy if only by association. He was therefore generally regarded as an expert. In a double-page spread to mark Princess Margaret's fiftieth birthday he dwelt almost exclusively on her romances and relationships, trotting out all the now-familiar names and concluding, 'Margaret remains trapped in the harsh limelight. Without ambition and brought up only to perform public duties, she is unable to answer her critics when she seeks respite from her lonely and unenviable life and faces a bleak future.

'On this day, our thoughts for the Princess should be those of compassion, not condemnation.'

On 6 November 1980 Roy Strong had noted that she invited herself to an exhibition at the Victoria and Albert Museum entitled 'Princely Magnificence'. He mused: 'It's a curious set she attracts in some ways ... Tennants, Roddy Llewellyn (his hair coiffured and behaving as a royal *manqué*) ... HRH was, as usual, straight on to the whisky and the cigarettes ... It was awful to hear HRH droning on about how wonderful Anthony Blunt was but I've endured worse evenings with her.'

On 7 April 1981 Strong recorded another glimpse of Her Royal Highness in his diary: 'There was a wonderful encounter between Marie Rambert[1] and HRH, a rare occasion when the person being presented was shorter.'

Although she generally held politicians in low regard, confiding in one friend, 'I hate them – they never listen,' Princess Margaret seemed to get on with Mrs Thatcher,[2] who was first elected Prime Minister in 1979. In view of the fact that Mrs Thatcher was supposed to be one of Her Majesty the Queen's least-liked prime ministers, this is perhaps surprising. However, Mrs Thatcher was,

1 Dame Marie Rambert (1888–1982). Founder and Director of the Ballet Rambert and influential teacher and lecturer.
2 Lady (Margaret) Thatcher (1925–). Agenda-changing Conservative leader who was first woman Prime Minister from 1979 to 1990.

apparently, the first Prime Minister ever to invite Princess Margaret to Chequers, and her robust right-wing views would have struck a chord with the Princess at least in one of her shriller moods.

In a private social sense Princess Margaret had become as contrary as she could seem in public. She felt the cold dreadfully and was so keen on cultivating open fires in her hosts' and hostesses' homes that friends would tell each other in a sort of light-hearted confidential code: 'We'll be bringing our stoker.' She also hated low lights because she liked to show off her skin which, even in middle age, was annoyingly good. Like her sister she had a near-perfect complexion.

In later life she often spent New Year with her friend and lady-in-waiting Janey Stevens. Mrs Stevens was given the use of rooms at Kensington Palace whenever she wanted in exchange for the Princess inviting herself to stay at Janey's Oxfordshire house whenever she wished. Although she visited at other times, New Year became a ritual fixed point in the Princess's calendar.

One year, after the clock had struck midnight and Angela Huth's husband, James Howard-Johnston, the darkest male present, had been dispatched outside for a lump of coal, the guests, including Margaret, linked arms for the singing of 'Auld Lang Syne'. Then the Princess fished in her handbag and produced a mobile phone – this in the days before such devices had achieved widespread popularity. Her fellow guests looked on in surprise as she dialled her mother's number and then wished her a Happy New Year on behalf of the assembled company. After a brief conversation she put down the phone, turned and smiled at her friends and said, 'Mummy asks me to wish you a Happy New Year too.'

One person who seemed to enjoy an endless licence as a sort of court jester was the ubiquitous Ned Ryan. Davina Alexander recalled one dinner when Ryan agreed to give the Princess a lift home to Kensington Palace. He was worried, however, that he was short of petrol and concerned lest he should run out. 'Never mind,' he laughed to Her Royal Highness, 'if that happens, I'll steer – you can push.' There were very few people she would have allowed to get away with such easy familiarity.

In April 1981 Princess Margaret went to Swaziland for the

sixtieth anniversary of King Sobhuza's accession. This was a little like the Tuvalu assignment in 1979. One couldn't help feeling that Princess Margaret had drawn another short straw. The occasion was not nearly grand enough for her sister the Queen. On the other hand it was a lot more fun and a lot less stuffy than some more important visits to smarter places.

Swaziland was not high on the list of important countries of the world and the British had only accorded the King the status of Paramount Chief for the first forty-six years of his reign. Britain only started regarding him as a king a year before Swazi independence. Princess Margaret was a useful emissary for occasions such as this where a royal presence was desirable but not one that was royal enough to suggest that the British were taking it quite as seriously as they might.

The royal party were to have stayed in a specially constructed village of straw huts, but this was not ready on time and the Princess and her party were lent a house by a wealthy South African. He left his faithful and extremely reliable major domo who had worked for him for ten years in charge. The welcoming letter said, 'With regard to drink there will be an ample supply of all kinds of whisky including the Famous Grouse whisky which I understand is Her Royal Highness' favourite drink.' The royal party itself brought along 144 bottles of mineral water, presumably Malvern.

The Princess was surprised to find that her room contained a double bed in the middle with an extraordinarily ornate headboard. When she asked Anne Tennant, her lady-in-waiting, to come and have a look, the two of them soon found a two-way mirror. The house and bedroom were obviously used for 'rest and recreation' of an exotic nature. South Africa had stiff laws about sexual entertainment. Swaziland, by contrast, was much more tolerant and relaxed. The King himself was reported to have fathered six hundred children and was escorted by a large number of bare-breasted local women who were somewhat ambiguously reported to be relations but were assumed by the British to be wives.

'I'm never ever going to give a medal to a man in a loincloth again,' said Princess Margaret afterwards. King Sobhuza was an enormous and jolly eighty-year-old who did not like wearing a lot of clothes. The night before she was due to present him with the Grand Cross of St Michael and St George the Princess asked him if he would be in uniform the following day. The ever-genial monarch was not much given to saying 'yes' or 'no', so he simply laughed and ignored the question.

He already had a KBE, of which he was extremely proud, and the GCMG, an even more honourable honour, had been personally approved by Her Majesty the Queen. An internal Foreign Office memorandum said of the investiture, 'I venture to suggest that it could be the crowning moment of the entire celebration of his Diamond Jubilee.'

Next morning King Sobhuza turned up wearing little more than a loincloth, a tiger-tooth necklace and a feathered headdress. There had been some concern about the headdress beforehand and Lady Anne had daringly asked the King if he would awfully mind not wearing his feathers, as they were liable to cause problems. His Majesty, true to form, simply laughed in a completely non-committal way, said nothing and turned up wearing feathers.

The Princess first of all had to slip the sash of the order over the King's head and shoulders, but she was quite unable to do so on account of the feathers. Lady Anne was sitting next to the Crown Prince and was eventually able to persuade him to step forward and remove his father's feathers. The Princess then slipped on the sash and picked up the Grand Cross, which she somehow had to attach to the regal form. The Princess was very small and the King was huge. After a little thought and with some presence of mind the Princess hung the cross on the tiger-tooth necklace and retreated. All were happy.

The official Foreign Office report confirms the more irreverent recollections of Lady Anne and Lord Napier.

Not that it was as easy as it sounds to confer the insignia of this order upon the King [reported the High Commissioner]. He was dressed in traditional costume which meant that there was only one thin round band of goat's skin running diagonally above his waist to which the badge of the order could be attached. The Princess had to be very careful indeed not to plunge it into the king's chest. Nor was it straightforward to put the sash of the order around his neck. Some 5 or 6 very long and tall feathers were embedded in his hair and Prince Gabhini, the Minister of Home Affairs, had to pluck one of these out smartly before the sash would go over his head.

It all sounds wonderfully strange. Princess Margaret said 'she would prefer anything other than look at sugar' when invited to inspect one factory and seemed to manage to avoid the pulp factory, which felled sixteen thousand trees a day. She was too unwell to sit through the second half of *The Merchant of Venice*, nor could she meet the cast afterwards. Richard E. Grant, the film star, who was growing up in Swaziland, later made a film about the country and recalled that the local theatrical company had not had enough white people to perform their production of *Camelot*, so a number of black actors had been obliged to 'whiten up' in order to avoid upsetting the Princess. 'Even so,' he said, 'she made her excuses and left in the interval. Said she wasn't feeling well, apparently.'

The Queen sent a goodwill message, signing off: 'I am, sir, My Brother Your Majesty's Good Sister, Elizabeth R', and the King described himself as 'Your Majesty's Good Brother'.

The High Commissioner was worried 'that if we are not fortunate a great deal of time will be taken up watching the Defence and Police Forces parading around the National Stadium', but in the event thousands of Swazi warriors, under the watchful eye of the Bishop of Mdzumba Hills, performed a battle dance first choreographed during the Bapedi Wars of 1879 when the Swazis had fought alongside the British. Their instructors came from Taiwan and Israel because, it was explained, 'King Sobhuza believes in sticking to his old friends.'

Perhaps the most remarkable success, however, was the rapport established between Princess Margaret and the senior African statesman present, namely Kenneth Kaunda, President of Zambia.[1]

---

1 Kenneth Kaunda (1924–). Prime Minister of Northern Rhodesia in 1964 and President of Zambia from 1964 to 1991.

The High Commissioner reported: 'When conversation lagged the President and the Princess had a private contest drawing upon their shared Presbyterian experience on who could remember most metrical psalms which they then sang together, frequently in unison!' Nor was this all. 'At one point with a twinkle in his eye he [Kaunda] began to refer to the past record of British imperialism only to find the Princess's elbows in his ribs.'

In a note to Lord Napier, Roger du Boulay[1] at the Foreign Office remarked laconically, 'Diplomacy in the proper sense of the word, takes many forms: this is the first time I have personally heard of metrical psalms as a valuable element in the diplomatic arsenal.'

As usual the Princess brought a veritable arsenal of presents. The King got a silver dish – a quaich – from Asprey's as well as a medium-sized photograph of the Princess and a larger, signed one of her sister the Queen. William, the chief of staff at the home of their South African host, got a ballpoint pen and a photo; his wife Phindile received a silver pencil. In return the King presented the Princess with fruit necklaces and bracelets. Mr Pik Botha,[2] the South African Foreign Minister, presented the Princess with flowers, sweets and thirty-two bottles of South African wine. It was agreed that Customs and Excise would provide 'the usual facilities' for the clearance of these items.

That same year the Princess appeared on *Desert Island Discs*, the famous BBC radio programme, invented by Roy Plomley.[3] One of her unexpected records was a track from a Herman's Hermits album, which she said she had heard in a traffic jam outside the Palace. Other tunes included a number by Tennessee Ernie Ford, a Welsh male-voice choir singing 'Guide Me, O Thou Great Redeemer' and the Band of the Highland Light Infantry playing 'Scotland the Brave'. Her book was *War and Peace* and

---

1 Sir Roger Houssemayne du Boulay (1922–). Career diplomat and Vice Marshal of the Diplomatic Corps from 1975 to 1982.
2 Pik Botha (1932–). South African Nationalist politician who served as Member of Parliament from 1977 to 1996.
3 Roy Plomley (?–1985). Writer and broadcaster who created *Desert Island Discs* and successfully concealed his date of birth.

her luxury item a piano. For someone who seemed so antipathetic to public orations and indeed to public performance of any kind she seemed surprisingly keen about appearing on the wireless. A few years later, in 1984, she even made a guest appearance on the long-running radio soap *The Archers*.

The conceit was that a fashion show in aid of one of her charities, the NSPCC, was being held at Grey Gables, the home of the *Archers* stalwart Jack Woolley. The actor playing Woolley, accompanied by the actress who played Caroline Grey, his long-standing girlfriend, duly presented himself at Kensington Palace along with William Smethurst, the producer. After all was set up, Smethurst retreated to a nearby room to perform all the requisite technical tasks while the actors and the guest star read their lines.

When they were finished Smethurst returned to deliver his notes. 'Perfect, ma'am', he cringed obsequiously. 'Just wonderful. I just wonder if, when we do it one more time, you might give the impression that you were, well, enjoying yourself.'

Her Royal Highness glared at him. 'Well I wouldn't be, would I?' she said.

On 20 June 1983 Princess Margaret opened an Oliver Messel exhibition and the ever-acerbic Roy Strong wrote, 'The HRH gang were there in force – Carl Toms, Derek Hart, Milton Gendel,[1] Jane Stevens etc ... There was a vast battery of photographers to get the photo they all longed for. Tony, having said that he'd just mingle with the crowd, did precisely what I thought he would. Immediately on HRH's entry he embraced her. Blaze of flashlights. In fact he's fascinated by her.'

Strong was a wonderful Margaret-watcher but, inevitably, much of the Princess's life passed unnoticed and unrecorded. One is always reading or hearing about how difficult it is for celebrities, who are constantly in the limelight and can never escape the scrutiny of the press and, in particular, the lenses of the paparazzi.

---

1 Milton Gendel (1918–). American art historian and photographer who came to Rome on Fulbright scholarship in 1949 and stayed ever since. Married Princess Margaret's friend Judy Montagu. He was godfather to the Gendels' daughter, Anna.

Even in middle age the Princess was a celebrated, recognizable figure; yet if she wanted to do normal, everyday things in an anonymous, unpretentious way it was perfectly possible.

Michael Palin,[1] the former Python, had a film out in the early eighties (1982) called *The Missionary*. He made a number of appearances in connection with its release and developed a happy working relationship with the manager of the cinema in the West End of London where it was showing. After a week or so Palin felt he had spent enough time dressed up, smiling and signing on the film's behalf. He was treating himself to a well-earned day off, mowing the grass in shirtsleeves in the garden of his North London home, when the phone went. It was the manager of the cinema telling him to drop everything, change into a suit and come quickly, quickly. Palin demurred, complaining that he'd done enough already and was taking time out.

'No, no,' explained the manager, 'Princess Margaret is in. She's watching the film and she says she'd like to meet you.'

Palin had never previously met the Princess, although she had been a favourite character for the Pythons during the show. A life-size model of the Princess had been constructed and had taken part in a number of sketches. When I spoke to him about it, Palin was vague about precisely why they had included the Princess in their sketches and suggested I contact Terry Jones[2] who would be much more likely to remember precisely why the Pythons had given the Princess a part. I should have known better. When I asked Jones if he remembered why, he replied, 'Well not really except that we had the Royal Dummy Princess Margaret shooting a tea tray with a harpoon (for some reason).'

Then, when the show had moved onstage at Drury Lane for a limited run, they had thought it would be fun to have a Royal Gala or Première. Recognizing that this was a far-fetched – indeed

1 Michael Palin (1943–). *Monty Python* writer and performer who cut his comic teeth at Oxford University and became Britain's best-loved television traveller.
2 Terry Jones (1942–). *Monty Python* writer and performer of serious historical disposition who diversified into television presentation to support this interest.

Pythonesque – idea, they had decided instead to resurrect the old Princess Margaret doll and put it in the Royal Box. There it had sat, waving and smiling before and during the show and providing a sort of surreal coda to the main performance. 'It was basically a bust of HRH with a costume hanging from it,' said Jones. The Pythons never had anything as boring as a logical reason for any of their material, but it is a mark of the Princess's profile that she was considered a suitable subject. It was also significant that she showed no signs of objecting.

That afternoon (in 1983) was Palin's first opportunity to meet the real Princess; so, cursing gently, he pulled on a suit and hurried down to the Haymarket in London's West End, arriving just in time to be greeted by his friend the manager as the house lights came on. The credits rolled and, to Palin's amazement, the diminutive figure of the Princess, attended only by a single lady-in-waiting, came tripping down the steps at the conclusion of the performance. The manager duly introduced the two and the Princess said how much she had enjoyed the film. She and Palin chatted happily together for a few moments and then the Princess left. 'I was surprised,' confessed Palin. 'I'd always assumed that if royalty wanted to watch a movie they sent out for a copy and showed it at home. But here she was, virtually on her own just like any member of the public. When she left she said she hoped we'd meet again but we never did.' Palin sounded rather wistful about it, as if he would have liked an invitation to Kensington Palace and would have accepted with alacrity. But it was never forthcoming.

On 9 May 1984 Roy Strong reported that Harold Acton[1] was looking forward to an eightieth-birthday party given by Princess Margaret. 'She had such a marvellous voice on the telephone, he said, so kind, so thoughtful, and such a bad press.' On this occasion she stayed in a hotel where she 'complained about the food the whole time. Nonetheless she was kept happy by morning visits to swimming pools. Her daughter came, so did the Weinbergs

---

1 Harold Acton (1904–1994). Aesthete, author and lover of Italy who lived in grand and beautiful circumstances near Florence.

and Norman Lonsdale, the new 'walker', who looked like a Rhodesian farmer. Everything, as usual, was arranged by Milton Gendel.' Gendel, who lived in Rome, remained a friend all her life and was her principal host on her many visits to Italy.

Her life was not always as exotic. Some time around now Matthew Parris,[1] then the Conservative Member of Parliament for West Derbyshire, reported a brief meeting in his constituency. In his memoirs he places it between a visit from Michael Brown, then MP for Brigg and Scunthorpe, who came for a wine-and-cheese evening with an exotic black man called Derek Laud and another from Edward Heath, campaigning in the 1984 European election. Parris recalls that 'Princess Margaret was nothing like as grand as Derek'. Evidently she came to open the new District Council Offices and at 10 a.m. was drinking gin and tonic while the MP was on instant coffee. Knowing that Parris was a long-distance runner, she asked him if he wore the 'strangely revealing shorts she had noticed on television'. He replied that one needed more to reveal if they were to be worth sporting. At which quip they both laughed and 'she drifted off, collecting another gin and tonic'. Later, according to Parris, she went to the north of the constituency to open some old people's sheltered bungalows, where she insulted the caterers by saying that the coronation chicken looked 'like sick'. The MP was not there at the time but repeats the story as if it were gospel.

They are a depressingly typical couple of paragraphs. In a short space of time Parris manages to convey the impression that Princess Margaret was prurient, drunk and rude. Presumably that was how she seemed to him. It seems highly unlikely that gin and tonic would have been available, even for the Queen's sister, at 10 a.m in the District Council Offices in Matlock. Besides, by the early eighties Princess Margaret had gone off gin and, when it came to alcohol, was drinking only whisky. The remark about 'sick' sounds too vulgar for someone as fastidious in her speech as Princess Margaret – besides which it seems uncharacteristic for her to say

---

1 Matthew Parris (1949–). Conservative MP from 1979 to 1986 who later became full-time author, journalist and broadcaster.

something hurtful to the cooks at a Derbyshire old people's community. She could be woundingly rude, but this doesn't sound like her sort of target. I'm more inclined to believe the query about the running shorts.

On 4 October Roy Strong accompanied her to Staffordshire. 'I did get my second honorary degree at Keele,' he recorded in his diary, 'which was nice, bestowed by Princess Margaret, who is now an old friend and who took me up to Keele and back on the royal plane which was a very funny experience. What the effect on the university was of the recipient of the degree arriving on the arm as it were of the bestower I cannot imagine. That was happy.'

Early in 1985 the Princess had a serious lung operation, gave up smoking and exchanged her Famous Grouse for Robinson's Barley Water. Five weeks later the *News of the World* published a photograph of her looking drawn and wan during convalescence on Mustique and painted a lurid picture of 'her fight to live again'. Viscount Linley was caught at Heathrow with his girlfriend Susannah Constantine and was quoted as saying breezily, 'She's on the road to recovery.' Elsewhere the IRA were apparently plotting to murder the Prime Minister, Mrs Thatcher, during a visit to the USA and Arthur Scargill[1] and his miners rejected an approach from Ian MacGregor and the National Coal Board. The exotic life of Princess Margaret battling away on her exotic island retreat was a perfect press diversion in hard times.

There was no escaping the fact that she was not in the best of health and also that, as she got older and her nephews and niece, the Queen's children, grew up and took on royal duties, Princess Margaret became a more and more peripheral figure in royal terms.

This was borne out, quite harshly, on 12 March that year (1985) when the Queen's private secretary Sir William Heseltine wrote to Lord Napier explaining that he had just received the draft letters patent from the Home Office dealing with the counsellors of

---

1 Arthur Scargill (1938–). President of National Union of Mineworkers from 1981 to 2002 and leader of famous strike.

state who would be on duty in the United Kingdom during a royal visit to Portugal later that month.

'I am reminded by this', wrote Heseltine, 'that, as a consequence of Prince Edward coming of age, Princess Margaret no longer occupies a place on the list of members of the Royal Family eligible to act as one of the Counsellors of State. I know that both my colleagues here at Buckingham Palace will be sad to register this fact since Princess Margaret has always been so very kind and helpful whenever she has acted in that capacity, and we have depended on her for so many years.'

Lord Napier wrote back formally and gracefully to say that the Princess was most grateful to Heseltine and his colleagues, but privately she was upset. Later Sir William explained:

> She loved doing those things, which she did as Counsellor of State, which she would have been doing had she been born before her sister. The Regency Act laid down the rules for Counsellors (it is tailored to each new reign, I think. Its provisions for Counsellors are also designed to cover the situation if the Sovereign is incapacitated). It says that the Counsellors are to be Prince Philip and Queen Elizabeth the Queen Mother and the four persons next in the line of succession, not disqualified by age. So, as her nephews and niece came of age Princess Margaret was knocked off the list. When the Queen was away, it was almost invariably the case that Prince Philip was too, so we were always having to look for someone to second the Queen Mother (any two could act). It was easy while Princess Margaret was on the list, but for all sorts of reasons, it was sometimes difficult to find a second Counsellor after she was made ineligible.

It seems sad and also inefficient for the Regency Act not to have been amended to allow Princess Margaret to continue in a role she enjoyed and at which she was clearly so conscientious. However, it seems not to have been contemplated.

Not for the first time one feels that the Princess was under-employed and under-appreciated. It is almost impossible to make a sensible assessment of her ability and intelligence because one's views are so clouded by the twin extremes of sycophancy and contempt that so often surrounded her. Her lack of formal education complicates the issue still further. She was a public figure in search of a role, but that role became more elusive as she grew older. She was also far too bright to be content with doing nothing or with merely going through royal motions. She was transparently bored by waving and smiling and seemed less biddable with age.

That same year she entered a *Sunday Telegraph*/BBC *Today* programme competition for mini-sagas. There were more than eighty thousand entrants. The oldest contributor was ninety and the youngest four. There was one from Wormwood Scrubs and also contributions from such established writers as Ian McEwan,[1] Martin Amis[2] and Laurie Lee.[3] In his introduction the writer, Brian Aldiss[4] began: 'Ours is a century which in trying to abolish art, spawns new art forms – from clerihews to computer games. Now here comes the mini-saga! What are mini-sagas? They are hot-rod versions of the *Odyssey*; a cross between graffiti and prose haiku; megalosaurus-sized mouthfuls, designed to tease reader and writer alike.'

Regarding the form of the mini-saga, there are three rules only. The story must be fifty words long, neither more nor less (the above introduction consists of fifty words, just to give you an idea); the title must be no more than fifteen; and a story should be conveyed, not simply a mood or anecdote.

The Princess's entry was posted, unsolicited, from Kensington Palace and was just signed HRH Princess Margaret. It suggests 'idle hands' at the same time as 'ability in the abstract' and ran as follows: 'A Happening From the Past: Sitting alone in the sun-

---

1 Ian McEwan (1948–). Author who won Booker Prize for Fiction in 1998 with his novel, *Amsterdam*.
2 Martin Amis (1949–). Controversial son of Kingsley, journalist and author whose first novel, *The Rachel Papers*, won the Somerset Maugham Prize in 1973.
3 Laurie Lee (1914–1997). Poet, author and Spanish Civil War participant who wrote slightly fanciful autobiographical *Cider with Rosie*.
4 Brian Aldiss (1925–). Critic and novelist, especially celebrated for award-winning science fiction.

warmed heather. An approaching noise of hooves and jingle on the unseen road. A feeling of presence – and they passed.

Checked, and there had been no horses anywhere near that day. Concluded it was ghosts of English or Scottish Cavalry 1745.'

The mini-saga has a ring of truth about it and sounds to me as if it was an experience drawn from life. I can only guess that something very like it happened one day somewhere in the hills above Balmoral. I am only guessing, but it sounds in character. There was a spiritual aspect to her that never occurred to distant observers.

In 1986 Princess Margaret's Oxford friend the novelist Angela Huth interviewed her for a book called *The Englishwoman's Wardrobe*. The book consisted of interviews with a dozen women mainly of a certain age, mostly upper-middle or upper-class, and stylish without being ridiculously so. They included one of the Princess's own ladies-in-waiting, Jane Stevens, who was also Marketing Director of Jacqmar; the actress Maria Aitken;[1] Lady Rothermere, known as 'Bubbles' and the estranged wife of the proprietor of the *Daily Mail*;[2] Hugh Trevor-Roper's wife and Angela Huth's step-mother, Lady Dacre;[3] the novelist Jilly Cooper;[4] Sue Lawley,[5] the broadcaster, and so on. The author tells us that they are a 'disparate group' united only in their general 'busy-ness'.

I actually think they are a remarkably homogenous group – the sort of people who are sufficiently in the public eye to need

---

1 Maria Aitken (1945–). Stylish actress and director, sister of sometime Cabinet minister and prison inmate, Jonathan.
2 Lady Rothermere, aka Bubbles (1933–1992). Former Rank starlet, Beverley Brooks, who married newspaper magnate and died of a heart attack in Nice.
3 Lady (Alexandra) Dacre (1907–1997). Younger daughter of Earl (Douglas) Haig who first married Rear-Admiral C. D. Howard-Johnston and subsequently the historian, Hugh Trevor-Roper (later Lord Dacre of Glanton).
4 Jilly Cooper (1937–). Racy journalist and then best-selling author of racy yarns.
5 Sue Lawley (1946–). Broadcaster and former presenter of *Desert Island Discs*.

to look good, who can afford to do so but, in a typically English way, are not – or were not – particularly interested in their clothes. They are all the kind of women whom a certain old-fashioned clubland hero would refer to approvingly as 'fine-looking gels'. John Betjeman would have approved. Joan Hunter Dunn would have fitted in perfectly.

'I always, always, have to be practical,' the Princess told her friend. 'I can't have skirts too tight because of getting in and out of cars and going up steps. Sleeves can't be too tight either; they must be all right for waving.' To illustrate this, the first photograph by Kenneth Griffiths shows the Princess posing in a doorway at her Kensington Palace apartment. The caption says, 'Suit in crushed velvet with a silk shirt by Sally Crewe of Sarah Spencer, who makes to order for the Princess. This is part of the Princess's collection of "working clothes", most of which consists of suits, or day dresses with long coats.'

She looks poised, royal and mildly alarming. Over the page she is more relaxed standing on the Joneses' slates in the hall of Apartment 1A with the famous Annigoni above a hall table covered with various items including a wicker basket containing a pink cyclamen. This caption reveals that Carl Toms, the theatrical designer and Snowdon's old friend, who was a significant figure in creating the Caernarvon Castle look for Prince Charles's investiture, occasionally designed something special for her. He was evidently still doing so seven years after the Snowdons' divorce. The gown, a creamy number with a bow at the breast, was 'for the ball the Queen gave at Windsor in 1985 to celebrate the clutch of twenty-first birthdays in the Royal Family'. Toms was a good designer for her because as he often worked in ballet he was used to designing clothes for small people.

Angela Huth wrote that the Princess attacked her wardrobe 'with practical zest, unfailing stamina and considerable humour'. She said that fittings were a bit like going to the dentist and she endured them twice a year: once to prepare for summer and once for winter. She could hardly ever dress solely 'for fun', she said. 'I have very few home clothes, mostly working clothes. My working clothes are like most people's best clothes. I wear last year's for some private occasions, but they're too grand for the country.'

Unlike most people she had to watch her back. She could be seen retreating as often as advancing; her clothes had to be as near crush-proof as possible; they had to photograph well; coats were good because you could take them off and still look smart while staying cool. In other words, she was always, more or less, on show and had to dress accordingly.

Some of her clothes got used over and over again. She had a peacock-blue cloak made by Sarah Spencer which she hoped would go on for ever. Other old favourites were given to the Victoria and Albert Museum, notably a pale-blue grosgrain New Look number made for her eighteenth birthday by Norman Hartnell, who also made another of her favourites, an evening dress with a huge tulle skirt adorned with butterflies. Her all-time best dress ever was her first Dior one: 'white strapless tulle and a vast satin bow at the back'. In it she could walk in any direction without falling over. It was never photographed.

In her twenties she was dressed mainly by Molyneux, Hartnell and Victor Stiebel, with a few designs by Dior and Jean Desses. Her mother also loaned her fur jackets. In the fifties she was introduced to the hairdresser René and to the milliner Simone Mirman by the Queen Mother's lady-in-waiting Lady Jean Rankin. These two did a lot to design a recognizable Princess Margaret style.

As she got older the clothes became more sedate. The old décolletage went and she was wary of becoming mutton dressed as lamb. Instead she showed off by choosing rich fabrics – velvets, satins and silks – especially for evenings. Never ever trousers and often long dresses when everyone else was in short. She liked to dress up and she was a great, rather old-fashioned, believer in the importance of 'grooming' and of accessories: make-up, hair-dos, bags, jewellery and even fingernails. As the posthumous Christie's sale demonstrated, she was particularly keen on brooches and fastidious about exactly how and where they were placed.

She never wore brown, which depressed her. She didn't like rough tweed on the one hand or frills on the other and preferred feathers to hats, though in the line of duty that wasn't always a preference she could indulge.

'I'm always conscious of what's in fashion,' she said, 'because, without following it too strictly, one must get the line right. For instance, for me, padded shoulders can't be too high. One has to adapt to what suits one. What I really enjoy is seeing how clothes are constructed: finding out how things are made and what of, and I enjoy going to dress shows. I dress for the public. I have to conform but I've *never* thought of myself as a leader of fashion.'

Instead she thought of herself as a victim of fashion writers and that this victimization was a recurring pattern for certain members of the Royal Family. It happened first, in her lifetime, with her Aunt Marina, the Duchess of Kent:

> They build one of us into a so-called leader of fashion, and then knock us down. They did it to my aunt, who was wonderfully elegant in the twenties and thirties. Then it was my turn. They tried to say I was a leader of fashion, which I hotly denied. How could I have been when I was not that smart. And now it's the Princess of Wales. In her interview with Alastair Burnet on television last year she said all the things I was saying twenty-five years ago. Clothes aren't her prime concern. They weren't mine. All the fashion writers persist in treating her as they did me, as if we were unreal figures from *Dynasty* with nothing better to think about. They criticize if the same things are worn twice, but also criticize if too much money appears to be spent on clothes. So it's hard to get it right, in their eyes.

The Huth article concentrated, of course, on just one aspect of her personality and it was also essentially uncritical. Of all her friends, Huth always seemed the most publicly loyal. Some thought that she glossed over the Princess's faults to an extent that was actually counterproductive.

A more dispassionate view came in November 1986 from another writer, Lady Selina Hastings.[1] Lady Selina, daughter of

---

1 Lady Selina Hastings (1945–). Biographer of Nancy Mitford, Evelyn Waugh, Rosamond Lehmann and (forthcoming) Somerset Maugham.

the Earl and Countess of Huntingdon, was, like Huth, a professional writer. She had worked as a journalist and written biographies of Nancy Mitford and Evelyn Waugh. She knew the Princess because she had enjoyed a relationship with Snowdon's friend the film-maker Derek Hart and she had sometimes dined at Kensington Palace when the marriage was at its most tempestuous. Lady Selina wrote a particularly shrewd and well-informed piece for the *Sunday Telegraph*, in November 1986, in which she accurately described the duality of the Princess's character and behaviour. She was particularly acute on the essential differences between Queen Elizabeth and her younger sister.

> The Queen [wrote Lady Selina] has no desire to participate in ordinary life, unlike her sister, no inclination to put on a cloak and play at being mortal. There she is up on her cloud and on her cloud, she knows very well, it is essential she remain. But Princess Margaret swoops down from the skies at the drop of a hat, and if she doesn't like what she finds, the cloak is thrown aside and mortals are expected to cower.
>
> It is not really playing the game. Royalty is something apart. What we actually see when Princess Margaret comes on to the platform is a little woman in a petal hat and a pair of peep-toe shoes; what we perceive is an almost sacred being. This is what makes it difficult. It is a well-known phenomenon that people go slightly barmy when in the presence of royalty: the slightest gesture, the most banal remark is invested with undue significance.
>
> The Queen knows this: Princess Margaret knows this – but she doesn't always choose to take it into account, having become adept at allowing left hand to do what right hand can't see.

In 1987 she visited the People's Republic of China. There was some concern in the Royal Visits Committee that this trip followed too closely behind that of her sister a few months earlier, but she was keen to go and so were both her children. In the end it was an epic family adventure, a reminder in a way of the South African visit of 1947, the only time when the little nuclear family of four had made a long journey abroad.

As so often, the details in the office correspondence are

revealing. The usual gastronomic minutiae were dutifully recorded. The Princess was now eating cream cakes for tea – but very small ones; she had no breakfast and just two courses for lunch – the others could have pudding if they wished; lapsang souchong was preferred at tea time with the cakes and perhaps equally small sandwiches. Should they bring their own tea? – an interesting variant on coals to Newcastle. There would be abundant lemons; they would bring their own lemon-barley and mineral water, but what about Famous Grouse?

Chopsticks posed problems. Lady Sarah would use them; her mother wouldn't. 'Please say firmly I can't manage them and use a knife and fork,' she scribbled in pencil, adding, 'Apparently they don't mind.' Lady Sarah didn't eat meat but liked fish and lots of fruit. She also enjoyed tea and Perrier water. Her brother ate meat and fish, enjoyed a fried egg at breakfast and drank vodka, white wine and Perrier.

There was concern over expense. On 11 January Snowdon wrote to Lord Napier in friendly terms, beginning, 'My dear Nigel' and signing himself 'Tony', to say that he thought it inadvisable for the taxpayer to be asked to stump up first-class fares for David and Sarah. Luckily there was a solution at hand because in Hong Kong the royal party would transfer to a reliable BA 146 of the Queen's Flight that would have flown out in short hops from the United Kingdom. The Snowdon children would hitch a lift.

The itinerary sounds like the best possible world tour: London, Northolt – Rome – Cairo – Bahrain – Muscat – Bombay – Calcutta – Bangkok – Hong Kong. The bill for this would, quite properly, be met from public funds and since there would be spare seats on the way out from Britain there would presumably be no objection to the presence of Viscount Linley, Lady Sarah and their friend and companion Elizabeth Vyvyan – who, once they'd met up with the Princess, could also double up as an extra lady-in-waiting.

There were hiccoughs in the planning as there always were. Some of the Princess's scribbles still sound tetchy: 'Scrub the reception if there are dinners ... Banquet? Oh dear.' And even, in response to a Foreign Office request for confirmation that she would be bringing her own decanter for use 'at all lunches and banquets', the obviously irritated rejoinder: 'Idiot! I never suggested anything of the sort!' The Chinese were persuaded to accept the Queen's Flight 146, despite what could easily have looked like a loss of face, but then insisted on putting a largish number of accompanying officials on board. This meant a complete reconfiguration of the passenger area on board the aircraft so that the passengers were reduced to 'a standard roughly between economy and club and way below anything we have ever previously considered acceptable for VIPs on a Royal Flight.'

Anouska Hempel supplied a bright-blue shot-taffeta evening skirt and jacket as well as a black-and-burgundy dress and jacket. The Foreign Office wrote: 'The Queen wore a hat for all events including sightseeing during her State Visit. But there will be no expectation on the Chinese side that Her Royal Highness will necessarily do likewise.' Li Peng[1] gave her Ching Lua cigarettes and the Embassy had 'a tactful word with the Chinese about the hardness of the beds and pillows at the Diaoyutai.'

In an early note to the Chinese Ambassador, Lord Napier said that the Princess would be interested in the following items: 1) Flowers; 2) The silk industry; 3) Ballet and other cultural matters; 4) The Terracotta Army; 5) The Great Wall.

The Princess's interests were treated with respect and the visit passed off satisfactorily. For those most concerned, it was as memorable as it sounds. For outsiders, it passed off almost completely unnoticed. Increasingly this was how it was as far as the Princess was concerned. She was being superseded by younger members of the Royal Family who were closer to her sister and the throne. Her own children had deliberately turned their backs on the traditional monarchy of which their mother had originally been such an integral part.

Margaret, in middle age, was becoming dangerously close to the status which she most affected to despise: 'minor' royalty.

---

1 Li Peng (1928–). Hardline Chinese politician who supported oppression of Tiananmen Square and was premier from 1987 to 1998.

SEVEN

THE NINETIES

———

'I was pleasantly surprised.
She couldn't have been nicer!'

I met Princess Margaret myself in the early 1990s when I was researching a biography of Prince Philip.

It was 15 November 1990 and I was 'bidden to luncheon' at Clarence House. Royalty would never do anything as prosaic as just ask you round for lunch, so I was 'bidden' and it was 'luncheon'. I had written to the Queen Mother and Princess Margaret asking if I could interview them. The reply was the invitation to lunch with the Queen Mother. A day or so later I got a letter from Lord Napier at Kensington Palace saying that Princess Margaret would be there as well.

The prospect was enthralling but also intimidating. The language seemed archaic and the Angela Huth observation about even guests as urbane and worldly-wise as Osbert Lancaster and Anne Scott-James shaking so much in anticipation of meeting royalty that the ice rattled against the sides of their gin-and-tonic glasses seemed horribly apt. 'Bidden' for 1 p.m., I arrived at two minutes to the hour and was ushered in by a uniformed footman and shown to a sort of staff common room, where there were a lot of people having drinks. I chatted to Sir Alastair Aird, the Queen Mother's Comptroller, to Sir Ralph Anstruther, her Treasurer, and to Sir Martin Gilliat. The South African Ambassador arrived. My heart sank. It was going to be a bun-fight.

Then, suddenly, the news came: 'The Queen is down.' My experience of dealing with the Royal Family is that a disconcerting number of things happen without your understanding quite what's going on or why or how, but I found myself being escorted down a long corridor by Alastair Aird, an equerry and a lady-in-waiting and then being ushered into a drawing room and introduced to the Queen Mother, Princess Margaret and a corgi. Just us.

The equerry brought me a dry sherry (it seemed the safe choice), and I found myself next to Princess Margaret and the corgi. The corgi looked at me ingratiatingly.

'I think she wants to be stroked,' said the Princess, who was smoking, left-handed, through a long black holder.

I said I'd heard about the royal corgis and wasn't sure it would be safe to stroke one. Princess Margaret laughed and said this one was perfectly safe, so I patted it nervously on the head.

I had never previously met the Princess and was at the time relatively incurious about her. Stories of smoking, drinking, possibly even drugs and one or two racy men-friends were commonplace and given credence by Fleet Street gossips such as Nigel Dempster. On this occasion, however, I was more interested in what Queen Elizabeth had to say about her son-in-law.

Like my friend Andrew Duncan twenty years before, my immediate reaction to the Princess was that she might be rather good fun. One would clearly have to have one's wits about one, but she gave the impression of being quick, sharp and mischievous. I tried to bear in mind that there was one often-forgotten truth about meeting any public person, royal or not: for the ordinary person doing the meeting the event is a once-in-a-lifetime moment, a red-letter day to be recalled for the whole of the rest of a life in often Pooterish detail. For the grandee, however, it's just another fleeting encounter in a crowded calendar.

Nevertheless I think some details of the moment are worth recalling. I also think it worth mentioning that, whereas practically all press comment about her was hostile, I enjoyed meeting her. It might be presumptuous to say that I 'liked' her.

I knew that she was soon to be guest of honour at the annual dinner of the Crime Writers' Association. As I was a member, I said something inane about it by way of trying to break more ice.

'Shall you be there?' she asked.

'Yes,' I said.

'Oh good!' she exclaimed smiling. 'So I shall have a friend!'

Overhearing this, the Queen Mother wanted to know what we

were talking about. When she realized we were both going to the Crime Writers' dinner she looked mildly envious.

'Lucky you!' she said as if she meant it. They both turned out to be keen crime readers and avid fans of P. D. James.[1]

In the event Princess Margaret intimated to the Crime Writers that she would very much like to meet Colin Dexter,[2] as she and the rest of her family were fans of his detective, Inspector Morse, and the TV series in which he was played by John Thaw. Came the day and Dexter found himself cordoned off with other VIPs behind a rope at the headquarters of the Law Society in Chancery Lane. He remembered being briefed by someone – an equerry, he presumed – and told that on first being presented to Her Royal Highness he should address her as 'Your Royal Highness' and that subsequently he should insert the word 'ma'am' as often as possible, making it rhyme with 'jam'. He and the other guests at the eight-strong top table were also advised that they should never initiate conversation but wait for the Princess to do so.

This made for a slightly stilted occasion. 'It was all very pleasant,' he recalled, 'but I wouldn't want to do it every evening.'

The Princess complimented him on Inspector Morse and said that she enjoyed the TV though she said nothing about having read the books. Gratified and emboldened, Dexter then said that he had been born just a month after the Princess and that he had always taken a great interest in everything to do with her. Because of this he was able to rejoice in the fact that the two of them shared an unusual delight in poached eggs. He had read about it.

The Princess looked at him as if he were mad. 'Poached eggs?' she said, 'I've never liked poached eggs.'

---

1 Baroness (P. D.) James (1920–). Hospital and Home Office administrator who turned to crime fiction in her thirties and has written best-selling series starring poetry-writing copper Adam Dalgliesh.

2 Colin Dexter (1930–). Teacher and Exam Board administrator who turned to crime in the seventies and produced best-selling (and successfully televised) series featuring red-Jaguar-driving Inspector Morse.

Princess Margaret was always alleged to be ill-at-ease with children, especially on public occasions such as this. The naturalness of her smile on this occasion seems to give the lie to the allegation.

Princess Margaret's love of the ballet was a lifelong passion. She was also much taken with the mesmerizing Rudolf Nureyev and his dance partner, Dame Margot Fonteyn, a couple much photographed by Lord Snowdon.

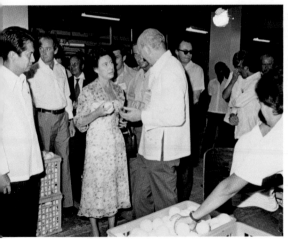

(*Top left*) It was not always easy to look properly fascinated while on duty. Here in the Philippines the Princess puts on a brave face while the enthusiastic director of a local factory talks tennis balls.

(*Top right*) There was frequent dancing of a local ethnic character as here in Tuvalu after a feast.

(*Middle*) More dancing, this time in Swaziland in 1981, where the wife of the manager of the local irrigation plant attempts to tell the Princess what is really going on. ('Mrs Clark explaining the meaning of the dance.')

(*Left*) Madam Marcos, wife of the Philippine ruler, had a similar reputation for flamboyance and occasional idiosyncrasy. Both women were said by observers to be acutely apprehensive about meeting the other.

(Top left) In 1978 the Princess succumbed to viral pneumonia before she was able to grant independence to the tiny Pacific country of Tuvalu. On the Hercules aircraft heading for hospital in Sydney, Australia, her lady-in-waiting, Davina Woodhouse (later Lady Alexander), was found to be suffering from severe insect bites. The Princess rose from her bed to minister to her.

(Top right) Lt. Col. Sir Eric Penn, Comptroller of the Royal Household and ex Grenadier Guards, lectures Professor Lord Plumb, the Cambridge historian and Master of Christ's College, Cambridge on the beach in Mustique while the Princess looks on.

(Above left) Also on Mustique the Princess combs the hair of her lady-in-waiting Lady Glenconner, wife of Colin Tennant (the island's owner) and daughter of the Earl of Leicester.

(Above right) Playing the piano and singing along was one of the Princess's favourite occupations. She liked singing everything from negro spirituals to blues but had eclectic taste and in the West Indies enjoyed nothing more than listening to Mozart on a crackly gramophone as the moon rose over the jet black sea. 'Magic' said one of her friends.

This was taken by Lady Antonia Fraser in the Marquess of Blandford's garden in 1964. The Princess is improvising a Balinese dance and flirting to camera.

The satirical magazine *Private Eye* enjoyed poking not so gentle fun at the Princess, none more so when she became involved with the much younger Roddy Llewellyn, professional gardener, amateur crooner and son of an Olympic gold-medal-winning equestrian. Here the *Eye* gives the couple front-page treatment.

The Princess disliked the famous Norman Parkinson triple portrait taken in 1980, seven years after another photographer captured the three women together at the Badminton horse trials, held annually at the home of the Duke of Beaufort, a regular refuge for all members of the family including the Princess.

This relaxed, informal picture was taken by her old friend Prue Penn when the Princess did not know she was being watched. It remains one of Lady Penn's favourite images and the way she likes to remember her.

The Princess's ashes lie along-side her parents at St George's Chapel, Windsor. The prayer around her memorial stone was personally composed by Her Royal Highness herself.

There was much 'motoring' on the Princess's first visit to her beloved Italy, chaperoned by Major Tom Harvey and his wife and subject to the unwelcome and unprecedented attentions of the paparazzi.

It was the Princess's custom to commission an annual birthday portrait. Many of the most striking were taken by Cecil Beaton, arch-rival of her future husband, Antony Armstrong-Jones, Lord Snowdon. The Princess's relationship with Beaton was not always smooth, but he took some of her most flattering photographs.

This picture was taken in May 1955 at the Guildhall when the City of London gave her a luncheon to celebrate her return from a tour of East Africa. The crowd is enormous and can be partly explained by the fact that speculation about her relationship with Group Captain Townsend was then at its height. The popular adulation was also due to her effervescent personality and stunning beauty.

Princess Margaret enjoying the proverbial joke with the poet John Betjeman, long-term partner of the Princess's lady-in-waiting, Lady Elizabeth Cavendish. It was 1958 and the Princess had just presented the poet with the Duff Cooper Memorial Prize at the house of playwright, Enid Bagnold.

Dexter sat next to his fellow crime writer Margaret Yorke[1] and remembered that she was not formally introduced to the Princess, which meant that, according to protocol, she was unable to take part in any conversation with her. Margaret Yorke said Dexter's memory was playing him false. It was true that she had not been introduced before the meal began, but this had swiftly been remedied by the Crime Writers' chairman, Catherine Aird,[2] who knew the Princess through a long association with the Girl Guides.

Margaret Yorke did some frantic eye-rolling, which Catherine Aird expertly and correctly interpreted, whereupon Margaret Yorke said, 'Your Royal Highness,' shook hands and they were off.

'We then had a wonderful time with a marvellous conversation,' the writer recalled.

> She was witty and charming. I had just been to Sweden and told her so. She thought I might not have liked this. I said I had had a lovely time, and then said, 'How's your Swedish, ma'am?' and she proceeded to count up to ten in Swedish. I said, 'How did you learn to do that?' and she said some of them (meaning the family) had just been to Sweden, and come back with this info.
>
> I probably shouldn't have asked her questions in my efforts to converse but she didn't seem to mind. Our chat was quite sparky. She drank only water throughout the meal. A full bottle of whisky was on the table in front of her and she made gestures to someone who must have been in the retinue and it was removed.
>
> She was absolutely at her best – those enormous blue eyes – but I felt very sorry for her as, before dinner, she looked like a little fairy from a Christmas tree, tiny, in her white embroidered dress, standing surrounded by deferential male writers.
>
> I was staying at the Overseas League in St James's Place and I felt like saying, 'I suppose you couldn't give me a lift, ma'am,' as

---

1 Margaret Yorke (1924–). Pseudonym of former Wren and Oxford College Librarian who turned to crime with popular crime novels without a serial character.

2 Catherine Aird (1930–). Pseudonym of Kim or Kinn McIntosh, prominent Girl Guide who has created series of crime novels featuring Inspector Sloan.

I knew she would be going that way ... and I might have a taxi problem. I did, and rather than wait for a bus in my finery – started to walk, parting from Hilary Hale [her editor at Little, Brown] at Waterloo Bridge, still hoping to pick up a taxi on the way. I ended up walking all the way back to the Overseas. An hour or two earlier I'd been sitting opposite Princess Margaret and here I was trudging home. I was laughing to myself all the way. I felt a great affection for her after that evening. She was lovely. And I had no trouble with the 'ma'ams', having been in the WRNS, where we called our officers 'ma'am'.

My Clarence House lunch was less formal and I have no recollection about having to wait to be spoken to before speaking, nor saying 'ma'am' to rhyme with 'jam'. There was a delay with the first course. This presented no problem. The Queen Mother simply said that in that case we'd better all have another drink. I stuck with the dry sherry. Hers involved gin and was pink. I guessed Dubonnet came into it as I had heard this was a favourite tipple. I suppose the Princess was on Famous Grouse.

Presently the first course was ready and we sat down at a round table. Alastair Aird, the equerry and the lady-in-waiting sat round one side. On the other I sat between the Queen Mother and Princess Margaret. The corgi sat on the carpet between me and the Queen Mother.

Sometimes in life – very occasionally – there are moments that you don't quite believe and when the only appropriate, private, response is: 'Look, Mum! It's me!' It should have been daunting beyond belief, but it wasn't. They couldn't have been friendlier, funnier, more relaxed, better at putting a nervous commoner-stranger at his ease. From time to time the Queen Mother dropped scraps of food into the corgi's appreciative mouth.

We ate oeufs en cocotte on a bed of mushrooms, a Portuguese chicken with a tomato-and-onion sauce, mashed potato and cabbage with a side salad with a blue-cheese dressing. Pudding was a chocolate mousse with some sort of brandy butter. We finished with coffee. Princess Margaret ate sparingly; her mother less so. The wine flowed. At the end of the meal cigarettes and cigars were offered but only Princess Margaret smoked.

The main point of the exercise was to talk about Prince Philip. 'So difficult talking about family,' said the Queen Mother and, although we did discuss the Duke, conversation ranged widely. We touched on animals: 'Dogs always forgive you,' she said, and then the ghastliness of animal-rights demonstrators. 'You used to wear a fur coat,' she said to Princess Margaret. 'If you did it now you'd have paint poured all over you,' said the Princess. 'Or be set on fire,' said her mother. And they both laughed. I mentioned the Queen's furrier, J. G. Links. 'What a nice man,' said the Queen Mother. 'He married a Lutyens,' said Princess Margaret.

The purpose of the lunch was to discuss the Queen's husband. 'Isn't it interesting that Prince Philip is so keen on poetry,' I said to Queen Elizabeth. She looked at me very quizzically and then leaned across to Princess Margaret and said, 'Did you know that he likes poetry? I never knew that about him. It just shows everyone's secret!' Princess Margaret didn't know either, and gave the impression that she still didn't believe it.

At one point Queen Elizabeth said that she owned the best picture of Prince Philip anyone had ever done. It was the study by Annigoni[1] for the portrait that hangs in Fishmongers' Hall. The finished work wasn't up to much but the sketch was brilliant. 'Philip and Annigoni didn't like each other,' she said. 'They presumably conversed in Annigoni's terrible fractured French. That's how he and Margaret communicated.' I was later told by Iris Peake, who was the lady-in-waiting at the time, that this was indeed how they had conversed and that Annigoni was a desperately slow worker. Miss Peake had taken a book to the sittings and kept her head buried in it.

Anyway, said Queen Elizabeth, would I like to see it? It was upstairs.

'Yes, please,' I said. And Princess Margaret, overhearing us,

---

1 Pietro Annigoni (1910–1988). Italian artist in traditional style who painted portrait of Queen Elizabeth II and her husband for the Fishmongers' Company in London as well as Princess Margaret for herself. He also painted Pope John XXIII and President John F. Kennedy.

said she had never seen it and could she come too. It seemed extraordinary that the daughter, so supposedly close to her mother and the subject of the same artist, should never have seen this sketch and even seemed to be unaware of it. Perhaps they were not as close as supposed. Or perhaps they just kept part of their lives in sealed and separate compartments.

When we had finished our meal the Queen Mother suddenly shot to her feet and ushered me and Princess Margaret outside. There was a lift and when the Queen Mother pressed the button a liveried footman fell out. Literally. It was like a moment from *Alice in Wonderland*. He must have been having a quiet doze. It was a very small lift and the three of us went up in it convulsed in giggles.

On the top floor we got out and went to look at the Annigoni sketch of Prince Philip. It is excellent but fierce. You could guess that the artist and subject didn't get on. Princess Margaret said it would make a marvellous cover picture but the Queen Mother and I looked at each other and agreed that it wouldn't really do. Too fierce and Germanic.

After we had contemplated and discussed it for a while the Queen Mother asked if I liked pictures, and when I said I did she said that rather than go back down in the lift she would show me her art collection on the walls of the staircase. So, slowly, we descended past her pictures. We paused a while at the Graham Sutherland[1] study. 'It's very good but he lost his nerve after the Winston Churchill fiasco. Someone's obviously told an awfully good joke.' 'No,' said Princess Margaret, '*you've* obviously told an awfully good joke.' I remember a Sickert.[2] And a Sisley.[3] 'I

---

1 Graham Sutherland (1903–1980). Religiously committed creator of numerous religious works including tapestry for Coventry Cathedral and portrait painter whose subjects included Somerset Maugham and a Winston Churchill destroyed on instructions of a furious Lady Churchill who much disliked it.

2 Walter Sickert (1860–1942). Eccentric English impressionist who said he preferred kitchens to drawing rooms and was championed by Canadian newspaper baron, Lord Beaverbrook, who amassed world's largest collection of his paintings.

3 Alfred Sisley (1839–1899). Impressionist artist friend of Renoir, Matisse and others who painted a series based on the small town of Argenteuil and was keen on sky.

always wanted a Sisley,' said the Queen Mother. 'I rather like it,' said Princess Margaret. 'I think it's boring,' said the Queen Mother. 'I know you do,' said Princess Margaret.

Eventually this magical tour was over and we were back at ground level.

'I'm afraid we haven't been able to help very much,' said Her Majesty, smiling, 'but if there is anything …'

'If you do think of something perhaps you could let me know.' I said.

'Oh we'll send telegrams,' she said, laughing.

At one point during the meal, after discussing P. D. James, the Princess asked if I read Colin Thubron.[1] I said I presumed she meant his travel books and she fixed me with a superior expression and said that she most certainly did not mean the travel books, she meant the novels. I had always heard these were dark and obscure. No, I said, I hadn't read them. She looked disappointed. 'Then what about Richard Holmes's newly published biography of the poet Coleridge? No, I confessed, I hadn't read that either. You must, she said, it's very good. It reminded her of a flight she had recently made by helicopter from, I think, RAF Chivenor. Suddenly the Princess had realized that they were approaching the Quantock Hills and that the village down below must be Nether Stowey, where Coleridge had once lived. She had made the pilot drop down and circle the house so that she could look. It was, to me, an extraordinary image. She seemed genuinely curious and well informed about books and yet when I mentioned this to Kenneth Rose, one of her most bookish friends, he looked pensive and then said quizzically, 'I've never really thought of Princess Margaret as someone who actually *finished* a book.'

She seemed, at the beginning of her seventh decade, to be cheerful and sprightly, and apparently unmarked by her earlier and serious lung surgery. It was by and large business as usual for her, though as with this, for me, memorable lunch the lines

1 Colin Thubron (1939–). Mildly obscure Old Etonian novelist and intrepid travel writer who roamed the Middle East and Asia in spartan circumstances and was created a Fellow of the Royal Society of Literature in 1969.

between business and pleasure sometimes seemed blurred.

When I saw her with Queen Elizabeth at Clarence House the Princess hardly ate, smoked non-stop using a long holder and drank whisky. Sure enough, those dusty files in Windsor Castle begin the 1990s with the familiar pencilled substitutions of salmon for beef, the stipulation of Famous Grouse on all occasions. 'It is noted that supper will be a buffet,' wrote a lady-in-waiting before a visit to Edinburgh. 'The Princess likes cold chicken, ham etc. Would it be possible to have some whisky available, as she does not take wine? The Princess prefers Famous Grouse with some still Highland spring water and a lump of ice.' Occasionally, there is a request for photographs – 'I'd like these six.' She liked to stick them into her album herself by hand and preferred them to be eight inches by five. The albums were specially bound at the Royal Archive in Windsor – a difficult and demanding task. Once there came a request for sustenance in the royal helicopter – 'something in chopper after'.

However, even in 1991, more than ten years before her death, Princess Margaret's health was giving cause for concern. For years she had smoked far too heavily for her health but during 1991 she cut the habit completely. Two thousand cigarettes were returned to their providers and she never lit up again. Damage, however, had already been done. There had, of course, been the earlier lung operation which seems to have been smoking related, and there were signs of incipient emphysema. She took steps slowly and paused every so often to admire the view.

She also took steps to reduce her alcohol consumption, which had always been well over the recommended safe limit. She completely cut out day-time drinking but as soon as the sun was over the yardarm she would have a glass of Famous Grouse. Once she had started, she continued and, as always, she tended to stay up late. By two o'clock in the morning she was not always coherent and a tendency to self-pity and a feeling of neglect became more pronounced. Concerns were voiced and even conveyed to the private secretary at Buckingham Palace.

The ballet loomed large – 'Nothing very interesting here ...

would Merle like a visit?' Dame Merle Park,[1] by now a valued friend, did and an outing to her Royal Ballet School in Richmond Park was duly arranged. The ballet continued to be her most apparent passion. A year or so later the American author Diane Solway was researching a biography of Rudolf Nureyev,[2] a particular favourite of the Princess and her husband, who had photographed him with strikingly successful results.

When she asked for an interview with the Princess, Diane Solway was told to present herself at Kensington Palace, where she would be given a few minutes of her valuable time. In the event, however, the minutes became hours, and Princess Margaret spoke knowledgeably and fervently about the great Russian dancer.

Thirty years after Nuryev's defection from the Kirov Ballet to Britain's own national company the Princess still spoke passionately about 'Rudi', who was so frequent a visitor to Kensington Palace that he was rumoured to be giving the Princess ballet lessons. 'He was not only free,' Solway reported the Princess as saying, 'but in *our* country and in *our* company.' There is more than a hint of a proprietorial tone in the italicized '*our*'. For the Princess, Britain and the Royal Ballet were both family businesses in a sense that they were not for the rest of us. And, three decades on, it sounds as if she was still, like many, more than a little in love with Nureyev. 'A creature from the moon,' she remembered, 'a new species of animal ... more beautiful than I can describe with his flared nostrils, huge eyes and high cheekbones.'

Later Diane Solway recalled that as the Princess voiced her appreciation of Nureyev she was looking at a photograph of him in a book that her visitor had noticed in the library. 'She was running her fingers up and down Nureyev's spine,' recalled Solway. 'It was the most sensual moment.'

---

1 Dame Merle Park (1937–). Rhodesia-born prima ballerina who retired as dancer in 1983 to become influential teacher as Director of the Royal Ballet School in Richmond Park on outskirts of London.
2 Rudolf Nureyev (1938–1993). One of the twentieth century's finest ballet dancers, defected from Kirov Ballet tour when on tour in Paris and formed famous partnership with Margot Fonteyn at London-based Royal Ballet. Promiscuously gay, he died of AIDS.

Earlier she had interviewed Snowdon several times but had assumed that he was no longer in contact with his ex-wife. She was surprised, therefore, when on one occasion he broke off their conversation to take a call from her. Afterwards he said that Solway really ought to see her. And so it was arranged.

The writer was apprehensive, particularly as she was told that the Princess didn't like Americans and insisted on being curtseyed to. She must also be addressed as 'ma'am' and not spoken to unless she spoke first. In the event Diane Solway ignored all this and they enjoyed a long and animated conversation. 'I felt she liked to be in the world,' she said, 'and I sensed that often she wasn't.' Apart from the enthusiastic talk of dance and dancers Solway remembered how proud the Princess seemed to be of the work of her son David Linley. More oddly, she was struck by the fact that even in her own house the Princess still entered her drawing room carrying a capacious handbag. It seemed such an odd thing to do.

The ballet was always a source of excitement and entertainment for the Princess, but other documents of the time illustrate the aching tedium of some of the visits the Princess – as indeed all royalty – was required to undertake. Sir Hector Laing, the boss of United Biscuits, for example, wrote to Muriel Murray-Brown, 'When we had the honour of entertaining Her Royal Highness at Dunphail in August I asked Princess Margaret if, having visited our Glasgow biscuit factory, she would like to see one of our crisp factories. She replied that she was not particularly interested in crisps but had enjoyed seeing the biscuit factory.'

After a hospital visit Lord McColl, of Guy's in London, wrote personally to say, 'It was a particular pleasure for me to meet you as my great friend Duke Hussey has often told me of your great kindness and consideration to him, always going out of your way to provide him with a chair to sit down at receptions.' Marmaduke Hussey,[1] commonly known as 'Duke' or 'Dukey', was a career

---

1 Marmaduke Hussey (1923–2006). Wounded at Anzio in World War II, after which he lost a leg; became chief executive at *Daily Mail* and then Times Newspapers before being appointed Chairman of BBC Governors from 1985 to 1996.

newspaperman who became Chairman of the BBC Governors. Having lost a leg at Anzio in World War II he was in frequent pain or discomfort. Not everyone noticed.

Harvey McGregor,[1] who liked to play the piano, though not perhaps as well as he hoped or indeed believed, was the Warden of New College and a friend. He invited the Princess to meet students in Oxford for lunch – just the sort of occasion the Princess enjoyed. She did the same at Cambridge with Jack Plumb at Christ's College. She derived pleasure from the company of the young and the bright, though observers often felt she preferred Cambridge to Oxford. 'Your presence was a delight,' wrote McGregor, after the event. 'It turned the occasion from a success into a triumph.'

The turn of phrase is felicitous; the sentiments sound obsequious but the Princess was fond of occasions such as this and if the mood seized her and everything went well she still had the ability to dazzle. A dinner at the Indian High Commissioner's had been postponed because His Excellency contracted pneumonia. The Princess was solicitous. 'Poor fellow,' she scribbled in an internal memo. 'Do send lots of sympathy and tell him to be very careful after.' This was translated, cleverly, into 'she herself suffered from pneumonia some eleven years ago ... on the Equator ... [and] knows well what an unpleasant time you will have gone through. I am asked to say ... take the greatest care ... lots of time taken in convalescence will not be wasted.'

The guest list at this intimate little dinner, agreed between Kensington Palace and the Indian High Commission, consisted of the Glenconners, the Vyvyans ('I said it best to put nothing for Brigadier Charles Vyvyan[2] unless it is just "a serving officer", said the instructions on background CVs, which are par for the course

---

1 Harvey McGregor QC (1926–). Lawyer and academic with doctorates from Harvard and Oxford Universities, wrote definitive *McGregor on Damages* and was Warden of New College, Oxford, from 1985 to 1996.
2 Major-General Charles Vyvyan (1944–). Academically inclined Winchester- and Balliol-educated Green Jacket who married one of Princess Margaret's ladies-in-waiting and ended his military career as head of British Defence in the United States.

on such occasions); also Mr and Mrs Robert Fellowes,[1] the Mexican Ambassador, Michael Caine[2] and his wife Shakira, Charles and Mrs Powell[3] (the Prime Minister's private secretary), Sir John and Lady Baring,[4] and the Swiss Ambassador – a last-minute substitute for Peter Morrison MP.[5] The Princess was asked who she would like on her right and chose Charles Powell.

After a visit to the Franz Hals exhibition at the Royal Academy, Janey Stevens wrote to the President, Roger de Grey, to say, 'The Princess loved the wonderful background colour ... I cannot wait to come back again to study in more detail and time the brilliance and bravado of the artist. What an incredible painter.'

Before a visit to the circus Annabel Whitehead wrote to say, 'You ask about the bouquet. I think it would be best if this were not to be presented by one of the clowns, or indeed an animal.' Afterwards she wrote a bread-and-butter letter that included the line, 'It is not often one can boast of seeing one's hostess hanging by her toes only minutes before handing out drinks – and all with a beaming smile.'

Later there was a problem with the ballet – 'They can't get Sadler's Wells to do *Façade* instead of *The Two Pigeons* and hope Princess Margaret will still come.' The pencilled scribble says simply, 'Oh yes!' After a visit to the Friends of the Elderly and Gentlefolk's Help Home near Haslemere the organizer wrote saying,

---

1 Lord (Robert) Fellowes (1941–). Private secretary to Queen Elizabeth II from 1990 to 1999; brother-in-law of Diana, Princess of Wales, and first cousin of Sarah, the Duchess of York.

2 Michael Caine, born Maurice Micklewhite (1933–). Film-star son of Billingsgate fish market porter who broke through with portrayal of aristocratic young officer in film *Zulu*.

3 Charles Powell (1941–). Private secretary to Prime Minister Thatcher from 1983 to 1990 and to her successor, John Major, from 1990 to 1991. Subsequently turned to lucrative world of international business. His Italian wife Carla is a celebrated hostess.

4 Sir John Baring, 7th Lord Ashburton (1928–). Scion of famous banking family who chaired the bank from 1985 to 1989.

5 Peter Morrison MP (1944–1995). Conservative MP for Chester from 1974 to 1992; protégé of Margaret Thatcher from well-established Tory family who spectacularly lost his touch and contributed to her demise.

'I do wish, Ma'am, that you could have been here on the day following to see what a wonderful effect your visit had. There was a glow in the house such as I have never before experienced. It certainly lifted everyone's spirits.' The local paper, the *Haslemere Herald*, carried a report headed: 'Warm Welcome for a Sparkling Princess'.

At the Chelsea Flower Show her party, travelling by Rolls-Royce and a small bus, consisted of the Willses, the Penns, the Llewellyns, the Lane Foxes, the Shelburnes, Drue Heinz, Lady Smith-Ryland, Lady Elizabeth Shakerley, Marigold Bridgeman and Janey Stevens.[1]

RAF Shawbury had to be told that the Princess was allergic to champagne and there was a slight disaster that caused her to write a memo to Lord Napier saying, 'Please may I put in a PLEA that the armed forces don't ever use coloured stinking smoke *ever* again under *any* circumstances. Not when I'm there anyway – it makes one cough.'

It's always educational to see how rather stroppy reactions get translated by accomplished diplomatic courtiers. As a result of his mistress's note Lord Napier wrote to the Defence Services Secretary, saying: 'I realise this may create a slight problem when troops are exercising or doing demonstrations in front of Princess Margaret, but earlier this week at Royal Air Force Shawbury quite a lot of green smoke canisters were discharged and unfortunately, at the critical moment, the wind changed and we, the spectators, were all enveloped in clouds of thick green smoke. You will, of course, I know appreciate that Her Royal Highness underwent a lung operation some years ago.'

---

[1] Many of these names will be familiar to assiduous readers of these pages and friendship apart they mustered an enviable degree of horticultural expertise. The Smith-Ryland gardens at Sherbourne Park in Warwickshire and the Earl and Countess of Shelburne's at Bowood in Wiltshire are well known public attractions; the American tinned food heiress Drue Heinz had notable gardens at her Scottish castle and her home in Italy as well as occasionally making gardening gifts to the Princess for Kensington Palace; Robin Lane Fox, quite apart from being an Oxford ancient historian and the father of the internet wunderkind, Martha of lastminute.com, is also the gardening correspondent of the *Financial Times*.

An apology and a promise were duly received by return. On another occasion Her Royal Highness remarked tartly, 'I've never read a more verbose letter. If my father had seen it he'd have told him to get on with it and give him the answer.'

Business, in other words, as usual. The archive files are, as always, a revealing yet tantalizing source of information. Because Lord Napier and the ladies-in-waiting always kept copies of their letters much of the correspondence is two-sided. The Princess, however, did not keep copies of her own invariably handwritten letters so that almost all that survives of her own writing in the official archives is scrawled notes in the margins of memoranda. So in some respects the picture that emerges from the files is incomplete. It is, however, remarkably consistent. The dry, laconic observations and corrections in the Princess's slightly loopy hand are much the same in the early nineties as they were in the late forties.

Misunderstandings frequently dog her. There was a wonderful example that first year of the 1990s at the commissioning of the Type 23 frigate HMS *Norfolk* in Plymouth on 1 June. Princess Margaret had launched her at Yarrow on the Clyde three years earlier. (Her party went west thanks to the RAF and gave a lift to the Duke and Duchess of Norfolk. 'Yes if there's room,' said the Princess when they asked. 'We mustn't leave them stranded.')

It was one of the Plymouth MPs, Alan Clark[1] of diary fame, who was the instigator of this misunderstanding. Clark was at the time Minister of State for Defence Procurement. It rained. A photograph of the Princess appeared in a local paper holding up her own umbrella with a uniformed admiral standing alongside her with his hands empty. Clark wrote a letter of stunning pomposity on behalf of his indignant constituents. Fuming away with indignation he wrote: 'I am in two minds as to whether or not to refer this complaint to the Minister of State for the Armed Services.' This was Archie Hamilton MP. The two were not close friends.

---

1 Alan Clark (1928–1999). Conservative MP, bon viveur, philanderer and historian but best known as effervescent and revealing diarist especially during his years as member of Mrs Thatcher's government.

Lord Napier passed the letter to his boss with the comment, 'I don't think I know Mr Clark! How would you like me to reply please?' The Princess replied, 'He's K. Clark's[1] son. How sweet of them to be indignant. Actually I insisted on holding it and isn't there something about people in uniform not holding umbrellas?' The minister did not receive a complaint from Alan Clark and the Princess was surely right about men in uniform not holding umbrellas. (It was almost certainly something her father the King had told her.) It could easily have become the sort of incident that would have made the Princess look ridiculous and spoiled, but it was she who defused it.

Three days later she attended the Royal Academy dinner. She obviously liked the Academy in general and Roger de Grey,[2] its president, in particular. It's fascinating trying to decode the thank-you letters. Sometimes they sound as if they are just going through the motions or even as if they are disguising a sense of disappointment such as is only overtly displayed – usually – in the press. Thus in a local paper in Berwick a few days after the dinner: 'Royal visitor disappoints the crowds'. It was bitterly cold and she didn't do as much walking about as people had hoped for. At the Academy dinner she had obviously felt more at home.

De Grey wrote, 'It was an occasion made twice as enjoyable by your enthusiasm, interest and sparkling performance through-out the evening. Everyone was delighted with you and everyone I have spoken to seemed to have had an opportunity to talk to you and enjoy your witty and pertinent observations about the arts in general.'

Occasionally one has a glimpse in the records of how and why the Princess might have felt taken for granted or even patronized. In early summer, for example, Sir Robert Fellowes, the Queen's private secretary, phoned to say that some senior Indian politicians

---

1 Sir Kenneth Clark (1903–1983). Father of Alan, Director of National Gallery, Surveyor of the King's Pictures and apparently omniscient presenter of TV series on *Civilisation*.
2 Roger de Grey (1918–1995). Elfin painter, inspiring art teacher and President of Royal Academy from 1984 to 1993.

including the Speaker of the country's House of Commons were visiting the country and wanted half an hour with a member of the Royal Family. It was deemed 'too political' for the Queen but perhaps Princess Margaret would like to meet them. Nothing too onerous. Ten minutes and a glass of orange juice would suffice. Her Royal Highness complied.

Old friends and admirers crop up. Norman St John Stevas – Lord St John of Fawsley[1] – who later told me that he found talking about his old friend too distressing to cope with, wrote as boss of the Royal Fine Arts Commission to ask the Princess to a party and dinner at the Garrick Club. 'Dearest Princess Margaret,' he began, signing off 'with love and best wishes and many blessings'. I sense Lord Napier being mildly irritated by these familiar effusions for in replying he picks Stevas up on a spelling error. 'May I perhaps mention that it is "SnowdOn" not "Snow-dEn".' Lord St John replies, 'I am afraid it was the dreaded word-processor.' In the event a good time was had by all, especially at the Garrick, though Anne Glenconner, in her bread-and-butter letter, writes that the Princess 'does hope her rather outspoken comments were taken in good part by the architects'. This makes it sound as if conversation was lively. Unfortunately not everyone took the Roy Strong line and gave back as good as they got.

Given that she had the reputation for not being much interested in food it's extraordinary how large catering looms.

For over thirty years Group Captain Townsend lay relatively low, carving out a new family life in exile in Belgium and France. One realizes how much of an exile he had become when listening to a recording he made for a BBC programme in 1978 at the time of the publication of *Time and Chance*. When he starts talking about the composer Mozart, he doesn't pronounce his name as most old boys of Haileybury would and call him 'Mowtsart' but pronounces him *à la française*: 'Msaart'. It's a small point but significant.

---

1 Norman St John-Stevas, Lord St John of Fawsley (1929–). Conservative MP for Chelmsford from 1964 to 1987, Master of Emanuel College, Cambridge, authority on Bagehot, oleaginous champion of Royal Family, and cat-lover.

Haileybury's most famous son, the Prime Minister Clement Attlee, would never have been guilty of such a linguistic solecism.

At the end of January 1992 Townsend wrote to Sir Martin Gilliat, Queen Elizabeth the Queen Mother's private secretary, to report on 'a bizarre visitor' who had called unexpectedly at his home, La Mare aux Oiseaux, just outside Paris.

> He was quite well-spoken [wrote Townsend] with a slight Welsh accent. He had practised as a solicitor, in Swansea (or was it Cardiff? I did not press for details), he told me; and his name was Philip Thomas.
>
> The purpose of his unannounced visit was to inform me that he had reason to believe that he was the son of H.R.H. Princess Margaret and that I might well be his father!
>
> I naturally told him that I could not discuss the subject of Princess Margaret on any account and the conversation, which was brief, turned to Welsh rugby. I gave him a glass of wine and sent him on his way, hoping that I shall not hear further from him.

In 1993 John Bindon died of cancer aged fifty. He was the small-time gangster and hoodlum who claimed to have had sex with Princess Margaret and to have procured cocaine for her. The rumours persisted after his death, perpetuated in print and never denied. There are still those who believe them. It's an occupational hazard of royalty.

On 26 February 1993 Philip Thomas, the self-proclaimed result of the Princess's premarital affair with the Group Captain, reappeared in Townsend's life by writing a long, somewhat rambling letter to Townsend recalling their conversation, in which the glass of unidentified wine had become three of Bordeaux. He made no reference to Welsh rugby but did refer to Townsend's learning to fly in Burma. Essentially he was asking for Townsend's help in getting the House of Windsor to answer his claims to royal blood.

Townsend's response was to write to his solicitor, Richard Sax of Rubinstein, Callingham, Polden and Gale, saying resignedly, 'It's that man again.' Townsend clearly believed Thomas to be at best 'a great bore' and at worst 'possibly dangerous'. As regards the evidence he produced concerning dates, Townsend wrote:

> Silly as this may be, I cannot resist the following observations: considering that (as he confirms) he was born in Swansea on 25 April 1956, it is not likely that P.M., whom he claims to be his mother would (as he also confirms) have made an official visit to Port Talbot on 26 April 1956.
>
> Again considering that P.M. and I last met – in the full glare of publicity – during the second half of October 1955 and that he was born six months later, it is nonsense for him to suppose that I am his father.

Sax replied that he didn't think that there was any chance of having Thomas sectioned under the Mental Health Act and that nothing done under English law would curtail Thomas's behaviour in France. Besides which, anything like that would be likely to lead to unpleasant publicity. His advice, therefore, was either to do nothing or to write a short letter asking Thomas not to try to communicate with Townsend again. The latter course was adopted and there is no evidence that he ever did.

From time to time Thomas did re-emerge still demanding DNA tests and insisting that he was the illegitimate son of Townsend and the Princess. Once, in 2005, he even appeared on daytime TV, where his claims seemed to be taken surprisingly seriously. The dates seem to speak for themselves. Townsend's only meeting with the Princess in the time preceding Thomas's birth was six months before Thomas was born, not nine. And the Princess made a well-documented official visit to Port Talbot only a day after Thomas's birth in neighbouring Swansea.

Townsend himself died in June 1995 in France. He was 81 and had stomach cancer. Before he died there was one final meeting with the Princess. It came after one of the HMS *Vanguard* reunions. Townsend and his wife Marie-Luce were staying with his old and loyal friends Eric and Prue Penn. Later Lady Penn recalled that it was a strange and mildly embarrassing meal as the Princess and Townsend talked quietly and intimately together while the other guests conversed among themselves and pretended that the effectively private conversation taking place in their midst was the most natural thing in the world. Marie-Luce tactfully made an excuse and did not attend. Afterwards, as Townsend drove away, she waved goodbye with a pocket handkerchief. Then, walking back into the apartment, the Princess turned to her private secretary and said words to the effect that he was just as she remembered him except that his hair had turned grey. At the time Townsend knew he was suffering from terminal cancer but, characteristically, shrugged it off as a temporary if tiresome ailment of little or no consequence.

Rumours of an illegitimate child failed to disappear. As late as December 2006 a man was claiming to be the son of Princess Margaret. This time his name was not Thomas but Brown and he was born a year earlier than the previous claimant – on 5 January 1955. He was an accountant from Jersey and he was prepared to submit to a DNA test, had taken his case to the High Court and was crossing swords with Farrers, the Queen's Solicitors. Buckingham Palace refused to comment on the grounds that the case was technically *sub judice*. The Palace were, for obvious reasons, obliged to take the case seriously and DNA testing would, presumably, settle the matter once and for all. I somehow sense, wearily, that the rumours will never quite dis-appear and that there will always be those who believe that the Princess, despite all the evidence to the contrary, left illegitimate children scattered about the globe. The later allegations seemed as improbable as the previous ones but, rather like the occasional claims concerning Anastasia, the 'missing' daughter of the Russian royal house, the story seemed remarkably persistent. At the time of writing it is 'unfinished business' and likely to remain so. Whatever happens, the rumours will not go away.

When Lord Snowdon more than once looked at me beadily and said, semi-rhetorically, 'I never really thought the Townsend business was all it was cracked up to be, did you?' It seemed, at the time – 2005 and 2006 – a strange question for the Princess's former husband to ask and yet it was a nice expression of the mystery that still surrounds the affair.

For a time I almost convinced myself that the implication

behind Snowdon's question was the truth. It seemed plausible to think that the Princess's love for the Group Captain was essentially an adolescent crush, begun, after all, when she was a teenager and he a married Battle of Britain hero with two sons. The Princess was obviously grief-stricken and bereft when her father died and naturally turned to the glamorous and much older Townsend for solace and comfort. However, when she realized the consequences of a permanent and legal arrangement she got cold feet and backed off, thankful, if the truth be told, that she had a cast-iron excuse for breaking off a relationship that had, as far as she was concerned, run out of steam.

I put this theory, which several people found quite convincing, to the writer Anne Edwards, who not only wrote a book called *The Two Princesses* but also had a close friendship with Townsend. In the last years of his life he was trying to complete a book about his family and Anne Edwards spent 'quite a bit of time working with Peter and interviewing him in his Paris flat'.

Ms Edwards thought I had the whole affair 'all wrong'. Like all those who knew Townsend and to whom I spoke, she thought Townsend was wonderful. She thought him 'a dear man'. She vividly recalled a moment, in Paris, when Townsend had told her that he was afraid he might carry some guilt about the Princess to his grave. The actual words he had used, according to Edwards, were: 'She believed I had betrayed her.'

Once he had said that, Townsend went to his files, pulled out a letter from the Princess and gave it to Edwards to read. It was written just before his marriage to Marie-Luce and was a response to Townsend's letter to the Princess telling her of his plans. 'It was an angry, bitter letter,' recalled Edwards, 'written in M's hand on her personal stationery. She did indeed accuse him of betraying their great love and the vow they had both made when she made her decision to remain in England (for she would have had to leave, had they married) that neither would ever marry another. She also asked him to burn all of her love letters to him. He had saved a few and quite impassioned they were (in later years he told me he had destroyed these as well as that last letter from her).'

Edwards agreed not to quote from or even to paraphrase any of the above when she wrote her book about the two princesses. She kept the promise and could not, when she was in touch with me, recall precisely what Margaret had written.

Later on, when Townsend was wondering whether he should sell his medals and give the proceeds to charity, he came to London on his own, without Marie-Luce, and he and Edwards shared a reflective lunch. Looking back, she says that Townsend never 'recovered fully from the treatment he received from the government and the Royal Family – being banished from the country he loved desperately and treated like a traitor when he had been one of Great Britain's finest war heroes and a great help to George VI'.

Edwards believes that Townsend was relieved, in the end, to escape from a situation that he came to find intolerable. She also believes that, although Townsend found happiness with his new wife and family, he behaved honourably towards Margaret, tried to help her through the crisis and convince her that what she was doing was right and for the best. She also told me that Townsend's first wife, not in the least friendly towards her, had always believed that Margaret had made all the running in the relationship and was, in effect, 'the predator'. 'Lucky escape?' remarked Andrew Duncan when he met the Group Captain in the late sixties. Townsend smiled but said nothing.

Edwards's personal opinion was that the Princess

married Tony out of pure spite towards Peter for marrying against their vow (which he had agreed to), being happy with Marie-Luce and having three children with her. She was head over heels in love with Peter – the sad thing was she was also arrogant, loved being a princess with all its perks, and perhaps even harboured the idea that she could continue to have a secret affair with him and still be able to carry on otherwise as before. Certainly she had a dismal romantic life from that time and never did find personal happiness.

It is incontestable that she never settled down with a perfect mate and her serious subsequent relationships ended miserably.

Yet would she have lived happily ever after as Mrs Peter Townsend? Most people doubt it, particularly if she had been condemned to do so in married quarters on an Air Force salary.

I am struck, as so often, by the way in which Ms Edwards, like everybody else nowadays, is so accepting of Townsend's behaviour. Tommy Lascelles's 'mad or bad' reaction to the news may have seemed insensitive to the Group Captain, as did that of the rest of the 1950s Establishment; yet the facts remain that Townsend was a serving officer in a position of trust and confidence at the Palace. He was also, when he embarked on a relationship with his boss's daughter, a married man, father of two small children and almost old enough to be his lover's father himself. Particularly given the almost unrecognizably stiff climate of those far-off times, his behaviour – above all his capacity for self-delusion – seems frankly bizarre.

Rumours of an illegitimate child, which grew stronger with the years, did the Princess's reputation no favours. Also, as she grew older, so the distant affair with Townsend seemed to acquire an increased importance until it effectively overshadowed almost everything else in the Princess's life. The older she became the more the Princess seemed to polarize opinion. On the one hand her friends and admirers, while acknowledging that she was seldom the easiest or most consistent person, were fiercely loyal. Others, usually those whose contact was relatively slight or distant, were extraordinarily venomous. In a letter – since published – of 30 April 1992 to the American writer Maya Angelou,[1] Jessica Mitford[2] revealed that her sister Nancy used to call the Princess 'the Royal Dwarf' and continued:

> I rather loathe the Royals, esp. Princess M. Many years ago, Bob [her husband] & I were at a dinner party at Edna O'Brien's

---

1 Maya Angelou (1928–). Fashionable black American writer. Prominent in Civil Rights movement, read poem at inauguration of President Bill Clinton.
2 Jessica Mitford (1917–1996). American-based writer and second youngest of fabulous Mitford sisters with uncharacteristic left-wing views and disposition. Known as 'The Queen of the Muckrakers'.

house[1] – all sorts of actors etc. at dinner. After dinner, a new crowd came, Gore Vidal[2] & followers, plus Princess M. The latter plunked herself next me on a small love-seat in the drawing room. 'How's Debo?' she asked in her silly little voice ... so I muttered 'I suppose she's all right,' edging away. Bob comes over, so I say, 'This is my husband Bob Treuhaft.' Bob: 'Typical English introduction! What's *your* name?' Princess M. comes over all royal & says 'Decca, please present your husband to me.' 'I can't think why you can't simply SAY your name,' says I. So she calls over a sort of Gold Stick character to do it right. 'May I present Mr. Treuhaft?' Such bosh ... When the princesses were little, I tried to spread a rumor in London that they'd been born with webbed feet which was why nobody had ever seen them with their shoes off; also, that Princess Lillibet (as Elizabeth was known by an adoring Brit. Public) was actually the Monster of Glamis ...

Calumnies about the physical characteristics of Queen Elizabeth and, more particularly, her younger sister are persistent and often unpleasant. The most obvious is the frequent allusion to their diminutive stature. *Private Eye* was always going on about 'the Royal Dwarf' and there is a letter from the actor Kenneth Williams,[3] dated 14 December 1975, to his friend Denis Goacher that is typical.

'While I was rehearsing at those awful rooms the BBC have at Acton,' he wrote, 'I saw Gordon Jackson [who played the butler in the popular TV series *Upstairs, Downstairs*] in the canteen. He said he had been lunching with the Queen the day before. When he congratulated Princess Margaret on Snowdon's documentary about midgets – 'The Little People' – she replied "not my cup of tea at all. Bit too near home I'm afraid" and he said "I suddenly

---

1 Edna O'Brien (1930–). Flame-haired Irish novelist and beauty, specializing in books of female angst and romantic difficulties with members of opposite sex.
2 (Eugene Luther) Gore Vidal (1925). Sardonic homosexual American novelist and aphorist domiciled mainly in Italy.
3 Kenneth Williams (1926–1988). Comic actor and diarist, best known for nasal-voiced and camp performances in twenty *Carry On* films.

realized, they're all TINY! The Queen, and Margaret, and the mum ...!'"

Some of what was written and said about the Princess was positively gruesome. In 1994, for instance, the novelist Edward St Aubyn[1] published the third of his Patrick Melrose trilogy under the title *Some Hope*. In it there is an account of a private dinner party at which Princess Margaret is a guest. (*A* guest is not entirely accurate, for on such occasions the Princess was seldom if ever just *a* guest but always *the* guest, to whom everyone else often bowed and curtseyed and generally deferred in a less obvious but nonetheless usually obsequious manner.) *The Times Literary Supplement* later wrote: 'The role of chief gargoyle is filled by Princess Margaret who is depicted as an ignorant, self-important reactionary.'

What makes this piece of writing so wounding is the fact that it is so obviously the product of first-hand observation. In fact it was one of the Princess's friends – or perhaps acquaintances – who first drew my attention to it, observing that it was the most accurate and telling description they had ever read.

We were both obviously mistaken about this for when I asked permission to quote from this remarkable passage, St Aubyn's agent told me that his author had asked him to make it clear that the Princess Margaret episode in his novel was not based on any personal or received experience. This makes it an even more extraordinary piece of writing. The friend (or acquaintance) of the Princess, who had watched her frequently over a number of years, thought the St Aubyn passage completely authentic and actually told me that if I managed to emulate the accuracy of it I would have managed something very special. And yet St Aubyn had described the Princess at dinner without any 'personal or received experience'. I remain amazed.

In the novel the Princess, who is clearly identified, remarks that politics remind her of windscreen-wipers moving as they do

---

1 Edward St Aubyn (1960–). Louche-sounding self-confessed former heroin addict and scion of ancient Cornish family, Man Booker Prize short-listed author of *Mother's Milk* in 2006.

inexorably from right to left and back again. Then she appears unable to identify the meat on her plate because it is concealed by some distasteful-looking sauce. Shades of the Princess being rude about the coronation chicken in West Derbyshire as reported by Matthew Parris.

Her host says that her guess of venison is correct, agrees that the sauce is disgusting and thinks to himself that he can remember checking with the private secretary that the Princess liked venison.

The Princess then pushes her plate to one side, picks up her cigarette lighter and says that she gets her venison from Richmond Park because at the suggestion of the Queen (not, characteristically, described as her sister) she had put herself on the list.

Worse is to come. Much worse. The French Ambassador is sitting on her right and, trying to be polite, enthuses about the venison dish and manages to flick some of it over the Princess's dress. Shades of Peter Martin/James Melville with the Famous Grouse all those years before in Kyoto.

The novelized Princess says nothing but looks peeved, puts down her cigarette and holder, takes her napkin between her fingers, presents it to the mortified Ambassador and orders him to wipe away the offending mess. And the diplomat does. He is utterly humiliated. His wife, furious, storms out but storms back. Her Royal Highness tells a ghastly patronizing story that includes a Mockney accent so contrived that only a Chinaman could have mistaken it for the real thing.

This last reminded me of a true story of the biographer Michael Holroyd, who was once sitting on the Princess's right at dinner, when she produced one or two imitations, including an Irish brogue to represent the author Edna O'Brien, who was also of the party. Holroyd dutifully laughed at the first two which he recognized but was mildly fazed by the third, which he didn't. Being polite however, he laughed dutifully and said, 'If I may say so, ma'am, I think that's your funniest yet.' It was only as he said the words that he realized this was no impersonation but the Princess speaking in her own voice.

'What happened then?' I asked.

'I seem to remember', said Holroyd, 'that she spent rather a lot of time talking to the person on her left.'

The fictional scene in St Aubyn's book is almost as gut-wrenching, concluding with some regal put-downs involving hymns and Noël Coward. Towards the end, however, the author allows himself a line that may be intended to be ironic but, for me at least, makes the authenticity even more chilling. He acknowledges the awfulness of the incident but remarks that, despite what happened, she could, if and when she put her mind to it, be one of the world's most charming women.

Edward St Aubyn felt unable to give me permission to quote from his book, which is a shame. His agent also told me that he would prefer me not to refer to it at all. In the circumstances I'm afraid I found this impossible. It is an astonishing feat of imagination and one which convinced even the most expert 'Margaret-watcher'.

Often, even in her sixties, she was not in the least monstrous but managed to charm. 'What a really nice letter,' she wrote that year after Sir William Gladstone[1] wrote to Lord Napier from his Flintshire castle. The Princess had been to an eisteddfod and particularly enjoyed some Sardinian dancers and a Ukrainian choir. 'I have never known of a visit by a member of the Royal Family which has been better fitted to the activities of such large numbers of diverse people in voluntary organisations or more widely appreciated,' wrote Gladstone. A little later Peter Purton from the Family Welfare Association thought her visit 'a wonderfully relaxed and colourful occasion and it was most warming to watch Her Royal Highness allow events to ebb and flow about her in such an informal way'. Even the anticipation of her presence produces euphoria. 'Whilst I cannot claim that there was actual dancing in the streets I can tell you that the rejoicing was great in the land when the news was noised that our Royal Patron would be with us on 23 September,' wrote the National Administrator of the Scottish Community Drama Association.

---

1 William Gladstone (1925–). Descendant of Victorian statesman, teacher and headmaster of Lancing College, Chief Scout between 1972 and 1982.

Although Princess Margaret never complained in public about being upstaged by her sister the Queen, one occasionally has glimpses of situations that might have caused resentment. Ever since the earliest days of the irritating – for her – age difference between the two sisters and the exclusion from such stimulating-sounding sessions as history tutorials with Sir Henry Marten, you can't help feeling that constantly being in her sister's shade must sometimes have become irksome.

One such occasion came at the Haberdashers' tercentenary service at St Paul's Cathedral on 7 November 1990. The Queen was notionally the Patron of the Haberdashers, whereas Princess Margaret was 'only' described as 'Citizen and Haberdasher'. Despite this the Queen seems to have had comparatively little, if anything, to do with the company during her reign, whereas Princess Margaret adopted them as one of her inner core of favourites. As Lord Napier remarked to Captain Barrow RN, Clerk of the Haberdashers, 'I am sure you know how greatly Princess Margaret enjoys visiting the schools.'

She was a very keen and conscientious Haberdasher. Nevertheless, because the 300th birthday was an important anniversary, the company wanted to invite their patron. Captain Barrow wrote to Muriel Murray-Brown saying they want to ask the Queen and Prince Philip to the service. Miss Murray-Brown passed the note to Princess Margaret and the Princess scrawled a sad little message in pencil in the margin. 'Please dissuade them!' she wrote.

This was another of those occasions when diplomacy and implicit understandings came into play. Lord Napier wrote to his counterpart at Buckingham Palace, Sir Robert Fellowes, and said, 'Her Royal Highness has asked me to say to you that she hopes that Her Majesty and His Royal Highness will not feel that there is a particular necessity to accept this invitation.'

The letter was shown to Her Majesty and Princess Margaret was assured that in the event of her being asked to the service Her Majesty would feel under no obligation to accept. Fellowes concluded: 'It was kind of you to let us know about this in advance in case they make an early approach.' So, aptly, Princess Margaret kept the Haberdashers to herself. It was a tricky situation, for many Haberdashers would have liked to be honoured by the presence of their Patron, the monarch. Yet it would have seemed desperately unfair for Princess Margaret to soldier on dutifully nurturing a meaningful relationship only to be usurped on the one occasion when it mattered most.

Time and again I catch a whiff of this sense of being taken for granted and of being a permanent stand-in or runner-up. She was always only the younger sister and sometimes an outsider. One can't help feeling that the Princess's quite natural feelings of being a permanent substitute are sometimes exacerbated rather than soothed.

On 27 November, for example, the Queen gave a party for foreign parliamentarians at Buckingham Palace. This was something she did every three years. This time Robert Fellowes phoned to say that Prince Philip was going to be away and 'Her Majesty wondered if Your Royal Highness could help'.

'Delighted,' scribbled the Princess, and she dutifully filled in for her brother-in-law. She would have been only human if she had not been entirely delighted, but she was a royal princess, and there was a code to observe. Whatever her private feelings might have been she was always scrupulously loyal to her sister the Queen, and to the whole concept of monarchy.

Not that she always did what other royals wanted. In November 1992 Prince Charles wrote her a 'Dear Margot' letter asking her, as a fellow royal colonel of regiments, to make her 'position clear' to the Defence Secretary Malcolm Rifkind[1] on the question of yet more defence cuts. Princess Margaret wasn't happy with the idea even though she couldn't quite put her finger on precisely why. 'I have a niggling feeling I don't want to write to him,' she confided to Lord Napier. 'So I won't.'

There are moments of course when the public events in which Princess Margaret was involved seem frivolous and irrelevant or at best enjoyable icing on a cake that involved other people's work

---

1 Malcolm Rifkind (1946–). Edinburgh lawyer and Conservative Cabinet minister, failed leadership candidate and MP for ultimate safe seat of Kensington and Chelsea in early 2000s.

rather than her own. From time to time, however, one glimpses something altogether more serious, unexpected and comparatively unknown. Other members of the Royal Family have sometimes made a considerable commotion when they have championed difficult or unfashionable causes but, despite what her critics sometimes thought, that was not Princess Margaret's style.

'I am keenly aware of the stigma and prejudice which still surrounds the subject and I am most grateful to Her Royal Highness for her support in this controversial area.' That was Margaret Jay, daughter of the sometime Labour Prime Minister James Callaghan, Leader of the House of Lords in a Labour cabinet and not the most likely Princess fan in the world. And she was writing as a member of the Council of London Lighthouse to express her gratitude to the Princess for 'the great interest which Her Royal Highness the Princess Margaret has taken in AIDS issues'. Subsequently Lady Jay told me, in an email, that her encounters with the Princess had been quite fleeting. 'I only came across her in passing at functions of the London Lighthouse, where I was on the council at the time,' she said. But she *did* come across her and she *did* write to say thank you.

Alongside this new and unfashionable concern there is continuing evidence of her enthusiasm and value for the organizations that meant most to her. After a lifetime of mutual support the Royal Ballet was the most significant of these. On 7 December that year she named the Margot Fonteyn Theatre at the Royal Ballet School at White Lodge in Richmond Park. Dame Margot, whom Princess Margaret had long admired, was too ill to attend. Afterwards the Chairman of the Royal Ballet's Board of Governors told her, 'I think the atmosphere on the day said it all. Your involvement with the Royal Ballet School and your visits to White Lodge mean so much to both students and staff. Your interest is of real encouragement to them all.'

In October 1993 her son, David Linley, married Serena Stanhope, only daughter of Viscount Petersham,[1] who had made a

---

1 Viscount Petersham (1945–). Property magnate, listed prominently in *Sunday Times* 'rich-list', and father-in-law of Princess Margaret's son, Viscount Linley.

fortune out of property. The following year – 1994 – her daughter Sarah married Daniel Chatto and a significant bonus was that the Princess thus acquired a new friend in her new son-in-law's mother, the theatrical agent Ros Chatto. 'I fell for her completely and immediately,' said Mrs Chatto:

> She was so nice and we had the theatre in common. She was extraordinarily well informed on everything to do with theatre. We went often and I never knew her to be wrong. She was sharp and clever and tremendously keen on asking questions. She liked to sit in the front row of the circle – not the royal box. And afterwards she would like to meet the cast. She loved it and they enjoyed it too. Sometimes we'd have dinner afterwards with some of the actors and she talked about plays and authors that interested her. She read reviews and was just tremendously enthusiastic and knowledgeable. We never had a dull moment.

There still seems a faint air of surprise in Ros Chatto's enthusiasm. The Princess generally suffered such a hostile press that relaxed, friendly, well-prepared performances often took people by surprise. On 30 June 1994, for instance, she opened the Antiquarian Book Fair, an event fostered by her lady-in-waiting Juliet Townsend, whose husband was himself an antiquarian bookseller. The chairman of the fair that year was an antiquarian bookseller from York called Peter Miller. Oddly enough, Miller's father Graham had once been a *New York Daily News* correspondent who had lost his job because he refused to write stories about the Princess and Peter Townsend, which he regarded as 'unpatriotic'. Perhaps partly because of this but also because of the Princess's generally unflattering reputation, Graham's son Peter was dreading the day.

'I was pleasantly surprised,' he recalled years later. 'She couldn't have been nicer and I really enjoyed the occasion quite a lot.'

The association had sent the Princess a catalogue and she, characteristically, though the organizers were not to know this, had annotated it so that when she arrived she knew exactly what she wanted to see. Miller had been dreading a sticky event, having to explain everything from scratch and being met with royal ennui.

Far from it. 'She was very well prepared,' he said, 'I remember that she particularly liked the P. G. Wodehouse and she was also very interested in the manuscript of Edward Lear's *Book of Nonsense*. She knew several of the pieces by heart and she was able to see where the manuscript version differed from the printed one.' The only bad moment was when some Italians broke through the semi-official cordon and presented her with a vast leather-bound volume 'for the royal library'. This was bad, but not as bad as one of the Italians attempting to kiss the royal hand. Miller remembered that this caused a particular frisson. 'She sprang back,' he said. The royal hand remained resolutely unkissed.

'Afterwards we had a little drink,' he said. 'She was jolly and she was intelligent and it was nice.' They had presented the Princess with a specially bound copy of an Edith Wharton book *Gardens Old and New*, in which the Princess expressed an interest slightly more distant and unconvincing than she had displayed for Wodehouse and Lear. Miller then took her down to her car and, as she drove away, the Princess gave him 'a really nice smile and a little wave'. He felt that everyone had enjoyed themselves; he was impressed; and, against his expectations, he liked her.

Early that year – 1994 – the Princess suffered a stroke. The first evidence of this in the office papers came in a letter that March from Lord Napier to Brigadier Jane Arigho[1] of Queen Alexandra's Royal Army Nursing Corps. 'All the Princess's official engagements have, of course, been cancelled for the time being following Her Royal Highness's recent stroke ... I am pleased to say that Princess Margaret is making good and steady progress in her recovery.'

Public comments continued to be disconcertingly hostile even in quarters where you would expect a level of politeness if not deference. In the *Daily Telegraph* in 1996, for instance, the Peterborough column wrote a distinctly gleeful little story about how the Princess, during a visit to Cheshire to see her old friends

---

1 Brigadier Jane Arigho. Became Matron-in-Chief Queen Alexandra's Royal Army Nursing Corps in November 2005.

the Sebastian de Ferrantis,[1] had mistaken a weed-covered pond for lawn and literally put her foot in it. A pained Lord Napier wrote to the editor of the *Telegraph*, Charles Moore,[2] to complain that there was 'not a word of truth in it'. In fact she had never even entered the garden in question. Moore made enquiries and discovered that indeed Napier was right and his paper had been mistaken. In his letter of apology the editor added, 'I regret the tone. A story such as this should be written amiably if at all.' Later he told me that at the time all concerned at the *Telegraph* were sure it must be true as it came from a reliable source and the facts of the Princess's visit to Cheshire seemed to corroborate it. Perhaps it is prissy to note that the Peterborough column never checked with Lord Napier and no correction ever appeared in the paper. When Napier showed the apology to his boss, she was jubilant if sardonic. 'Keep it!' she scribbled. 'It must be unique.'

Despite her occasional legendary hauteur she loved staying with friends such as Roddy and Tania Llewellyn, the Penns, the Huths or Anne Glenconner who had relatively normal houses and none of the live-in staff of royal palaces or grand stately homes. She liked washing up. If something were spilt she always had a clever remedy of a Mrs Beeton/Women's Institute nature. She was full of unexpected tips such as how to ensure perfect scrambled eggs by adding a raw egg at the final moment of cooking. Above all, she hated undue formality on such weekends. She liked everyone to be relaxed and 'normal'. Her absolute hatred was the hostess who would suddenly say that they had friends coming in for drinks or a meal. She would feel, usually correctly, that she was being exploited and 'shown off'. She would protest that she was not 'on duty' and she would sometimes, under these circumstances, behave badly. Unlike some public figures, even royal ones, she liked, on occasions, to switch off, to lounge about, be casual and behave, as far as she

---

1 Sebastian de Ferranti (1927–). Millionaire socialite boss of hi-tech companies with desirable residence in Cheshire.

2 Charles Moore (1956–). Patrician Conservative journalist who edited the *Spectator*, the *Sunday* and *Daily Telegraph*s between 1984 and 2003 when he resigned to freelance and work on his official biography of Mrs Thatcher while affecting a Trollopian regard for fox-hunting and old rectories.

could see, like everyone else. Kitchen meals and intelligent small-talk were sometimes what she craved more than anything.

On 9 July 1998 Lord Napier finally stood down. He had done the job for a quarter of a century and Princess Margaret was reluctant to accept his going. She insisted that his successor should be a peer. Hence Viscount Ullswater,[1] aka, depending on your disposition, 'Nicky' or 'Dullswater'. Ullswater was a former whip in the House of Lords but by the time he arrived the Princess was unwell and reluctant to accept change. She was not happy about a new man in her life, even if only as her private secretary

On reflection and with the benefit of hindsight Napier would not have retired when he did. He and the Princess had grown comfortable with each other, used to each other's ways, accepting of eccentricities and foibles, and mutually trusted. It was not Ullswater's fault that he was never fully accepted. 'Her confidence had been knocked for six,' said Ullswater. 'Her loss of confidence made things extremely difficult.'

For two months he stood in alongside Napier in order to learn the ropes, but they weren't the old familiar ropes. This was new, unfamiliar territory and precisely the wrong time for such a crucial change. No matter how diplomatic, charming and adroit Lord Ullswater might be, he was never able to win his mistress's confidence in her newly vulnerable state. As she had done in the past when faced with adversity, she turned her face to the wall. She simply wouldn't allow any of her male friends to come and see her and she restricted female visitors to close friends such as Ros Chatto, Pru Penn and her trusted ladies-in-waiting.

She simply wasn't sure about the wretched Lord Ullswater. During the handover period, for instance, Lord Napier arranged for two officers of her Royal Anglian Regiment to come in to mark the transfer of command from one to the other. 'When you receive the two officers tomorrow at 12.30 may I bring Nick with me please, so that he may see how it is done?'

---

1 Viscount Ullswater (1942–). Conservative peer who succeeded Lord Napier and Ettrick as Princess Margaret's private secretary and was still en poste at her death in 2001.

'Yes,' she replied, 'as long as he talks too.'

This sounds unpromising and there is sometimes a note of tetchiness in exchanges between the new private secretary and Her Royal Highness that was not in evidence before. He was naturally solicitous because, as he explained to one of her hosts, 'Her Royal Highness is making good progress but is still convalescing'. She, on the other hand, sometimes insisted on being treated as before. Once, for instance, the new private secretary arranged for the normal pre-lunch drinks to be dispensed with in favour of something more sedentary. The Princess objected. He replied, 'The idea of seated drinks before lunch was for Your Royal Highness's comfort. However, I have informed them that you would prefer to undertake this standing up.'

Her reply sounds far less patient than the average response to Ullswater's predecessor. 'Otherwise how could one circulate?' she asked petulantly.

'She was still very keen on the ballet,' said Ullswater, 'but she couldn't go out much. The NSPCC liked her to take their council meetings so I would go along to represent her.'

The team remained otherwise unchanged. Ullswater looked after what he calls 'the public side' and he relied on Annabel Whitehead to supervise 'the private side'. For a while it seemed that she was recovering. Plans were made for foreign visits and public engagements and before very long she seemed almost restored to her former self.

'Madam,' wrote Lord Hartington,[1] heir to the Duke of Devonshire, 'It was wonderful to see you at the Sotheby's summer party fully returned to health and stickless to boot.' He went on to ask her to present the trophy after the Queen Elizabeth II stakes at Ascot and promised: 'I can absolutely guarantee a box full of cheery souls and a good lunch.' This seems to have been achieved. At her own request her Tipperary property-dealing friend Ned Ryan was of the party. A good time seems to have

---

1 12th Duke of Devonshire (formerly Marquess of Hartington) (1945–). Hereditary landowner and pillar of horse-racing establishment who was Senior Steward of Jockey Club from 1989 to 1994.

been had by all though Lord Hartington, who by 2006 had become the Duke of Devonshire, forbore to comment.

There was now a cautious optimism and she even went to Mustique. There, however, disaster struck. 'That bloody foot,' said one of her friends.

The scalding of her feet remains something of a mystery for the simple reason that it was completely unwitnessed. The only person present was the Princess herself and she was too shocked and confused to give a coherent account of what happened. More to the point, she was too shocked and confused to know.

As far as everyone else was concerned, the events were dreadfully straightforward. It happened in February 1999 at the beginning of the usual long holiday on Mustique. The rest of the house party at Les Jolies Eaux were enjoying a lethargic breakfast and wondering what they were going to do on another languid day on the island paradise when an agitated cook came into the room to say that there was steam coming out from under the locked bathroom door and she was afraid the Princess was inside. The Princess's personal detective broke down the door, finding her distressed and badly scalded. He carried her out.

The problem seems to have been caused by the controls to the water supply, which were old, unnecessarily complicated and should have been changed. 'In some ways she was very old-fashioned,' said Annabel Whitehead, who was lady-in-waiting at the time and present when the accident happened. The controls consisted of concentric rings which regulated temperature and water supply as well as determining whether the bath taps or the overhead shower were being used. The Princess's intention seems to have been to use the shower to wash her hair, so she got into the bath and turned on the controls. Tragically she got it wrong and instead of a lukewarm shower she got jets of boiling water from the bath taps directed straight at her feet. She was too shocked to move until she was rescued. The effects of the hot water would have been horrific anyway but they were exacerbated by the fact that the Princess had for years suffered from Raynaud's disease, itself probably brought on by years of heavy smoking. This affects circulation to the body's extremities and would have made her feet particularly vulnerable to burns such as these.

The Princess's own stubbornness and famous hauteur now contributed to the severity of her illness. No one present had the strength or authority to override her basic decision, which was that there was nothing seriously wrong with her, that she didn't need to return to the United Kingdom. It was accepted that the local Mustique general practitioner, Doctor Bunbury, was perfectly capable of looking after her. It was not until weeks later, after she had had to move out of Les Jolies Eaux to a friend's house because her son, David, had let the house to tenants and didn't feel able to put them off, that Anne Glenconner phoned Her Majesty the Queen at Balmoral.

As a result Concorde was scrambled and the Princess flew home, but she was far from well. She really should have had skin grafts but she absolutely refused such drastic treatment and, not for the first time, both metaphorically and literally, turned her face to the wall. She spent a long time convalescing at Balmoral and after she moved back south Lord Ullswater wrote to Doctor Douglas Glass, who tended to her in Scotland, 'All of us would wish to thank you and your nurses for your untiring support and attention to the Princess while she was at Balmoral over the last month or more.'

Gradually and up to a point she recovered. The Corrieneuchin Project, a scheme for helping sexually abused children in Aberdeen, asked her to open the project for them and she replied to Lord Ullswater, 'I'll go as soon as possible, as I started the whole idea and promised to do it.' She went on 28 September. The *Aberdeen Press and Journal* reported that it was her first public engagement since the accident. Later she managed a reception for the Pottery and Glass Traders' Benevolent Institution at the Savoy but was only happy when she realized it was on the ground floor and only one or two steps had to be negotiated.

As Colonel-in-Chief she was guest of honour at a party given by the Royal Highland Fusiliers, who were 'thrilled' and 'delighted to see how well she looked'. She needed to fly to an engagement of the Royal Society for the Prevention of Cruelty to Children and Lord Ullswater wrote asking for a special aircraft on the grounds that 'Princess Margaret suffered injuries to her feet earlier in the year which have not entirely healed. With reduced mobility travelling by commercial flights would be unsuitable.'

Although she managed a reduced programme of engagements, she never regained full mobility and remained in pain. She had become a permanent invalid, a shadow of the vibrant, sparky woman who had embarked on the decade with such apparent optimism.

EIGHT

THE END

'I regret the tone ...'

B y the time the twenty-first century began it was widely reported that the Princess had lost the will to live. The burns to her legs were not healing. To start with she seemed optimistic and even saw a specialist from the Priory, the fashionable London clinic, at the suggestion of her daughter Sarah, and an Indian-born holistic healer and nutritionist suggested by Prince Charles, who had consulted him himself. Whether or not it was as the result of the ministrations of these two or just a return of her former *joie de vivre*, in mid-March she managed dinner at the fashionable Caprice in Mayfair with Ned Ryan and her cousin Elizabeth Shakerley,[1] sister of Lord Lichfield, the photographer. Later, in a TV interview with Sir David Frost,[2] Shakerley recalled the occasion, with the Princess in 'fantastic form' and looking radiant in a red-and-gold jacket. She said it was how she would like him to remember her.

Soon afterwards the Princess enjoyed Kensington Palace meals with her sister, and her mother, separately. Then, however, she suffered a second stroke on 27 March and another minor one at Windsor Castle on Easter Monday. The second was diagnosed as a ministroke, or transient ischaemic attack, but it came disturbingly soon after the earlier full stroke. Recovery was

---

1 Lady Elizabeth Shakerley (née Anson) (1941–). Founder of event organisers, 'Party Planners', sister of royal lensman Lord (Patrick) Lichfield and 'minor' royal.

2 Sir David Frost (1939–). Lifelong broadcaster who cleverly metamorphosed from angry young star of *That Was the Week That Was* to avuncular friend of famous.

slow. The sight in one eye had gone and she had virtually lost all movement on her left side. She was only able to move around in a wheelchair and for a while at least could neither read nor write.

At least one old friend, Angela Huth the novelist, who, with her husband the Oxford don James Howard-Johnston, stepson of Lord Dacre aka Professor Hugh Trevor-Roper, had often entertained the Princess, seemed almost to be jumping the gun by writing a premature obituary for the *Daily Telegraph*. Many friends of the Princess thought her tribute fulsome. In their judgement the Princess was not well served by the suggestion that she was a paragon of virtue. She was much more complicated than that. Huth's piece, which appeared on 19 January 2001, was headed, 'Royal who sought culture in her companions', and it began with the always provocative claim that the author was 'one of the Princess's closest friends'.

She began by drawing attention to the Princess's undeniable talent for friendship coupled with what Huth described as 'an innate wisdom'. She explained that her advice 'is sometimes brusque, often funny and almost always apt. Her disapproval of something is blunt, which gives weight to her approval.' This sounds perilously close to euphemistic obituary double-speak. It has the same subtext as: 'She never suffered fools gladly', or 'She was never afraid to speak her mind', both of which translate into real-life 'On occasions she could be very rude.'

Huth had originally met the Princess forty years earlier when married to Quentin Crewe, restaurateur, bon viveur and friend of Lord Snowdon. They had been to the ballet with the Snowdons and later asked round for what sounds like a merry meal at Kensington Palace. The Crewes returned the hospitality by giving a party 'crowded with writers, actors, singers, artists – the sort of people to whom the Snowdons were naturally drawn'.

George Melly[1] sang and other guests included Edna O'Brien

---

[1] George Melly (1926–). Gravel-voiced *chansonnier*, raconteur and character with fine line in frocks and hats.

and Shirley MacLaine,[1] a couple of Rolling Stones,[2] Kathleen and Ken Tynan and a barefoot *chanteuse* Sandie Shaw.[3] The Princess apparently danced non-stop and stayed till dawn.

Huth remembered subsequent evenings at Kensington Palace where John Betjeman would tell stories, Noël Coward and Peter Sellers would exchange jokes, Dudley Moore[4] would play piano and Cleo Laine and John Dankworth would sing. The Princess often joined in. Huth was extravagant in her praise of the royal voice though others were not always quite as enthusiastic.

> The Princess and I were pregnant with our daughters at the same time [wrote Huth]. I had to stay in bed for five months before Candida was born and Princess Margaret was advised not to leave London in the last stages of her pregnancy. She came up with the idea that, as I was stuck in bed, she and Tony should come round on Saturday evenings, set up the projector in the bedroom and watch films. After two weeks of this entertainment, I was forced to confess I had run out of help to cook supper and was not allowed to do it myself.
>
> 'Don't worry,' she said, 'we'll send it round.'
>
> Thereafter, a van would arrive from Kensington Palace to deliver a delicious cold supper, after which we would watch the next film.

Shades of the curious picnic at Hampton Court that the Princess described in that anthology. Sometimes Princess Margaret and her apologists display a self-defeating lack of self-awareness. Help with cooking, palatial meals sent round in vans and bed-bound

---

1 Shirley MacLaine (1934–). Gamine and goofy American film star, sister of Warren Beatty, comedienne, outspoken advocate of minority causes and believer in reincarnation.
2 Rolling Stones (1960s–). Once dangerous-seeming rock group of astonishing longevity still going comparatively strong in 2000s.
3 Sandie Shaw (1947–). Essex girl-singer who shot to fame after winning Eurovision song contest singing 'Puppet on a String'.
4 Dudley Moore (1935–2002). Diminutive *Beyond the Fringe* veteran, comic and pianist who became Hollywood film star and died of progressive supra-nuclear palsy.

home movies are not the stuff of ordinary lives. It is easy to seem charitable when one has only to snap one's fingers and get someone else to do the work.

The two women went through their divorces at the same time, not, in Huth's recollection, complaining but suffering in a stiff-upper-lipped silence. Afterwards Huth went to live alone in a Wiltshire cottage for some years.

'Concerned that I was "all right", she came down with her daughter Sarah to inspect the place,' wrote Huth, in her *Telegraph* article. 'Candida and I entertained her with a sausage casserole at the kitchen table. She wanted to be shown every nook and cranny, complained only that it was rather too hot and left satisfied by my wellbeing.' This contradicted the popular notion, suggested Huth, that she was 'the guest from hell'. She rejected this idea, referring to 'all the years of her coming to stay with us' and averring that she had never been anything but a particularly appreciative guest although 'admittedly, having her for the weekend is not quite like having anyone else: for a start, detectives have to come, too. More flowers than usual, probably, are arranged and the candlesticks given an extra buffing. Most essential of all is the choice of others to invite to lunches and dinners. Lively minds are what she likes and thrives among and are not hard to press into coming.'

In 1978 Huth had married Howard-Johnston, a fellow of Corpus Christi College, and moved to Oxford. When Princess Margaret came to stay,

> She particularly liked to see Dame Iris Murdoch[1] and her husband John Bayley.[2] She loved listening to Iris talk about philosophy, retaining all she could. Each time a new Murdoch novel appeared, she would pounce upon it, but, to my amazement, she also made headway into Iris's last tome on philosophy. 'I had to read it with the *Encyclopaedia Britannica* beside me,' she confessed. 'It was difficult, but worth the effort.' Ever ready to leap upon

---

1 Dame Iris Murdoch (1919–1999). Oxford philosopher and novelist whose lingering death from Alzheimer's disease was captured in print and film.
2 John Bayley (1925–). Professor of English, married to Iris Murdoch.

opportunities of further education, she taxed a friend of ours from Oriel College, a history don, quite hard when he came to dinner. 'I'd like to know,' she said, 'every pope, in order, from the beginning. Hang on, while I get a piece of paper.'

The challenged guest settled down to the list, forgetting only one pope, who was luckily supplied by Katherine Duncan-Jones,[1] an English don at Somerville.

Huth finally conceded, as if realizing perhaps that she had over-egged the pudding, 'Of course, the Princess has her foibles, but as she is the kind of friend I myself hope always to be to her, I'm damned if I'm going to mention them. I have tried to write about her as I have seen her: a remarkable friend, for a very long time.'

The historian from Oriel was Jeremy Catto[2] and it wasn't popes, of whom the Princess was not fond, that she asked about, it was Holy Roman Emperors. Catto said that he didn't reel them off either. Instead he went through them methodically and in chronological order rather as if he were conducting a tutorial. Each emperor was given his dates, fate and so on and Princess Margaret wrote everything down in her notebook. Catto thought this odd, but eventually she revealed her reasons. She was due to stay with the Wittelsbachs, who now had a dukedom but had once been kings of Bavaria. She was perfectly aware that the family were heirs to the residual Stuart claim to the British throne and, in Doctor Catto's words, 'wanted some ammunition if they teased her with it, which they probably did. She planned to tell them off – "You behave."'

Another history tutor who found himself at one of these princessly dinners in the Howard-Johnstons' rambling Victorian house on Headington Hill was the Balliol College medievalist

---

1 Katherine Duncan-Jones (1941–). Fellow of Somerville College, Oxford, and biographer of Sir Philip Sidney and William Shakespeare.
2 Dr Jeremy Catto (1939–). Long-serving Fellow of Oriel College, Oxford, and author of multi-volume history of Oxford University.

Maurice Keen.[1] Keen remembers sitting next to the Princess on the sofa after dinner when cameras were suddenly produced and photographs were taken.

'I don't understand this sort of thing at all,' muttered Keen, donnishly.

The Princess smiled at him and drawled, 'Oh I understand it all perfectly. I was married to a photographer once.'

On 6 March 2001 Lord Ullswater was writing to the Architects' Benevolent Society, 'I am sure you will have read in the newspapers that Her Royal Highness has cancelled her public engagements until the end of April.' But the same day he was wondering if she would consider a public engagement in September, to which she felt able to reply, 'Yes.'

She also accepted an invitation from her old friends Johnny Dankworth and Cleo Laine to open a new Laine Dankworth Centre at their converted stables at Woburn Sands. She even responded with characteristic asperity when Lord Ullswater asked if she would like to be received by the Lord Lieutenant. 'Certainly not,' she scribbled.

Some of her friends privately thought it a pity that she didn't die earlier when her quality of life seemed so diminished and her capacity for enjoyment so impaired. 'It wasn't always easy to feel sympathy,' confessed her friend Prue Penn. 'She'd sit in the bedroom looking utterly miserable. The things she asked me to read ... there was a Trollope. A frightfully dull book. No men came at all. She couldn't bear to be seen by men. When she went to sleep I stopped reading. 'I'll go, nurse,' I'd say. 'She's asleep.'

'I'm not,' she'd say.

She eventually died at six-thirty on the morning of 9 February 2002, at Sister Agnes', as King Edward VII's Hospital for Officers is more generally known, asleep with her son and daughter at her bedside. She was 71 years old. It was, in the end, a peaceful death.

---

1 Dr Maurice Keen (1930–). Equally long-serving Fellow of Balliol College, Oxford, winner of Wolfson History Prize and author of numerous scholarly works on medieval history.

Later the coffin, draped in her own personal standard, was taken back to 1A Kensington Palace, where it lay for forty-eight hours in her bedroom before being moved on at night. Every window in the courtyard was candle-lit, and every occupant of the palace stood silently to watch together with a small crowd of friends and supporters. The Linleys and the Chattos were joined by their friend and the Princess's lady-in-waiting Liz Vyvyan. Hugo Vickers was there, issued like everyone else with a candle, though his blew out four or five times and he abandoned it.

As six o'clock struck the hearse moved out of the yard, where it was joined by the Duke of Kent, Prince and Princess Michael – the Gloucesters – neighbours and workers from other parts of the palace. The Queen's piper and another from the Royal Highland Fusiliers played a lament all the way to the High Street. As they passed the Gloucesters' house, the tiny hundred-year-old Duchess of Gloucester sat in the porch with her nurse to watch. She was well wrapped up against the February cold and wore a black felt hat.

For a further forty-eight hours the body of the Princess lay at the Queen's Chapel, Marlborough House. Thence it was taken to Windsor, where the coffin, still draped in the Princess's personal standard, lay overnight in the nave of St George's Chapel guarded by two of the Military Knights of Windsor in scarlet swallowtail coats with black armbands and cocked hats.

Her funeral took place on the afternoon of Friday 16 February attended by a congregation of 450. Her now ancient mother, frail and only weeks away from her own death, came in a wheelchair. She had flown by helicopter from Sandringham and then rested for a while at Royal Lodge. It was exactly fifty years to the day since the funeral of her husband, Princess Margaret's father King George VI, whose remains lay in the side chapel waiting to be joined by those of his wife and daughter.

Lord Snowdon arrived independently, limping heavily and grumbling because the Lord Chamberlain had told him there would be no steps. He had joined the Linleys and the Chattos at the Deanery. At one point he came face to face with Roddy Llewellyn, his wife's sometime boyfriend. Llewellyn seemed eager to talk. Snowdon cut him dead. Later Llewellyn had no recollection of the incident.

Her sister the Queen led the mourners, who included her nephew Prince Charles and her two great-nephews, her niece Princess Anne and husband Commodore Tim Laurence.[1] Former ladies-in-waiting were well represented. Dames Judi Dench,[2] Maggie Smith[3] and Cleo Laine brought some theatricality to the occasion. The bearer party was from the 1st Battalion the Royal Highland Fusiliers, alternatively known as Princess Margaret's Own Glasgow and Ayrshire Regiment.

Queen Elizabeth the Queen Mother entered by the North Door accompanied by a black-cloaked canon. She was wearing deep black with a light veil and her eyes shone brightly. Hugo Vickers, who saw her very close up, thought she seemed both 'impressive and demonic'. The overriding impression was that she was determined to attend the funeral and to do so with dignity and composure. Vickers 'detected a kind of steely resolve that was more involved with her own attendance of the ceremony than any sympathy she might feel for her dead daughter. It was a mixture between her wonderful resolve and perhaps a tiny hint of triumphalism.'

The family followed – Linleys, Chattos, Waleses, Queen and Prince Philip. Then the procession including the Dean of Windsor and the Archbishop of Canterbury entered the Choir.

Princess Margaret had chosen the music herself: some of Tchaikovsky's *Swan Lake*, two good old-fashioned hymns – 'Immortal, invisible, God only wise' and 'When I survey the wondrous cross'; the choir sang Psalm 23 and the Nunc Dimittis. Lord Linley read from Romans 8 and the Archbishop of Canterbury read her favourite prayer, 'Enter my heart, O Holy Spirit, come in blessed mercy and set me free'. Finally there was a last

---

1 Rear-Admiral Tim Laurence (1955–). Career naval officer and second husband of the Princess Royal, whom he married in 1992 after three years as equerry to Queen Elizabeth II.
2 Dame Judi Dench (1934–). Grande dame of English theatre.
3 Dame Maggie Smith (1934–). Grande dame of English theatre.

post and reveille sounded by a trumpeter from another of her regiments, the Hussars and Light Dragoons, and the coffin was borne away to a waiting hearse as a piper played 'The Desperate Struggle of the Bird'. It was all over in forty-five minutes; dignified, simple, traditional and much as she herself would have wished.

The organist, Roger Judd, played on for a while and then stopped when he thought everyone must have left. The church was absolutely silent. When he looked up he saw that every seat was still occupied. The silence was sombre and complete.

The indefatigable Poet Laureate, Andrew Motion,[1] penned a commemorative poem called 'The Younger Sister'. 'The luxuries', it began, 'of course and privilege – The money, houses, holidays, the lot ...' It ended with the extremely debatable notion that the Princess was 'a woman in possession of the fact "That love and duty speak two languages."'

Before long her body, reduced to ashes in the antiseptic and almost completely unwitnessed anonymity of Slough Crematorium, was back in St George's Chapel. Her mother did not long survive her and so Princess Margaret was able to rest alongside her beloved parents, commemorated with a prayer of her own composition. This was engraved on a memorial slab of granite from Caithness. It ran:

> We thank thee Lord who by thy spirit
> Doth our faith restore
> When we with worldly things commune
> And prayerless close our door
> We lose our precious gift divine
> To worship and adore
> Then thou, O Saviour, fill our hearts
> To love thee ever more.
> Amen.

The little side chapel is behind bars so members of the public gain only a vague idea of what lies within – a paradox of accessibility

---

1 Andrew Motion (1945–). Conscientious Poet Laureate from 1999 appointed only for a ten-year term, also apart from writing verse and biography of fellow-poet Philip Larkin, critic and academic.

and distance which reflects the Princess's life. She liked to be noticed and appreciated but she did not, on the whole, like ordinary people to get too close. As in life, so in death. You can look at her memorial but only from afar.

The obituaries were mostly in a range from grudging to venomous. Kenneth Rose, who had liked her in life, wrote a considered, magisterial and even-handed piece for the *Daily Telegraph* in which he said that 'in a life devoted to public duties and private passions Princess Margaret was cruelly exposed to the whims of popular opinion'. He contrasted the friendly way in which the mass murderer Harold Shipman was described in the press with the vilification meted out to Princess Margaret. Even when her second stroke had left her bedridden, unable to eat and practically blind, one tabloid had crowed, 'She's spoilt and ill-mannered and over the years has drunk enough whisky to open a distillery.'

The spiteful valedictories were in bizarre contrast to the deferential platitudes that had welcomed her birth. Yet, if the truth be told, neither her coming nor her going was as central to the national life as she herself might have wished. Certain as she was in her belief about the significance of monarchy and of her own place within the family, it would have seemed galling to be perceived as a marginal figure in a diminished institution.

'What a dreadful life,' said one acquaintance who had observed her closely throughout. 'Would I have coped with it any better than she did? I sometimes wonder.'

On Friday, 19 April 2002, a magnificent service of thanksgiving and remembrance was held at Westminster Abbey. The Princess's real wish was for a performance of Fauré's *Requiem*, pure and simple, without adornment and embellishment, but this was generally thought to be a bit much and a compromise was arrived at so that 'the service [was] set around the Requiem by Gabriel Fauré'.

The performance was almost more like a grand religious concert than a religious service. The soloists were Dame Felicity Lott[1] and

---

1 Dame Felicity Lott (1947–). Soprano universally known as 'Flott' and with a marked liking for Benjamin Britten's settings of traditional English songs.

Bryn Terfel[1] backed by the choirs of Westminster Abbey, King's College, Cambridge, and St George's Chapel, Windsor. The organist played Bach, the Academy of St Martin-in-the-Fields performed Tchaikovsky, everybody sang 'Thine be the glory' and 'Ye holy angels bright'. Lord Linley read from Corinthians asking: 'O grave, where is thy victory?'; Felicity Kendal[2] read a short piece by William Penn, which concluded: 'This is the comfort of friends; that though they may be said to die, yet their friendship and society are ever present, because immortal.' Finally, the bells of the Abbey Church were rung.

In the years after her death the image of Princess Margaret began to change, as her life started to become a part of history rather than of the contemporary scene. The little girl and the glamorous younger woman emerged from the shadows cast by the sad, crippled figure in the wheelchair. Magazines and newspapers wrote about the 'Princess Margaret look'; pictures reappeared of Margaret in her prime appearing attractive and funny. She seemed to acquire context.

Even the congenitally hostile were forced into a sort of reassessment, however grudging. In March 2006 the *Guardian*, for instance, published a photograph of the Princess looking glamorous in a tightly waisted frock under the heading: 'Fashion for Grown-ups'. The writer, Catherine Bennett, revealed rather surprisingly that she had read the memoirs of the former royal butler Paul Burrell. (She liked the story of Princess Margaret checking the TV for warmth when she came in after a late night. Burrell claimed she did it to make sure the staff hadn't been watching when her back was turned.) Bennett managed to be grouchy in a knee-jerk manner, referring to 'Fags, obviously; then maybe gin, boyfriends and her final cautionary appearances in a wheelchair'. Even Bennett, however, was forced to admit that the new Burberry

---

1 Bryn Terfel (1965–). Welsh baritone who started with Mozart but diversified into Wagner while enjoying popular success and celebrity.
2 Felicity Kendal (1946–). Gamine actress who starred as tight-jeaned, green-wellied Barbara in TV comedy *The Good Life*.

designer, Christopher Bailey,[1] had selected the Princess as 'the muse' for his new collection, shown in Milan. Bailey was concentrating on 1966, when even the *Guardian* had to concede that she 'looked rather nice'. Not that Bennett could stomach Bailey's claim that the 'Princess Margaret look' was 'refined and grown up'. 'Refined?' asked an incredulous hackette. 'Would that be the same battered old broad who made such a twerp of herself with Roddy Llewellyn?' It would clearly take more than a Princess Margaret-inspired fashion collection in Milan to change the mind of some people, but even so it was evidence that, in death, the Princess's image was reverting to something more glamorous than that of her declining years.

A number of events conspired to keep her in the public gaze, the most controversial of which was the auction of her property at Christie's, the London auction house, on 13 and 14 June 2006. This was mainly the work of her son Viscount Linley, who not only inherited much of his mother's property, together with his sister Sarah, but was also, fortuitously, a director and later hands-on executive chairman of Christie's.

The widespread mood of misgiving was most effectively and surprisingly evoked by Kenneth Rose, the historian and journalist who was not only an old friend of the Princess but was regarded by many as a consistent supporter of the Royal Family come hell or high water. What they perhaps forgot was that Rose was also an old friend of Lord Snowdon, whom he had taught briefly when Rose had been an Eton beak and Snowdon, then Armstrong-Jones, a pupil at the school. Snowdon was alleged to be bitterly opposed to the sale of many of his wife's possessions, particularly wedding presents, which he reasoned were as much his as hers. He was reported to have remonstrated with Christie's – shocking observers because he seemed unable to discuss the matter with his own son and daughter. When I asked him, at the end of 2006, how close he was to his son David, he said that he spoke to him on the

---

1 Christopher Bailey (1971–). Yorkshire-born, Royal College of Art educated, designer poached from Gucci in his late twenties who transformed Burberry from traditional to trendy.

phone or in person at least once a day. He also added, musingly, that his new job as executive chairman of the Christie's, which had so successfully auctioned his mother's effects, was 'quite grown up'.

Writing in the *Daily Telegraph* the day before the sale, Rose asked, 'There is something melancholy – isn't there? – about turning over the possessions of the well-remembered dead.'

Much of Rose's article took the form of a fairly gentle and characteristic rumination. At the end of the piece, however, he became surprisingly tart.

> Lord Snowdon [he wrote] always loyal to the memory of his first wife, does not hide his disapproval not so much of the sale as its extent. A few of the items, he recollects, belong to him alone; more were given jointly to him and the Princess.
>
> His children cannot be expected to pay inheritance tax on a hoard of rarely used chattels, but the legatees should have kept the neatly inscribed cards that accompanied some of the presents – 'For darling Margaret, from her loving Grannie Mary'.
>
> And what of the feelings of those who dutifully forked out to give birthday and wedding presents, and now see them go under the hammer to the highest bidder – all ranks of her regiments, the crew of the Royal Yacht *Britannia*, staff and pensioners at Balmoral, Birkhall and Sandringham? On future occasions, surely, they will know what to do with their money.

It is ironic that the crew of the Royal Yacht *Britannia* actually did not dip into their pockets for a Snowdon wedding present because of the way in which they felt exploited when their leave was cancelled and they had to take the couple on their honeymoon cruise to the Caribbean. Had they known that 'their' gift would be auctioned for the benefit of the couple's children, their action might have been even more drastic.

Rose said that 'quite a lot of people' welcomed his verdict and it was widely shared by commentators in the press. There were exceptions. The Queen apparently agreed and it was said that Buckingham Palace was anxious to avoid the controversy surrounding Michael Fawcett,[1] who sold off gifts he had received while working for the Prince of Wales. These were found to have been official presents and Fawcett was acquitted of any financial impropriety but acquired the unfortunate nickname of 'Fawcett the Fence'. Whether as a result of the Queen's intervention or not a number of the items were sold in aid of charities, in particular the Stroke Association. This was particularly favoured by Lord Linley and Lady Sarah in view of their mother's several strokes in her final years, but Lord Linley was known to be bitter that earlier attempts to help the association had met with widespread indifference in the press. Those few donors questioned by the press tended to be diplomatic. The New Zealand government whose pair of silver kiwis in the sale were a wedding present, said simply and graciously, 'We are pleased that the proceeds from our gift are going to a good cause.'

Apart from presents of the sort Kenneth Rose described in his article, the greatest controversy surrounded the Annigoni portrait, which had hung in the hall of Apartment 1A Kensington Palace and had been substituted with a copy made by Historic Royal Palaces. Not that the painting was to everyone's taste. Simon Heffer, the newspaper columnist not generally thought of as an art critic, wrote, 'If it had been of my mother I'd have sold it. Perhaps because one has seen it so often and become inured to it, I have never minded Annigoni's iconic portrait of the Queen; but, my word, he was having the mother of all off-days when he painted her sister. Not to put too fine a point on it, the painting is bloody awful, rather like something painted by some old dear who has taken several courses of art lessons rather late in life.' Christie's, quoting the opinion of Sir Alfred Munnings, President of the Royal Academy, that Annigoni was 'the greatest painter of the age', placed a reserve of £200,000 on the painting. It was eventually sold to that well-known character 'a mystery buyer' for £680,000.

---

1 Michael Fawcett. Aide to Prince Charles who resigned after internal enquiry found that he had not been declaring gifts including a watch worth several thousand pounds.

The mystery buyer turned out to be Lord Linley himself, after the first day's sale raised far more than he or Christie's had expected. Another oddity was what was described as 'The Royal Ascot Balustrading'. This was the wrought ironwork that had been dismantled in 1963 when the Duke of Norfolk had announced the rebuilding of all the stands at Ascot racecourse. The ironwork was offered in two lots; the first, with a reserve of over £8,000, was the ironwork actually in situ in the former private gardens at Kensington Palace, while the second was a job lot of assorted ironwork in Christie's warehouse at Nine Elms Road valued at between £2,000 and £3,000. Historic Royal Palaces took the view that the former was a fixture or fitting and not therefore something that should have been part of the sale. In any case, they argued, the former was in such a parlous state that it couldn't have been removed from the palace without falling to bits.

The agency, who were responsible for the apartment and for showing it off to the public, were not best pleased either at having to compete in this open sale for items such as the dining-room table – itself a wedding present from the British Army – which they wanted to display in the apartment.

They were not the only ones. A number of the Princess's old friends would have welcomed the opportunity to purchase items of jewellery they particularly liked but were deterred by the prohibitive guide prices in the catalogue. Perhaps the most poignant sight was that of Major the Lord Napier and Ettrick attending the second day of the sale in the hope of buying the battered leather briefcase with the Princess's 'M' monogram on the side. It had been bought one day when the Princess had realized that they were still using old cases with her sister's initials 'ER' stamped on their side. Suddenly she had told Napier to organize the purchase of a new replacement and to have her own 'M' cipher stamped on it. Napier had done as he was told and carried it round the world during his twenty-five years of service to the Princess. The case carried a guide price of £50 and Napier privately vowed that he would bid as much as £800 to secure 'his' case. In the event it was sold for £1,440 and Lord Napier went home to Wiltshire empty-handed.

Christie's were extremely conservative in their estimates. The firm argued that absolute accuracy was impossible and that therefore all valuations should be based on the intrinsic value of the jewels or the artefacts themselves, with just a small added value for their royal celebrity status. This was clearly misleading if not naïve. The very first item – a ruby, cultured-pearl and diamond necklace given to the Princess by her grandmother, Queen Mary, on her second birthday, was estimated by Christie's at between £1,200 and £1,500. It went to another 'mystery buyer' for £27,600. An aquamarine-and-diamond cluster ring estimated at between £400 and £600 went for £28,800. A Louis Vuitton jewellery case valued at £500 sold for £21,600. A world record £1.24 million was realized by a Fabergé clock that the Princess had kept by her bedside – it had been estimated at between £600,000 and £800,000. The famous Poltimore tiara, favoured by the Princess because it added inches to her diminutive stature – raised £926,400 against a top estimate of £200,000 – and so on.

The heirlooms were originally expected to raise about £3 million but in the end they went for £13,658,000, which triggered additional tax problems. Originally the Princess's estate had been valued at about £7.6 million, on which about £3 million tax was due. The extra profit, inevitably, meant extra tax to pay.

The reason given for the sale was that Lord Linley and Lady Sarah had to find millions of pounds in death duties and needed to sell off some of their mother's valuables to do so. Once the sale of their mother's possessions had gone so well, it was estimated that they would have to pay more than £3m more in tax. On the other hand, their net profit from the whole exercise would have been more than £8m. Much was made of the items which *were* sold, but friends of the children were quick to point out, defensively, that no one had said anything about treasured possessions that were *not* included in the sale.

However, the overriding impression was that the publicity surrounding the sale was badly handled. The two children were, of course, perfectly entitled to sell off their mother's bequests and they *had* been confronted with a hefty tax bill, but there was a widespread impression that they had been greedy and insensitive.

Many of the items in the sale went abroad, where some of them had been exhibited before the auction, notably in Moscow, Geneva, Hong Kong and New York. Most details of the sale remained mysterious, but very few of the Princess's possessions were destined to remain in her former home at Kensington Palace. Historic Royal Palaces were able to purchase the pair of 'Blackamore Torchères' that used to flank the entrance to the dining room and between which the Princess was often photographed. They were also able to buy some of the turquoise glassware that she was fond of collecting, three bottles of Kensington white wine made in 1976 from her own grapes in the garden and a set of menu cards, a hundred sheets in all, dated from September to March and containing the chef's alternative suggestions for lunch and dinner. The Princess has carefully indicated her preference with a cross against the preferred dishes. That's all.

'Interestingly,' remarked Lee Prosser, the Historic Royal Palaces curator, 'several of the Duke of Sussex's bookcases turned up with the blurb that they'd been removed by Princess Louise in the 1930s. Funny that, when we have a picture of them in situ in 1960.'

Another interesting little postscript came from Joan Collins[1] the actress, of all people, writing a diary column in the *Spectator*. A few years earlier La Collins had apparently taken up silver-box-collecting. A friend had told her that Princess Margaret was having a clear-out and wanted to get rid of some 'junk'. Would Joan be interested? Yes, Joan was interested, so the friend brought round 'a beautiful and rather large embossed square silver box for which I cheerfully coughed up £600'. A month later the Princess had another 'clear-out' and the actress paid over an undisclosed sum for a second, smaller box. When she opened the first box Collins discovered a small engraved card which said, 'Presented to HRH Princess Margaret and Antony Armstrong-Jones on the occasion

---

1 Joan Collins (1933–). Evergreen Rank starlet who retained youthful looks into her seventies while adding occasional journalism and books to thespian portfolio.

of their visit to ———'. The columnist didn't give the name of the country 'to save international embarrassment'.

She tacked on a codicil about Princess Margaret coming round late one evening with the aforementioned friend, drinking a large quantity of Collins' Famous Grouse, having an animated conversation with Roger Moore[1] and giving 'a small glint of recognition' when she saw her discarded silver boxes. Her hostess 'quickly doused' this with more whisky, but that's not the point of the story, which is that if their mother was already selling off official presents given jointly to her and her ex-husband in her lifetime it's difficult to blame the Snowdon children for carrying on the family tradition.

One blogger has commented waspishly, 'The eighties are gone Joan, along with the career, so forget about embarrassing the late Princess to keep your name in the news.' An incandescent Ned Ryan phoned Liz Vyvyan to say that he would have known about any such transaction and that none could have taken place. In any case, even if she had sold off a silver box she would never have sold it to 'a person like that'.

Ryan was quoted in an article on 'The Royalist' website written by Joanne Leyland. She alleged that Ryan told her, 'It's a load of bunkum.' He added, 'It's perfectly true that I did once take Princess Margaret around to Joan Collins's flat in Belgravia for a drink after we'd had dinner. That was about twenty-odd years ago. But I certainly never sold any of the Princess's silver – or anything else. The story is completely invented.' A few days later Ryan phoned me to say that he had been woken by a phone call – presumably from Joanne Leyland – but had no recollection of what he had said nor to whom he was talking. 'Joan's a friend of mine,' he said, adding that she should have spoken to the press about 'Her Royal Highness'. She hadn't, of course. It was a signed article so she could hardly complain of having been misquoted or

---

1 Roger Moore (1927–). Winsome successor to Sean Connery as cinematic James Bond, the secret agent originally created by Ian Fleming, husband of Princess Margaret's acquaintance Ann. Moore made seven Bond films between 1973 and 1985.

indeed exploited in any way. Ryan was clearly embarrassed by the affair.

It was noticeable that great efforts were made to establish 'provenance', though sometimes there were mistakes. A trinket that Colin Glenconner had picked up in an Indian market and given to the Princess and which he was anxious to buy back was presented with a card suggesting that it had been a present from Queen Mary. It proved too expensive for Glenconner. Later, when many of the Princess's books were auctioned separately by a London specialist, a bookplate was inserted into the front of every volume saying that it had been her property and adding the dates of her birth and death. This looked like sharp practice to this outsider, but to those within the trade it is, apparently, common practice. The establishing of provenance is all-important, I was told by one expert. How you achieve it is immaterial.

Confusion of a different sort surrounded the dedication of a memorial garden in Oxford. This was in the grounds of the Rothermere American Institute next to Mansfield College and was personally opened by Her Majesty the Queen in May 2006. Most of the Princess's surviving ladies-in-waiting were present and had their photograph taken together with Princess Margaret's two children. However, there were some who thought the choice of memorial was a touch curious. The Princess was generally thought to have liked Cambridge more than Oxford – preferably in the company of her great friend Professor Jack Plumb; she had nothing particularly to do with the Rothermeres or their newspapers – mainly the *Daily Mail* – and despite her relationship with Roddy Llewellyn most people would have thought of her as a theatre-goer and especially a ballet-lover rather than a horticultural person.

The garden was designed by Anouska Hempel, wife of the financier Sir Mark Weinberg, proprietor of a chic design company at whose dinner table the Princess first met her friend Ned Ryan. Hempel, described as 'a close friend', used yew, box and stone and concentrated on what the *Mail* itself described as a 'monastic, contemplative ambience'. There are lighter notes, such as pineapples on plinths, but Hempel was keen to emphasize the quiet, religious side of her old friend's character. 'She was very Church of England,' she said.

Many observers were surprised that her old friend Roddy Llewellyn was not consulted. Llewellyn continued to advise the Princess on gardening even after his marriage to Tania. The Princess always got on well with her. They hit it off from the moment they first met and Margaret always addressed her by her proper full Russian Christian name which was Tatiana. This was actually a form of endearment, almost like a private code designed to exclude outsiders who were often baffled. Prue Penn, another good friend, was sometimes called Prue; never Prudence which she would rather have liked – enjoying the archetypal Puritan combination of Prudence and Penn; but most often 'Lady Penn'. Thus Princess Margaret would say such things as 'Lady Penn always wears a tiara for dinner' or 'I expect Lady Penn would like to sit in the front row'. This perplexed others who thought the two were good friends and couldn't understand the apparent formality. Prue and Tania, however, understood implicitly.

Henry Wrong, the first director of the London Barbican Centre and a long-standing friend of the Princess, was the man behind the Oxford memorial garden. 'It had to be Oxford or Cambridge,' he explained, 'and I didn't want Cambridge because of Norman St John Stevas.' He felt that Lord Stevas boasted enough about his relationship with the Royal Family and also that the Princess enjoyed her visits to Oxford just as much as those to the other place, whether she was staying with her old friend Angela Huth or another friend, the former President of Magdalen College Anthony Smith.[1] The project had not been entirely plain sailing, but Wrong was gratified that Her Majesty the Queen had attended the dedication party and written him a long thank-you letter in her own hand. He was also pleased that no less than eight former ladies-in-waiting had come to Oxford for the great day and that, what's more, he had the photograph to prove it.

Critics thought Oxford was an odd choice for a memorial,

---

1 Anthony Smith (1938–). President of Magdalen College, Oxford, 1988–2005.

sensing that if either of the ancient English university cities should provide a venue, then she would have preferred Cambridge. One friend, hearing that the Oxford garden included lavender and rosemary, commented sardonically, 'At least they got something right.' Others said that although there was no doubting the Princess's fondness for Anouska Hempel they had completely different tastes.

At Glamis Castle the Earl of Strathmore was planning another memorial garden, but there seemed to be no plans for a memorial scholarship or indeed bequest of any kind to the Royal Ballet, which had been, surely, her favourite cause.

One of the many curiosities of the Princess's life is that it seems to require judgement. On the whole and with reservations the average life is seen, even by obituary writers, as a muddled collection of pluses and minuses, successes and failures, with no clear verdict required or delivered. Margaret who deserves, surely, to be treated in the same way, is a rarity who apparently demands evaluation.

Sitting in the drawing room of her house in Windsor Great Park – a sort of green-belt equivalent of the Aunt Heap – Margaret's cousin Margaret Rhodes, née Elphinstone, said thoughtfully, 'The Almighty gets the right people to be born first. Thank heaven she wasn't the eldest. It would have been disastrous the other way round.'

This slightly begs the question of the extent to which the Princess was shaped by being born second and therefore always in the shadow of her sensible and dutiful elder sister. Nature or nurture? Had she been born before Elizabeth they would both – surely – have been very different people. 'I do think her life was sad,' said Mrs Rhodes. 'She was unfulfilled.'

This is a frequent judgement. John Julius Norwich, who once knew her quite well but drifted away, not least because, like others, he couldn't bear the interminable late nights, was equally certain. 'I've never known an unhappier woman,' he said.

Repeat verdicts such as these to others, however, and the reaction is utterly different.

Prue Penn, a very long-standing and very loyal friend, remembered the laughter. 'At a dinner party she'd catch my eye and we'd get the giggles until the tears ran down our faces. We couldn't stop. She was a great giggler.'

Lady Penn used to send her 'Rebus letters' along the lines of the ones Lewis Carroll sent his child friends. Princess Margaret used to love receiving them, though she never returned the compliment. Lady Penn's were carefully, beautifully constructed – a complex amalgam of words and pictures, a clever code. The Princess kept Prue's letters, which are works of art in their way, and after her death Lady Sarah gave them back to her. They are an eloquent memento of a friendship.

Even those closest to her acknowledged that she was contrary and contradictory. 'To sum up,' said Johnny Johnston, 'when she was nice, she was very very nice. When she was awkward she was very awkward. As far as I was concerned, I always felt that her view was: "There's no need to be nice to this chap. He works for my sister." If she was on good form in Scotland, for instance, she'd turn up on time and she might, if she was on good form, say "Johnny, come and sit next to me," or sometimes Queen Elizabeth would say, "Johnny, do go and sit next to Princess Margaret." And it would be all right if she was on good form … You'd try to jolly her along and she wouldn't try so much.'

Years after her death her old friend Anne Glenconner and her much newer friend Ros Chatto both said they still missed her terribly. So did her lady-in-waiting Liz Vyvyan. In fact all the ladies-in-waiting said the same – as did her former husband Lord Snowdon; and her Oxford friend Angela Huth. 'The people who knew her best were devoted to her,' wrote Lady Elizabeth Cavendish. 'It was the fringe friends who could be so unpleasant. It is also true that the people who worked for her loved her too. She was, I think, the most loyal person I have ever met and of course to me a wonderful friend. I know or at least I think I know that no matter what I had done she would have been there.'

Even a few years after her death the media seemed ready to treat her as if she was a historical or even mythical figure and one who could be portrayed in any way that suited the film-makers.

A Channel 4 biopic screened in the autumn of 2005 opened with a disclaimer saying, 'Some of the following is based on fact.' The *Guardian* interviewed the film's scriptwriter, Craig Warner, and reported that 'he looked puzzled when asked if he had a shred of evidence for several scenes in the film, such as the Duke [of Edinburgh] cheerfully remarking that the only consolation for the stultifying boredom of royal tours is "there's always a bit of striking totty about". He said he'd done the research over a year ago, and could not remember.'

I was staying in Scotland with Lady Penn in the aftermath of the screening and she was surprised when, in the film, the Roddy Llewellyn character told the Margaret character that he was about to marry someone called Prue. In real life Roddy married a girl called Tania and the couple remained on good terms with the Princess until her death. As a result of the film's curious invention Lady Penn's phone line was busy with friends wishing her a happy anniversary. There was even an amused one from her 'husband' Roddy Llewellyn himself.

Princess Margaret's wedding present from Colin Glenconner, Les Jolies Eaux on Mustique, was sold on by her son Viscount Linley and was available for hire in 2006 for $24,000 a week, falling to just $16,000 after 30 April. It had been renovated virtually beyond recognition. 'Fashion', quipped a journalist called Mimi Spencer, extolling this bargain escape (*Guardian*, 7 January 2006), 'is about to have a Princess Margaret moment. Come spring, the more style-savvy among us will be tripping about in duchesse satin coats, accessorised with a ciggie holder, and a quart of gin and Dubonnet.'

EPILOGUE

After the publication of my book on Prince Philip I was asked to contribute to a radio obituary by the BBC. The interviewer was the late Brian Redhead.[1] Redhead was an intelligent broadcaster with an original approach to the job. One of his finest achievements was that, on having been confronted with an inarticulate German road-traffic specialist who had been unable to say more than *Ja* or *Nein*, he had managed to speak for a long period on the theme of 'what the professor is actually saying'.

At the end of the interview Redhead leaned forward and I expected him to ask the question everyone else always did, which was: 'Did you like him?' Instead, however, he wanted to know, 'Do you feel better for having known him?'

It's a much more satisfactory question for a biographer and because of its surprising originality it has the merit of making one actually think rather than producing an instant reaction. However, now that I have spent a long time getting to know Princess Margaret, I have to confess that I would revise my answer to the question, in her case, to a sad 'not really'. Someone who knew her very well read through the whole of my first draft and said a little wistfully, 'Sad, really.' Because they end in death I suppose all lives contain an element of sadness. When they are preceded by enfeebling or debilitating illness, as was the case with the Princess, the sense of sadness is deepened.

----

1 Brian Redhead (1929–1994). Journalist, mainly for the *Guardian*, and broadcaster, best known as terrier-like interrogator on BBC radio *Today* programme.

By no means everyone I spoke to, however, thought that hers was a sad life. Several, especially her close women friends emphasized her gaiety, laughter, loyalty and sense of fun while completely failing to detect that lack of fulfilment and sense of waste that others thought they saw in her. The positive qualities are there and there are others too. She had a strong religious faith, a genuine love of the arts and particularly dance; she possessed a sense of duty and royalty and a fierce protective instinct when it came to anything to do with her sister the Queen.

I wonder, naturally, about that other question: Did I like her? In real life I scarcely knew her but enjoyed what little I saw. I am not sure it is an appropriate question for a biographer. We are not supposed to like or dislike those about whom we write. Yet it is a question that is asked and that one asks oneself and, at the risk of seeming presumptuous, I think I do. That is not the same as saying one sympathizes with everything that she did or said or seemed to believe. She could be inconsiderate, rude, insensitive and spoiled. Conversely she could be fun, thoughtful, considerate, witty and good company.

Philip Howard,[1] author of a sharp and often perceptive analysis of the British monarchy published in the late seventies when people like him either pretended that the Snowdon marriage was in good order or were genuinely ignorant of the truth, suggested that the couple could have 'built a bridge across the chasm between the monarchy and the artistic and intellectual worlds'. Maybe so, but for various reasons it did not happen.

Instead, as Howard perceived, 'It was psychologically natural for the lively younger sister to become the royal equivalent of an *enfant terrible*. She is short of the exquisite discretion and majestic humility we demand from our monarchs. When attacked, her instinct is to bite back.'

This was probably true in 1977 and the Princess did not

---

1 Philip Howard (1933–). Eton- and Oxford-educated *Times* news-feature writer, literary editor, etiquette pontificator, classicist and expert on language and words as well as author of books on the River Thames, the Black Watch and *The Times* newspaper.

change a great deal in the quarter of a century left to her.

I realize, incidentally, that although I have dealt at length with the Princess's apparently defining relationship with Peter Townsend and with her tempestuous marriage to the Earl of Snowdon, I have said comparatively little about the Princess and sex. I have mentioned the heavy drinking and heavy smoking but said little or nothing about other drugs, such as cocaine.

At this point, I confess, a certain weariness comes over me. It happened when I was writing about Prince Philip. Everyone wanted to know about his alleged 'girlfriends' and when I professed ignorance or scepticism they became lofty and omniscient. I remember several times discussing the question with the *Daily Mail* diarist Nigel Dempster, who would ask me what I was writing about the air hostess from Bombay or the actress in Miami or the millionairess in Buenos Aires. When I said, 'Nothing,' Dempster looked outraged, but when I asked why he, after all his years as *Mail* diarist, had written nothing about such people, he replied, 'That's different.' He never explained exactly why and I don't believe him.

Princess Margaret also suffers from the same sort of persistent allegations. People like John Bindon, whom I have mentioned, claimed to have had relationships with her. Reviewers, to whom I have also alluded, refer casually to her 'nymphomania' as if it were a well-known fact.

I happened, in this connection, to be reading *Slow Man*, a novel by the Nobel Prize-winning author J. M. Coetzee, and came across a paragraph that sums up what I feel on this subject: 'Gossip, public opinion, *fama* as the Romans called it, makes the world go round – gossip not truth,' he wrote. 'But what counts as sexual intercourse nowadays? And how do we weigh a quick deed in a dark corner as against months of fevered longing? When love is the subject, how can an outside observer ever be sure of the truth of what has gone on?'

Her Royal Highness Princess Margaret Rose was the daughter of a king and the sister of a queen. She never forgot this and she never let anyone else forget it. Being royal, at a time when being royal mattered more than it later did, defined her in ways beyond anyone's control.

Had she been a commoner, she would have been quite different. But for her to be a commoner was inconceivable. She was the last of a breed but also, in a sense and up to a point, the first of a new breed too.

'Trivial stuff,' said Kenneth Rose, the eminent historian and royal biographer, 'but so (except for the Sovereign) are the lives of all members of the royal family.'

Perhaps part of Princess Margaret's problem was that when she was born and when she was growing up she was made to feel that she mattered; yet by the time she died the world that put her on that pedestal had vanished. Roy Strong – self-confessed 'devoted monarchist' and once a seemingly devoted acolyte – felt guilty about his own disillusion but he was not untypical: 'The problem is my attitude to the Royal Family changed in the 1980s. In the days of deference you automatically deferred, but that world went and the new line I took was that they had to earn my respect.'

This was a change not restricted to Sir Roy Strong and it impinged particularly hard on a princess who celebrated her fiftieth birthday at the beginning of the eighties and who, in many ways, behaved in the same way that princesses behaved at the time of her birth and before.

In the end, like so many lives, it was conditioned by a series of unanswerable 'what-ifs'. What if her uncle had not abdicated? What if her sister had never been queen? What if she had inherited instead? What if she had been allowed to marry Group Captain Townsend? What if she had been more abstemious?

History demonstrates, of course, that she was Her Majesty the Queen's little sister, that she was not able – for whatever reason – to marry the man she loved, that she smoked and drank too much, that she could be wonderfully loyal and life-enhancing yet, almost in the same breath, wilful and rude. She lived a life of privilege, never had a conventional job, seldom behaved in the way most people behave. She could exasperate even her most loyal admirers but could inspire great love.

She was, above all, complex and contrary, and, though often bored, seldom dull.

In the end, even one of her closest friends and admirers was moved to comment when, surveying her life as a whole, 'So what?' The life that had begun with such optimism and high spirits ended sadly and on the periphery. She who had once filled centre stage died in the wings.

She left behind memories, many of them happy. Her children, conspicuously not royal in the sense that their mother felt herself to be, won wide approval for their apparent normality and niceness. To some they seemed her greatest credit.

NOTES

The purpose of these notes is to give the reader some idea of what informs the text and how it came to be written. As I explained in the Acknowledgements at the beginning of the book there are some people who have only confided in me on the understanding that their identity is not revealed. This poses difficulties for me and for the reader but it's a fact.

Partly for this reason I have not provided the sort of notes which cite detailed chapter and verse and then explain 'confidential source' or 'private information'. I find these sorts of notes pointless and frustrating. I am doubtful in general about highly specific source notes. If you gave genuine explanations for every tiny piece of information and interpretation you would more than write the book all over again. I also feel the need for an element of trust. If I say that on such-and-such-a-date so-and-so-happened you have to trust me to be telling the truth. If not, you might as well give up reading.

I do, however, think it useful and interesting to have a general idea about how I came by information, what sort of researches I carried out, the identities of those I consulted and the circumstances under which I did so.

These notes are a gloss and an explanation. They are by no means essential reading but they are, I hope, a useful and interesting background to the text, and they represent my best efforts to explain how I went about writing Princess Margaret's story.

CHAPTER ONE: THE THIRTIES

Back numbers of *The Times*, stored in the basement at the London Library, were an invaluable source of information about events taking place in the world at the same time as various milestones in Princess Margaret's life. They were also useful as evidence of changing ways in which royalty was reported by that most authoritative and conservative of newspapers, at least until its take-over by Rupert Murdoch in the 1980s. Many of the changes that took place then and thereafter were necessary and beneficial, but it is depressingly clear from looking at the back numbers that whereas in earlier times *The Times* was a genuine newspaper of record and as such a valuable historical tool, that has long ceased to be the case.

'Google' hasn't exactly taken the place of *The Times* but it, along with other search engines, websites and elements of the World Wide Web, has become an invaluable aid.

I visited Glamis on a winter's day in 2005, accompanied by Lady Penn, an old friend of the Queen and her sister, who was married to Colonel Eric Penn, sometime Comptroller of the Royal Household. When we called in on Mary, the Dowager Countess of Strathmore, she suggested that we motor down the castle drive just opposite her dower house, which Princess Margaret often visited in later life, and pause at the point where the castle first comes into view. There we should just gaze and admire.

She was right. A few hundred yards down the drive you pass over the brow of the hill and the castle appears before you. It was a crisp day in 2005 and the hills behind the castle were lightly dusted with snow. The castle itself looked immense, tall and turreted and gauntly menacing, utterly un-English and more reminiscent of one of Ludwig's Bavarian Schlosses or a French chateau than an English country house. Above all, though, it looked grand. There is nothing even faintly middle-class about this place.

At the beginning of the twenty-first century the 14,000-acre Glamis estate was still being used as a shooting lodge but in a far more commercial way. On the December day that I was there Mark Phillips, first husband of the Princess Royal, could be found lunching in a dungeon along with his son Peter and a group of businessmen, all there for a day blasting away at pheasant. Commercial details of the shooting as well as of weddings, champagne receptions and various other activities can all be found on the castle website: www.glamis-castle.co.uk. We adjourned for coffee with 'the shooters', but Lady Penn, Lady Strathmore and I enjoyed an excellent self-service lunch along with visiting and paying members of the public in the Victorian kitchens. We also spent a few moments in the modern shop full of rugs and whisky and other attractively presented souvenirs. Glamis has been open to the public since 1950 and like most other 'stately homes' is now run very professionally as a tourist attraction with the family relegated to relatively modest private quarters while the public are allowed to roam through the grand state quarters. It very much wasn't like that in 1930 when Princess Margaret was born there. In those days it was, essentially, a holiday home and, perhaps for that reason, always seemed particularly welcoming to the young princesses. It was a place where they were always on holiday.

Even more than most houses now open to the public Glamis impresses with its stony grandeur. We spent some time climbing up and down ancient stone staircases, walking through baronial drawing rooms and a great dining hall, where the family were, unusually, to celebrate a Christmas meal together, and inspecting the private chapel where her mother had originally wanted Princess Margaret to be christened. Afterwards we went round to the wing that has been retained by the present Earl and his wife as a private residence. This contains the bedroom where Princess Margaret was actually born. Unlike most of the rest of the castle it is quite modest, one might even say ordinary.

As I have demonstrated in the bibliography, I have relied quite heavily on the book about her charges by the royal sisters' governess Marion Crawford. I am in a quandary about this. Miss Crawford wrote the book after she had left royal service and against the strongly expressed wishes of her former employer, Queen Elizabeth. It has long been clear that the Royal Family bitterly regretted what they regarded as an act of betrayal. Crawfie, for her part, seems to have believed – or was encouraged to believe – that she should have had a more generous pension and been rewarded by being made a Dame rather than a Commander of the Royal Victorian Order. It now seems to be accepted that she overvalued her status.

Crawfie's writing career eventually came to grief when she wrote an account of a trooping-the-colour parade that turned out to be a complete fiction. She wrote it before the event, which, unfortunately for her, was cancelled because of a rail strike and never took place. For this reason alone her veracity has to be questioned and a number of experts, notably Queen Elizabeth's unofficial biographer Hugo Vickers, have alleged that her editors and maybe others, including her unpopular husband, may have encouraged her to invent colourful 'facts' when the truth was insufficiently dramatic or when she simply didn't know it.

Vickers devotes an entire chapter to 'Crawfie', her dodgy-sounding husband, a retired 'major' called George Buthlay, and the supposedly unscrupulous Bruce and Beatrice Gould, joint editors of *The Ladies' Home Journal*, who allegedly got their claws into the vulnerable ex-governess and tinkered with her copy. Because of this, 'Incidents were inserted which never happened and words put into the mouths of those who never said them.'

Sometimes it is easy to identify Crawfie's 'mistakes'. Her description of the Yorks' Piccadilly mansion as typically middle-class is plainly absurd. I am told by others in a position to know that her claim, for instance, that his daughters curtseyed to King George VI immediately after his accession is complete nonsense.

The problem is, however, that while Miss Crawford's revelatory book was deeply deplored by those it portrayed, there has never been a detailed public rebuttal of what she wrote. We know that Queen Elizabeth – *both* Queen Elizabeths – disapproved of Crawfie writing her book, but we don't know which parts of the book are true and which parts are fiction. I have done my best to separate the two and I have treated the governess's tale with extreme caution. The problem, however, is that much of the time she is not just the *primary* but the *only* source. She was also, for a crucial period, very close to the princesses – indeed it is this closeness and its repudiation that caused the grief. It is not so much the falsehood that upsets those who were the subject of her book as the truth.

CHAPTER TWO: THE FORTIES

Crawfie is once again precariously invaluable for this period in the Princess's life, as are such hagiographic volumes as Lisa Sheridan's John Murray wartime celebration and the Pitkin Pictorial issued to mark her nineteenth birthday. Both need to be treated with a degree of circumspection, but they are still useful. I have treated such sources with more than a pinch of salt, but I can't say where all the salt comes from. I hate it when authors are evasive like this and shelter behind such bromides as 'confidential information' or 'private source', but it is a fact of biography that from time to time people are prepared to help only on an unattributable basis. Inevitably this makes the reader suspicious and often, I believe, those suspicions are justified. However, there are occasions when, as a writer, one is faced with a choice between not revealing one's source and not getting the information. When that happens I'm afraid I follow the 'off the record' course. I do so with extreme reluctance and I know that some readers will be sceptical. I'm sorry about this and can only ask you to trust me. I don't do it often, and only when it seems inescapable.

The long letters from Princess Margaret to her grandmother Queen Mary are all in a single file at the Royal Archives in Windsor Castle, but the copyright in them belongs to the Princess's next of kin. I am grateful to Viscount Linley, her son, for giving me permission to quote them in full. In the late 1940s, as the Princess begins to undertake more public duties, the Archive material becomes more extensive. I record my appreciation to Her Majesty the Queen for being allowed to consult these files in my acknowledgements. I am also indebted to Pam Clark and her staff at Windsor Castle for all their help in making the documents accessible. My grateful thanks are recorded elsewhere.

A condition of consulting material in the archives is that one submits material for checking and approval. This I did, though Pam Clark found checking everything I submitted unusually difficult not least because of 'the absence of references' which sometimes made it difficult for her to find the relevant files. I naturally take full responsibility for any errors. My notes were handwritten as were many of the notes and letters in the Archives. Although I have, I think, been punctilious in my recording there are moments when I have been – necessarily I think – selective and even tidied up grammar and syntax. Miss Clark has been meticulous about correcting me wherever possible. The Archives were not willing for me to quote the whole of the two letters Princess Margaret wrote to Queen Mary in 1947 because I 'was not writing an official biography'. I regret this but have reluctantly omitted the second half of both letters as requested.

Lady Violet Bonham Carter's diaries were sporadically useful, as was Lord Montagu of Beaulieu's autobiography. His personal recollections recounted over a London lunch with my editor, Ion Trewin, were also invaluable.

Sir Edmund Grove, one of a very few survivors of the 1947 South African tour, gave me the benefit of his memory and Dermot Morrah's contemporary published account was a great help, as were Peter Townsend's published recollections. Back numbers of *The Times* provided first-hand accounts of South Africa, Holland and much else besides. These, of course, are never intimate, but they are particularly interesting because they constituted the main source of information for many members of what later became known as 'the Establishment'.

Viscount Norwich's diaries provide a shrewd contemporary glance. His son, John Julius Norwich, drew my attention to Dorothy Shay, and, indeed, sang several of her songs, word-perfect, over lunch one day at the Frontline Club in Paddington. Information about the fate of the wheelbarrow from Eastbourne came from James Kidner, assistant private secretary to the Prince of Wales in 2004.

Clara Knight, the royal nanny in the thirties and early forties, was a problem. Her nickname was produced because her charges had trouble pronouncing 'Clara' correctly. Their version, probably Princess Elizabeth's, was 'Allah', 'Alah' or 'Alla'. The Queen's biographer Sarah Bradford favoured the first spelling; Crawfie, Hugo Vickers and Anne Edwards the second, and Robert Lacey the third. Hugo Vickers had her dying in 1941, Crawfie and Sarah Bradford in 1945, Anne Edwards in 1947. Sarah Bradford said it was from meningitis, Anne Edwards a sudden heart attack.

None of these is an insubstantial enough writer to dismiss out of hand; yet the discrepancies are significant.

CHAPTER THREE: THE FIFTIES

All sorts of people have ventured into print to give their accounts of 'the Townsend affair' and there are even more who are keen to express their opinions verbally even if their version is circumstantial and based on a view from the upper circle – always assuming they were even in the theatre. Easily the most authoritative stories are in Townsend's own account later published in his autobiography and the alternative version confided to his recently published diaries by the Queen's private secretary Sir Alan Lascelles. They agree on many points but differ quite sharply on others.

I had two enjoyable lunches with Lord Snowdon as well as several phone conversations. A mutual acquaintance remarked, 'Tony is impossible to pin down, isn't he? I can picture your "intriguing" and "slightly inebriated" lunches completely. As you say, "charming but ..." He is the past master at apparent intimacy that betrays nothing.' He did, in fact, tell me a number of things that I found very revealing, but talking to him about the past was always, I felt, rather like playing a very genteel and amusing game of cards. His were nearly always kept close to his chest!

Most of the details of 'the Townsend affair' come from their accounts by Sir Alan Lascelles, the Queen's private secretary, during the crucial period and by Group Captain Townsend himself. They don't always agree. I also talked to the elder of Townsend's two sons, Giles, who was as charming as I guessed his father to have been. He confirmed that most of what he knew came from his father's published version of events, which he accepted as gospel. He was adamant about the fact that the break-up of his parents' marriage had nothing at all to do with Princess Margaret. It had fallen apart, as far as he could tell, long before any romantic attachment between his father and the Princess.

CHAPTER FOUR: THE SIXTIES

Much of this chapter is based on research in the Royal Archives and on the various official documents stored there. I relied extensively on a number of published sources, identified in the bibliography, and I am grateful to Weidenfeld & Nicolson for permission to quote from Roy Strong's diaries. I also had conversations with Sir John Dankworth, Ned Sherrin, Lieutenant Colonel Sir John Johnston and others.

I was able to visit 1A Kensington Palace after the Princess's death and after her son and daughter-in-law, Viscount and Viscountess Linley, had left. Despite the impression of emptiness there was still some of the Princess's past in the place even though her sister the Queen was concerned that the apartment should not become simply 'a shrine'. The floor of the hall was still black-and-white-chequered marble and slate said to come from the Armstrong-Jones family quarries in North Wales, though there are those who say that there never were family quarries and that the Jones fortune, such as it was, came from the manufacture of patent pills. The ancestor who invented the pills was known, apparently, as 'the pill roller of Trenador'.

The hall also contained the famous Annigoni portrait, which hung there during Princess Margaret's lifetime. In fact this was a copy and there was a certain amount of ill-feeling about it because Historic Royal Palaces were keen to have a copy made but, in their view, Viscount Linley, who had the original after his mother's death, was reluctant to allow it out of his custody. It was a full six months before a copy could be made and his stipulations over security meant that the agency had to pay £2,000 even before the copy was actually made. Elsewhere there was another portrait of the Princess, a present from Imelda Marcos, painted by a Filipino who obviously did not have the advantage of first-hand sittings. The result is that the Princess has what her brother-in-law Prince Philip would have described as 'slitty eyes'. She disliked the painting so much that she used to shake her fist at it. The Princess's personal standard was also hanging in the hall, loaned by her daughter Lady Sarah Chatto.

Outside, the garden remained much as it had been in the Princess's day, featuring the wrought-iron railing salvaged from Ascot racecourse. In the distance one could make out a concrete fountain, described tersely by the curator as 'another bit of Roddy'. Actually it had nothing to do with Llewellyn but was based on a fountain at Glamis Castle and had been paid for, generously, by her rich and philanthropic friend 'Drue' Heinz, widow of an eponymous 57 Varieties tycoon. It was not a success, not quite the same as the original and led to complaints from their neighbour the Dowager Duchess of Gloucester. It interfered with her plumbing

Llewellyn always advised on her gardens after he came into her life in 1973 and he was largely responsible for the plantings in Mustique and for making the gardens at Kensington Palace more informal and relaxed. It was he who put a big mirror into the garden wall making the space seem much greater than it actually was. She liked plants that smelled; she adored roses, had a soft spot for a shrub whose shed leaves produced a smell like strawberry jam when you walked over them, and she loathed 'mauve'.

She was always interested in gardening and the Chelsea Flower Show was an annual event in the Princess's calendar. She usually took a party of about twenty and they travelled to and from the show in an ancient green Buckingham Palace bus. This could only just squeeze through various gates on the route and apprehensive passengers would breathe in deeply and hug their chests as they negotiated such entrances and exits. After the formal business of inspecting the flowers on display she and her guests would take the bus home to Kensington Palace. There, ladies would remove their hats and everyone would take off their shoes in order to wander casually and barefoot over the lawn. She always insisted that her grass be mown so that there was an inch or so of grass on which it was a springy, bouncy pleasure to amble about in bare or stockinged feet. The relative length also meant that her grass was nearly always green.

Inside there was little left of the Princess. One or two things simply couldn't be moved. The kitchen, for instance, had a terribly *House and Garden* canopy and extractor fan over the stove; the ovens were set in slate. There was Formica everywhere. It felt as it obviously originally was: a piece of *echt*-1960s Design Centre design – the sort of thing Snowdon did most effectively.

There was an odd sense of lingering resentment directed partly at the Princess's son and heir Lord Linley, who was felt to have made off with items to which he did not really have a right. 'There was a huge Gothick bookcase in here. Linley took it,' was one not untypical aside. Actually that seems to be a mistake and it has gone to the Queen. Kate Mortimer filled me in with information about her father's time as Bishop of Exeter though, sadly, Margaret Rhodes, with whom the Snowdons stayed in Devon, remembered little or nothing about it.

CHAPTER FIVE: **THE SEVENTIES**

Andrew Duncan expanded on what he said in his book, published at the time. Freddy Burnaby-Atkins entertained me to an enjoyable lunch at his home in Wiltshire and put his side of what sounds like a contentious story. From the moment that he took over from the Colonel, Lord Napier has been a sympathetic and authoritative source. He and various ladies-in-waiting were there or thereabouts, particularly on public occasions and also behind public scenes.

The Independence celebrations on Tuvalu were first revealed in the papers at the Royal Archives, but after I had read the accounts there they were filled out by the personal recollections of Anne Glenconner, Davina Alexander (née Woodhouse), Lord Napier and Messrs Cortazzi (now Sir Hugh) and Snodgrass from the Foreign Office. They were all there.

CHAPTER SIX: **THE EIGHTIES**

The Archives and various newspaper cuttings formed the basis for my account of the Canadian visit at the beginning of the decade; the Archives provided most of the material concerning the visit to the King's Royal Hussars in Germany; Elizabeth Vyvyan and Lord Napier provided entertaining glimpses of the visit to Madam Marcos in the Philippines. My attention was drawn to *The Picnic Papers* by John Julius Norwich. I also spoke to Angela Huth and to Ned Ryan about their friendships with the Princess. The 1981 celebrations surrounding the sixtieth anniversary of the accession of King Sobhuza are recorded in some detail in the Royal Archives at Windsor, but both Anne Glenconner and Lord Napier, who were there, provided further insights and details as well as corroborating the original account. I should say that there is conflicting evidence about what precisely the King was wearing when the Princess invested him with the Grand Cross of the Order of St Michael and St George. The one thing on which all agreed is that it was not a lot.

Michael Palin himself told me about his encounter with the Princess after she had been to a matinee of his film *The Missionary*. Matthew Parris's account of her visit to his Derbyshire constituency in 1984 comes from his memoirs. Sir William Heseltine commented on his 1985 memorandum about being a counsellor of state in an email to me dated 4 November 2005. Angela Huth lent me a copy of her book *The Englishwoman's Wardrobe*. Selina Hastings sent me her *Sunday Telegraph* piece of November 1986. Lord Napier and Elizabeth Vyvyan amplified the documents concerning the visit to China in 1987.

CHAPTER SEVEN: THE NINETIES

Citing myself as the prime source for my account of lunch with Princess Margaret and Queen Elizabeth the Queen Mother at Clarence House in November 1990 may seem self-indulgent or even narcissistic but also happens to be true. So I make no apology for doing so. The account of the Princess's dinner with the Crime Writers' Association relies heavily on eyewitness accounts from Colin Dexter and Margaret Yorke, both of whom sat at her table, though recollections differ in some respects.

I spoke on the telephone to Diane Solway in New York. She wrote a biography of Rudolph Nureyev for my editor Ion Trewin in the course of which she interviewed the Princess at Kensington Palace. I thought her recollections were very interesting and it was a different way of tackling Princess Margaret's enthusiasm for the ballet, about which she was genuinely knowledgeable.

As so often, material from the Royal Archives has been essential for reconstructing the basic routines of royal life and giving a sense of the time-consuming and detailed planning of even the most apparently mundane engagements. Sometimes, however, written information comes from other sources. The letter from Peter Townsend concerning Philip Thomas, for instance, is not in the Royal Archives, though I have seen it.

Other informants in this section include Baroness Jay (a brief email) and Peter Miller, the York bookseller, to whom I talked on the telephone. Where possible I have identified the source of information in the text and given as far as possible the circumstances under which the information was conveyed. I had emails from and telephone conversations with Charles Moore, former editor of the *Daily Telegraph*; I saw Viscount Ullswater at his home in Norfolk – and so on

CHAPTER EIGHT: **THE END**

The Angela Huth material comes from her article in the *Daily Telegraph*. The story about Jeremy Catto was in an email from Dr Catto himself and the Maurice Keen anecdote was told during a conversation with Doctor Keen in Oxford. Hugo Vickers provided a first-hand account of the funeral procession, the funeral and the memorial service. I visited the tomb of Princess Margaret and her parents at St George's Windsor with Lord Napier and Major-General Sir Michael Hobbs, Governor of the Military Knights. Information about the auction at Christie's comes from a variety of sources including the auction house itself. Lee Prosser of Historic Royal Palaces provided some interesting sidelines in a series of emails. I spoke on the phone to Ned Ryan about the Joan Collins story, stayed a couple of nights with Lady Penn at her home in Scotland and saw Margaret Rhodes at her home in Windsor Great Park one morning. The late Johnny Johnston, who lived nearby, saw me after lunch. Kenneth Rose was an engaging and informative lunch-time companion and also wrote me several letters.

SELECT BIBLIOGRAPHY

Allison, Ronald and Riddell, Sarah (eds), *The Royal Encylopedia* (Macmillan, 1991).

Aronson, Theo, *Royal Subjects* (Sidgwick and Jackson, 2000).

Beaton, Cecil, *The Unexpurgated Diaries*, ed. Hugo Vickers (Weidenfeld and Nicolson, 2002).

——, *Beaton in the Sixties: More Unexpurgated Diaries*, ed. Hugo Vickers (Weidenfeld and Nicolson, 2003).

Bonham Carter, Violet, *Champion Redoubtable 1914–1945* (Weidenfeld and Nicolson, 1999).

——, *Daring to Hope 1946–1969* (Weidenfeld and Nicolson, 2000).

Botham, Noel, Margaret, *The Last Real Princess* (Blake, 2002).

Bradford, Sarah, *Elizabeth* (Heinemann, 1996).

——, *George VI* (Weidenfeld and Nicolson, 1969).

Brandreth, Gyles, *Philip and Elizabeth* (Century, 2004).

Clarke, Gerald, *Truman Capote* (Simon and Schuster, 1988).

Clarkson, Wensley, *Bindon* (Blake, 2005).

Coetzee, J. M., *Slow Man* (Secker and Warburg, 2005).

Colville, John, *The Fringes of Power: Downing Street Diaries* (Hodder and Stoughton, 1984).

Cooper, Duff, *The Duff Cooper Diaries 1915–1951*, ed. and intro. by John Julius Norwich (Weidenfeld and Nicolson, 2005).

Coward, Noël, *The Noël Coward Diaries*, ed. Graham Payne and Sheridan Morley (Weidenfeld and Nicolson, 1982).

Crawford, Marion, *The Little Princesses* (Cassell, 1950).

Dempster, Nigel, *H.R.H the Princess Margaret: a Life Unfulfilled* (Quartet, 1981).

Duncan, Andrew, *The Reality of Monarchy* (Heinemann, 1969).

Fleming, Ann, *The Letters of Ann Fleming*, ed. Mark Amory (Collins Harvill, 1985).

Gathorne-Hardy, Jonathan, *Half an Arch* (Timewell, 2004).

Gillen, Mollie, *Royal Duke* (Sidgwick and Jackson, 1976).

Gladwyn, Cynthia, *The Diaries of Cynthia Gladwyn*, ed. Miles Jebb (Constable, 1995).

Grenfell, Joyce and Graham, Virginia, *Letters*, ed. Janie Hampton (Hodder and Stoughton, 1997).

Hart-Davis, Rupert and Lyttelton, George, *The Lyttelton–Hart-Davis Letters, vol. 5, 1960* (John Murray, 1983).

Henderson, Nicholas, *Mandarin* (Weidenfeld and Nicolson, 1995).

Hillier, Bevis, *John Betjeman – New Fame, New Love* (John Murray, 2002).

Hoey, Brian, *Her Majesty* (HarperCollins, 2001).

——, *Snowdon* (Sutton, 2005).

Howard, Philip, *The British Monarchy* (Hamish Hamilton, 1977).

Kenward, Betty, *Jennifer's Memoirs* (HarperCollins, 1992).

Lascelles, Sir Alan, *King's Counsellor: Abdication and War*, ed. Duff Hart-Davis (Weidenfeld and Nicolson, 2006).

Lees-Milne, James, *A Mingled Measure: Diaries 1953–1972* (John Murray, 1994).

Lewis, Jeremy, *Cyril Connolly* (Jonathan Cape, 1997).

Longford, Elizabeth, *Darling Loosy* (Weidenfeld and Nicolson, 1991).

Morrah, Dermot, *The Royal Family in Africa* (Hutchinson, 1947).

Morris, Jan, *Coronation Everest* (Faber and Faber, 1958).

Parris, Matthew, *Chance Witness* (Viking, 2002).

Paxman, Jeremy, *On Royalty* (Viking, 2006).

Pimlott, Ben, *The Queen* (HarperCollins, 1996).

Rose, Kenneth, *Kings, Queens and Courtiers* (Weidenfeld and Nicolson, 1985).

Sheridan, Lisa, *Our Princesses at Home* (John Murray, 1940)

Sherrin, Ned, *The Autobiography* (Little, Brown, 2005).

Shew, Betty Spencer, *Royal Wedding* (Macdonald, 1947).

Strong, Roy, *The Roy Strong Diaries 1967–1987* (Weidenfeld and Nicolson, 1997).

Townsend, Peter, *Time and Chance* (Collins, 1978).

Tynan, Kenneth, *The Diaries*, ed. John Lahr (Bloomsbury, 2001).

Vickers, Hugo, *Elizabeth the Queen Mother* (Hutchinson, 2005).

——, *Cecil Beaton* (Weidenfeld and Nicolson, 1985).

Warwick, Christopher, *Princess Margaret. A Life of Contrasts* (André Deutsch, 2002).

Williams, Kenneth, *Letters*, ed. Russell Davies (HarperCollins, 1994).

INDEX

Oxfordshire, 229

Pacific Ocean, 202, 211
painting, 26–7
Palestine, 57
Palin, Michael, 235–6, 323
pantomimes, 30
Paris, 52–3, 154–7, 168, 268
Park, Dame Merle, 257
Parker, Lieutenant Commander Mike, 55–6, 88, 91; and Snowdon, 111–12, 125
Parliament, 95
Parris, Matthew, 237, 273
Partington, Harold, 118
Partridge, Frances, 114
Peacock, Andrew, 204
Peake, Hon, Iris (Mrs Dawnay), 97, 118, 156–7, 253
Peake, Lady Joan, 55
Peel, Lady Delia, 47, 54, 56, 66
Pembroke, Earl of, 115
Penn, Sir Arthur, 58, 71
Penn, Colonel Sir Eric, 185, 261, 266, 280, 315
Penn, Lady Prue, 94, 185, 261, 266, 280–1, 291, 305–8, 315, 324
Penn, William, 296
People, 98, 100, 102
Perth, 62
Peshawar, 2
Petersham, Viscount, 277
Philip, Prince: meets Princess Elizabeth, 21; engagement, 44; and George VI, 55; visits East Africa, 88; and 'Townsend affair', 93, 95, 101; and Snowdon, 111–12, 125, 127; and family name, 126; attitudes towards, 158; and PM, 201; supports Queen, 224; serves as counsellor of state, 239; author's biography of, 248–9, 253–5, 309; love of poetry, 253; Annigoni sketch, 253–4; PM stands in for, 276; attends PM's funeral, 293; alleged 'girlfriends', 308, 311
Philippines, 206, 211, 225–6, 322
Phillips, Captain Mark, 186–7
Phipps, Simon, 133

photographs, of PM, 85, 225, 233, 296; by Dorothy Wilding, 56–7; by Beaton, 81–2; by Snowdon, 102, 112; by Antonia Fraser, 150; by Griffiths, 242; and choice of clothes, 243
piano playing, 26–7, 59, 82–3, 164, 169, 195, 234
picnics, 226–7, 288
Pilcher, Sir John, 160, 162–3
Pimlott, Ben, 89
Pinter, Harold, 171
Pipkin (dachshund), 25
Piston, Walter, 139
Pitkin Pictorials, 14
Pitkin Princess Margaret's Nineteenth Birthday Book, 11, 85
Plas Dinas, 110
Plomley, Roy, 233
Plumb, Sir John ('Jack'), 185, 194, 227, 259, 304
Plunket, Patrick, Lord, 64, 106, 177
Plymouth, 262
poetry, 253
Poitier, Sidney, 212
Polo, Marco, 29
Poltimore tiara, 119, 187, 301
ponies, 31, 40
Poole, Sir Reginald, 10
Port Carling, 221
Port Elizabeth, 38
Port of London, 73
Port Talbot, 266
Porte, A. P., 48
Portobello Road, 183
portraits, of PM, 226, 299, 320
Portsmouth, 123
Portugal, 239
Potter, Frederick, 63
Pottery and Glass Traders' Benevolent Institution, 284
Potts, Sir Stanley, 71
Powell, Charles and Mrs, 260
Pownall, Lieutenant General Sir Henry, 64–5
prayers, 144–5
Prescott, Lena (L. R.), 71, 76, 79
presents, 16–18, 29–31, 33, 44
press, 51–3, 67, 78, 234, 249, 295; and